W9-CBZ-862

American Portraits
Biographies in United States History

American Portraits:

Biographies in United States History

VOLUME II

Stephen G. Weisner
Springfield Technical Community College

William F. Hartford
Independent Scholar

Boston, Massachusetts   Burr Ridge, Illinois   Dubuque, Iowa   Madison, Wisconsin
New York, New York   San Francisco, California   St. Louis, Missouri

McGraw-Hill

A Division of The McGraw·Hill Companies

AMERICAN PORTRAITS

Copyright © 1998 by The McGraw-Hill Companies, Inc. All rights reserved. Printed in the United States of America. Except as permitted under the United States Copyright Act of 1976, no part of the publication may be reproduced or distributed in any form or by any means, or stored in a data base or retrieval system, without the prior written permission of the publisher.

This book is printed on acid-free paper.

Photo credits appear on page 319 and on this page by reference.

3 4 5 6 7 8 9 0 DOC/DOC 9 0 9

ISBN 0-07-069142-8

Editorial director: *Jane Vaicunas*
Sponsoring editor: *Lyn Uhl*
Developmental editor: *Monica Freedman*
Marketing manager: *Anne Mitchell*
Project manager: *Karen M. Smith/Alisa Watson*
Production supervisor: *Jon Christopher*
Designer: *Larry J. Cope*
Photo research coordinator: *Keri Johnson*
Compositor: *Ruttle, Shaw, & Wetherill*
Typeface: *10/12 Palatino*
Printer: *R. R. Donnelley & Sons Company*

Library of Congress Cataloging-in-Publication Data

Weisner, Stephen G.
    American Portraits : Biographies in United States History /
Stephen G. Weisner, William F. Hartford.
        p.   cm.
    ISBN 0-07-069141-X (volume 1). —ISBN 0-07-069142-8 (volume 2)
    1. United States—Biography.   I. Hartford, William F.
II. Title.
CT214.W45   1998
973'.09'9   97-24794
[B]—DC21

http://www.mhcollege.com

For my mother, Anne Weisner, 1921–1993

Contents

UNIT THREE

Preface

American Portraits is a two-volume collection of biographical profiles designed to supplement the textbooks used in college-level survey courses. We adopted this format for several reasons. One is a belief that biography provides a particularly valuable tool for introducing students to the excitement and wonder of history. Life-writing forcefully reminds us that, beneath the abstractions, history is about the aspirations and struggles of flesh-and-blood human beings; it further enables us to identify with these individuals as they seek to give meaning to their lives. In so doing, biography restores a sense of immediacy to the study of the past that is often lost in textbook generalizations. Accordingly, the articles in this anthology have been selected not only for their readability—though that was certainly a consideration—but also for the interest they are likely to generate. It is our hope that, in reading these essays, students will learn more about themselves as well as the people whose lives are profiled.

We also believe that biography provides an especially effective means of exploring the social and cultural diversity that has figured so prominently in the American experience. In the not-too-distant past, U.S. history was largely the study of middle-aged white males who had attained positions of political, military, or social distinction and whose forebears hailed from the British Isles. This is no longer the case, and textbooks today devote increasing attention to both women and men from a variety of cultural groups and social classes.

Biography cannot expand the breadth of this coverage. It can, however, deepen our understanding of these people. To cite but two examples from this anthology, Alvin M. Josephy's examination of the obstacles Tecumseh encountered in his efforts to achieve Indian unity sheds light on the diversity of Native American life; and Cletus Daniel's portrait of Cesar Chavez shows how factors such as religion and ethnicity shaped the development of this leader's unique brand of trade unionism.

On a related matter, biography adds depth to our understanding of major historical themes. Most of the essays selected for this anthology thus have a dual purpose: to profile the life of a given individual and to explore how that person influenced and was influenced by broader historical forces. For example, Patricia Horner's article on Mary Richardson Walker describes the trials and tribulations of a female pioneer in the Oregon Country; however, it also raises important questions about the ways in which environment and culture limited women's self-activity in frontier areas.

As for the structure of *American Portraits,* we have divided the essays in each volume into three or four units. Each unit begins with an introductory essay that is designed to help put the portraits into topical and chronological perspective. To provide additional context for the lives profiled in the anthology, we have prepared headnotes for every article. We also have selected a document to accompany each chapter and thus broaden the scope of coverage. Discussion questions follow, to help focus attention on the main issues raised in each chapter's portrait. Finally, each chapter concludes with a brief bibliography that offers suggestions for further reading.

Acknowledgments

Thanks go to Chris Rogers for signing on to this project. At McGraw-Hill, History Editor Lyn Uhl, and Monica Freedman, Development Editor, provided encouragement and support. Former student Susan Wyzik, now a colleague, helped by critiquing articles. At Springfield Technical Community College Dr. Andrew M. Scibelli, President, and especially John H. Dunn, Executive Vice President, aided the cause with an adjustment in my teaching schedule. Thanks to the late Tom Boyle, also from STCC, whose calm and comforting demeanor will always be remembered. A final expression of thanks to my wife Jane, and daughters Sarah and Hannah.

Stephen G. Weisner
Springfield Technical Community College

William F. Hartford
Independent Scholar

Introduction

The late nineteenth century was a period of expansion and growth in most parts of the nation. With the construction of a transcontinental railroad network, enterprise flourished on the agricultural, ranching, and mining frontiers of the West. And in the East, cities grew at an astonishing rate as waves of "new" immigrants poured into the country from Eastern and Southern Europe. The pace of industrialization also quickened, propelled by the formation of massive new corporate entities that substantially increased the output of numerous industries. By the century's end, no informed observer doubted that the United States soon would displace Great Britain as the world's leading economic power.

Not everybody benefited from these advances. Among the casualties, no one suffered more than the Native Americans who stood in the way of westward expansion. Although most tribes agreed to relocate on reservations, they often found that the government's promises of decent living conditions were a cruel hoax. When some tribes subsequently rebelled, federal forces intervened, ruthlessly suppressing all expressions of dissent. In his essay on Philip Sheridan, the general most responsible for implementing Indian policy in the postbellum West, Paul Andrew Hutton sheds light on the darker side of regional development.

As federal officials gradually recognized that the reservation policy was not working well, they sought to replace it with an assimilation program designed to strip Native Americans of the "barbaric" traditions of their cultural past. The new approach targeted Indian youths, many of whom were placed in off-reservation boarding schools, where they were expected to internalize the values of white society. Despite the patronizing assumptions that informed the program, some students profited from the experience. One of them was Susan LaFlesche Picotte, the daughter of an Omaha chief, who went on to become the nation's first Native American woman doctor. Her education and subsequent work on behalf of her people are the subject of an essay by Valerie Sherer Mathes.

Although relatively few women of any ethnic background became physicians during the late nineteenth century, many did make their mark in the teaching profession. By 1870 more than one of every two instructors in the nation's primary and secondary schools was a woman. In some regions, they even used their background as teachers to enter politics. This was especially so in the West, where women such as Minnesota's Sarah Christie Stevens won election to school superintendencies throughout the period. In her essay on Stevens, Jean Christie provides an insightful profile of a dedicated woman who was a social activist and public official as well as a housewife.

Native Americans were not the only group for whom Gilded Age developments brought more sorrow than fulfillment. This was also a dismal time for African Americans, particularly those ex-slaves who remained in their southern homeland. With the restoration of traditional white rule during the 1870s, the hopes raised by emancipation began to fade amid mounting racial oppression. As they did, southern blacks became increasingly reliant on their own independent institutions. Of these, none had a greater influence on African–American life than the church, whose ministers often provided leadership on political and social as well as spiritual matters. In his essay on the African Methodist Episcopal bishop, Henry McNeal Turner, John Dittmer examines how one black churchman responded to the deteriorating position of regional African Americans.

In most areas outside the South, where economic development lagged throughout the period, the release of entrepreneurial energies made the Gilded Age an era of extraordinary material growth. Leading the way were huge, multidivisional enterprises that used the latest technology to take advantage of economies of scale. In so doing, some of the new corporations not only crushed smaller competitors, but they established effective monopolies in given industries. Few Gilded Age firms proved more adept at this often brutal game than John D. Rockefeller's Standard Oil Company, which by century's end refined more than 80 percent of the oil produced in the United States. In his essay on the oil tycoon, William Manchester attempts to move beyond the robber baron stereotype and provide a rounded portrait of Rockefeller by exploring his private life as well as his business career.

Not surprisingly, the widespread social change taking place in Gilded Age America affected the world of letters. This was particularly the case among writers drawn to the new literary realism of the period, many of whom sought an outlet for their creative impulses in the nation's growing urban centers. One such writer was Stephen Crane, who based his first novel, *Maggie: A Girl of the Streets* (1893), on his experiences in New York City. In the course of providing a fascinating portrait of this gifted novelist whose reckless behavior resulted in his early death, Stephen Oates describes how Crane withstood the disappointing response to *Maggie* and went on to write one of the most acclaimed works of the era, *The Red Badge of Courage*.

Philip H. Sheridan

At the start of the Civil War, Native Americans still controlled much of the trans-Mississippi West. But this soon changed, as western Indians found themselves caught between two great population movements. On one hand, miners from the Pacific Coast poured east into the Rocky Mountains. At the same time, a seemingly endless stream of eastern settlers pressed westward onto the Great Plains. Meanwhile, the completion of a transcontinental railroad in 1869 gave added impetus to both migrations. This was only the beginning. As additional railroad lines crisscrossed the region in subsequent years, the buffalo gradually disappeared, thus depriving the Plains Indians of their primary source of food, clothing, and shelter.

Their entire way of life threatened, Native Americans did not passively accept these developments. During the Civil War years, the Plains Indians of Minnesota and the Dakotas killed nearly 1,000 pioneers in attacks on frontier settlements. Afterward, tribes further west sought to protect their hunting grounds by disrupting the road-building activities of the U.S. government. To end the bloodshed, federal authorities initially negotiated treaties that promised to provide Native Americans of the region some measure of security by establishing protected reservation areas. But not all tribes accepted the policy, and in 1871 Congress arbitrarily declared that the U.S.

government had the authority to confine all Plains Indians to reservations, regardless of their wishes.

   Even had all western Indians agreed to relocate on reservations, the program probably would not have worked. Because of the mismanagement and
corruption that all too often characterized the federal administration of reservation areas, many Native Americans soon found that such life offered a bleak
future at best. Not surprisingly, several tribes chose to fight rather than submit. Thus began a new round of Indian wars that continued throughout the
1870s and beyond.

   A major figure in those conflicts was an army general named Philip H.
Sheridan. One of the great heroes of the Civil War, Sheridan began his military career on the Plains; afterward he returned to the region with fixed ideas
about how to deal with his Native American adversaries. In the essay that
follows, Paul Andrew Hutton provides an insightful portrait of this sometimes ruthless military commander, whose commitment to order often over-
rode any ethical considerations that might obstruct the accomplishment of his
aims. In so doing, Hutton tells us much about the costs of progress in the
postbellum West.

Philip H. Sheridan

Paul Andrew Hutton

They buried Philip Henry Sheridan, commanding general of the United States
Army, on August 11, 1888, in Arlington Cemetery. His grave, on a high, green
knoll near the Custis–Lee Mansion, faces eastward toward the city of Washington. Lavish eulogies poured forth from that city, where Congress had tardily
voted him a fourth star only weeks before his death, and from throughout the
nation. They rang with the familiar names of battle sites—Stones River, Missionary Ridge, Winchester, Cedar Creek, Five Forks, Appomattox—that had
established Sheridan as the youngest member of the Union's trinity of great
captains. But strangely absent from this outpouring of mournful praise was
any mention of the task that had dominated the first 7 and last 20 years of the
general's career—the conquest of the American frontier.

   Phil Sheridan had been, in fact, the republic's preeminent frontier soldier.
He had commanded a larger frontier region—the vast Division of the Missouri—for a longer period of time than any other military officer in the nation's history. He had given overall direction to the final, and greatest, Indian
campaigns waged on this continent. Between 1867 and 1884, his troops fought
619 engagements with the western Indian tribes, completing the subjugation of
America's native peoples and the conquest of their lands, which had been set

Source: Reprinted by permission from Paul Andrew Hutton, "Phil Sheridan's Frontier," *Montana
The Magazine of Western History,* vol. 38 (Winter 1988), pp. 16–31.

underway almost 400 years before. At the same time he actively promoted the movement of hunters, stockmen, miners, farmers, and railroaders into these newly appropriated regions, using his military power and political influence to bring some order to this rapid, oftentimes chaotic, expansion westward. The American West during the 1870s and 1880s was in a real sense Phil Sheridan's frontier.

Sheridan's origins gave little hint of the vital role he was to play in his adopted nation's future. The exact place and date of his birth is unknown. He confused the issue himself, claiming both Albany, New York, and Somerset, Ohio, on various official documents, before finally deciding that Albany on March 6, 1831, sounded best. It seems almost certain that he was born either in County Cavan, Ireland, where his parents were tenant farmers, or on the boat en route from Liverpool. He was an infant when his parents, John and Mary Sheridan, settled in the hamlet of Somerset, Ohio.

Sheridan's later life was greatly influenced by the education he received in Somerset's one-room schoolhouse. He particularly admired an itinerant educator named Patrick McNaly, a drunken brute who believed that education could be beaten into students. Sheridan recalled with admiration that the Irishman consistently punished every "guilty mischief-maker" by whipping the whole class when unable to identify the actual culprit. This effective tactic made a deep impression on young Phil, as did the overall power of education. "The little white schoolhouse of the North made us superior to the South," he later remarked. "Education is invincible."

At 14, his schooling over, Sheridan secured a position as clerk in a local general store at $2 a month. He rose quickly to become bookkeeper in Somerset's largest dry-goods shop, a mighty responsibility for one so young, for almost all business was transacted on credit. Although dedicated to his bookkeeping chores, the lad was often lost in daydreams of martial glory, especially after the outbreak of the Mexican War. His greatest hero as a youth had been Somerset's Revolutionary War veteran who was trotted out every Fourth of July

black codes   Laws passed in Southern states in 1865–1866 that restricted the rights of newly freed slaves.

Custer's 1868 Washita fight   A military engagement that pushed the Cheyenne and Arapaho toward final capitulation and removal to a reservation.

Baker's 1870 Piegan massacre   Colonel E. M. Baker's attack on Chief Red Horse's camp that killed nearly 200 Indians, including Red Horse and many children, with the loss of only one soldier.

Red River War   The war that brought an end to effective Indian resistance on the southern Plains.

Great Sioux War   The war in which U.S. troops defeated Sitting Bull and Crazy Horse, but not before Custer and his contingent were annihilated at the Battle of the Little Big Horn.

Rosebud   A battle against General George Crook's northbound column during the 1876 Sioux campaign that bolstered the Indians' confidence.

to be admired by the citizenry. "I never saw Phil's brown eyes open so wide or gaze with such interest," noted his boyhood chum Henry Greiner, "as they did on this old Revolutionary relic." On another occasion Greiner and Sheridan interrupted their play to gawk admiringly at a tall, carrot-topped West Point cadet who was courting one of the young ladies at Somerset's St. Mary's Female Academy. The lady, Ellen Ewing, would eventually marry that fledgling soldier from nearby Lancaster, and her beau, lanky William Tecumseh Sherman, made a deep impression on young Phil Sheridan.

Learning that the 1848 appointee from his district to West Point had failed the entrance examinations, Sheridan hurriedly appealed to Congressman Thomas Ritchie offering to fill the vacancy. The congressman, who knew Sheridan's father well, promptly returned a warrant for the class of 1848, which elated Sheridan but horrified his family. Not only was West Point generally viewed by westerners as a bastion of aristocracy, special privilege, and militarism, all out of keeping with the ideals of the republic, but it was also firmly Episcopalian. John Sheridan took Phil in hand to the Church of St. Joseph where Dominican Father Joshua Young advised: "Rather than send him to West Point take him out into the backyard, behind the chicken coop, and cut his throat."

John Sheridan brooded over this sound if drastic advice for some time, but finally relented and allowed the boy to go. Phil traveled to the military academy with future general David S. Stanley. Stanley remembered Sheridan as "small and red faced, [with] long black wavy hair, bright eyes, very animated and neatly dressed in a brown broadcloth suit." At the academy, the long locks were soon shorn and the simple suit replaced by the "plebe skin," or brown linen jacket, of a freshman cadet. Poor Sheridan, Stanley noted, was "the most insignificant looking little fellow I ever saw."

West Point was an unhappy place for Sheridan. Gray buildings melded into a rocky landscape under foreboding wintry skies, reinforcing the discipline and monotonous regimen of cadet life. The traditional hazing frayed his volatile temper, and his grades suffered. The refined mannerisms and aristocratic temperament of the southern clique that dominated academy social life irritated him. While he found solace in the company of three other Ohio cadets—George Crook, John Nugen, and Joshua Sill—his rural, Irish–Catholic, Whig roots left him constantly insecure and ill at ease.

His frustrations broke forth late one afternoon on the drill field in September 1851. Virginian William R. Terrill ordered Sheridan to align himself properly in the ranks. Instead of obeying the order Sheridan lunged at Terrill with his bayonet. When Terrill reported the incident to his superiors, Sheridan sought him out and attacked him, but this time with his fists. An officer intervened and saved the wiry, five-foot-five Sheridan from a thrashing by the much larger Virginian. Saved from expulsion by a previously unblemished record, Sheridan received only a year's suspension. Unrepentant, he harbored deep resentment at all those involved in the incident. He brooded for 9 humiliating months back at his Somerset bookkeeping job before returning to West Point in August 1852, where he compounded his poor grades with a bitter attitude that left him only 11 demerits away from expulsion when he graduated 34th in a class of 52 in July 1853.

Brevet Second Lieutenant Sheridan was assigned to the First Infantry and ordered to Fort Duncan, Texas, perhaps the most desolate and primitive post on the frontier. Nevertheless, he found the fort an improvement over West Point and busied himself with amateur ornithology and hunting expeditions. He was soon transferred to his friend George Crook's regiment, the Fourth Infantry, and sent to Fort Reading, California, at the northern tip of the Sacramento Valley. The region was overrun by the dregs of humanity in search of a quick fortune in the goldfields. The miners and squatters terribly abused the local Indians, while their political representatives—most notably ambitious young Isaac Stevens, governor of Washington Territory—pushed through specious treaties to force the tribes off their coveted lands.

Crook, who had been in the Pacific Northwest since 1853, characterized the situation as "the fable of the wolf and the lamb." It was not infrequent, Crook noted, "for an Indian to be shot down in cold blood, or a squaw to be raped by some brute," and the white criminals to escape unpunished. Then, when the Indians were pushed beyond endurance and struck back, the soldiers "had to fight when our sympathies were with the Indians." Sheridan's sympathies, however, were not with the "miserable wretches" native to the region, for he felt their "naked, hungry and cadaverous" condition to be the natural result of the overthrow of savagery by civilization.

A gold discovery and influx of miners at Colville, Washington Territory, finally drove the Yakima and Rogue River Indians to war. Sheridan marched north in October 1855 with a detachment of 350 regular troops and a regiment of Oregon mounted volunteers under the command of Major Gabriel Rains. Sheridan's introduction to Indian fighting was a dismal affair, with the Yakimas easily avoiding the pursuing troops. On one occasion Sheridan, in command of the advance column, pursued a party of fleeing Indians for two miles before discovering them to be a company of Oregon volunteers. Winter snows mercifully ended the campaign, and Sheridan spent the next few months at Fort Vancouver.

While the reorganized troops were busy preparing for a spring invasion of the Walla Walla Valley, the Yakimas struck the first blow on March 26, 1856, attacking white settlements at the Cascades, a vital portage on the Columbia River. With 40 dragoons and a small cannon, Sheridan rushed upriver to the rescue aboard a little steamboat. Although they outnumbered the soldiers, the Indians only skirmished before withdrawing when more troops arrived on March 28. Slightly wounded by a Yakima bullet that grazed his nose before killing a soldier standing beside him, Sheridan had his first victory over the Indians and his first military honor when General Winfield Scott commended him in general orders.

After his victory at the Cascades, Lieutenant Sheridan and his troops occupied the nearby village of the Cascade tribe, easily rounding up the demoralized Indians. The Cascade men protested their innocence, but Sheridan found freshly burned powder in several of their old muskets. He hauled 13 of the men before Colonel George Wright, and a drumhead court-martial immediately sentenced 9 of them to death. The soldiers fastened a rope to a nearby cottonwood tree, stacked two barrels underneath, and unceremoniously hanged the Indians. Among those executed was Tumult, a Cascade Indian who had warned several settlers of the impending attack and had guided an elderly white man to safety. Sheridan noted with satisfaction that this "summary punishment inflicted on the nine Indians, in their trial and execution, had a most salutary effect on the confederation, and was the entering wedge of disintegration." Somerset schoolmaster McNaly's legacy was ever the directing influence in Phil Sheridan's use of force to effect the will of his government.

Sheridan's remaining years in the Pacific Northwest were spent quietly at the Grande Ronde Indian Reservation, guarding the several tribes who lived there. He learned the Chinook language while there, aided no doubt by Frances, a Rogue River Indian girl who lived with him on the reservation. This liaison, however, seemed to have no moderating influence on his prejudice toward the natives. He was proud of the harsh tactics he employed on the reservation to suppress traditional customs. "We made," he later noted,

> a great stride toward the civilization of these crude and superstitious people, for they now began to recognize the power of the Government . . . I found abundant confirmation of my early opinion that the most effectual measures for lifting them from a state of barbarism would be a practical supervision at the outset, coupled with a firm control and mild discipline.

It was difficult to concentrate on the duties at hand, for the news from the East was increasingly worrisome. Pony Express riders carried the sober details of Fort Sumter westward across the plains to western posts. Sheridan fretted that the war would end before he could return east. He was delighted to depart Portland in September 1861 as a newly minted captain in the Thirteenth Infantry and was anxious to see action, confiding to a friend that if the war lasted long enough he might "have a chance to earn a major's commission." The small-framed, 30-year-old frontier captain was a latecomer to the war. Ulysses S. Grant had already won fame as the victor at Fort Henry and Fort Donelson, William T. Sherman was now in command of a division, and George Crook's political connections had secured him the colonelcy of an Ohio volunteer regiment by the time Sheridan took command of a desk at General Henry W. Halleck's Missouri headquarters. His bookkeeping skills paid rich dividends as the young staff officer quickly straightened out the confused accounts of Halleck's predecessor, General John C. Frémont.

Sheridan's impressive staff service brought him to General Sherman's attention. He recommended Sheridan be given command of one of the Ohio volunteer regiments, but the governor declined to make the appointment. Russell Alger, the future secretary of war, then a captain in the Second Michigan Cavalry, succeeded where Sherman had failed, using his considerable political influence back home to have Sheridan appointed colonel of his regiment. On May 27, 1862, Sheridan jumped from regular army captain to volunteer army colonel, beginning one of the most meteoric rises in American military history.

The new colonel fought a masterful battle at Boonville, Missouri, against a force over four times the size of his own, prompting General William Rosecrans and four of his brigadiers to telegraph Halleck that Sheridan deserved a promotion and was "worth his weight in gold." Promoted to brigadier general of volunteers in September 1862, Sheridan quickly won a high reputation in army circles for his bulldog tenacity and reckless courage. His fierce counterattack at Stones River turned seeming defeat into an important but grisly Union victory and won him a second star in the volunteer army. It remained for his bold charge up Missionary Ridge, however, to secure him General Grant's esteem and guarantee his future. The press would dub Sheridan's assault on the seemingly impregnable Confederate positions on the crest of Missionary Ridge in November 1863 as the miracle at Missionary Ridge.

General Grant, who had watched the assault in amazement, was delighted. "Sheridan showed his genius in that battle," Grant later declared,

> and to him I owe the capture of most of the prisoners that were taken. Although commanding a division only, he saw in the crisis of that engagement that it was necessary to advance beyond the point indicated by his orders. He saw what I could not know, on account of my ignorance of the ground, and with the instinct of military genius pushed ahead.

When Grant went east in March 1864 as commander of all Union forces, he took Sheridan with him to command the Army of the Potomac's cavalry. Sheridan quickly defeated Confederate cavalry commander J. E. B. Stuart at Yellow Tavern and earned an independent command in the Shenandoah Valley. With orders to block the advance of General Jubal Early's Confederates up the valley and seal off the rebel breakbasket once and for all, Sheridan won battles at Winchester and Fisher's Hill and secured a brigadier's star in the regular army as a reward.

His greatest triumph, however, came at Cedar Creek. Sheridan was 14 miles to the north, at Winchester, when his army was taken by surprise on October 19, 1864. Galloping to the sound of the guns, he rallied his routed forces to crush Early's Confederates. "Sheridan's Ride," as it was called, became one of the most memorable episodes of the Civil War, soon celebrated in poem, story, and painting.

With the rebel army destroyed, Sheridan and his "robbers," as his army was thereafter known, ravaged the Shenandoah Valley so that it would never again support an invading army from the south. A crow, Sheridan boasted, would have to carry his own rations when crossing Virginia's most bountiful valley. "I do not hold war to mean simply that lines of men shall engage each other in people," Sheridan declared, in defining the strategy he would apply both in the Shenandoah and later on the frontier. "This is but a duel, in which one combatant seeks the other's life; war means much more, and is far worse than this." The key to strategic success in war lay in ravaging the enemy's homeland, depriving him of the resources to make war, and destroying the will of the people to resist, "for the loss of property weighs heavy with the

most of mankind; heavier often, than the sacrifices made on the field of battle."
As he later advised Prussian Count Otto von Bismarck in 1870:

> The proper strategy consists in the first place in inflicting as telling blows as
> possible upon the enemy's army, and then causing the inhabitants so much
> suffering that they must long for peace, and force their government to demand
> it. The people must be left nothing but their eyes to weep with over the war.

President Abraham Lincoln had hesitated to agree to Sheridan's Shenandoah command, believing the general too young and inexperienced. The president had once described Sheridan as "a brown, chunky little chap, with a
long body, short legs, not enough neck to hang him, and such long arms that if
his ankles itch he can scratch them without stooping." Lincoln now confessed
that he had always thought a cavalryman should be "six feet tall, but five feet
four seems about right," he declared, subtracting an inch from Sheridan's already diminutive size. His reelection hopes given a timely boost by the victory
at Cedar Creek, the president promoted Sheridan to major general in the regular army.

Realizing that the war would soon be over, Sheridan hurried south to re-
join Grant. At Five Forks his troops destroyed the right flank of Lee's army,
and at Appomattox he blocked the Army of Northern Virginia's line of retreat.
On Sunday, April 9, 1865, 34-year-old Phil Sheridan, the Union's finest combat
commander, walked with General Grant into the McLean house at Appomattox to accept the surrender of Lee's army.

The war over, Grant immediately sent Sheridan to the Texas border with
orders to provide material and moral support to the forces of Benito Juárez in
their struggle with Maximilian, the puppet of the French emperor, Louis
Napoleon. Sheridan relished the opportunity to confront French troops in battle, but the Department of State restrained him. Sheridan still aided Juárez by
declaring huge quantities of arms and ammunition as surplus or condemning
and depositing them on the Rio Grande for Juárez's troops. The French soon
abandoned Maximilian, and the imperialist adventure swiftly moved to its
melancholy finale.

Although preoccupied with border affairs, Sheridan kept a wary eye on
civil matters in Texas and Louisiana. He distributed troops at critical points to
suppress night-riding white terrorists and assist civilian authorities in enforc-
ing the law. Before the war, Sheridan's mind, as he put it, had never "been disturbed by any discussion of the questions out of which the war grew" and he
had been animated at the outbreak of the rebellion only to preserve the Union.
The war had radicalized him, so that by the time of Appomattox he was one of
the most stridently Republican and bitterly anti-Southern generals in the army.
Enraged by the various vagrancy and apprentice laws—**black codes**—enacted
in Texas, Sheridan angrily declared that they resulted in "a policy of gross injustice toward the colored people on the part of the courts, and a reign of law-
lessness and disorder ensued." Although hardly enlightened in his racial
views, Sheridan determined that he would protect the blacks. Now that they

had been given their freedom, "it was the plain duty of those in authority to make it secure" and "see that they had a fair chance in the battle of life."

Sheridan further angered unreconstructed Texans. When asked by a reporter at Brownsville, Texas, what he thought of the Lone Star state, Sheridan acidly replied: "If I owned hell and Texas, I would rent Texas out and live in hell!" Sheridan also argued with Texas Governor James Throckmorton over troop assignments. The governor wanted troops transferred from the interior of the state to protect frontier settlers from raiding Comanches. Sheridan refused to move any men, noting that "if a white man is killed by the Indians on an extensive Indian frontier, the greatest excitement will take place, but over the killing of many freedmen in the settlements, nothing is done."

Sheridan's determined defense of blacks in Texas and Louisiana, his bitter disputes with local politicians, his forceful suppression of white terrorism, and his enthusiastic application of the Reconstruction policies of the congressional Radical Republicans, led President Andrew Johnson to dismiss him from his command on July 31, 1867. Reassigned to command the Department of the Missouri, which included present-day Kansas, Oklahoma (Indian Territory), New Mexico, and Colorado, the embittered Sheridan would find the task of frontier defense equally difficult work, but far more congenial to his temperament.

Peace on the frontier was tenuous at best. Although the 1867 Treaty of Medicine Lodge had established reservations for the Cheyennes, Arapahos, Kiowas, Comanches, and Kiowa-Comanches in the Indian Territory, the Indians had in general failed to settle on the reservations. Congress had been preoccupied with the impeachment of President Johnson and had failed to appropriate the necessary funds to meet the government's treaty obligations. It hardly surprised Sheridan when a Cheyenne war party raided white settlements along the Saline and Solomon rivers in Kansas in August 1868. Sheridan thought that the only way to ensure a lasting peace was to see the Cheyennes "soundly whipped, and the ringleaders in the present trouble hung, their ponies killed, and such destruction of their property as will make them very poor."

Sheridan determined on a winter campaign to crush the Indians. Although campaigning against Indians during winter was hardly a novel idea, Sheridan's campaign was universally greeted as a bold, innovative plan. He was convinced that his well-fed and well-clothed troopers could challenge the severe climate long enough to strike a decisive blow. Winter limited the Indians' mobility, their greatest advantage over the soldiers. With their ponies weakened by scarce fodder they would seek the comfort of their traditional winter camps and be lulled into a false sense of security. Distance and climate had always protected them, but the westward advance of the railroads had ended that advantage, allowing supplies to be shipped rapidly to distant depots and stockpiled for prolonged campaigns.

Sheridan was well aware of the vital role to be played by the railroads in bringing order and peace to the frontier, and he was determined to remove the Indian barrier that impeded the rapid advance of the lines. Thus, he concentrated his forces against the Cheyennes, Arapahos, and Sioux who ranged near the Kansas Pacific and Union Pacific lines and paid only passing attention to the Kiowas and Comanches, who traditionally raided south into Texas and New Mexico. Self-interest and past fellowship tied the soldiers and railroaders together, for most of the railroad construction bosses, surveyors, and engineers were former soldiers with close ties to the military establishment. Grenville M. Dodge, chief engineer of the Union Pacific, had commanded an army corps during General Sherman's Atlanta campaign. William J. Palmer, president of the Kansas Pacific, and W. W. Wright, superintendent of the same line, were both former Union army generals. These personal relationships naturally resulted in close cooperation between the soldiers and the railroadmen. Military escorts for surveying parties and construction crews were readily provided, and Sheridan often made large troop transfers to oblige the needs of the railroads.

This alliance was only natural considering the heavy federal investment in the railroads. It was in the best interests of the government, the military, the capitalists, and the people to have the roads completed as rapidly as possible. For the military, the lines promised rapid and inexpensive transport of troops and supplies and consolidation of numerous scattered posts. More importantly, the transcontinental lines would split the northern Indian tribes from the southern ones, spell doom for the great buffalo herds, and bring in more settlers. In 1867, General Sherman correctly foresaw that the completion of the transcontinental railroad was "the solution of the Indian question."

Throughout late 1868 and early 1869 Sheridan directed a masterful winter campaign against the Cheyennes and allied tribes. In sharp encounters at the Washita in November 1868, at Soldier Springs the following month, and at Summit Springs in July 1869, Sheridan's troopers broke the power of the Cheyennes and compelled them to settle on a reservation in Indian Territory. The campaign won Sheridan an enviable reputation as an Indian fighter.

After Grant took office as president in March 1869, he appointed Sheridan lieutenant general and gave him command of the Division of the Missouri. This vast command extended from Sheridan's Chicago's headquarters on the east to the western borders of Montana, Wyoming, Utah, and New Mexico on the west and from the Canadian line on the north to the Rio Grande on the south. Most of the Indian population of the United States lived within the boundaries of Sheridan's division: Sioux, Northern Cheyennes, Southern Cheyennes, Kiowas, Comanches, Arapahos, Utes, Kickapoos, and Apaches all battled Sheridan's troopers. Before he left his frontier post to become commanding general of the army in 1883, Sheridan planned and directed the greatest Indian campaigns of the century.

Sheridan's pragmatism and elastic ethics made him the perfect frontier soldier for an expansionist republic. He ruthlessly carried out the dictates of his government, never faltering in his conviction that what he did was right. He viewed all Indians as members of an inferior race embracing a primitive culture. He felt them to be inordinately barbarous in war, which he attributed to a natural, ingrained savageness of the race. They formed, in Sheridan's mind, a stone-age barrier to the inevitable advance of white, Christian civilization.

Sheridan not only favored this advance, but he also proudly saw himself as its instrument.

Although he denied uttering it, the infamous quote that "the only good Indian is a dead Indian" became synonymous with Sheridan and his Indian policy. Although the sentiment certainly did not originate with the general, it nevertheless has the ring of typical Sheridan rhetoric. Exactly as he had done in the Shenandoah Valley in 1864, Sheridan proposed to undermine the Indians' economy and impoverish them, as well as kill warriors in battle. Sheridan believed that the essential first step in his total war against the Indians was the destruction of the great buffalo herds. Not only did buffalo provide a rich commissary for the plains tribes, but the herds also gave the Indians reason to continue their traditional seasonal movements, which led them off their reservations and into collision with whites. Several treaties, such as the 1868 Fort Laramie Treaty with the Sioux, gave the Indians the legal right to hunt in certain areas off the reservation so long as the buffalo ranged in sufficient numbers to justify the chase. Sheridan hoped to quickly reduce the buffalo population and thus terminate this hunting right.

The general applauded the activities of the white hunters who began slaughtering the buffalo in the early 1870s for their hides. In 1875, when the Texas state legislature was considering a bill to protect buffalo in Texas, Sheridan protested. Instead of outlawing the slaughter, Sheridan declared, the legislature should strike a bronze medal with a dead buffalo on one side and a discouraged Indian on the other and bestow it on the hunters. "These men have done in the last two years, and will do more in the next years, to settle the vexed Indian question, than the entire regular army has done in the last 30 years," the general declared.

> They are destroying the Indians' commissary; and it is a well-known fact that an army losing its base of supplies is placed at a great disadvantage. Send them powder and lead, if you will; but for the sake of a lasting peace, let them kill, skin, and sell until the buffaloes are exterminated. Then your prairies can be covered with speckled cattle, and the festive cowboy, who follows the hunter as a second forerunner of civilization.

After the destruction of the southern herd during the early 1870s, Sheridan worked to ensure the same fate for the northern herd. In 1881, when the government considered protecting what was left of the herds, Sheridan vigorously opposed such action. "If I could learn that every buffalo in the northern herd were killed I would be glad," the general wrote the War Department. "The destruction of this herd would do more to keep Indians quiet than anything else that could happen. Since the destruction of the southern herd, which formerly roamed from Texas to the Platte, the Indians in that section have given us no trouble."

Sheridan's sponsorship of several civilian hunting parties onto the plains—such as the millionaire's hunt of 1871 and the Grand Duke Alexis hunt in 1872—furthered his policy of exterminating the buffalo while at the same time he curried the favor of powerful, influential citizens. An avid sportsman, Sheridan liked to combine business with pleasure on these western jaunts. Nevertheless, they were a calculated part of his overall strategy to defeat the defiant western tribes.

With their economic base destroyed, western Indian tribes would have no choice but to retire to the reservations allotted to them by the government. Sheridan believed the concentration of the tribes and their segregation from the whites to be essential to the establishment of order on the frontier. He thus agreed with the reservation policy and supported President Grant's so-called Peace Policy out of loyalty to his old commander, but he vehemently disagreed with what he viewed as the overly mild treatment of the Indians on the reservation. "An attempt has been made to control the Indians, a wild and savage people, by moral suasion," Sheridan noted in 1874, "while we all know that the most stringent laws have to be enacted for the government of civilized white people."

The Civil War had taught Sheridan how easily the social order could be disrupted, and he had come to believe that the application of force was essential to guarantee stability. "I have the interest of the Indian at heart as much as anyone, and sympathize with his fading out race," Sheridan wrote, "but many years of experiences have taught me that to civilize and christianize [sic] the wild Indian it is not only necessary to put him on Reservations but it is also necessary to exercise some strong authority over him." Sheridan believed that only the army could exercise this control, and he repeatedly but futilely recommended that supervision of Indian affairs be transferred from the Department of the Interior back to the War Department where it had been until 1849.

The Indian Bureau's protection of Indians that Sheridan believed were guilty of depredations frustrated him, while the lack of a firm national consensus on the righteousness of his Indian campaigns deeply troubled him. During the Civil War, a grateful nation applauded his every action, but now he drew bitter criticism for pursuing similar tactics against the western Indians. The public condemnation of his direction of **Custer's 1868 Washita fight** and Baker's 1870 Piegan massacre on the Marias deeply wounded Sheridan.

Sheridan could never fathom why so many opposed his methods. His experience in previous Indian campaigns where conventional military methods had been employed and failed had convinced him by the early 1870s that the army could not "successfully fight Indians on the principle of high-toned warfare; that is where the mistake has been." "In taking the offensive," he once explained to Sherman in defense of his methods,

> I have to select that season when I can catch the fiends; and if a village is attacked and women and children killed, the responsibility is not with the soldiers but with the people whose crimes necessitated the attack. During the war did any one hesitate to attack a village or town occupied by the enemy because women and children were within its limits? Did we cease to throw shells into Vicksburg or Atlanta because women and children were there?

Sheridan could not cope rationally with eastern criticism, repeatedly relying on a string of Indian atrocity tales to discredit those who opposed his tac-

tics. He pointed to "good and pious ecclesiastics" as the agents of frontier disorder, castigating them as

> the aiders and abettors of savages who murdered, without mercy, men,
> women, and children; in all cases ravishing the women sometimes as often as
> 40 and 50 times in succession, and while insensible from brutality and exhaus-
> tion forced sticks up their persons, and, in one instance, the 40th or 50th savage
> drew his saber and used it on the person of the woman in the same manner.

He viewed his soldiers as defenders of female virtue—the heart of civilization—who sacrificed everything to destroy "murderers and rapers of helpless
women." Sheridan repeatedly trotted out these atrocities—committed by
Cheyennes during the 1868–1869 war—in his debates with the eastern humanitarians. "I do not know exactly how far these humanitarians should be excused on account of their ignorance," he wrote, in 1869, "but surely it is the
only excuse that gives a shadow of justification for aiding and abetting such
horrid crimes."

This use of such graphic diatribes gives some insight into Sheridan's background, his unconventional nature, and his quick reliance on any tactic to discredit his enemies. No story was more traditional in American history or more
effective in rallying support to the western army than the plight of captive
frontier women. Unmarried until age 44 and then taking a wife young enough
to be his daughter, Sheridan fully subscribed to Victorian notions of man as
woman's protector. He was mortified when unable to save the captive Clara
Blinn and her child, who the Arapahos murdered at the Battle of the Washita in
1868; and he was elated at Custer's 1869 rescue of two women held by the
Cheyennes during the same campaign. Nonetheless, he saw these women as
forever tainted by their captivity. In 1872, Sheridan refused to authorize the
payment of five ponies to ransom Mary Jordan from the Cheyennes. "I cannot
give my approval to any reward for the delivery of this white woman," Sheridan declared. "After having her husband and friends murdered, and her own
person subjected to the fearful bestiality of perhaps the whole tribe, it is mock
humanity to secure what is left of her for the consideration of five ponies."
Mrs. Jordan's captors murdered her.

Sheridan's bizarrely convoluted logic dictated that the Indians be destroyed *before* such outrages could occur, *before* the social fabric could come undone, *before* the race could be polluted. It was a no-win situation for Sheridan.
"We cannot avoid being abused by one side or the other," he mused in 1870. "If
we allow the defenseless people on the frontier to be scalped and ravished, we
are burnt in effigy and execrated as soulless monsters, insensible to the suffering of humanity. If the Indian is punished to give security to these people, we
are the same soulless monsters from the other side." Sheridan consciously,
even combatively, made his decision to support the settlers who resided on the
extended frontier line encompassed by his military division:

> My duties are to protect these people. I have nothing to do with Indians but in
> this connection. There is scarcely a day in which I do not receive the most

heart rendering [*sic*] appeals to save settlers . . . and I am forced to the alternative of choosing whether I shall regard their appeals or allow them to be butchered in order to save myself from the hue and cry of the people who know not the Indians and whose families have not the fear, morning, noon, and night, of being ravished and scalped by them. The wife of the man at the center of wealth and civilization and refinement is not more dear to him than is the wife of the pioneer of the frontier. I have no hesitation in making my choice. I am going to stand by the people over whom I am placed and give them what protection I can.

Such sentiments endeared Sheridan to the westerners, who soon came to regard him as their special advocate. They saw the question clearly. "Shall we Williampennize or Sheridanize the Indians?" asked the Columbus, Nebraska, *Platte Journal* in 1870. An angry Texan's letter in 1870 to the *Chicago Tribune* clearly expressed the position of many westerners: "Give us Phil Sheridan and Send Philanthropy to the devil!" But Indiana Congressman Daniel Voorhees spoke for many in the East when he rose in the House to denounce the "curious spectacle" of President Grant "upon the one hand welcoming his Indian agents in their peaceful garments and broadbrims coming to tell him what they have done as missionaries of a gospel of peace and of a beneficent Government, and upon the other hand welcoming this man, General Sheridan, stained with the blood of innocent women and children!" Wendell Phillips, the famed Boston reformer, could not have agreed more, declaring at an 1870 Reform League meeting: "I only know the names of three savages upon the Plains—Colonel Baker, General Custer, and at the head of all, General Sheridan."

Undeterred, Sheridan planned and directed a series of harsh campaigns during the 1870s that broke the back of Indian resistance and opened the frontier to rapid white occupation. In the largest of these campaigns, the **Red River War** of 1874–1875 on the southern plains and the **Great Sioux War** of 1876–1877 on the northern plains, he employed the same overall strategy that had succeeded in his 1868–1869 winter campaign. In each case he attempted to employ winter as an ally—although both campaigns saw summer fighting—and to have converging columns trap the Indians. Recognizing the difficulties of distance and terrain, he never expected these columns to meet or work in concert. Rather, they would keep the Indians insecure, off-balance, and constantly moving. In neither of these campaigns did the Indians suffer much loss of life in battle, but rather were defeated by starvation, exposure, stock and property losses, and constant insecurity. These campaigns reaffirmed the effectiveness of Sheridan's philosophy of total war, for it was concern over the suffering of their families that brought the warriors in to the reservations to surrender. If Indian women and children had been allowed to find sanctuary on the reservations—which they were not—or if the soldiers had been prohibited from attacking the Indian villages, then Sheridan's strategy could not have been successful. Only by making war on the entire tribe—men, women, and children—could Sheridan hope for quick results. Although brutal, this strategy was eminently successful.

So wedded to his converging-columns, winter-campaign strategy, Sheridan often refused to consider alternatives. Sheridan's conservatism, combined with his underestimation of the tenacity, courage, and ability of his Indian foes, could lead to disaster, as it did at both the **Rosebud** and Little Big Horn in 1876. In these most conventional of battles, where large numbers of troops and Indians maneuvered for control of open battlefields, the Indians simply outgeneraled Crook and Custer. Only after Sheridan turned to occupying the Sioux hunting grounds, to constant harassing tactics, and to military control over the agencies did the Indians suffer defeat as a result of starvation and exhaustion.

Sheridan, who during the Civil War had proven to be quite original in his approach to military problems, failed for the most part to provide innovative or imaginative leadership for the frontier army. The long shadow cast by the Civil War was part of the problem. Instead of looking to the future, Sheridan and many other army officers were far more captivated by the glorious past. The conflict on the western frontier was simply not a "real" war to the men who had won their stars in the great struggle of 1861–1865. Traditionalism set the tone of Sheridan's little frontier army.

After the Great Sioux War the nature of Indian campaigning changed. Sheridan's soldiers no longer marched into strange country against a foe of unknown numbers. Instead, his troopers ringed the Indian reservations with their forts, guarding against outbreaks. Clearly on the defensive, the Indians never could muster much strength. "Indian troubles that will hereafter occur will be those which arise upon the different Indian reservations," Sheridan declared in 1879, "or from attempts made to reduce the number and size of these reservations, by the concentration of the Indian tribes." The characteristic type of campaign after 1877 was the pursuit of Indian fugitives over a large expanse of territory. Such was the case with Chief Joseph's Nez Perce band in 1877 and with the Northern Cheyennes of Dull Knife and Little Wolf in 1878.

To guard against these outbreaks Sheridan could muster few troops. In the Departments of the Missouri, the Platte, and Dakota, he had but one man for every 75 square miles of territory, while in the Department of Texas he had but one for every 120 square miles of territory. His infantry companies averaged 40 men, while the cavalry and artillery did only slightly better with 60 and 50 men, respectively. Sheridan complained that three or four of his companies were "expected to hold and guard, against one of the most acute and wary foes in the world, a space of country that in any other land would be held by a brigade."

Keeping the peace on the Indian frontier remained Sheridan's primary duty throughout his years as commander of the Division of the Missouri, but even when there was Indian unrest his troops were quickly pulled from the frontier to meet various threats to national order. Sheridan and his troopers were called to duty, for example, during 1875 when he was placed in charge of Louisiana, during the tense election crisis of 1876, and during the railroad labor strife of 1877. Indian wars were already anachronistic to Gilded Age Americans, and the requirements of frontier expansion were usually subordinated to more pressing political or economic needs in the East.

Sheridan spent much of his time with the establishment, construction, maintenance, and abandonment of forts within the Division of the Missouri. A parsimonious Congress never appropriated enough funds to build vital new posts or to keep established forts in even a modest state of repair. Western communities competed for forts, depots, or headquarters offices, and some frontier community boosters even fabricated Indian scares to bring in troops, with a resulting gain to the local economy from construction and supply contracts. Sheridan often confronted irate citizens, congressmen, and even his own officers over troop transfers or the location, construction, and budget of forts and depots. Sheridan guarded his meager resources, spending funds only on those projects that he considered in "the public interest." He resented accusations that his actions retarded development in the western territories, for just the opposite was true. When Montana's territorial delegate chided Sheridan over his refusal to construct new posts, the general angrily reminded him that "nearly everything done for the opening of a way to Montana for the last two years has been ordered by me, or on my recommendation."

Sheridan was one of the West's greatest boosters, actively promoting western lands and constantly encouraging settlement. Despite his warm approval of the activities of western capitalists, he never sold his favor to any business interest and his name was never tainted with scandal. He was quick to point out to frontier promoters that "if the wishes of the settlers on the frontier were to be gratified, we would have a military post in every county, and the Army two or three hundred thousand strong." He had enormous power over the frontier economy, and when he could justifiably do so he worked to assist struggling western communities. One of his proudest accomplishments was to "have been connected with the great development of the country west of the Mississippi river by protecting every interest so far as in my power, and in a fair and honorable way, without acquiring a single personal interest to mar or blur myself or my profession."

Along with his promotion of western growth, Sheridan also developed a deep interest in the cause of conservation during his final years as commander of the Division of the Missouri. He had long had a special interest in the Yellowstone National Park region and had sponsored several exploring expeditions into the area. During an 1882 trip to Yellowstone National Park, Sheridan was enraged to learn of the slaughter of the park's wildlife by hide hunters. He was further disturbed to learn that the Department of the Interior had granted monopoly rights to develop the park to a company affiliated with the Northern Pacific Railroad. In contradiction to his earlier encouragement of the slaughter of the buffalo and his long support of the Northern Pacific, Sheridan now vigorously raised his voice in opposition. "The improvements in the park should be national," he declared in 1882, and if the Department of the Interior could not operate and protect the park, he would. "I will engage to keep out skin hunters and all other hunters," he told the administration, "by use of troops from Fort Washakie on the south, Custer on the east, and Ellis on the north, and, if necessary, I can keep sufficient troops in the park to accomplish this object, and give a place of refuge and safety for our noble game."

•••••

As part of his crusade to protect Yellowstone National Park, Sheridan organized a presidential excursion to the park during the summer of 1883. President Chester Arthur's trip, which was guided by Sheridan and accompanied by Secretary of War Robert Lincoln, Senator Vest, Governor Crosby, and other dignitaries, attracted wide publicity. It resulted in blocking efforts by the railroad to run a spur line into the park, reducing the company's leases in the park from 4,400 acres to only 10 acres, and defeating an attempt to return the park to the public domain. Sheridan failed to expand the park, but in August 1886 he had the satisfaction of ordering a company of the First Cavalry to take charge of the park, inaugurating 32 years of able military administration. When Sheridan rode to Yellowstone's rescue he achieved the finest moment of his last years and secured a national treasure for posterity.

On November 1, 1883, General W. T. Sherman retired from the army and Phil Sheridan moved to Washington to assume the position of commanding general. By law, however, Sherman's four stars retired with him, leaving Sheridan with the rank of lieutenant general. Sheridan found his new position frustrating, for the office was devoid of any real authority. The commanding general had no vital responsibilities in time of peace, because various bureau chiefs actually administered the army and reported directly to the secretary of war. Despite his relative youth, Sheridan's health had been slipping for years and he now withdrew more and more from the public limelight to spend time with his wife, Irene Rucker Sheridan (they were married in 1875), and their four young children. He spent much of this time working on his memoirs, which he completed in March 1888.

•••••

On May 22, 1888, just after his return from Chicago to inspect the site for Fort Sheridan, the 57-year-old general collapsed from a severe heart attack. A string of heart attacks of increasing seriousness followed. This news prompted Congress to revive the grade of general of the army, and President Grover Cleveland promptly signed the commission so that Sheridan joined Washington, Grant, and Sherman in holding the four-star rank. His spirits buoyed by the promotion, even though his body was now frail and emaciated, he requested that he be taken to his seaside cottage at Nonquitt, Massachusetts. Throughout July he calmly waited, looking out over the lovely summer sea of Buzzard's Bay, as his condition worsened. He faced the end without fear or despair, for Sheridan knew neither. He had dealt in death all of his adult life—he was too familiar with it to fear it when it came for him on the Sabbath evening of August 5, 1888.

His legacy, as with all of humankind, is a mixed one. Hardly cerebral, he nevertheless possessed a truly continental vision for the republic. He was determined to open up the West and unite it with the rest of the nation. He could be cruel and vindictive in this enterprise, and this found expression in his frontier military policies. Knowing nothing but a soldier's life, Sheridan tended to view every situation in light of how military power could establish order. Deeply affected by the chaos of Civil War, he was quick to apply force against all those who opposed his government's wishes—be they unreconstructed rebels in the South, striking laborers in the East, or Indians in the West.

Despite his racism, brutality, and conservatism he was in many ways the perfect soldier for his times. He ruthlessly carried out the dictates of his government, confident that his harsh tactics brought on a quicker peace and thus an end to warfare for all. He conquered and subjugated the Indians, opening their rich lands to a wildly expansive and exploitative generation. He then sought, in his simple, blunt way, to impose order on that mad push westward and was at times somewhat successful.

By the time Phil Sheridan passed from the scene his frontier was gone as well. That final, rapid push westward—in all its brutality and all its glory—remains his great legacy. "He was," as the Bard said, "a man, take him for all in all, I shall not look upon his like again."

THE PLAINS INDIANS AND THE PASSING OF THE BUFFALO

Most of the Plains Indians' economic and cultural activities revolved around the buffalo. In addition to being their main source of food, clothing, and shelter, the buffalo also played a central part in their ceremonial practices. When Philip Sheridan decided to target the great herds for extermination, he could not have done more to disrupt the traditional way of life of his Native American foes. In the selection below, taken from an Indian folktale related to anthropologist Alice Marriott, a Kiowa woman named Old Lady Horse tells us what the loss of the buffalo meant to her people.

The End of the World: The Buffalo Go

Everything the Kiowas had came from the buffalo. Their tipis were made of buffalo hides, so were their clothes and mocassins. They ate buffalo meat. Their containers were made of hide, or of bladders or stomachs. The buffalo were the life of the Kiowas.

Most of all, the buffalo was part of the Kiowa religion. A white buffalo calf must be sacrificed in the Sun Dance. The priests used parts of the buffalo to make their prayers when they healed people or when they sang to the powers above.

So, when the white men wanted to build railroads, or when they wanted

Source: "The End of the World: The Buffalo Go." Kiowa, from *American Indian Mythology* by Alice Marriott and Carol K. Rachlin. Copyright © 1968 by Alice Marriott and Carol K. Rachlin. Reprinted by permission of HarperCollins Publishers, Inc.

to farm or raise cattle, the buffalo still protected the Kiowas. They tore up the railroad tracks and the gardens. They chased the cattle off the ranges. The buffalo loved their people as much as the Kiowas loved them.

There was war between the buffalo and the white men. The white men built forts in the Kiowa country, and the woolly-headed buffalo soldiers [the Tenth Cavalry, made up of Negro troops] shot the buffalo as fast as they could, but the buffalo kept coming on, coming on, even into the post cemetery at Fort Sill. Soldiers were not enough to hold them back.

Then the white men hired hunters to do nothing but kill the buffalo. Up and down the plains those men ranged, shooting sometimes as many as a hundred buffalo a day. Behind them came the skinners with their wagons. They piled the hides and bones into the wagons until they were full, and then took their loads to the new railroad stations that were being built, to be shipped east to the market. Sometimes there would be a pile of bones as high as a man, stretching a mile along the railroad track.

The buffalo saw that their day was over. They could protect their people no longer. Sadly, the last remnant of the great herd gathered in council, and decided what they would do.

The Kiowas were camped on the north side of Mount Scott, those of them who were still free to camp. One young woman got up very early in the morning. The dawn mist was still rising from Medicine Creek, and as she looked across the water, peering through the haze, she saw the last buffalo herd appear like a spirit dream.

Straight to Mount Scott the leader of the herd walked. Behind him came the cows and their calves, and the few young males who had survived. As the woman watched, the face of the mountain opened.

Inside Mount Scott the world was green and fresh, as it had been when she was a small girl. The rivers ran clear, not red. The wild plums were in blossom, chasing the red buds up the inside slopes. Into this world of beauty the buffalo walked, never to be seen again.

QUESTIONS

1. Why did Sheridan have such a negative opinion of the Plains Indians? In what ways did his views of African Americans differ from his views of Native Americans? In what ways were they similar?

2. To what extent did Sheridan's Civil War experience influence his conduct of the Indian wars? How would you describe his philosophy of war?

3. What role did railroads play in Sheridan's military strategy against the Plains Indians? What prompted such an ardent proponent of progress to become a conservationist?

4. What were Sheridan's views of women? In what ways did these views shape Sheridan's conception both of himself and of his mission on the post–Civil War frontier?

5. What influence did Sheridan have on the times in which he lived? What challenges does a biographer who has chosen to write about Sheridan confront? Would your portrayal of the famous general be positive or negative?

BIBLIOGRAPHY

The most recent biography of Sheridan is Roy J. Morris, Jr., *Sheridan: The Life and Wars of General Phil Sheridan* (1992). Studies that focus on Sheridan's post–Civil War career on the Plains include Paul Andrew Hutton, *Phil Sheridan and His Army* (1985); Randolph Keim, *Sheridan's Troopers on the Borders: A Winter Campaign on the Plains* (1985); and Stan Hoig, *The Battle of the Washita: The Sheridan–Custer Indian Campaign of 1867–1869* (1976). For more general treatments of the late nineteenth-century Indian wars, see Robert M. Utley, *Frontier Regulars: The United States Army and the Indian, 1866–1891* (1973); William H. Leckie, *The Military Conquest of the Southern Plains* (1963); and Dee Brown, *Bury My Heart at Wounded Knee: An Indian History of the West* (1970), which examines the conflicts from a Native American perspective.

Susan LaFlesche Picotte

The Indian wars had ramifications that extended well beyond the Plains region. They were also felt in Washington. During the early 1880s, government
officials gradually recognized that federal inability to protect Indian lands
from the incursions of white settlers had made a mockery of the reservation
policy. In its place, Washington moved toward an assimilation program designed to "civilize" Native Americans: by dissolving their tribal organizations and by integrating them into the broader society. The legislative centerpiece of this new approach was the Dawes Severalty Act of 1887, which broke
up communally controlled tribal lands and provided 160-acre allotments to
individual families. To ensure that Native Americans remained on these plots
and did not sell them to speculators, the government retained title to the allotments for 25 years.

Although many federal officials doubtless believed assimilation would improve the lives of
Native Americans, no one bothered to consult them about the
change of policy. And the assumptions underlying the new
program represented the worst
forms of cultural chauvinism.
Having to maintain their own
property, it was believed, would
both force Native Americans to
discard the "barbaric" habits
of their tribal past and promote
acquisition of those moral-
pecuniary values—temperance,
thrift, industry, and the like—
that white society so highly
prized.

In implementing the new policy, Indian Bureau officials took a number of steps to speed the pace of assimilation. One was the suppression of traditional tribal rituals such as the Sun Dance. Another focused on Native-American youths, many of whom were dispatched to off-reservation boarding schools, where they received instruction designed to separate them from their cultural past. For many students the experience left much to be desired. All too often they found themselves in a miserable situation for which they were totally unprepared: Those who resisted the school routine had a terrible time; yet those who adapted were frequently considered outsiders when they returned home.

There were, however, some exceptions. One was Susan LaFlesche Picotte. The daughter of an Omaha chief who believed Native Americans had no alternative but to accept assimilation, she made the most of her years at Virginia's Hampton Institute, later becoming the nation's first Indian woman doctor. Despite her accomplishments, Picotte did not forget where she came from, and her subsequent career demonstrated that assimilation did not require an abandonment of one's past. In the essay that follows, Valerie Sherer Mathes describes the obstacles Picotte had to surmount in order to become a physician, while providing an in-depth examination of this remarkable woman's selfless work among her people.

Susan LaFlesche Picotte
Valerie Sherer Mathes

"Plenty of air and sunshine—that is Nature's medicine, but I have hard work to make my people understand," Susan LaFlesche, the first Indian woman physician, once remarked. Susan's people, the Siouan-speaking Omaha, had their origins in the Ohio and Wabash River area but had subsequently migrated westward to eastern Nebraska. Following the passage of the Indian Removal Act in 1830, they began ceding their claims to eastern lands. By 1854 they gave up their rights to hunting grounds west of the Missouri River and retained only a small tract bordering the river. In return for ceded lands, they received annuities, a grist mill, a blacksmith shop, and protection from hostile tribes. The treaty also gave the Board of Foreign Missions of the Presbyterian Church four quarter sections of land to continue missionary work among the tribe.

The Presbyterians had established their first permanent mission at Bellevue, Nebraska, in 1845, but when the Omaha cession required the Indians to move to their new reservation, the missionaries followed. In 1858 they built a new mission house as well as a boarding and day school where Omaha children, including those of Joseph LaFlesche, were educated.

Source: Nebraska History, Winter 1982, pp. 502–25. Reprinted by permission of Nebraska State Historical Society.

The son of a French fur trader and his Indian wife, Joseph in 1853 was the last recognized chief of the tribe. Aware that the Indians would eventually have to learn the ways of the whites, in the 1850s he hired white carpenters to construct a two-story frame house near the site of the new mission. By abandoning the Omaha traditional earthen lodge, Joseph became an example for his people to follow. He laid out a town site, fenced 100 acres, and divided the land into smaller fields in order that each man in his village could farm.

Joseph took another step in adopting white ways when he refused to have his daughters tattooed and his son's ears pierced. He explained, "I was always sure that my sons and daughters would live to see the time when they would have to mingle with the white people, and I determined that they should not have any mark upon them that might be detrimental in their future surrounding."

Joseph was remarkably astute, for several of his seven children not only mingled with whites but played important roles in bridging the gap between the two cultures. One son, Francis, became a well-known ethnologist with the Bureau of American Ethnology; Susette, the eldest daughter, became a prominent Indian-rights leader; and Susan, the youngest daughter, became the first Indian woman to graduate from a medical college and practice modern medicine.

•••••

Susan's education began at the Omaha Agency and the Presbyterian Mission School. In September 1879 she and her sister Marguerite entered the Elizabeth Institute for Young Ladies in Elizabeth, New Jersey. In 1882, after three years in New Jersey, the sisters returned to the reservation. Susan spent the next two years working at the mission school and for a six-month period taught a class of small children. In 1884 Marguerite and Susan entered Hampton Normal and Agricultural Institute in Hampton, Virginia.

The education of Indians at Hampton began in 1879 when Richard Henry Pratt, a young Army officer, arrived with 22 Indian students from Fort Marion, Florida. Well known for its education of Negro freedmen, Hampton had been established by General Samuel Armstrong in 1868. Armstrong welcomed the Indian students warmly, thus beginning a long and successful experiment in Indian education at Hampton.

For the next two years Susan and Marguerite, dressed in uniforms, drilled on the parade ground and were imbued with the educational philosophy of Armstrong. He believed that labor was "a spiritual force, that physical work not only increased wage-earning capacity, but promoted fidelity, accuracy, honesty, persistence and intelligence."

•••••

Graduating from Hampton on May 20, 1886, as salutatorian, Susan's address was entitled "My Childhood and Womanhood." General Byron M. Cutcheon, Civil War medal of honor winner, also presented her with the Demorest prize, a gold medal awarded by the faculty to the graduating senior who had achieved the highest examination score in the junior year. Dressed simply but neatly, "Susan looked well, spoke clearly and everyone was delighted with her," wrote Alice Cunningham Fletcher, an ethnologist who had journeyed from Washington, D.C., to join the more than 1,000 people in the audience.

Susan's education to this point was little out of the ordinary, but her decision to attend medical college was unique. The fact that she eventually became a medical practitioner was not unusual, for in some western tribes there were medicine women and female shamans. All native medical practitioners gained their skills through visions and trances brought on by fasting as well as by special training. While Indians could acquire healing skills at any point in their lives, women could not engage in healing until after menopause. What set Susan apart was her desire to graduate from a medical college, an accomplishment few women could hope to achieve, especially Indian women. Later, too, she would practice medicine many years before the onset of menopause on the Omaha reservation.

At Hampton, Susan had been encouraged to concentrate on academic subjects rather than vocational skills. Both General Armstrong and Dr. Martha M. Waldron, the school physician, believed Susan capable of attending medical college. But first it was necessary to raise funds for tuition and expenses. Alice Cunningham Fletcher and Sara Thomson Kinney, wife of the editor of the *Hartford* (Connecticut) *Courant*, would solve that problem.

Alice Fletcher was familiar with the LaFlesche family, having worked closely with Francis as her major informant on Omaha culture, and having been tended by young Susan during an attack of inflammatory rheumatism in 1883. While serving as missionary, teacher, and government official for the tribe, Miss Fletcher had also been a frequent visitor to reform gatherings at Lake Mohonk, New York. There she met Sara Kinney who, after some persuasion, agreed to approach the commissioner of Indian Affairs about the possibility of Susan's continued education.

The Woman's Medical College of Pennsylvania, located in Philadelphia, ultimately admitted Susan as a "beneficiary student." Established initially as the Female College of Pennsylvania "to instruct respectable and intelligent *females* in the various branches of medical science," it opened its doors on October 12, 1850. By the time of Susan's attendance, it was known as the Woman's Medical College of Pennsylvania.

• • • • •

On learning of her good fortune, young Susan wrote to Mrs. Kinney from Hampton in June that it made her happy to have so many mothers caring for her. "It has always been a desire of mine to study medicine ever since I was a small girl," she wrote, "for even then I saw the needs of my people for a good physician." She intended to teach the women of her tribe a few practical points about cleanliness, cooking, nursing, and housekeeping. In closing Susan noted that she and Marguerite hoped to spend most of the summer working among the sick at the church.

Suffering from motion sickness, a weary Susan alighted from the train in Philadelphia in early October. She was met by Mrs. Seth Talcott, chairman of the business committee of the association and Dr. Elizabeth Bundy, an instructor of anatomy at the college. Susan was placed in suitable housing at the YWCA, with which she was extremely pleased, and was provided with necessary supplies and clothing. For the next three years she sent home lively and interesting letters to her sister Rosalie about the people she met, her courses, and the sights she saw.

• • • • •

In her first year Susan attended lectures in chemistry, anatomy, physiology, histology, materia medica, general therapeutics, and obstetrics. Students were expected to take notes. Apparently Susan had difficulty with chemistry, for she borrowed a chemistry notebook almost every morning after lecture from a second-year student, Sarah Lockery. Although attendance was not mandatory, Susan and the others rarely missed classes, especially on examination day, for they had to pass 90 percent of their tests.

In addition to attending lectures, the students went to a weekly clinic at the Woman's Hospital. Susan humorously described an incident in which female students had been joined by male students of the Jefferson Medical College. Just as the surgeon prepared to operate, a young man fainted and had to be removed from the room. "I wasn't even thinking of fainting," wrote Susan, nor for that matter were any "of the girls." Susan and her fellow students must have truly enjoyed that day, for they had often been teased about being faint hearted. Apparently Susan never minded dissecting cadavers and jokingly informed Rosalie she was "going to wield the knife tonight—not the scalping knife though."

• • • • •

Unlike most Indian women of the 19th century, Susan was afforded the opportunity to learn about mainstream cultural activities. She frequented the Philadelphia Academy of Art, commented on the paintings of Benjamin West, became fond of musical performances, and attended literary and theatrical events, including "The Mikado" and a performance of Lily Langtry in "Wife's Peril." Accompanied by her brother Francis, she witnessed the Philadelphia Mummer's Parade, commenting that the masqueraders dressed as Indians looked "pretty well for Indians."

She especially enjoyed getting out of the city and walking through Fairmount Park collecting pine cones, but she did not ignore her Indian friends and visited Marguerite at Hampton at every opportunity. She also visited the Indian boys at the Educational Home in West Philadelphia as well as the Indian children at Philadelphia's Lincoln Institute. She attended missionary meetings, went to church, and joined her friends in various social activities. Well respected by her fellow students, Susan was chosen corresponding secretary of the Young Women's Christian Association. Out of a feeling of indebtedness for their support, she spoke before several branches of the Connecticut Indian Association. In October 1887 she visited the Hartford group, meeting for the first time many of the women whom she lovingly called her "mothers."

•••••

Susan graduated on March 14, 1889, at the head of a class of 36 young women. In his commencement address Dr. James B. Walker praised Susan highly:

> Thoughtful of a service to her people, child though she was, she permits not the magnitude of her task to stay the inspiration, but bravely, thoughtfully, diligently pursues the course, and to-day receives her fitting reward. All this without a precedent. She will stand among her people as the first woman physician. Surely we may record with joy such courage, constancy, and ability.

Following a competitive exam, Susan was elected one of six women to intern at the Woman's Hospital for four months beginning in May. She took a brief vacation before her internship. Spending several days with her Connecticut "mothers," she was kept busy speaking before branches in Farmington, Guilford, New Britain, Norwich, Waterbury, and Winsted before she made a quick trip home.

Susan returned to the reservation permanently in late 1889. She accepted an appointment as physician at the government boarding school on August 5, but in December Omaha Agent Robert Ashley requested that she be allowed to treat the adults of the tribe as well. Commissioner Thomas Morgan complied with his request. Although there was already another physician at the reservation, within three months of her coming, Susan cared for most of his Indian patients because she spoke their language. When the other doctor left, she was in charge of the health care of all the 1,244 tribal members.

The government built an office for her at the school. A spacious building, it contained a drug counter, cabinets full of games and scrapbooks and picture books as well as magazines. Some branches of the Women's National Indian Association donated books and other reading matter to her library. Before long her office was full not only of school children but of adults, who came to ask her advice on business matters, personal affairs, and questions of law. Especially on cold rainy days, the older Omaha could be found spending a pleasant hour either visiting with Susan or looking through the magazines.

Susan's living quarters were provided at the government school, where Marguerite was the principal teacher. Although most of their work was centered at the school, Susan and Marguerite also carried on their father's work, directing the tribe along the path to assimilation. They advised the tribe, encouraging couples to marry by license and with the sanction of the church. Christian services were soon being held over the dead. Thus Susan was serving not only as physician but also as nurse, teacher, social worker, general adviser, and interpreter for church services.

Religion had always been an important part of Susan's life, and partly for that reason the Women's National Indian Association appointed her medical missionary to her tribe. She attended church services on Sunday mornings, where she and Marguerite often assisted by singing and interpreting. Sometimes they spoke before church groups on various topics. Christian Endeavor meetings were held for the young people on Sunday evenings, prayer meetings were held on Wednesdays, and Sunday school was held for the children in the schoolhouse before church.

But it is the medical record of this young Omaha woman that is legendary. Her patients, scattered over the 30x45-mile reservation, were reached by a network of poor, dirt roads. During her first year she was unable to make as many house calls as she wished because she did not have a team. If a patient was only a mile or so away, she walked. If the distance was greater, she hired a team, but patients often came to her. She finally purchased a team and buggy. In a talk at Hampton in 1892, Susan told her audience that the roads were so bad that a single horse could not pull a wagon. "After trying for some time to go about on horseback," she said, "I broke so many bottles and thermometers that I had to give that up."

During the first winter there were two epidemics of influenza. Although there were no fatalities among the adults, two babies died. With the arrival of summer, her patient load lessened. During July 1891, she saw only 37 patients; in August the number rose to 111; and by September it soared to 130. She started out every morning before eight o'clock, drove six miles in one direction, returned to the office by noon and then set out again on more rounds, returning sometimes as late as 10 P.M. with an exhausted team. Although she never spoke of her own weariness, her reports began to reflect more and more days taken off because of illness. She treated both acute and chronic cases ranging from influenza, dysentery, and cholera, to an epidemic of conjunctivitis, an eye ailment spread because of unsanitary conditions. After she had instructed her patients to use separate towels and basins, the epidemic subsided. At the end of her second year, she summed up her experiences by saying, "I am enjoying my work exceedingly, and feel more interest in, and more attached to my people than ever before. I have not a single thing to complain of, for . . . my life here is a very happy one."

December 1891 brought an especially bad epidemic of influenza, *la grippe* as she called it. Susan saw a total of 114 patients that month during the epidemic. She wrote that the disease

> raged with more violence than during the two preceding years . . . Some families were rendered helpless by it, sometimes all the family but one or two being down with it. Almost every day during the month I was out making visits. Several days the thermometer was 15 to 20 degrees below zero, and I had to drive myself.

•••••

January 1892 brought no relief as Susan cared for 120 cases in three weeks. The last week of the month she took off to care for members of her immediate family. When ladies from the Morristown, New Jersey, auxiliary of the Women's National Indian Association sent Susan money for the sick, she added it to funds of her own to buy food for her patients. From October 1891 to the spring of 1892, Susan saw more than 600 patients. The hard rides were becoming increasingly exhausting, but she never refused to make a call unless she was bedridden herself.

With the arrival of summer 1892, Susan took a well-deserved month of rest and attended Hampton's 24th anniversary. She gave the commencement address entitled "My Work as Physician Among My People." While in the East, she had an opportunity to meet more members of the Women's National Indian Association. As their medical missionary, she now had to make annual reports. In May she spoke before the Washington, D.C., auxiliary on the spread of intemperance among her people. One of her earlier reports had stressed the drinking problem, noting that the Omaha could obtain whisky almost as easily as water. Laws were needed to prevent crimes attributed to alcoholism, she believed: "If a drunken Indian smashes a buggy and assaults a woman and child by beating them and nothing is done, what can prevent him from doing it again." The temperance movement was beginning to occupy much of her thought.

During the fall of 1892, Susan continued her arduous round of house calls, attending to children and numerous walk-in patients, but her own health began to suffer. She had complained of numbness and breathing difficulties in college but thought it was psychological. Possibly it was an early indication of the disease that would later take her life. By the first of January 1893, she was bedridden. "Susie has been sick for several weeks, her ears have been troubling her very much, she says she has pain in her head and the back of her neck constantly," wrote Rosalie to Francis. On October 20, 1893, she resigned as government physician because of her health and that of her mother, who had recently become critically ill.

In the summer of 1894, Susan surprised her family by announcing her forthcoming marriage to Henry Picotte, a Sioux Indian from the Yankton Agency and brother of Marguerite's late husband, Charles. Charlies had died in 1892, and probably sometime shortly thereafter Thomas Ikinicapi, Susan's first love, died of tuberculosis. Only Marguerite and Rosalie knew of "TI," as Susan called him, for she had placed her education and career before marriage. After she graduated and began to practice, she met Henry, "a handsome man with polite, ingratiating manners, and a happy sense of humor." Susan fell in love with him. When she expressed her desire to marry, her friends and the Heritages [close family friends] were upset. Learning of the intended betrothal on June 30, Mrs. Heritage wrote expressing regret, for she did not think it wise owing to Susan's poor health. Marian also wrote Rosalie of her concern over the matter. "It is because I wish for Susie only the best things in this world with the least suffering and trouble that I wish she had decided not to take this step," she wrote.

Personal letters written by Susan about her romance with Henry have not survived, but there are numerous letters in which she revealed her feelings for TI. They had met at Hampton, and although he was deeply interested in Susan, she had decided that her career must come first. She visited Hampton several times while a student at the Woman's Medical College and spent as much time as possible with TI. She was afraid that he might return to Hampton already married but wrote Rosalie that [this] would not break her heart, for she was not "made that way." She added, however, "He was *without exception* the handsomest Indian I ever saw."

Her 1886 Christmas visit to Hampton found TI constantly by her side, as handsome as ever. They attended a band concert, and brought in the New Year together. At one point during her visit, TI was so overcome with emotion on seeing her that "he had his handkerchief up to his face and his eyes were shining—I felt so sorry for him—I felt like crying," she wrote. When her carriage departed Hampton, he stood with a handkerchief over his eyes again. He looked so forlorn that Marguerite broke down and another friend wrote that he "acted as if he had lost his right hand."

In his letters TI told Susan he thought of her constantly. Her good friend, Hampton teacher Cora M. Folsom, was convinced that there was no one good enough for Susan, and encouraged her to have only a "platonic friendship" with TI, for she feared he was getting into "deep waters" over her. "He is so respectful to me & I like him for that & for his faithfulness," wrote Susan in reply.

In January 1887, Susan and a friend had gone to the Educational Home in West Philadelphia to visit the Indian boys. While there a young Dakota Sioux had paid a great deal of attention to her, but Susan wrote she did not "care to go with any one and . . . remembered someone at Hampton and wondered what he would think to see so much attention lavished upon [her]." When she attended morning service and Sunday school in the afternoon, the young Sioux sat next to her holding out his hymnal. She remarked to Rosalie, "That is the end of it I hope. I haven't any time or patience for such things nowadays. Doctors don't have much time, you know, and he will have to keep his place."

Several days later she wrote, "I shall be the dear little old maid you know and come and see you . . . and doctor and dose you all." In the very next sentence, nevertheless, she spoke of TI: "Sometimes it seems to me I can see *him* looking at me with such a look—sometimes a smile on his face as he says, 'Come on Susie.'" But afraid her older sister might become concerned, Susan assured her that TI had helped her, had been a good influence, and that she only hoped her influence over him would be half as good. "I want to be his *friend*," she wrote, "and help him—I am a better girl for having gone with him." She ended by assuring Rosalie that "nothing will come of it dear, so be easy and at rest." One wonders if her life would have been the same had TI lived and had they married, but that was not to be.

Susan, when almost 30, apparently decided she was tired of being an old maid. Following her marriage to Henry, she began to participate more directly in Indian life. She and Marguerite, who had remarried, drew even closer, both having their first babies within a few months of each other. Within a year Susan was seriously ill again. "Susie had been very sick; I had given up all hopes of her when she commenced to improve," wrote Rosalie to Francis.

• • • • •

Despite her poor health she became an active temperance speaker in place of her father. In 1856 Joseph LaFlesche had organized a police force of Omaha

Indians who administered corporal punishment to any member of the tribe found drunk. Until his death in 1888, there was very little liquor on the reservation, but since that time liquor flowed freely, church attendance suffered, and farm work was often neglected.

As a young student at the medical college, Susan had attended lectures by noted temperance leaders including Frances O. Willard. She was, therefore, exposed to the temperance movement and the effects of alcoholism early in her medical career. Later as a physician she saw the effects of alcohol from both medical and personal angles. Tragically, her husband had begun to drink excessively, and consequently she became even more active in the movement. During the four years she had tended the ill of the Omaha tribe, Susan always felt perfectly safe in making her appointments, but the increased use of alcohol had begun to change the situation. "Men and women died from alcoholism, and little children were seen reeling on the streets of the town," she wrote. "Drunken brawls in which men were killed occurred and no person's life was considered safe." Women pawned their clothing, and men spent rent money on liquor instead of provisions and machinery. Congress passed a law that improved the situation and a commissioner or deputy was assigned to enforce it, but his removal encouraged bootleggers to return. A death caused by alcoholism on January 26, 1900, prompted Susan to write to William A. Jones, commissioner of Indian Affairs, asking what advantage any money saved from the removal of the deputy would be if her "people . . . [were] to be demoralized mentally, morally, and physically."

• • • • •

Domestic brawls were common, and Indian lands were sold for money to purchase liquor. One Indian, she explained, sold his land in 1904 for $6,000, and in one year spent the money, treating his friends to liquor, giving them money, and buying himself three buggies. She enumerated the deaths attributed to liquor from 1894 to 1914, beginning with an individual who fell from a buggy and was not missed by his drunken companions until the next morning, when his frozen body was discovered. The government's efforts to keep liquor off the reservation had failed miserably. Susan urged that the detectives appointed to patrol the reservation not be local men, and above all, should be moral, impartial, and above receiving bribes.

Whatever small victories she achieved elsewhere were not equalled at home, and in 1905, owing to complications from drinking, Susan's husband died. She was left as the sole support of an invalid mother and two small boys. For the remainder of her life, she continued her struggle against alcohol. Following her husband's death, the Presbyterian Board of Home Missions appointed her missionary to her tribe, the first Indian to hold such a position. She was furnished housing along with a small stipend.

The degenerative ear disease from which she had suffered for years made her increasingly deaf; and the pain now extended down into her back. She continued, nevertheless, serving as teacher, preacher, field worker, and physician at the agency's Blackbird Hills Presbyterian Church. She held church services, read the Bible in her native tongue, interpreted hymns, and held simple Christian services for those who died.

In November 1906, Susan and Marguerite's husband, Walter Diddock, purchased house lots in the newly established town of Walthill, carved out of Indian land by the railroad. Largely through Susan's work, the Secretary of the Interior Department ruled that no liquor could be sold in towns once a part of the Omaha Reservation, another small victory in her long struggle over alcohol. On her town lot Susan had a modern home built, complete with fireplace, furnace, windows for light and fresh air, and an indoor bathroom. Upon its completion, Susan, her sons Pierre and Caryl, and her mother moved in. Once settled, Susan and Marguerite entered the social structure of the town, becoming charter members of the new chapter of Eastern Star. Susan, a major organizer of the new Presbyterian Church, also taught in its Sunday school. Her home was on occasion filled with family and friends, for she enjoyed entertaining.

The two sisters supported community projects, lectures, concerts, and special events at the county fair. At the latter Susan was in charge one year of the Indian department. She continued to be active as president of the church missionary society, urging townspeople and businessmen of Walthill to become sufficiently interested in projects to give freely of their money and time. Soon many people began attending the monthly church meetings of the study circle, which held talks on topics ranging from Mexicans to Negro freedmen. Concerts were held to raise money for missionary work.

Susan also became politically involved when the government arbitrarily decided to extend the trust period for the Omaha an additional 10 years because it considered Indians in general uneducated and backward. This was, however, not true of the Omaha, who had a higher literacy rate than most tribes. "They are independent and self reliant . . . [and] as competent as the same number of white people," noted Susan. Their last allotment papers had been delivered in 1885, and the 25-year trust period, during which time they could not alienate their land, should have ended in 1910. The decision to extend the trust term caused numerous hardships for the Omaha. In addition, a new system of supervised farming was instituted. The Winnebago and Omaha Agencies were consolidated, thus requiring longer travel distance for tribal members to transact agency business. A. G. Pollock, well-respected Omaha superintendent, was removed. Protests arose from both whites and Indians over the additional supervision. "Every business action of the individual is supervised and hedged about with red tape and paternal restrictions," wrote the editor of the *Walthill Times.* All the Omaha wanted was to lease their lands and draw upon their monies themselves. But, as Susan had predicted, the entire tribe rebelled, depending upon her to free them of these new regulations.

• • • • •

In February she was the unanimous choice of the Omaha men and women as one of the delegates to argue their case before the Secretary of the Interior Department and the attorney general of the United States. When she originally declined to do so because of poor health, tribesmen threatened to place her bodily on the train. "The Omahas depend on me so, and I just have to take care of myself till this fight is over," she wrote to her friend Miss Folsom. Despite a severe case of neurasthenia (nervous frustration), which prevented her from digesting food, Susan protested the red tape which made it difficult for the Indians to get their own money and the problems imposed in travel to the new combined agency. Her efforts and those of the rest of the delegation were successful, and most of the Omaha were deemed competent to rent or lease their lands and to receive monies.

Susan occasionally wrote articles which contained light humor. Invited by the Burt County Farmer's Institute to speak on "Primitive Farming among the Omaha Indians," she put the history of tribal farming on paper. "There was no need for suffragettes in those days," she wrote, "for the produce of these gardens always belonged to the woman." Her final draft was read by Marguerite on February 13, 1912, in Decatur, Nebraska, during one of the most successful meetings the association had ever held. Susan continued recording the traditions of her people by writing an article on the origin of corn for the local newspaper.

Susan always returned, nevertheless, to her first love, medicine. She was one of the organizers of the Thurston County Medical Association, served several terms on the health board for the town of Walthill, and was a member of the State Medical Society. For three years she served as chairman of the state health committee of the Nebraska Federation of Women's Clubs, working to get health-related bills through the state legislature. She began to study tuberculosis more intensively, giving lectures on the subject at the Indian church as well as to local townspeople.

• • • • •

Another one of Susan's important successes was the campaign to eradicate the "troublesome household pest," the fly. Describing it as the filthiest of all vermin, Susan designed an attractive anti-house fly poster encouraging people not to allow flies in their houses or near food. By sprinkling lime or kerosene where flies might collect, she pointed out, their breeding places could be eliminated; she also encouraged the use of screens for doors and windows. Fly traps were soon available at local hardware stores.

Susan had always dreamed of a hospital where she could care for her patients and avoid the long trips to hospitals in Omaha or Sioux City. After several efforts to interest local philanthropic organizations in building a hospital, she approached the Home Mission Board of the Presbyterian Church. It granted $8,000. The Society of Friends (Quakers), through the Presbyterian Church, gave an additional $500. Marguerite and her husband donated an acre of land, and equipment and furnishings came from other individuals and organizations. A benefit concert was held to raise additional funds, and the hospital opened in January 1913. It contained two general wards with a capacity of 12 beds, five private wards, maternity ward, operating room, two bathrooms, kitchen, and reception room. Both

Indians and whites were admitted, and in 1915 a total of 448 patients were cared for, 126 of them Indians. The presence of the hospital made it possible for Susan to reduce her patient load and avoid long drives in inclement weather.

Death took Susan LaFlesche on September 18, 1915. The infection in her ears had worsened steadily, and by 1914 was diagnosed as "decay of the bone," probably cancer. Susan underwent two operations, the first in February 1915 and the second the following March. By June her brother had been informed by the surgeon that she had only a month or so to live. Her sons, Caryl and Pierre, were home from school that summer and they and Marguerite's eldest daughter helped care for her. Caryl was the only one Susan would trust to give her hypodermic injections and medicines.

Her value to the community had been so profound that the *Walthill Times* of September 24 added an extra page to carry special eulogies of Susan. Funeral services were held on Sunday morning, September 19, in her home, where friends and relatives surrounded her casket. The simple service was performed by three Presbyterian clergymen, the Reverend C. H. Mitchelmore, pastor of the Walthill Presbyterian Church, which Susan had helped to organize; the Reverend George A. Beith, pastor of the Blackbird Hills Mission, where she had spent years of hard work; and Dr. D. E. Jenkins, a member of the Presbyterian Board of Home Missions, which she had served for many years. The closing prayer was given in the Omaha language by one of the older members of the tribe. Interment took place at the Bancroft Cemetery, where she was laid to rest beside her husband. The Amethyst Chapter of the Eastern Star conducted a moving graveside service.

> Hardly an Omaha Indian is living who has not been treated and helped by her, and hundreds of white people and Indians owe their lives to her treatment, care and nursing . . . We are confronted here with a character rising to greatness, and to great deeds out of conditions which seldom produce more than mediocre men and women, achieving great and beneficial ends over obstacles almost insurmountable.

After her death the Walthill Hospital was in tribute renamed the Dr. Susan Picotte Memorial Hospital by the Home Mission Board.

"AMERICANIZING" NATIVE AMERICANS

Though often well meaning, the people in charge of late nineteenth-century Indian policy viewed Native American culture through an ethnocentric prism

Source: Twelfth Annual Report of the Board of Indian Commissioners (1880), pp. 7–9, in Francis Paul Prucha, ed., *Americanizing the American Indians: Writings by the "Friends of the Indian," 1880–1900* (Cambridge: Harvard University Press, 1973), pp. 193–96.

that distorted all their plans. This was especially so with regard to educational matters, as can be seen in the excerpt below from the 1880 report of the Board of Indian Commissioners. Given the assumptions behind such programs, it was little wonder that so many Native American youths resisted the assimilationist teachings encountered in government schools.

The most reliable statistics prove conclusively that the Indian population taken as a whole, instead of dying out under the light and contact of civilization, as has been generally supposed, is steadily increasing. The Indian is evidently destined to live as long as the white race, or until he becomes absorbed and assimilated with his pale brethren.

We hear no longer advocated among really civilized men the theory of extermination, a theory that would disgrace the wildest savage.

As we must have him among us, self-interest, humanity, and Christianity require that we should accept the situation, and go resolutely at work to make him a safe and useful factor in our body politic.

As a savage we cannot tolerate him any more than as a half-civilized parasite, wanderer, or vagabond. The only alternative left is to fit him by education for civilized life. The Indian, though a simple child of nature with mental faculties dwarfed and shriveled, while groping his way for generations in the darkness of barbarism, already sees the importance of education; bewildered by the glare of a civilization above and beyond his comprehension, he is nevertheless seeking to adjust himself to the new conditions by which he is encompassed. He sees that the knowledge possessed by the white man is necessary for self-preservation. He needs it to save him from the rapacity and greed of men with whom he is forced to come in contact; he needs it just as much to save him from himself.

It is this, supplemented and reinforced by a pure morality and the higher principles of Christianity, that is to enable him to resist the old currents of habit, which, like a mighty river, would otherwise sweep him to certain destruction.

• • • • •

If suitable boarding and industrial schools could be established and properly managed, a compulsory attendance of the youth enforced, as is practiced by some of the governments of Europe, the next generation of Indians would unquestionably be found far in advance of what may be expected from many years of schooling under the present, imperfect, and unsatisfactory methods.

To expect them to attain civilization without these advantages is to look for impossibilities; to deny them these opportunities is to perpetuate their present helpless semibarbarous condition.

The influence of the education of the child is most beneficial to the parents. Gradually they come to perceive the immense advantages of education over ignorance, and they are eager to encourage their children to secure a boon which will eventually enable them to compete successfully with the more favored white man.

The Indian has demonstrated his record for courage, endurance, and loyalty, elements of true manhood, and with proper facilities will show himself equally capable of a true civilization.

Industrial schools once established, the methods suggested by experience as the wisest and most successful should be adopted for bringing them to the highest possible state of efficiency; these are the dictates of economy as well as justice and humanity.

If the common school is the glory and boast of our American civilization, why not extend its blessings to the 50,000 benighted children of the red men of our country, that they too may share its benefits and speedily emerge from the ignorance of centuries?

QUESTIONS

1. What influence did her years at Hampton Institute have on Picotte's life? Why did her white sponsors show such great interest in Picotte? Why do you think Picotte was able to overcome the internal conflicts that troubled so many Native American youths who attended off-reservation boarding schools?
2. Why did Picotte want to become a physician? Why did other Omahas consult Picotte on business and legal matters as well as medical problems?
3. What were the greatest problems that Picotte encountered as a practicing physician? Why did she become an ardent temperance advocate? What steps did Picotte take to reduce alcohol consumption among the Omahas?
4. In what ways did Picotte's medical practice most likely differ from that of white physicians of the period? What were her most important achievements as a doctor?
5. How do you think Picotte would have responded to the sentiments expressed in the 1880 report of the Board of Indian Commissioners? What would the commissioners have thought of Picotte?
6. Which aspects of Picotte's life did you find most interesting? If you were asked to write a biographical profile about Picotte, in what ways would your portrait differ from the one presented in this chapter?

BIBLIOGRAPHY

There are no full-length biographies of Picotte, but her family is the subject of Norma Kidd Green's *Iron Eye's Family: The Children of Joseph LaFlesche* (1969). Also see Dorothy Clarke Wilson's fictionalized biography of her sister, *Bright Eyes: The Story of Susette LaFlesche, an Omaha Indian* (1974). Studies of late nineteenth-century Indian policy and the operation of the assimilation program include Francis Paul Prucha, *American Indian Policy in Crisis: Christian Reformers and the Indian, 1865–1900* (1976), and Robert Winston Mardock, *The Reformers and the American Indian* (1971). For more on women physicians during the period, see Mary Walsh, *"Doctors Wanted: No Women Need Apply": Sexual Barriers in the Medical Profession, 1835–1975* (1977), and Regina Markell Morantz–Sanchez, *Sympathy & Science: Women Physicians in American Medicine* (1985).

Sarah Christie Stevens

Throughout much of the nineteenth century, teaching provided one of the few avenues through which women could exercise public influence. Although some people had initially objected to the widespread employment of women teachers, such resistance quickly wilted. It did so for both ideological and economic reasons. On one hand, women in the classroom posed no threat to the behavioral norms prescribed by the cult of domesticity. Teaching, it was argued, not only constituted a "natural extension" of women's maternal duties; their purportedly greater virtue and religiosity also made women uniquely qualified to shape young minds that were all too susceptible to the baneful influences of a corrupt world. Meanwhile, financially strapped school administrators soon realized that they could reduce operating costs by

paying women teachers about half as much as their male counterparts. By 1870, women comprised more than 50 percent of the teaching force in the nation's primary and secondary schools.

The professional lives of most nineteenth-century women teachers were anything but enviable. Many people believed that women had a greater capacity for self-sacrifice than men, and more than a few school boards seemed intent on putting that dubious notion to the test. In addition to low pay, which was the norm everywhere, women teachers frequently had to contend with loneliness, overwork, and *substandard classroom conditions. This was especially the case in frontier communities, where students of all ages crowded one-room schoolhouses that were sometimes no more than a sod hut.*

Despite such privations, many women eagerly sought teaching positions. They did so in part because alternative sources of professional employment were scarce or nonexistent. Teaching also had its rewards. For some women, a stint in the classroom offered a welcome period of independence before marriage; for others, instructing the young provided a lifetime of fulfillment. And while they were always markedly underrepresented in supervisory positions, increasing numbers of women became school administrators during the post-bellum period. In 1872, Kansas voters elected the nation's first woman school superintendent. Women in other states achieved similar distinction in later years.

One of these women was Sarah Christie Stevens, a former teacher who in 1890 won election to the school superintendency of Blue Earth County, Minnesota; two years later, however, she lost her bid for another term. Stevens's accomplishments and setbacks are the subject of the essay that follows. In it, Jean Christie furnishes an inspiring account of an energetic woman who successfully combined the roles of educator, social reformer, elected official, and housewife. In addition, she explores the ways in which Stevens's public life was influenced by her domestic responsibilities: how they prompted her to assume a more active public role and yet limited what she could achieve in that—for nineteenth-century Americans—avowedly male sphere.

Sarah Christie Stevens

Jean Christie

"I am determined on having an education," young Sarah Jane Christie told her father in 1862. Like many of her contemporaries, this Wisconsin farm girl had set herself to achieve the knowledge and intellectual training that offered self-fulfillment and, for some, held out the promise of advancement in the world. For boys, indeed, education might prove to be, if not the sufficient, at least the necessary condition for upward mobility, the crucial step beyond manual labor, the foundation for a variety of occupations and careers. For girls, schooling opened a narrower range of opportunities, including above all, teaching in the common schools. That activity, it was widely admitted, fell within the proper sphere of single females who as yet had no children of their own. Some women ventured to argue that they should be able to participate in choosing boards of education and even asserted that the presumed feminine talent for

Source: Reprinted from *Minnesota History,* vol. 48, pp. 245–54. Copyright 1983 by The Minnesota Historical Society.

child care qualified them not only for classroom teaching but for supervision of schools as well.[1]

Such a woman was Sarah Christie Stevens, whose early ambitions finally culminated in a modest success: her election in 1890 as superintendent of schools in southern Minnesota's Blue Earth County. Numerous family letters reveal much of her personality and of the circumstances that enabled a farm wife to become a school administrator. They portray her as articulate, intense, and self-assertive, yet in some respects insecure, a conscious and spirited champion of women's abilities who nevertheless retained certain conventional ideas of women's role. The voluminous family correspondence documents the experience of an individual, but it also illustrates society's expectations of women and suggests both the limitations on their activities and the opening of wider opportunities during the latter part of the 19th century.

Born in Ireland in 1844 to a Scottish father and Scotch–Irish mother, both industrial workers, Sarah Jane Christie was brought in 1846 to settle on a farm newly cleared from the forest in Clyman Township, Dodge County, Wisconsin. Her mother, Elizabeth Reid Christie, died in childbirth in 1850, and Sarah, the only daughter, spent her early years with four brothers. They were cared for by a self-effacing stepmother in a household dominated by their father, James, a man of little formal education but of intense intellectual interests. Like her two nearest brothers, Thomas and Alexander (Sandy), Sarah grew up with a drive to learn, an ambition to make an honorable career, and an aspiration to "do great good in the world."[2]

Won over by Sarah's passionate entreaties, her father sent her to nearby Wisconsin Female College at Fox Lake in September 1862. When his funds ran low, two of her brothers

Ignatius Donnelly   A reformer, author, and public official who played a leading role in the founding of the Populist party.

ad hominem   An attack on an opponent's character rather than an answer to his or her contentions.

Sherman Law   The requirement that the Treasury purchase each month an amount of silver about equal to United States silver production, paying for it with notes redeemable in gold or silver.

[1]Sarah to James Christie, November 11, 1862, in James C. Christie and Family Papers, 1823–1949. Minnesota Historical Society (MHS), hereafter cited as Christie Papers. Richard N. Current, *History of Wisconsin*, vol. 2, *The Civil War Era, 1818–1873*, 528–30, 533 (Madison, 1976).

This article was adapted from a conference paper given for the Women Historians of the Midwest in St. Paul in 1982. I wish to thank the MHS staff for its indispensable assistance, in particular Dallas Lindgren, Bonnie Palmquist, and Duane Swanson. Much of the chronology in this article is based on an intensive reading of the Christie Papers.

[2]For brief sketches of family members, see Inventory, Christie Papers; the quotation is from Sarah to Bessie Stevens, October 23, 1902. Other correspondence among Sarah and her family reflects such values. See, for example, Sarah's assessment of a new position in 1873: "If I succeed it will be a grand good thing for me . . . & I may be the means of doing good to others"; Sarah to James, September 13, 1873, Christie Papers. Unless otherwise noted, all letters cited in this article are from the James Christie Papers.

contributed to her expenses out of their pay as soldiers in the Union Army. Her stay at the college introduced her to many new experiences. At the urging of a professor, she joined the Baptist church. An ardent Unionist, as were her family and friends, she participated eagerly in the Soldiers Aid Society, a homefront organization that made bandages, sewed, and cooked delicacies to send the troops. A visit to the state prison at Waupun left her with "very sad feelings," for the system, she observed, provided no good influences and did not offer the convicts "any chance of amendment at all." Previously a stranger to the arts, 18-year-old Sarah saw her first oil painting (at the home of two male students) and commented to her father that "I never knew what singing or music was till I came here and now I can hear the music going every hour in the day."[3]

She also began the study of algebra—"I love it," she declared. To her father's warning against this "masculine attainment," she replied: "I cannot see as it is any more *that*, than a Feminine attainment . . . It is they [men] who keep women where they are. It is the education which a woman gets and the false ideas that are crammed into them, that keep women where they are. Now I believe that the weakness of women lies in their education. They have the same power given them that is given to men, and if they were cultivated and strengthened, in the same way, and direction, woman would be just as able to make her way through life as man is." She resisted social pressure to marry and, in spite of her family's fears that study would ruin her health, declared her intention to pursue a scholarly life.[4]

Although she had hoped to continue on to college, lack of money made this impossible, and Sarah left Fox Lake in late 1863. In 1867 she did spend a term, apparently, studying at the high school in Watertown (countering her landlady's efforts to marry her to a local young man), and for some time she clung to the vision of higher education.[5] Even in her secondary schooling, then, there were gaps; and yet she acquired considerable familiarity with the middle-class culture and an intellectual base for further reading and self-education. Her letters demonstrate a sizable vocabulary and an acquaintance with current issues and trends of thought.

Sarah had early announced her intention of becoming a teacher, which

[3]Sarah to James Christie, November 3, 1862; January 5, 1863, Sarah to Sandy, January 23, 1863. Wisconsin Female College (sometimes called Fox Lake College or Seminary) was in reality a secondary school and took in both female and male students. Later called Downer, it eventually merged with Milwaukee College. See Grace Norton Kieckhefer, "Milwaukee Downer College Rediscovers Its Past," in *Wisconsin Magazine of History*, 34:210–14, 241 (Summer, 1951). Sarah's half-brother William and brother Tom fought through the entire Civil War in the Minnesota First Battery of Light Artillery; later Sandy, born in 1846, also enlisted; *Minnesota in the Civil and Indian Wars, 1861–1865*, 650 (St. Paul, 1890). General information on Wisconsin is derived chiefly from Current, *History of Wisconsin*, vol. 2, see especially p. 371.
[4]Sarah to James, November 11, 1862. Sarah corresponded with Sergeant James Dempsey of the 17th Wisconsin Infantry, who was killed in October, 1862, at the battle of Corinth. How much he meant to Sarah, or whether his death affected her decision, is not revealed in the letters. *Roster of Wisconsin Volunteers*, vol. 2, p. 61 (Madison, 1886).
[5]See Sarah's letters of May 10, [18], 1867.

brother Tom (a year older) assured her was "one of the highest and most important of Human pursuits." On July 1, 1863, after creditably passing an examination given at Fox Lake, she obtained a recommendatory certificate issued by the normal school regents that entitled her to teach in any common, intermediate, or grammar school in Wisconsin. By the winter of 1863–1864 she was prepared to enter seriously upon her vocation. Although in reality—once she had decided against marriage—she had little choice among alternative means of support, she embarked upon teaching with exalted, if vague, visions of a fulfilling future.[6]

Her hopes soon collided with actual conditions, however. Haphazardly organized, lacking any regular road to advancement, teaching in a one-room school hardly offered a "career"; though many women and men entered it, few remained for more than a few years before leaving for other occupations—in the case of women usually for marriage. Nor were teachers expected to stay long in any one school district; like most of them, Sarah moved from one to another in constant search of higher pay and smaller classes. Everywhere women were paid less than men, and she resented the fact. Casting about, she dreamed of becoming a doctor, embarked in 1869 on an ill-fated dressmaking enterprise in Beloit, Wisconsin, and at one time, impressed by a visit to a Catholic hospital, alarmed her Protestant family by proposing to join the Sisters of Charity.[7]

Sarah once remarked of herself and her brothers that "we are all too sanguine . . . always attempting too much and falling short." The family struggled with slim finances. Her oldest and youngest brothers, William and David, whose schooling was brief, remained on the land in Minnesota and Montana. After spells of schoolteaching, the more ambitious Tom and Sandy went on to college: Sandy studied at Harvard and obtained a scientific post in the United States Coast Survey; Tom, reorienting his life after a religious conversion, graduated from Congregationalist Beloit College and from Andover Theological Seminary. Like many others in that era of Christian expansionism, he went forth as a missionary and eventually headed a school in Turkey.[8]

From 1869 to 1871, Sarah and Tom kept house together in Beloit, an outpost of New England, where he attended the college (not yet open to women); she, after the disastrous dressmaking venture, returned to teaching in the nearby rural districts and in the graded schools of the town. Her Beloit salary for instructing 40 children was $6.00 a week.[9]

Partly, at least, through careless management and openhanded ways of liv-

[6]Tom to Sarah, August 6, 1862, and certificates dated April 3, July 1, 1863, Christie Papers.
[7]Sarah to Sandy, May 17, and to James, July 2, both in 1869. The one room schools have their defenders, among them Wayne E. Fuller, who insists that the old educational system "promoted democracy, strengthened community life, unabashedly taught generations of Midwesterners the three R's, and made the Middle Border the most literate part of the nation throughout the years." See his *The Old Country School: The Story of Rural Education in the Middle West,* 245 (Chicago, 1982).
[8]Sarah to Sandy, October 2, 1870, and Inventory, Christie Papers.
[9]Here and below, see Sarah to Sandy, October 2, 1870. Numerous letters furnish only hints as to the source of Sarah's troubles.

ing, both young people ran heavily into debt. Tom enjoyed hunting and canoe-
ing expeditions with classmates (for which Sarah prepared food) and seems to
have spent improvidently on hiring carriages and other luxuries while courting a succession of young women. Besides the business failure, Sarah befriended several younger women so generously that her father suggested that
she was running a charitable institution. Even so, how she came to owe large
sums remains mysterious; conceivably Sandy, though he was given to dramatic imaginings, was correct in suspecting that she had fallen into someone's
power and was being blackmailed. For brother and sister the outcomes differed. When in desperation Tom decided to abandon his studies and do manual labor so that he could pay off the creditors, a sympathetic professor came
to the rescue by finding him a well-paid high school position in Beloit. With a
striking sense of family responsibility and at some sacrifice, Tom and Sandy
(who was teaching in various Wisconsin schools) helped out their sister, but
they could not pay off all her debts.

In 1873, perhaps through acquaintances at Beloit College, Sarah obtained
an interview with the Reverend James W. Strong, president of Carleton College, and impressed him so favorably that he appointed her an instructor at
that six-year-old coeducational Congregationalist institution in Northfield,
Minnesota. She was grateful to God: "What I am astonished at is, that in all my
weariness, suffering & discouragement, that I didn't turn aside & marry for a
rest—a home—as so many poor women do. But somehow I have been saved
from that."[10]

The work was taxing. As an instructor in English and German she taught
other subjects as well, for a total of five courses, had to stay up at night to blow
out the dormitory lights at 10 o'clock, and rose at four in the morning to prepare for classes. (To keep one jump ahead, one imagines.) In addition, she
found herself helping Mrs. Strong with her children and nursing many of the
college "boys" through an epidemic of measles. She also made friends, especially with some of the older students.

For reasons that are not clear, Sarah left Carleton in 1875. After applying to
various colleges, including the University of Michigan, which was "not ready"
to employ any lady to teach, she held a position at Wheaton College in Illinois
till 1877. That experience ended in disaster when creditors pursued her and the
college paid them off in lieu of salary.[11]

During the 1860s, her father, half-brother William, and youngest brother
David had joined thousands of other early Wisconsin settlers in a move to the
west, and in the winter of 1876–1877 a discouraged Sarah retreated to the
homestead of James and David in Blue Earth County, Minnesota. Financial
need and restless temperament, however, sent her once more into schoolrooms
as far away as Iowa City, Iowa.

---

[10]Here and below, see Sarah to James, May 24, 1874. On Carleton College, see Merrill E. Jarehow,
Private Liberal Arts Colleges in Minnesota: Their History and Contributions, 21–24 (St. Paul, 1973).
[11]Here and below, see University of Michigan to Sarah, April[?], 1876; Sarah to Sandy, September
27, 1878; David to Sandy, January 14, 1877, David B. Christie and Family Papers, 1871–1933, MHS.

Early in 1879, in her middle 30s, Sarah married William L. Stevens, once a pioneer and now a relatively prosperous farmer, a widower with four children who was 19 years older than she. It was perhaps a marriage for security, but also of affection for one whom she described as "a wise man & a good one . . . a good husband to me—always thoughtful and kind." Her home was still in Blue Earth County, near Good Thunder. Even though married, she planned to continue teaching—"I will pay my own debts by my own work"—and for a term or two she did so, but pregnancy put an end to that.[12]

In the 1880s, Sarah's mind should have been "at rest." She was settled now with home and husband, four stepchildren, and soon two daughters of her own. Caring for the family and running a household frequently augmented by hired men, she sometimes helped in the fields—one July she ran the horserake for three days to harvest the barley—but she assured Sandy that "We hire all the heavy work done." She aided and counseled neighbor women and advised her ailing father on medication and diet. But somehow she made time to read current publications such as *Harper's, Scribner's, Century,* and *Atlantic* that she exchanged with Sandy who was still in Washington with the Coast Survey.

Energy and unfocused ambition kept Sarah from contentment. In the eyes of brother Sandy, her existence was "a sort of penitentiary life for one of her activity of faculty." She read medicine and sometimes indulged in hope of practicing. (She considered herself as well qualified as most of the doctors around.) Ever mindful of the importance of education, she arranged a way for William's daughter Estella to earn expenses at Iowa College (later Grinnell)—a plan that the girl rejected—and considered anxiously how best to ensure that daughters Bessie and Mary would have more opportunities for learning than the local district school could provide.[13]

The Baptist church, to which she still belonged, the temperance cause, and the Farmers Alliance movement afforded some outlets for her energies. Voicing the grievances and the demands of farmers increasingly dominated by railroads, bankers, and Wall Street, the Alliance movement had grown during the hard times of the late 1880s; in 1890 its Minnesota chapters formally adopted the principles of the National Farmers, or Northwestern, Alliance and for the first time entered politics directly as a third party. Sarah and, more actively, her husband were associated with the local groups, which in Blue Earth County found their center of strength in Good Thunder. In the church, a Ladies' Mission Circle affiliated with the Woman's Baptist Home Mission Society met regularly to sew for freedmen's schools in the South or for working girls in the cities; Sarah was elected secretary in 1886.[14]

[12]Here and below, see Sarah to Sandy, July 21, 1879; February 20, 1880.
[13]Iowa College to Sarah, November 25, 1881; Sandy to James, December 12, 1888.
[14]Minutes of the Mission Circle, 1886, Christie Papers. On the Alliance movement in Minnesota, see especially William Watts Folwell, *A History of Minnesota,* 3:169–171, 187–189 (revised ed., St. Paul, 1969); Lawrence Goodwyn, *Democratic Promise: The Populist Moment in America,* 582–587 (New York, 1976). See also Thomas Hughes, *History of Blue Earth County and Biographies of Its Leading Citizens,* 191, 265 (Chicago [1909]). Alliance demands included the secret ballot, government ownership of the railroads, an income tax, free textbooks, and equal pay for equal work by men and women.

The Woman's Christian Temperance Union (WCTU) demanded the suffrage, freedom to participate in public affairs, and general respect for the abilities of women. Its crusade for "social purity" tended in some aspects to counter the prevailing prudery. One Blue Earth group, for example, advocated "mothers talking freely with their children, their boys as well as their girls, casting aside all Modesty, and telling them before they learned it from other children of which they surely would." Sarah joined the Good Thunder WCTU, became its secretary, and gave lectures on "Temperance Hygiene." Further, the state WCTU appointed her superintendent of its Mothers' Meetings.[15]

That Sarah should join the women "screeching" at public meetings greatly perturbed her father James. In one letter, he took advantage of the news that her children were ill with whooping cough to insist that "there are but few married women, Mothers, who can give their thought and time to almost anything outside of the Home duties, for their [sic] is danger that when they do they will become too much taken up with them to the serious detriment of their family affairs." And he begged her not to dissipate "the generating power of the feminine heart."[16]

Though she loved her father, Sarah again refused to be put in her place. Other, younger, male relatives, including Sandy and her stepson Buell, as well as her loyal husband, supported her aspirations. Since antebellum years when feminists had first challenged traditional restrictions, women's public activities had gained some guarded public acceptance. Throughout the region lyceums had presented such lecturers as Mary Livermore, Susan B. Anthony, or Elizabeth Cady Stanton, so that few persons still viewed the spectacle of female speakers as in itself bizarre. In Minnesota, although full suffrage seemed for the moment unattainable, certain local opportunities had been opened: In the mid-1870s women had gained the school franchise and admission to educational office, and there were 10 or 11 female superintendents in the then 78 counties of the state.[17]

With a base among women's groups, the local Alliance, and the Prohibition party, Sarah Christie Stevens decided to try for election in the fall of 1890 as county superintendent of schools. The post Sarah sought was not only administrative but also political, since the holder was chosen by the voters every two years. So, at the age of 45, she plunged into electoral politics.

Circumstances favored her that year. The Alliance party, risen "to new heights of membership in the early months of 1890," and the Prohibition party, both of which welcomed women as members, nominated her; among her many acquaintances it was not hard to round up individual backers. Moreover,

[15]Minute book for Vernon Center, July 2, 1891, in Minnesota WCTU Records, 1862–1979, in MHS, program. Mankato teachers' meeting, January 19, 1889, Sarah to James, February 5, 1889, and E. L. Condit to Sarah, October 9, 1889—all in Christie Papers.

[16]James to Sarah, October 2, 1888, July 1, 1889. James Christie wrote from Bridger Canyon, Montana, where his son David, in a successful attempt to cure his asthma, had taken up a ranch. James died there early in 1890.

[17]Minnesota, *Laws,* 1875, p. 18; Marilyn Ziebarth, "Woman's Rights Movement," in *Minnesota History,* 42:225 (Summer, 1971); Superintendent of Public Instruction, *Seventh Biennial Report,* 1891–92, 92–134, 146 (St. Paul, 1892).

and of crucial importance, the local Democrats were supporting most of the candidates put forward by the Alliance. The *Review*, Mankato's Democratic paper, for example, backed her bid for election, saying that Sarah offered "ability, fidelity, and an earnest enthusiasm for the cause of popular education."[18]

As the argument for Sarah ran, a country resident such as she was the proper person to have charge of the country schools; furthermore, a woman would make the most appropriate director of a system that guided the development of children. Confronting the issue of gender, Sarah asserted her rights on the basis of a modified traditional ideology. In one "scholarly address" at Garden City she cited historical cases in which, she said, women had "successfully administered affairs without losing their womanly graces," and made the point that they now had a duty to accept the responsibility that accompanies the privilege of voting. To her aid came Eva McDonald of Minneapolis, journalist and "girl orator," to urge the claims of Mrs. Stevens and of the whole Alliance ticket. As reporters observed, "ladies worked in getting out voters . . . with the energy of male politicians."[19]

Angry accusations also marked the campaign. The Reverend F. L. Patterson, Republican candidate for superintendent, and his supporters charged that his Alliance opponents had bought up certain newspapers and had gone so far as to poison his Newfoundland dog. They complained that Sarah had vilified her rival (her friends insisted that she had never uttered a derogatory word), and at the end of the campaign, Patterson declared that he had "had to contend against a villainous conspiracy . . . [and] scandalous stories."[20]

In the outcome, the Republican ticket was "lost sight of" and Blue Earth "joined the ranks of those counties . . . which have placed their school interests in the hands of a lady." Out of a total vote of 6,858 she had won by 301. As a sympathetic local editor analyzed the vote: "She ran well in the country towns, especially where she is best known. Our foreign born people, except the Irish, are averse to a woman's holding office, and the Germans and Scandinavians generally voted against her. The Irish supported her heartily, as did most of the Americans. The women in our city [Mankato] mostly voted against her, excepting the most intelligent and progressive, while those in the country supported her." But the campaign had been so bitter that some on the defeated side remained irreconcilable.[21]

[18]Goodwyn, *Democratic Promise*, 259; *Review* (Mankato), September 2, 1890. Accounts of Sarah's three campaigns are drawn chiefly from correspondence, notes on the 1894 campaign, clippings in the Christie Papers, and local newspapers (*Amboy Herald, Good Thunder Herald, Lake Crystal Mirror, Lake Crystal Union, Mankato Free Press*) which were examined most carefully for the periods from late summer to mid-November of the election years.

[19]Letter to editor, *Mankato Journal*, October 25, 1890; *Review*, November 11, 1890; accounts in news columns of the *Journal*, Christie Papers. See also Rhoda R. Gilman, "Eva McDonald Valesh, Minnesota Populist," in Barbara Stuhler and Gretchen Kreuter, eds., *Women of Minnesota: Selected Biographical Essays*, 55–76 (St. Paul, 1977).

[20]*Lake Crystal Union*, October 22, November 12, 1890; *Enterprise* (Mapleton), November 7, 1890; *Register* (Blue Earth), October 30, 1890.

[21]*Register*, November 13, 1890; John C. Wise to Sandy, November 10, 1890.

Jubilantly, Sarah and her family moved to the county seat, Mankato, where a system of graded schools and "the Normal" would provide better education for her children. (They seem to have rented the farm.) In spite of her outward self-assertiveness, Sarah suffered from an awareness of her own deficiencies that might not have troubled a more run-of-the-mill male politician. She turned for counsel to several persons, including Professor A. F. Bechdolt, head of the Mankato schools, and her brother Sandy in Washington. Sandy poured out advice: He suggested books for her office and dispatched many volumes from his personal library, drafted speeches for teachers' meetings, and anxiously adjured her not to "give gossips a chance to wag their tongues—observe in strictness all the rules laid down in this evil world for regulating the relations of the sexes."[22]

As county superintendent, Sarah was to oversee the 137 "common" ungraded schools, each in its own district under its own elected board of trustees. (Graded and high schools were not under her jurisdiction.) She drew a salary of $1,000 per year, slightly higher than the state average. Singlehanded, she had to visit the schools; examine and certify teachers and further their training; spur trustees to improve buildings, grounds, and equipment; encourage the planting of trees on Arbor Day; and gather statistics for an annual report to the state superintendent in St. Paul. In a biennial report, her superior recognized the difficulties confronting a county superintendent: "Attending faithfully and conscientiously to all his other duties and exercising only a general supervision over the individual schools, he finds himself the hardest worked and most underpaid officer in the state. To ask him to give each district the careful salutary inspection needed is to ask for an impossibility."[23]

At the end of 1891, the county, with a population of 29,210, had 130 frame and 7 brick common school buildings. Almost half sat on the prairie ungraced by trees; thanks probably to the efforts of Sarah, who was sensitive to natural beauty, the number of treeless schoolyards was reduced from 64 in 1891 to 32 in the following year. At a time when school districts were only beginning to provide free textbooks, the 137 schools in Sarah Stevens's jurisdiction had 1,362 books—about ten apiece—in their libraries.[24]

The school year, consisting of three terms, fall (sparsely attended), winter, and spring, averaged 6.1 months in 1891 and 7 months in 1892. Total enrollment in 1891 amounted to 3,337 persons of ages from 5 to 21, of whom 1,934 were between 8 and 16 years old. State law required the latter group to attend for 60 days during the year, but enforcement was another matter and many did not meet even this modest requirement. It was taken for granted that male teachers, who constituted 27 percent in 1891, would be paid more than the females: In that year they received monthly wages of $35.82 and $26.35, respec-

[22]Sandy to Sarah, November 10, 23, 1890. Bechdolt's influence is clear in Sarah's undated speech notes for 1890 and 1891.

[23]Superintendent of Public Instruction, *Eighth Biennial Report*, 1893–94, 28–29 (St. Paul, 1894).

[24]With one exception, the figures here and in the following paragraph are found in, or derived from Superintendent of Public Instruction, *Seventh Biennial Report*, 170, 174, 180, 182, 184, 186, 190. For county population, see United States, *Census*, 1890, *Population*, part 1, p. 195.

tively. (This gap was slightly larger than in the state as a whole.) The staff lacked both continuity and training. Most were not even graduates of high school or normal school, and college graduates were rare indeed; their teaching certificates were awarded on the basis of tests administered by the county superintendent. The turnover was truly astonishing: In 1891, only 31 percent of Blue Earth County's teachers had stayed in the same district for as much as one year or more; in 1892, 46 percent had done so. Over the state the respective figures were 35 and 40 percent.

As the incoming superintendent, Sarah was determined to enhance the skills and to elevate the intellectual level of teachers and students. Already, state-sponsored, week-long institutes held every year or two provided some training for teachers and awarded certificates to those who attended with diligence. Sarah organized numerous shorter meetings at various places in the county. On a Friday evening and Saturday morning some 14 or 15 authoritative persons, perhaps from the Mankato system or the Normal School, would discourse on a variety of subjects: music, a course of reading for teachers, manners and morals, chemistry of common things, arithmetic, calisthenics, writing, school government, primary reading, history, "general mental exercises," geography, and local geology. She herself would speak at these gatherings, expatiating on "the importance of the common schools for American democracy," or advising more specifically on aims and methods. She urged teachers to specialize in making the pupils good readers. They themselves must read and study and thoroughly master their subjects; if not, they would not be interested themselves and, in turn, would be unable "to get up any very lively interest on the part of pupils." In arithmetic, she insisted, they must explain basic principles rather than rely on rote learning. Good order, of course, was crucial and, following the counsel of Professor Bechdolt, she instructed them to exact entire and instant obedience from their pupils. In mitigation of such authoritarian precepts, however, she constantly exhorted the teachers to stimulate the children's own desire to learn.[25]

For teachers, school trustees, and parents, Sarah held meetings to discuss such matters as "school supplies, textbooks, school libraries, and how to promote a more regular attendance of pupils." Addressing the trustees, she explained the school laws, pleaded for accurate records, asked for improvements to buildings and for more dictionaries in the libraries, and advocated free textbooks, both to save money (through certain economies of purchasing) and to promote democracy among the children of rich and poor, of concerned and of indifferent parents. Her short-lived paper, *Blue Earth Co. Education*, served as a vehicle for news and announcements. In its pages she suggested that each school should purchase a flag: The stars and stripes, she believed, "stand for liberty the world over . . . The pupils . . . should be made to understand this, and be made familiar with their country's flag, and with its history."[26]

[25]See for example, "Announcement of Institute for Blue Earth County," March 23, 1891, and "Program for Teachers' Meeting," January 16 and 17, 1891, and undated notes, in Christie Papers.
[26]Notice of educational meetings, April and May, 1892, Christie Papers, *Blue Earth Co. Education*, May and June, 1892. There were apparently only two issues of this paper; copies in MHS.

Desirable innovations came readily to her mind. Some, like kindergartens and industrial schools, could only be goals for the distant future. But she could and did introduce a modest health measure, as she circulated a local physician's article on the care of children's eyes and instructed teachers to administer tests for refraction errors. In another direction, she introduced a series of examinations in the various "branches" taught in the common schools, so that in time a pupil could obtain a certificate to ensure admission to a secondary school. In initiating this practice she participated in a movement that was spreading through the Middle West to measure and to recognize a certain level of achievement, whether, for most children, to mark the completion of formal education or, for others, to facilitate the passage from elementary to more advanced training in high school or academy.[27]

Part of the superintendent's duties was the often arduous task of traveling throughout the county to visit all the district schools. In 1891, Sarah reported 138 visits, calling at some schools more than once and leaving 35 unobserved. Strangely, in the following year she included no figures for visits in her annual report, although at a later date she claimed to have made 141. Whatever the precise numbers, she seems to have neglected some of the more remote districts—a serious mistake. (This may be partially explained by the fact that early in the year her daughter Mary went through an illness so severe that, Sarah wrote, "I had an awful fear in my heart, that it was possible I would have to lose her.")[28]

Although throughout the whole region county superintendents found it difficult or impossible to inspect all the schools. Sarah's dereliction left an opening to her rivals and seemed to lend substance to a common complaint expressed, for instance, by a new state superintendent who answered an inquiry from Sarah in August 1892, when, preparing to run again, she no doubt hoped for a favorable reply. He wrote that there were women county superintendents of schools in Minnesota who "give as good satisfaction as the same number of men holding similar positions." But he added: "You ask if they [women superintendents] are in every way as well qualified as men. I think not. While in most particulars I think they accomplish their work as well as men in similar positions, they are not as well able to endure exposure in the winter in riding over prairies and through the woods to visit schools."[29]

As her term drew to an end in 1892 she began her campaign for reelection, though in conditions less favorable than two years before. She had now compiled a record to be judged by; moreover, the Minnesota Alliance movement was breaking apart as a sizable wing refused to follow **Ignatius Donnelly** into

---

[27]Fuller, *Old Country School,* 213–215.

[28]Sarah to Frank Stevens, February 6, 1892.

[29]W. W. Pendergast to Sarah, August 27, 1894. In *The Old Country School,* especially 192, 193, Fuller contends that the relative absence of supervision was not to be regretted, since it allowed the teachers greater flexibility and opportunity to use their own judgment and personal understanding of their students. This puts a lot of faith in the abilities of teachers who, moving constantly from one school to another, must in many cases have lacked the opportunity to gain any deep acquaintance with individual students.

the People's party. According to the *Good Thunder Herald*, an Alliance newspaper, the movement of 1890 had little in common with the People's party of 1892 which "had no time for the humble needs of our farmers" but supported the Omaha platform, "that indecent libel upon this great and prosperous nation, that curious conglomeration of all impracticable visions." Members of an abortive, anti-Donnelly "Alliance Party" of Minnesota failed to find willing candidates and, presumably, drifted back toward the Republican party. Hoping that all groups would agree on her for superintendent, Sarah presented herself as a nonpartisan educator, but Democrats and Republicans each put up their own candidate and she was left with the nominations of the Prohibitionists and of what remained of the People's party.[30]

Personal accusations again marred a contest entwined with issues not directly related to the schools. Sarah pointed to "many original lines of work" that she had embarked on. In a fiery speech at Mankato, the famous Kansas Populist leader Mary E. Lease asserted that "Our schools should be out of politics and when a community has a successful woman county superintendent, she should be sent back to the office again and again." Following another, *ad hominem* line of attack, some of Sarah's supporters made the potentially damning statement (indignantly denied) that her chief opponent, 30-year-old Republican George W. Scherer, former editor of the German-language *Mankato Post*, had once joined a society in New Ulm that believed "neither in Christ, man, or the devil." They also spread stories of his intemperance, to which his more forthright adherents replied that indeed he was not "the goody goody sort, but a straight, intelligent, and capable man." Ignoring Sarah's boasted improvements, Scherer and his friends zeroed in on her failure to visit all the schools and, in a statement with obvious implications, pledged that he would "give his entire time to the duties of the office." Perhaps even more important, Republicans put him forward as the candidate of solid "men who stand high in business circles."[31]

Sarah Christie Stevens lost the election: she had 2,055 votes, Scherer 2,968, and David E. Fleming, the Democratic candidate, 1,562. In addition to her own mistakes, the county's politics had taken a conservative turn that worked to her detriment. Or, rather, the county and the state had returned after a brief aberration to their normal Republican allegiance. Nationally, Democrat Grover Cleveland gained the presidency with 277 electoral votes to Benjamin Harrison's 145, while the Populist candidate, General James B. Weaver, showed remarkable strength with 22 votes. But in Blue Earth and in Minnesota, Harrison won the majority, his party garnered most state offices, and Weaver trailed far behind.[32]

[30]*Good Thunder Herald,* July 6, September 28, 1892. On the 1892 election and the Omaha platform, see John D. Hicks, "The People's Party in Minnesota," in *Minnesota History,* 5:542–547 (November, 1924).
[31]*Good Thunder Herald,* September 14, 21, 1892; *Mankato Daily Free Press,* October 26, November 1, 1892; *Lake Crystal Union,* October 5, November 2, 1892; *Lake Crystal Mirror,* November 4, September 9, 1892. The New Ulm society was, of course, the Turners.
[32]Minnesota, *Legislative Manual,* 1893, 342, 468.

Locally, if those Sarah and her husband considered the "best people" favored her, others disliked precisely the "goody-goodies," suffragists, and Populists she stood for. Understandably, even her brother Tom, who had supported her in so many ways, admitted that "there are many things about the whole business that make me sometimes wish Sarah had never entered on public life."[33]

Yet in 1894 she tried again. Logically, the nationwide depression that began in 1893 should have brightened the prospect for election of a candidate allied with the Populist protest of hard-hit farmers. Like her neighbors, Sarah and her husband were "really & truly very hard up—we owe all the banks and they are coming down *hard*." She blamed the "rings that hold the gold and wealth of the country—to *force* the repeal of the silver clause in the **Sherman Law**." Holding the Republicans responsible, she might well suppose that others, many worse off than she, would recognize that the People's party stood for them and their interests.[34]

Sometimes accompanied by Sandy, who had lost his job the previous year and had come west for a visit, she canvassed vigorously, calling on acquaintances and speaking twice a day in the little school districts. Comparing her record with that of her successor, she insisted that she had made more visits than he and had accomplished for the schools much more of permanent value. "Good growth is silent and slow, like that of grass and trees." The image she projected may be suggested by the letter written in her support by "A Woman Voter" for whom Sarah Christie Stevens—a "grand and noble woman"—was "one of those vigorous and robust women of which Blue Earth county is proud to boast."[35]

The effort failed. In spite of the depression Republicans made a clean sweep in county and state, and defeat by a wide margin ended Sarah's public career. Back on the farm, she sold eggs, experimented with growing ginseng, and embarked on several unsuccessful business ventures. Leaving her Baptist affiliation, she became an Episcopalian. Fragmentary diaries paint vignettes of her daily life: She rejoiced that the flowering almonds were in bloom; friends dropped by for a whole day's visit; a tramp took supper; a neighbor boy brought her a dozen duck eggs—"Eddie would take nothing, saying as I tried to make him take a quarter—'no, you have given us so many things.' I conclude therefore that apples cast about freely return in duck eggs after a while."[36]

Like her three married brothers, she knew the sorrow of losing a child, for her daughter Mary died of tuberculosis at 18. Her other daughter, Bessie, attended the medical school at Hamline University. Although her choice of

[33]Tom to Sandy, November 8, 1892. Through the whole Great Lakes region the Populists "did unexpectedly poorly"; Goodwyn, *Democratic Promise,* 321.
[34]Sarah to David, October 19, 1893, David Christie Papers. Both the Prohibition and the People's party endorsed woman suffrage that year; Folwell, *Minnesota,* 3:200.
[35]Sarah's undated notes, Christie Papers, letter to the editor, *Mankato Free Press,* October 5, 1894.
[36]The vote: Scherer, 3,162, Stevens, 1,166, W. R. Thompson (Dem.), 1,323; Sarah Stevens, Diary, 1894, in Christie Papers; *Legislative Manual,* 1895, 346, 463.

occupation was unusual, and she belonged to a small female minority at the medical school, she encountered little hostility and judged her male classmates to be "thorough gentlemen." Her gratified mother hoped that "you will make your mark in a good & great way on those lines—I am sure you must have inherited some of my life ambitions." Thus Sarah found vicarious fulfillment of an early dream.[37]

Although shifting political alignments weighed heavily in Sarah's initial election and in her subsequent rejection at the polls, her gender surely played some part. Toward the end of the 19th century, changing mores, reflected in the laws, permitted a woman to hold public office; yet both prejudice and her own life situation obstructed her public career. Always bitterly resentful of unequal pay and unequal opportunities for women, Sarah spoke scornfully of the "arbitrary medieval principles" exemplified in such statements as "'wimmin ain't fit to hold office,'" which indicated, she bravely insisted, "a benighted condition of the individual which is not likely to be sustained by a majority of votes in an enlightened community." No doubt she encountered such crass attitudes, and her robust, womanly, and reformist style was precisely what many voters detested. Yet by those closing years of the century, male tolerance of women's "outside" activities had developed to a point where persons who considered themselves "enlightened" would express their opposition in more subtle terms. Old politicians were "amused," said one journalist in 1890, at the contest among the "ladies" to bring out the "lady voters." With seeming respect but delicate disparagement, George Scherer's supporters spoke of Mrs. Stevens as an "estimable lady," and observed with obvious truth that personal accomplishments were desirable but not sufficient for the superintendent of schools. Though on the one hand, aggressiveness may antagonize voters, ladyhood may also cripple the aspirant to office.[38]

Furthermore, the arguments over Sarah's visits to the school point both to a false perception and to a reality of female existence. To combat the assumption of fragility, a woman superintendent would have been wise to exert extraordinary efforts to reach *all* the districts, and yet, because of her responsibilities for a household and children, this might have been impossible. Now and then, in Sarah's letters, we catch a hint of impatience with the burden of household duties, but whether in her own mind she ever envisioned a feminist rejection of woman's domestic role, we cannot know. Outwardly she conformed and utilized the argument of women's special gifts. But when she asserted that the motherliness of women made them peculiarly fitted to supervise the common schools, opponents could counter by suggesting that maternal duties made them *un*fit for the task. Handicapped by gender as well as by the decline of the local Alliance movement, she needed to prove herself more effective than any

---

[37]Bessie to Sarah, September 22, 1902; Sarah to Bessie, October 24, 1902. Bessie married a classmate, Dr. Hugh Monahan, and they practiced together in northern Minnesota and later in Minneapolis.
[38]Notes for "An Appeal to Voters," October 24, 1892, Christie Papers; *Lake Crystal Union*, November 5, 1890; *Lake Crystal Mirror*, November 4, 1892.

man—which is only to say, she would have had to be a Superwoman—a familiar dilemma.

Who will manage the household? Who will take care of the children? Today we are only beginning to solve these problems. At least we can ask such questions, as in her time Sarah Christie Stevens could not.

NINETEENTH-CENTURY TEACHERS

Compared with their frontier counterparts, women teachers in late nineteenth-century urban schools worked in much more comfortable physical settings. At the same time, though, they were often subject to "petty and minute supervision." As education became increasingly bureaucratized, the growing number of irksome administrative tasks imposed on them made many long for those simpler days when instruction took place in a one-room schoolhouse. The unknown teacher who penned the following poem almost certainly would have agreed to such a transfer.

Twas Saturday night, and a teacher sat
    Alone, her task pursuing:
She averaged this and she averaged that
    Of all her class were doing.
She reckoned percentage, so many boys,
    And so many girls all counted,
And marked all the tardy and absentees,
    And to what all the absence amounted.

Names and residence wrote in full,
    Over many columns and pages;
Yankee, Teutonic, African, Celt,
    And averaged all their ages,
The date of admission of every one,
    And cases of flagellation,
And prepared a list of the graduates
    For the coming examination.

Her weary head sank low on her book,
    And her weary heart still lower,
For some of her pupils had little brain,
    And she could not furnish more.
She slept, she dreamed; it seemed she died,
    And her spirit went to Hades,
And they met her there with a question fair,
    "State what the per cent of your grade is."

Source: Mary Abigail Dodge, *Our Common Schools* (Boston: Estes & Lauriat, 1880), in Nancy Hoffman, ed., *Woman's "True" Profession: Voices from the History of Teaching* (Old Westbury, NY: The Feminist Press; New York: The McGraw-Hill Book Company, 1981), pp. 255–56.

Ages had slowly rolled away,
    Leaving but partial traces,
And the teacher's spirit walked one day
    In the old familiar places.
A mound of fossilized school reports
    Attracted her observation,
As high as the State House Dome, and as wide
    As Boston since annexation.

She came to the spot where they buried her bones,
    And the ground was well built over,
But laborers digging threw out a skull
    Once planted beneath the clover.
A disciple of Galen wandering by,
    Paused to look at the diggers,
And plucking the skull up, looked through the eye,
    And saw it was lined with figures.

"Just as I thought," said the young M.D.,
    "How easy it is to kill 'em—"
Statistics ossified every fold
    Of cerebrum and cerebellum.
"It's a great curiosity, sure," said Pat,
    "By the bones can you tell the creature?"
"Oh, nothing strange," said the doctor, "that
    Was a nineteenth-century teacher."

QUESTIONS

1. Why did Stevens believe education was so important for women? Why did she became a teacher? What satisfactions did Stevens derive from teaching?
2. How did Stevens's life change after marriage? In what ways did Stevens's domestic concerns inspire her to become more involved in public affairs?
3. Why, as a candidate for school superintendent, did Stevens feel compelled to cite
   examples of women who had "successfully administered affairs without losing
   their womanly graces"? Why did some women, especially those in urban areas,
   vote against her in the 1890 election? What factors were most responsible for her
   election as school superintendent? To what extent was gender a factor in her defeat
   for reelection in 1892?
4. What were Stevens's main priorities as school superintendent? In what ways did
   Stevens's conduct of the superintendency reflect her experience as a teacher? How
   do you think she would have responded—as a teacher and later as a superintendent—to the bureaucratic impositions described in the poem?
5. A comparison of Stevens's life with that of Susan LaFlesche Picotte raises interesting questions about race and gender in late nineteenth-century America. In what
   ways did the two women face similar kinds of obstacles? Which of the two women
   posed a greater challenge to the cultural norms of the society in which she lived
   and worked?

BIBLIOGRAPHY

Although there is no full-length treatment of Stevens's life, a growing number of studies provide additional information about women's activities during her lifetime. Two fine accounts of women's experiences in the postbellum West are Julie Roy Jeffrey, *Frontier Women: The Trans-Mississippi West, 1840–1880* (1979), and Joanna Stratton, *Pioneer Mothers: Voices from the Kansas Frontier* (1981), which contains generous excerpts from a rare collection of autobiographical writings. Nancy Hoffman's *Woman's "True" Profession: Voices from the History of Teaching* (1981) has a fine bibliography, in addition to reprinting valuable source materials. For more on women's involvement in the temperance crusade, see Ruth Bordin, *Women and Temperance: The Quest for Power and Liberty, 1873–1900* (1981), and Barbara Leslie Epstein, *The Politics of Domesticity: Women, Evangelism and Temperance in Nineteenth-Century America* (1981). Eleanor Flexner presents an in-depth treatment of women's campaign for political equality in *Century of Struggle: The Woman's Rights Movement in the United States* (1959); developments in Minnesota are examined by Marilyn Ziebarth in "Woman's Rights Movement," *Minnesota History* 42 (Summer 1971).

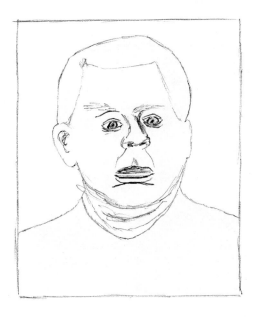

Henry McNeal Turner

Following the end of Reconstruction in 1877, the position of African Americans in southern society steadily deteriorated. To be sure, major changes did not occur overnight. The region's white-dominated governments were initially restrained by fears of northern reaction and uncertainty as to what system of race relations they wished to institute in place of slavery. But such questions were soon resolved. During the 1880s, the new system began taking shape, as state after state enacted a wide range of Jim Crow laws that required physical separation of the races at public facilities. Nor was this all. Beginning in Mississippi in 1890, southern state governments also moved to deprive African Americans of their voting rights through a combination of devices such as poll taxes, white primaries, and racially biased literacy tests.

Socially isolated and forced to rely on their own resources, southern

blacks turned increasingly to what would become the most important institution in postbellum African-American society: the church. With emancipation, the secret churches of slavery came out of hiding and experienced tremendous growth. As they did so, black churches not only met the spiritual needs of their parishioners but took on a broad range of secular functions: promoting economic cooperation and development; providing food and shelter to the poverty-stricken; educating people of all ages; and serving as a general haven in a hostile white world.

Churches further served as

an important training ground for the development of a leadership class. Not allowed to participate in the broader society, ambitious African Americans sought advancement by channeling their energies into racially based institutions. The ministry thus became a primary avenue for social mobility, and ministers were highly respected and powerful members of their communities, whose influence extended to secular as well as religious matters. That black clergymen later played a dominant role in the modern civil rights movement was hardly surprising.

One of the most prominent—and the most controversial—black churchmen of the late nineteenth century was an African Methodist Episcopal bishop named Henry McNeal Turner. After service as a Civil War army chaplain, Turner settled in Georgia, where he struggled to give the promise of emancipation real meaning. He soon found, however, that all too little had changed. And as discrimination and oppression obliterated earlier hopes, he became a leading proponent of African emigration ventures that would enable southern blacks to flee "this bloody, lynching nation." In the essay that follows, John Dittmer traces the evolution of Turner's thought, showing how it was informed by a theological interpretation of history that merged religious themes and secular concerns in a coherent whole.

Henry McNeal Turner

John Dittmer

Outside of the African Methodist Episcopal **(AME) church**, where he is venerated as one of the pillars of that denomination, Henry McNeal Turner is best known today (when he is known) as a combative black nationalist who promoted ill-fated schemes to send black Americans "back to Africa." He was the "forerunner of **Marcus Garvey**." But important as that was, Turner's significance as a black leader rests upon much more than his impassioned advocacy of African emigration. More than any other public figure of his day, he encouraged identification with the African homeland, instilling confidence and pride among Afro-Americans "inferiorated" by centuries of slavery. Yet Turner also committed himself to the ongoing black struggle for freedom and dignity inside white America. His public life encompassed one of the most turbulent periods in Afro-American history, from the latter days of slavery to the nadir of black life at the outbreak of World War I.

Viewed in terms of individual achievement, Turner's career was a nineteenth-century American success story. Rising from humble origins, he gained

Source: From the *Black Leaders of the Nineteenth Century.* Copyright 1982 by the Board of Trustees of the University of Illinois. Used with the permission of the author and the University of Illinois Press.

national recognition as an important Reconstruction politician and, after the failure of that democratic experiment, quickly moved up through the ranks of the AME church hierarchy. Later, as senior bishop, he became one of the most influential and outspoken black churchmen. Turner believed that in the post-war South religious leaders must become involved in the secular life of the community, and thus he saw his mission as both spiritual and political. In the 1880s Turner emerged as a leader of the African emigration movement, and his unrelenting support of that cause gained him a wide audience and a major voice in the debate over the Afro-American's future. He was the preeminent black nationalist of the period, and his appeals to race consciousness and pride, coupled with his blistering attacks on white society, won him the respect of thousands of American blacks.

At the same time Turner was one of the most paradoxical public figures of his era. The champion of the inarticulate black masses, he did not effectively represent their interests during the early period of his political ascendancy after the Civil War. The same man who pleaded for black unity was unwilling to compromise with other leaders and was himself a divisive force in the black community. His criticism of white America, as it developed over the years, was more biting and incisive than that of his contemporaries, yet Turner openly consorted with racist politicians, not all of whom supported his emigrationist platform. It is difficult, even today, to reconcile many of these apparent contradictions. Turner kept his own counsel and did not leave behind memoirs or correspondence that might shed light on the complexity of his thought.

The contradictions in Turner's public life were reflected in his personality. A large, powerful man, crude and awkward of manner, Turner evoked the image of the two-fisted frontiersman. He was a spellbinding orator whose cruel irony and penetrating sarcasm withered his ideological enemies. Yet this rough facade masked a sensitive, deeply religious man whose spiritual mission was to alleviate the suffering of his people. This messianic vision at first manifested itself in the optimistic belief that white political leaders would live up to the promises made in the imme-

AME church A black church founded by Richard Allen in 1816 following a confrontation over segregated seating in a Philadelphia white Methodist church.

Marcus Garvey A black nationalist leader who emphasized black pride and achievements and founded a "back to Africa" movement in the early 1920s.

escutcheon A cast of arms, made to resemble a shield.

Union leagues Organizations originating in the North during the Civil War that insisted upon equality before the law and full participation by blacks in the political and economic life of the South.

diaspora The dispersal of a people from their native homeland.

Boer War A war between the British and Dutch for control of South Africa at the turn of the 20th century.

Orange Free State A province in east central South Africa.

diate postwar period. The collapse of Reconstruction and the subsequent failure of the federal government to safeguard black Americans' constitutional rights dashed Turner's hopes, left him profoundly cynical about the motivations of all white people, and reinforced his conviction that blacks could achieve their just destiny only by returning to the African homeland. The contrast between his youthful optimism and later bitter disillusionment tells us as much about America in the half century after Appomattox as it does about the intellectual odyssey of Henry McNeal Turner.

On Emancipation Day in 1866 a large audience of freed slaves turned out in Augusta to hear a young preacher named Henry Turner deliver the commemorative address. At 32 already one of the major figures in black Georgia, Turner had worked his way up from the cotton fields to a position of state leadership in the AME church. He was clearly a man to be reckoned with, and his presence in Augusta was proof of how far blacks might carry their aspirations. Emancipation itself had created an atmosphere of excitement and anticipation, and the citizens attending this meeting were expecting an oration equal to the joyous occasion. Their speaker did not disappoint them.

In his address Turner rehearsed the history of racial injustice in America, but his tone was upbeat, focusing on the contributions of Africans and Afro-Americans to the advancement of civilization. He urged his listeners to take pride in achievements won in the face of adversity. The young minister saw the Civil War as a turning point and, along with many other black activists, looked to the future with optimism. Using the American flag as his symbol, Turner observed that while in the past "every star was against us; every stripe against us," now "we can claim the protection of the stars and stripes. The glories of this faded **escutcheon** will ever bid us go free." He concluded with the advice that, so far as southern whites are concerned, blacks should "let bygones be by-gones . . . Let us show them we can be a people, respectable, virtuous, honest, and industrious, and soon their prejudice will melt away, and with God for our Father we will all be brothers."

That Turner would face the dawn of Reconstruction with such misguided optimism was due in part to his own successful rise from obscurity. Although he was born free in South Carolina in 1834, family necessity dictated that Henry be sent to work alongside slaves in the cotton fields, so he too felt the overseer's lash. Determined to escape the plantation environment, Turner saw education as a way out. With the help of several friendly whites he learned to read and write, and while still in his teens he caught the attention of officials of the white Methodist Episcopal Church-South, who enlisted him as an itinerant minister. Turner traveled freely throughout the Deep South in the mid-1850s, preaching to slaves and free blacks, and his powerful sermons attracted whites to his meetings as well. Then in 1858 he learned of the AME church, and the idea of an all-black denomination exerted strong appeal. Assigned to the AME mission in Baltimore, Turner began a rigorous program of educational training, studying Latin, Greek, Hebrew, and theology with several professors at Trinity College. Appointed deacon in 1860 and elder two years later, the young minister moved to Washington, where he pastored Union Bethel Church, the largest black congregation in the city.

In Washington, Turner developed friendships with leading antislavery congressmen such as Benjamin Wade, Thaddeus Stevens, and Charles Sumner, contacts he would cultivate during his years as an active politician. He gained national attention when Abraham Lincoln appointed him the first black army chaplain. Turner served with distinction, accompanying troops into battle while ministering to their spiritual needs. After the war he moved to Georgia to work with the Freedmen's Bureau, but racial discrimination soon led to his resignation. He then accepted Bishop Daniel A. Payne's offer to become presiding elder and superintendent of the AME missions in Georgia.

Banned from the South for over 30 years, the AME wasted no time in dispatching over 70 missionary-organizers into the states of the Old Confederacy in a massive effort to win over the former slaves who had been members of white-run denominations. Returning to Georgia in 1865, Turner found many freedpeople still prisoners of old slave habits. They exhibited little racial pride and were fearful of antagonizing their former masters. From the outset Turner realized that by necessity his mission would be political as well as religious. A largely self-educated intellectual, he retained the common touch and sought by courageous example to raise the consciousness of free blacks. Throughout his life he would speak to the condition of impoverished blacks, and they would remain his natural constituency and major base of support.

Turner threw himself into his organizational work with unsurpassed energy and enthusiasm. Of his efforts in the field one black Georgian wrote: "I never saw a man travel so much, preach and speak so much and then be up so late of nights . . . drilling his official men. Surely if he continues this way, and lives the year out . . . he has nine lives." There was some question as to whether Turner would "live the year out," for many southern whites did not take kindly to this invasion of black organizers. Tempers flared on both sides. In Macon, after white Methodists won a court victory giving them control of church property, they awoke to find the church burned to the ground. Turner received a number of death threats and welcomed protection from armed supporters as he traveled throughout the rural South. (What was at stake here was more than church property or the souls of freedpeople. For whites, the sight of black men and women organizing to take charge of their destiny did not bode well for the future of white supremacy.)

Turner saw the necessity of striking fast, while the South was off-balance, and he licensed preachers "by the cargo," declaring that "my hastily made preachers have been among the most useful." The efforts of the AME missionaries met with instant and spectacular success, as they recruited thousands of converts. Early in 1866 Turner claimed that Georgia had been secured for the AME church, stating, "I have visited every place it was safe to go, and sent preachers where it was thought I had better not venture."

A man of Turner's talents quite naturally became involved in secular matters, including the burning question of civil and political rights. When asked by the Republican Executive Committee to organize black voters in Georgia, he retraced his steps across the state, writing campaign broadsides, organizing **Union leagues**, and speaking at freedpeople's conventions. His message was always the same: "We want power, it can only come through organization, and organization comes through unity." Crucial to his success in mobilizing the black vote were the AME churches he had founded the previous year. In these often isolated communities the minister, in addition to preaching the gospel, educated and politicized parishioners. The church was the only institution capable of providing secular leadership, and it quickly became the focal point of black political life as well.

Describing himself as "a minister of the gospel and a kind of politician—both," Turner could look back with satisfaction on the two years since the war's end. He had established the AME church in Georgia on a solid footing and laid the groundwork for his future leadership of that denomination. While his claim that he "organized the Republican party in this state" was somewhat exaggerated, his grass-roots organizing campaign was unprecedented; indeed Georgia would not again see anything like it until the civil rights movement a century later. At 33 Turner was the most influential black religious and political leader in Georgia, the state with the largest black population. As an elected member of the state constitutional convention in late 1867, he looked forward to working with white men of good will to shape a new government responsive to the needs of all its citizens.

Like many grass-roots organizers who would follow him, Turner proved more effective in the field than in the legislative halls. Throughout the long deliberations leading to Georgia's Reconstruction constitution, his stance was both conservative and accommodationist. Consistently supporting planter interests, he introduced a resolution to prevent the sale of property of those owners unable to pay their taxes, and he supported a petition to Congress to grant $30 million for planter relief. He also introduced a resolution providing financial assistance for banks, supported poll tax and education requirements for suffrage, and even attempted to persuade the convention to take up a petition for the pardon of Jefferson Davis. Perhaps Turner summed up his convention performance best when he later ruefully observed that "no man in Georgia has been more conservative than I. 'Anything to please the white folks' has been my motto . . ."

Aside from his key convention role in establishing a public school system, Turner did not address the concerns of his black constituents. He avoided the issue of land reform, despite widespread interest among freedpeople for "40 acres and a mule." Indeed, by protecting planter property he helped reduce the amount of land for purchase at reasonable prices. His stand for suffrage restrictions would have drastically reduced the potential black electorate, and his failure to push for a constitutional amendment making absolutely clear the right of blacks to hold public office contributed to the expulsion of all black members of the state legislature.

The accommodationist position taken by Turner and the other black delegates rested in part on political expediency. Over three-fourths of the nearly 170 convention delegates were conservative white southerners. Blacks, who made up no more than 20 percent of the total, felt the need to compromise to maintain any political influence. But such assumptions also stemmed from the rather naive faith of Turner and most other blacks at the convention that white Georgians would agree to meaningful black participation in government. As members of the educated black elite they assumed to know what was best for the illiterate black masses, and they were confident of their ability to deal with seasoned and powerful white politicians. They were wrong on both counts.

After satisfying the requirements of the Congressional Reconstruction Acts of 1867, Georgia was readmitted to the Union and in April 1868 held elections for governor and state legislators. Conservative white Democrats and Republicans dominated the new General Assembly, but 32 blacks did win election, including Henry Turner. During his brief tenure in the legislature, Turner served with greater distinction than he had at the constitutional convention. Now openly suspicious of the agenda of white lawmakers, he increasingly saw his role as that of defender of the rights of freedpeople. Along with other black legislators he introduced bills to provide state subsidies for black higher education, to charter black cooperative stock companies, and to create a black militia to offer some protection against Klan violence. Aware of the nature of economic exploitation against blacks, Turner was among the first to make effective use of the term "peonage" to describe the widespread practice by which many landlords held on to unwilling tenants. He offered legislation to protect sharecroppers, to enact an eight-hour work day, and to abolish the convict lease system.

As he moved away from his accommodationist stance, Turner's relationship with white politicians became confrontational. The state's most articulate black leader, he was singled out for abuse. Angered by slanderous attacks on his character, and upset by the failure of white Republicans to support pro-black legislation, Turner lashed back at his critics. His speech during the debate that led to expulsion of all black legislators, the most powerful of his career, was a manifesto for human rights: "I am here to demand my rights and to hurl thunderbolts at the man who would dare to cross the threshold of my manhood . . . Never, in the history of the world has a man been arraigned before a body clothed with legislative, judicial, or executive functions, charged with the offense of being of a darker hue than his fellow-men . . . The great question, sir, is this: Am I a man?" Turner went on to defend the Negro against charges of inferiority ("I hold that we are a very great people") and to voice contempt for the "treachery" of the white race. At the close of his address he led the black delegation out of the chamber, turned to face his colleagues one last time, and contemptuously scraped the mud off his shoes.

This would not be Turner's legislative swan song. Under protection of federal bayonet the black representatives would gain readmission, and Turner would serve during the 1870 General Assembly session. But by the time he returned, Radical Reconstruction in Georgia had been so effectively undermined that there was little chance for the black delegation to have any impact. The Democrats quickly consolidated their power. After lobbying unsuccessfully for further federal intervention, Turner called upon his old friends in Congress to secure him appointive office. These efforts to obtain federal patronage met such intense white resistance—as when President Grant appointed him post-master of Macon—that Turner retired from active political life in the early 1870s. Deprived of his political power base, disillusioned by federal indifference to white violence and voter fraud, Turner returned full-time to his religious duties.

Except for church historians, scholars have given Turner's religious career and beliefs short shrift. For over a half century the church was the central concern in his life, providing him with his livelihood and a strong base of operations in the black community. Moreover, his theological interpretation of history laid the foundation for his early political optimism, his evolving black nationalism, and his ultimate obsession with African emigration.

Bishop Turner's theology was grounded in the Bible, particularly in the teachings of the Hebrew prophets and in the gospel of Jesus. A firm believer in the omnipotence and sovereignty of God, Turner said: "There is a God that runs this universe: and a nation and people are no exception." Given this fundamentalist view of the relationship between God and humanity, Turner had to come to terms with the tragic history of the African peoples since the **diaspora**. In so doing he developed a messianic vision which had as its keystone the concept of God's Providential design for people of African descent. Throughout his ministerial career Turner insisted that slavery was a "Providential institution." God was "not asleep or oblivious to passing events" but knew that the slave regime "was the most rapid transit from barbarism to Christian civilization for the Negro." Thus God permitted the enslavement of Africans and placed them under the trusteeship of white Americans. It was whites' brutal treatment of slaves that subverted divine will and purpose and was "an insult to God." It would take the Civil War to "satisfy the divine justice and make slavery despicable in the eyes of a country which loved it so dearly and nurtured it so long." This logic led Turner at first to see Reconstruction as a conversion experience for whites in which they would undergo a change of heart. Convinced that "all great convulsive courses have been succeeded with liberative consequences," he held out the olive branch to southern whites, hopeful that together they would build the new Jerusalem.

The bitter experience of Reconstruction soured Turner on elective politics but did not shake his faith in God's Providential design. The bishop simply adapted the model to fit new circumstances. His experience with the evils of slavery, the racism of northern troops, and the perfidy of both South and North after the war convinced Turner that God's plan for the Negro did not include a positive role for whites. From the outset of his ministry he had believed the church must develop racial pride and consciousness among millions of blacks beaten down by centuries of oppression. Now, beginning in the late 1880s, Turner viewed this mission with a great sense of urgency and began to develop a black theology of liberation grounded in the basic tenets of Christianity.

To achieve this end, Turner realized, blacks must reject all teachings of the white church that confirmed their inferior status. He was particularly sensitive to the symbolic significance of "whiteness" in Christian teachings and discouraged singing of such verses as, "Now wash me and I shall be whiter than snow," explaining that the purpose of washing was to make one clean, not white. More dramatic was his assertion, often repeated, that "God is a Negro." When this statement drew criticism from whites—and from a few blacks—Turner patiently pointed out that historically every race of people had portrayed God in its own image; but he also lashed out at those whites and "all of the fool Negroes" who "believe that God is a white-skinned, blue-eyed, projecting-nosed, compressed-lipped and finely-robed *white* gentleman, sitting upon a throne somewhere in the heavens." Turner was deeply disturbed by the negative influence of white Christianity upon the black psyche: He knew that "Christianity" reflected the values of the greater society, and he despaired of any significant improvement in the self-image of Afro-Americans so long as they were subjected to daily indoctrination by the dominant culture. "As long as we remain among the whites," he wrote in 1898, "the Negro will believe that the devil is black . . . and that he [the Negro] was the devil . . . and the effect of such sentiment is contemptuous and degrading." This is one of the reasons, Turner concluded, "why we favor African emigration."

The black exodus was both the culmination and cornerstone of Turner's theology. It linked his messianic vision of the AME Christian mission and his African dream of a strong and proud black nation, free from the corrupting influence of white society. He had always believed that God's providential plan was to Christianize Africa. As early as 1866 the young minister expressed interest in emigration, and after Reconstruction it became his consuming passion. Contrary to critics' charges, Turner never contended that all Afro-Americans would choose to return to the land of their ancestors. But "millions of the Negro race" would emigrate, bringing with them the message of Christ crucified and (paradoxically) the benefits of Western civilization. To comprehend Turner's black nationalism and the depth of his dedication to Africa, then, one must examine both within the context of his strong religious beliefs.

Turner's election to the bishopric in 1880 culminated 22 years of active service for the AME church in a variety of positions. After five years of religious and political organizing in Georgia, he resigned as elder to become pastor of a large Savannah congregation. In 1876 the Methodist hierarchy called him to Philadelphia to become business manager of the nearly bankrupt AME Book Concern. Turner impressed his superiors with his administrative skills and made good use of the opportunity to write for publications, edit the *Christian Recorder*, revise the church hymnal, and compile the *Catechism of the AME Church.* He also used his position to political advantage, traveling from conference to conference to meet influential black Methodists.

Turner became bishop over the objections of his former patron, Bishop Daniel A. Payne, and other northern-based church leaders. The pious and idealistic Payne was uncomfortable with this crude, awkward preacher-politician from the South. Turner's support came from the southern rank-and-file AME members and their pastors, many of whom he himself recruited into the ministry. In charge of the Georgia Conference, the denomination's largest, Turner and his followers became a powerful voice for the AME church's southern majority.

Church leadership gave Turner a forum denied him in the 1870s. He enjoyed the rough-and-tumble ecclesiastical politics. One of his contemporaries remembers him as "always looking for a fight." Another recalled that he "was no kid glove leader, and no hat box bishop. There was nothing of the smell of the parlor and drawing room about him." Turner saw himself as the leader of the masses but not one of them. He wielded power autocratically, eschewing familiarity. One minister who addressed Turner as "brother" at a convention got a sharp reprimand, as Turner stopped the proceedings with an explosive, "I want you to understand, I am the BISHOP."

Turner's private life centered around his spacious home at 30 Younge Street in Atlanta. Even here the outside world intruded, for amid a mountain of books, journals, and manuscripts, a clerical staff was on hand to do the bishop's bidding. Married four times, Turner survived three wives and all but two of his children. He did not normally refer to his personal tragedies, but in 1893 he did inform newspaper readers that in the 10-year period just ended he had lost his mother, his eldest daughter, his first wife, his youngest daughter, and his second wife. His final marriage at age 73 to his private secretary, Laura Pearl Lemon, a divorcee, evoked a storm of criticism in the AME bishopric, but Turner survived the attempts to remove him from office. A firm believer in the institution of marriage, he once wrote to his son John that "bachelors are a public nuisance."

Although his attitude toward husband–wife relations appears to have reflected the mores of the Victorian age, Turner was ahead of his time in advocating an expanded public role for women. While serving in the Georgia legislature he introduced a bill giving women the vote, and in 1888 he ordained a woman as deacon in the AME church. (The Council of Bishops immediately rescinded the appointment, claiming that the Scriptures did not authorize such action and grumbling that it was an act "without a precedent in any other body of Christians in the known world.") Turner persisted in involving women in the activities of the church, founding the Women's Home and Foreign Mission Society, praising black women because they "intend to make a fight for their rights," and opening the columns of his newspapers to women writers. Turner received strong support and little criticism from women in the AME church; he in turn was proud to recognize their contribution and worth.

As senior bishop for 20 of his 35 years in the episcopacy, Turner put his stamp on the church in numerous ways. An iconoclast at the head of a vast bureaucracy, he scorned regulations that did not serve his purposes. Thus, when faced with the need for strong local leadership in the new AME mission in South Africa, he created the post of vicar-bishop—an office unknown to Methodism. Turner's pragmatism continually caused conflict with his fellow bishops. He also ruffled feathers on the congregational level with attacks on emotionalism in the pulpit and insistence on rituals and [the] use of clerical vestments to promote formality and dignity in worship services. But his major contributions to the church lay in the fields of education and foreign missions.

Like most black leaders Turner saw education as the key to progress, and from the beginning of his ministry he stressed the need for well-trained ministers and teachers. Moreover, since he believed that education could be either a means of social control or a potent weapon for liberation, he insisted that schools be organized and run only by blacks, without interference from white teachers or trustees. Under Turner's leadership the AME transferred most of its educational activities to the South, establishing a dozen schools and colleges during the last two decades of the nineteenth century. The centerpiece of the system was Morris Brown College in Atlanta. Turner took special interest in this institution, serving for a time as its chancellor, overseeing its expansion, and at one point mortgaging his personal property to keep the college afloat. In 1900 the college's board of trustees established Turner Theological Seminary in honor of the contributions of the senior bishop.

While not nearly so well publicized as his promotion of African emigration, Turner's missionary work on the continent produced tangible results for the AME church and facilitated the rise of black consciousness in South Africa. The conviction that the AME church had an obligation to Christianize Africa was not original with Turner, but early efforts to do so had failed because of the church's meager economic resources and the more immediate task of evangelizing the freedpeople in the South. The crusade to convert Africans began in earnest in the late 1880s, when Bishop Turner became president of the AME Missionary Department and expanded its jurisdiction to include Africa. Late in 1891 he made his first trip to Africa, drawing upon his considerable organizational skills to establish annual conferences in Sierra Leone and Liberia. Then, and in two subsequent visits in 1893 and 1895, Turner ordained preachers, elders, and deacons, established schools and churches, and won over hundreds of converts to African Methodism. Welcomed by large crowds wherever he went, Turner responded enthusiastically and in a series of widely read letters promoted both African missions and emigration.

The AME church's major gains came in South Africa, where Turner became involved in the racial politics of that strife-torn region on the eve of the **Boer War**. AME church interest stemmed directly from establishment of the South African Ethiopian church in 1892 by African religious leaders upset by the color bar in white churches and stirred by nationalistic feelings of "Africa for Africans." The two religious bodies had so much in common that in 1896 the Ethiopian church sent a delegation to Atlanta to arrange a merger. Turner appointed Reverend James W. Dwane, leader of the Ethiopian group, as superintendent of the newly created AME church in South Africa and authorized his return to Africa to work on the transition of the clergy and members of the Ethiopian mission into the AME denomination.

Two years later Turner made a five-week triumphal tour through South Africa, traveling over a thousand miles from Cape Town to Pretoria, meeting with Paul Kruger, the president of the **Orange Free State**, and organizing the Transvaal and Cape Colony conferences. Although he received a polite reception from government officials, they became suspicious that he and American AME missionaries were pursuing goals more political than religious. The "race solidarity" and "race regeneration" messages brought by these missionaries alarmed colonial administrators, who began placing restrictions on the ministers. Turner was specifically accused of arousing nationalist passions among the Zulus, and after the Zulu revolt failed in 1906, AME missionaries were barred from most of Natal and Transvaal.

Turner's South African campaign also got him into trouble with his fellow bishops back home. The controversy erupted with the appointment of Dwane as vicar-bishop. Turner argued that the position was not inconsistent with Methodist tradition, but the AME episcopacy repudiated his action. The Dwane affair was but one of a series of issues that had been dividing Turner and the more traditional bishops (the majority of them did not share his enthusiasm for African emigration), and in the 1890s his power in the church began to decline. But by then Turner had once again reimmersed himself in the secular world, promoting and organizing black migration to Africa, renewing his interest in state and national politics, and making his bid to fill the leadership void left by Frederick Douglass.

For Afro-Americans the decade of the 1890s was the low point of their post–Civil War experience. Acts of racial violence had reached a new high, the courts were continuing their retreat from the constitutional guarantees afforded American citizens, and the depression of 1893 further tightened the chains of crop lien and peonage. Traditional black leaders appeared unable to come to terms with these catastrophic developments. Douglass was now an old man (he would die in 1895), and his assimilationist ideology, based on black political empowerment, had failed to anticipate the depth and virulence of white racist sentiment. The time was ripe for new leadership, and Henry McNeal Turner was ready to make his move.

Save for Douglass, Turner was as well known and as well respected as any black leader. His appeals to black pride and his famous denunciation of the U.S. Supreme Court for its decision in the 1883 civil rights cases had won him a large audience. Turner understood better than most the implications of that ruling, which declared unconstitutional the Civil Rights Act of 1875. That "barbarous" decision should be "branded, battle-axed, sawed, cut and carved with the most bitter epithets and blistering denunciations that words can express . . . It absolves the allegiance of the Negro to the United States." His position as senior bishop provided a strong power base in the black community, and his organizing skills and oratorical prowess would serve him well in a bid for national leadership. Turner also had a program, one based on the realities of the past three decades of American history: The Afro-American dream of assimilation had failed; it was time for blacks to found their own nation in Africa.

Although he continued to demand equal rights for blacks in America, African emigration was the heart and soul of Bishop Turner's program. His first trip to Africa in 1891 was an emotional and exhilarating experience, one that confirmed his feelings about Africa as the homeland. Upon his return he persuaded the AME church to establish a monthly newspaper, the *Voice of Missions,* which quickly became the personal voice of Henry Turner. Under his editorship the *Voice* achieved a wide circulation. The monthly devoted its columns to attacks on racial discrimination, essays on black history and achievement, and, above all, articles promoting African colonization. Turner soon began receiving hundreds of letters from poor southern blacks, eagerly requesting information on passage to Africa. Convinced by this outpouring of interest that his idea was one whose time had come, he pushed forward with plans to settle colonies in Liberia, where the black government would welcome Afro-Americans. Middle-class blacks here remained either lukewarm or hostile to emigration, with their spokespeople usually unequivocal in their opposition.

To rally middle-class support for his crusade, Turner sent out a call for a national convention of Afro-Americans, to meet in Cincinnati in November 1893. With the Democrats back in the White House, the decline of Douglass, and the failure of organizations such as the Afro-American League to unify and galvanize black leadership, a political vacuum now existed that Turner purported to fill. Though the call specifically stated that the convention would "have no application to party politics," he made it clear that "the Negro cannot remain here in his present condition and be a man . . . for at the present rate his extermination is only a question of time."

The response to the convention call was gratifying. Turner's emphasis on the need to rally against racial injustice struck a common chord, and many prominent blacks responded. When the bishop rose to make the keynote address, nearly 800 delegates and a large group of local blacks were in the audience. The occasion afforded Turner a unique opportunity, yet he opened the meeting with a curious speech. He began by reiterating his concept of slavery as a providential institution and then went on to observe that during the Civil War the "Negro was as loyal to the Confederate flag as he was to the federal." Turner devoted much of his talk to the increase in lynching and, more specifically, the question of rape as its primary cause. Though he attacked the "rape defense," Turner did argue that blacks must assume responsibility for dealing with rapists in their midst. Only at the end of his speech did he address the issue of emigration, coupling it with an eloquent plea for the development of a "consciousness that I am somebody, that I am a man . . . that I have rights . . . that I am entitled to respect, that every avenue to distinction is mine."

The audience received Turner's speech warmly, but his somewhat muted emigrationist appeal failed to sway convention delegates, who rejected a committee report recommending that black Americans "turn their attention to the civilization of Africa as the only hope of the Negro race." To avoid a showdown vote he would have lost, Turner sent the report back to committee for revision. Bishop Turner's efforts to unify the delegates around a nationalist and emigrationist program had failed. While he adamantly denied having called the convention to promote his program, the black press was correct in labeling the outcome as a personal defeat for the bishop. Turner was never comfortable in the role of conciliator, and his rebuff by representatives of the black elite in Cincinnati affected him in much the same way as his earlier humiliation at the hands of white Georgia Reconstructionists. Never at home in bourgeois society, Turner reverted after Cincinnati to his familiar polemical style to answer his black critics.

•••••

What angered Turner most about the attacks of black opponents was their exaggeration and distortion of his position on emigration and Africa. As early as 1883 he lamented, "Every solitary writer who has been trying to excoriate me for my African sentiments has done so under the hidden idea, 'He wants us all to go to Africa.'" Simply stated, Turner's goal was that a significant minority (his numbers varied) of blacks should "found and establish a country or a government somewhere upon the continent of Africa." Beyond that Turner was vague in his statements concerning the form of government and the nature of the economic system in his proposed African state. There was more truth to the charges that the bishop exaggerated the appeal of Africa to attract emigrants ("And gold dust can be switched up by women and children in marvelous quantities along the shores of rivers and creeks after heavy rains . . ."); yet he did make a point of telling prospective settlers of the difficulties they would initially face and insisted that blacks should not emigrate without sufficient funds to maintain themselves until they found employment.

In the end the most persuasive arguments against African colonization came from the emigrants themselves. In the mid-1890s two boatloads of colonists left the United States for Liberia amid much fanfare and press coverage. Months later reports of disease, malnutrition, and death started filtering back. As the first colonists returned to America with horror stories of life in Liberia, the newspapers reported every tragic detail. Black opponents of emigration seized upon these reports to discredit both the movement and its chief promoter, Bishop Turner. Not all colonists had bad experiences in Africa, however; a few stayed and prospered. But returnees reinforced stereotypes of the "dark continent," and Turner could not dispel that image. His assertions that those who came back had selfish motives, exaggerating their plight to justify their defection and win sympathy back home, were undermined when he labeled them as "shiftless no-account Negroes . . . accustomed to being fed and driven around by white men . . ." It appeared that Turner, to repair the damage of unfavorable publicity, had resorted to blaming the victim. Although he continued to press for African emigration, the failures of the early expeditions, along with the solid opposition of most black leaders, prevented the bishop from rekindling the spirit of the early 1890s, when thousands of poor southern black sharecroppers shared his African dream of a homeland free from the tyranny of white supremacist rule.

In addition to his work with African missions and for colonization, Turner found time to become active once again in state and national politics. His retirement from active political life in the 1870s had not been total: Occasional comments on national affairs and his widely read denunciation of the U.S. Supreme Court in 1883 had won him a large audience. While he never regained his early zeal for party politics (almost all of his later political pronouncements included the disclaimer that the Afro-American's stay in this country was "a temporary one"), in the 1890s he began to speak out more frequently on issues facing black Georgians. As the decade ended he was vehemently denouncing the new United States imperialism in Cuba and in the Philippines.

For the last quarter century of his life Henry McNeal Turner was a political maverick. The most important black member of the small Prohibition party, he agreed to be a delegate to the party's 1888 national convention. In Georgia, Turner was not alone among black leaders in supporting Democrat William J. Northen for governor in 1892, for Northen was a southern moderate who promised increased funds for black schools and a state antilynching law. The bishop joined most black spokespeople in resisting the appeals of Tom Watson's Populists. More comfortable with powerful Democrats than white insurgents, Turner also questioned the Populist commitment to interracial politics. Ideologically, the Populists had little to offer him, for the bishop never concerned himself much with economic alternatives to corporate capitalism.

Turner received much notoriety—and a degree of political influence—for his support of Democratic candidates running for national office. The bishop was almost alone among blacks in his support of Grover Cleveland's 1892 bid for the presidency. Turner wrote to Cleveland endorsing Georgia editor Hoke Smith for secretary of the interior and was rewarded by having three of his relatives appointed to jobs in the interior secretary's office. (This information surfaced in the 1906 Georgia gubernatorial campaign, embarrassing candidate Smith, by this time one of the state's champion race-baiters.) When Turner actively supported Democrat William Jennings Bryan in his unsuccessful presidential campaigns, the bishop drew fire from black Georgia's political establishment. Republican to the core, leaders such as William A. Pledger, editor of the *Atlanta Age* and the first black Republican state chairman in Georgia, and attorney Judson Lyons, who, as register of the United States Treasury, was the nation's highest black appointee, viewed Turner's actions as heresy, and the black press excoriated him for his crimes.

The bishop's alliance with stand-pat conservative Democrats in Georgia and in Washington does not lend itself to easy explanation, for unlike Senators Morgan and Butler, the Northens and Smiths did not support Turner's plans for African emigration. They were, at best, racial paternalists and had no program for addressing the range of problems facing black Americans. Turner never attempted to reconcile his vehement attacks on American "democracy" with his support of politicians who embraced the status quo in race relations. His endorsement of Democratic candidates enabled him to settle some scores with white and black political foes, provided him with a forum for his emigrationist views in the white press, and gained him some access to important politicians. But in the long run Bishop Turner did not look upon his political activity as preparing the way for meaningful and lasting black participation in the American system. Events at the turn of the century only strengthened his conviction that white America was on a collision course with people of color, both at home and abroad.

Although well into his 60s and in failing health, Turner seemed to grow angrier and more militant with age. Enraged by escalating white violence against defenseless blacks, the bishop responded with a *Voice of Missions* editorial titled, "Negro, Get Guns": "Let every Negro in this country, who has a spark of manhood in him supply his house with one, two, or three guns . . .

and when your domicile is invaded by the bloody lynchers or any mob . . . turn loose your missiles of death and blow the fiendish wretches into a thousand giblets . . ." This was too much for the white press, which accused him of fomenting race war. Although he backed off some here, Turner's nationalistic message remained clear and strong. He carried his analysis a step further when the United States, acting upon its imperialistic impulses, declared war on Spain in 1898.

Turner had opposed American intervention in Cuba, but when the McKinley administration moved to crush the Aguinaldo independence movement in the Philippines, the bishop's rage knew no bounds. Labeling the war there the "crime of the century," Turner castigated blacks who volunteered to help put down the insurrection: "I boil over with disgust when I remember that colored men from this country . . . are there fighting to subjugate a people of their own color . . . I can scarcely keep from saying that I hope the Filipinos will wipe such soldiers from the face of the earth . . . to go down there and shoot innocent men and take the country away from them, is too much for me to think about, and I will write no more, for I cannot stand it."

His increasingly outspoken behavior further eroded Turner's support in the church hierarchy, and while he successfully resisted efforts to "encourage" his retirement as senior bishop, he did lose control of the *Voice of Missions* in 1901. Unabashed, he founded his own personal journal, the *Voice of the People*, and continued to put forward a broad black nationalist platform with African emigration as its centerpiece. But circulation of the new monthly remained small, and Turner's fiery appeals now met more apathy than hostility. Still, Bishop Turner remained a commanding presence. When black Georgia's political and intellectual leaders met in Macon in 1906 to form the Georgia Equal Rights Association, Turner was selected to head the group, which included such strident activists as Augusta editor William J. White and Atlanta University's W. E. B. Du Bois.

The Georgia Equal Rights Convention was something of a last hurrah for Bishop Turner. He would live on for nearly a decade, and his name would surface from time to time, usually at the center of some minor controversy. But age and infirmity—as well as American history—had taken their toll. A once herculean frame had grown portly, and his broad shoulders were drooped. Yet as he rose to address his colleagues assembled in Macon, he was again the Turner of old. In his deep booming voice he thundered his most famous lines: "I used to love what I thought was the grand old flag, and sing with ecstasy about the Stars and Stripes, but to the Negro in this country the American flag is a dirty and contemptible rag. Not a star in it can the colored man claim, for it is no longer the symbol of our manhood rights and liberty . . . Without multiplying words, I wish to say that hell is an improvement on the United States where the Negro is concerned." For Henry McNeal Turner the flag had always stood as a metaphor for the American dream. His remarks at Macon represented a final judgment upon a nation that had consistently disappointed him, along with millions of other black Americans.

Turner remained active in the church until the end. He died in Ontario,

Canada, on April 8, 1915, at the age of 81, after suffering a heart attack. He had gone there against the advice of his physician to preside over the Quarterly Conference of the AME church.

The estimated 25,000 mourners who attended Bishop Turner's funeral in Atlanta represented a cross-section of black America, with a number of prominent figures leading the procession. The eulogies praised his church and missionary work, along with his contributions to black education, but made only passing reference to his early political career and his emigrationist activities. Most of those paying their respects were poor blacks. They were not asked to make speeches, but they recognized in Turner's life the embodiment of their spirit. Whether or not they shared in his African dream, they endorsed his appeals to racial pride and applauded his bold, incisive attacks on American society. Bishop Turner was, in Du Bois's words, a "charging bull," the "last of his clan: mighty men, physically and mentally, who started at the bottom and hammered their way to the top by brute strength."

Henry McNeal Turner was a leader who defies easy categorization. A deeply religious man with the political instincts of a street fighter, an intellectual whose natural constituency existed in the shacks of unlettered sharecroppers, Turner could be maddeningly inconsistent in his political behavior, but he was unswerving in his advocacy of black nationalism and African emigration as the only righteous road to freedom and dignity. He was an agitator and a prophet, who articulated the hopes and frustrations of three generations of Afro-Americans trapped along the color line.

IDA B. WELLS AND
THE ANTI-LYNCHING MOVEMENT

The late nineteenth century was the heyday of American lynching. The most frequent victims were southern blacks suspected of real and imaginary offenses that ranged from discourtesy to murder. During a period when white southern society evinced acute concern about matters of racial control, lynching became the most vicious of the various means employed to keep African Americans in their place. Of those who sought to combat this horrific development, no one did more to keep the issue before the public than Ida B. Wells, a black writer, suffragist, and founding member of the National Association for the Advancement of Colored People (NAACP). After a Memphis mob lynched three of her friends in 1892—a year that witnessed 230 such killings—she used her position as editor of the Memphis Free Speech *to launch what would be a lifelong crusade against this barbarous practice. In the extract that follows, Wells speaks of the incident that prompted her activism in the course of urging other African Americans to take a more aggressive stance against lynching.*

Source: Ida B. Wells, *Southern Lynch Law in All Its Phases* (New York: The New York Age Print, 1892), pp. 22–24.

Self-Help

To Northern capital and Afro-American labor the South owes its rehabilitation. If labor is withdrawn capital will not remain. The Afro-American is thus the backbone of the South. A thorough knowledge and judicious exercise of this power in lynching localities could many times effect a bloodless revolution. The white man's dollar is his god, and to stop this will be to stop outrages in many localities.

The Afro-Americans of Memphis denounced the lynching of three of their best citizens and urged and waited for the authorities to act in the matter and bring the lynchers to justice. No attempt was made to do so, and the black men left the city by thousands, bringing about great stagnation in every branch of business. Those who remained so injured the business of the street car company by staying off the cars, that the superintendent, manager, and treasurer called personally on the editor of the *Free Speech,* asked them to urge our people to give their patronage again. Other businessmen became alarmed over the situation and the *Free Speech* was run away that the colored people might be more easily controlled. A meeting of white citizens in June, three months after the lynching, passed resolutions for the first time condemning it . . .

• • • • •

The appeal to the white man's pocket has ever been more effectual than all the appeals ever made to his conscience. Nothing, absolutely nothing, is to be gained by a further sacrifice of manhood and self-respect. By the right exercise of his power as the industrial factor of the South, the Afro-American can demand and secure his rights, the punishment of lynchers, and a fair trial for accused rapists.

Of the many inhuman outrages of the present year, the only case where the proposed lynching did *not* occur, was where the men armed themselves in Jacksonville, Florida, and Paducah, Kentucky, and prevented it. The only times an Afro-American who was assaulted got away has been when he had a gun and used it in self-defense.

The lesson this teaches and which every Afro-American should ponder well, is that a Winchester rifle should have a place of honor in every black home, and it should be used for that protection which the law refuses to give. When the white man who is always the aggressor knows he runs as great a risk of biting the dust every time his Afro-American victim does, he will have greater respect for Afro-American life. The more the Afro-American yields and cringes and begs, the more he has to do so, the more he is insulted, outraged and lynched.

• • • • •

Nothing is more definitely settled than he must act for himself. I have shown how he may employ the boycott, emigration and the press, and I feel that by a combination of all these agencies can be effectually stamped out lynch law, that last relic of barbarism and slavery. "The gods help those who help themselves."

QUESTIONS

1. What place did the Civil War have in Turner's theological interpretation of history? Why did he support planter interests at Georgia's constitutional convention following the war? Why did his later initiatives as a Georgia state legislator differ so markedly from his performance at the convention?
2. Turner's career spanned a period of extraordinary change in African-American society. Identify a major turning point in his life and explain why you think it was significant.
3. How would you describe Turner's views on the relationship between religion and society? In what ways did his religious beliefs influence his actions as a politician and racial leader?
4. What were Turner's greatest strengths as a religious leader? Why did he get along so poorly with his fellow bishops within the African Methodist Episcopal church? Given the often troubled nature of these relations, how was Turner able to become such a powerful figure in the church?
5. What developments prompted Turner to become an outspoken proponent of African colonization? Why did middle-class African Americans tend to oppose African emigration? What was Ida B. Wells's likely reaction to emigration proposals?
6. What did Wells mean when she said that African Americans were "the backbone of the South"? What was the main theme of her statement? How do you think Turner reacted to her message? In what ways did the two black leaders' views of American life differ?

BIBLIOGRAPHY

The only book-length biography of Turner is M. M. Poston's *Life and Times of Henry M. Turner* (1917), an outdated and uncritical work that should be supplemented by Edwin S. Redkey, ed., *The Writings and Speeches of Henry McNeal Turner* (1971). Redkey has also provided a searching examination of Turner's emigrationist initiatives in *Black Exodus: Black Nationalist and Back-to-Africa Movements, 1890–1910* (1969). Those wishing to learn more about the controversial churchman can consult the relevant sections of the following studies: Leon F. Litwack, *Been in the Storm So Long: The Aftermath of Slavery* (1979); Edmund L. Drago, *Black Politicians and Reconstruction in Georgia: A Splendid Failure* (1982); Clarence E. Walker, *A Rock in a Weary Land: The African Methodist Church During the Civil War and Reconstruction* (1982); Henry J. Young, *Major Black Religious Leaders, 1755–1940* (1977); August Meier, *Negro Thought in America, 1880–1915* (1963); and John Dittmer, *Black Georgia in the Progressive Era, 1900–1920*.

John D. Rockefeller

During the last third of the nineteenth century, the U.S. economy grew by leaps and bounds. A major contributing factor was the extension of the railroad network. The construction and operation of railroads required vast quantities of steel, iron, coal, and other products. And as the railroads expanded, these industries also experienced substantial growth. Even more important, as rail lines gradually penetrated all regions of the country, a national market began to take shape. This in turn spurred the creation of ever larger productive units that combined organizational innovations with the newest technology to take advantage of economies of scale. In so doing, the new corporations established formidable market positions at the expense of smaller, less efficient firms.

One example was the Carnegie Steel Company, which by 1890 outpaced all other producers in that industry, and which in 1901 combined with its 10 largest competitors to form the U.S. Steel Corporation. Another was John D. Rockefeller's Standard Oil Company. As early as 1870, Standard controlled nearly 40 percent of the oil industry; by the turn of the century, it owned most of the nation's pipelines and refined more than 80 percent of the oil produced in the United States. Had these firms achieved such dominance on the basis of efficiency alone, the enormous power they wielded would have excited alarm. As it was, they often employed a variety of unscrupulous tactics to drive competitors to the wall. And where some

observers lauded the new corporate chieftains as captains of industry who had imposed stability on a chaotic economic system, others viewed them as mean-spirited plunderers who wantonly destroyed peoples' lives in their single-minded pursuit of wealth. In the words of historian Hal Bridges, "they were a set of avaricious rascals who habitually cheated and robbed investors and con-sumers, corrupted government, fought ruthlessly among themselves, and in general carried on predatory activities comparable to those of the robber barons of medieval Europe."

In the essay that follows, William Manchester gives us an opportunity to assess the validity of these competing interpretations. His examination of the business career and private life of John D. Rockefeller reveals a complex and somewhat eccentric individual who is not easily categorized. Indeed, there is much in Manchester's portrait of the oil tycoon to support the contentions of both critics and defenders of the new corporate elite. Readers will thus have to draw their own conclusions as to whether Rockefeller was a robber baron, cap-tain of industry, or something apart from the images suggested by these de-scriptive terms.

John D. Rockefeller

William Manchester

Fifty-six floors above Manhattan's Rockefeller Center, William Couper's bust of America's first billionaire gazes out stonily on the private offices of his four sur-viving grandsons. Those who knew him in his later years find the likeness strik-ing, for at the end of his life John Davison Rockefeller (1839–1937) had a remark-ably graven look. He is remembered as a wrinkled, bony nonagenarian who distributed 20,000 dimes to strangers—he started with nickels but found them too heavy—and spent his last days among the black parishioners of the Union Baptist Church in Ormond Beach, Florida, chanting prayers and reedily affirm-ing in his quavering tenor that when the roll was called up yonder, he'd be there.

Like so much else in his extraordinary career, this final tableau is decep-tive. All his life John D. deftly masked his real self from an inquisitive public. Leafing through an album of photographs of him is like reviewing the dis-guises of a celebrated character actor. His use of his hair is illustrative. When side whiskers were the fashion, John D. wore them. After they went out and long mustaches came in, he went to the barber, and when shorter mustaches became the vogue he went again, always emerging the image of the average businessman.

This protean performance became impossible after a series of illnesses brought on by anxiety over the government's determination to disassemble his

Source: Reprinted by permission of Don Congdon Associates, Inc. Copyright © 1974 by William Manchester.

beloved Standard Oil trust. All his hair fell out, including his eyebrows. To his horror, his bald head glittered like a knob of buffed marble. He wore a skullcap for a while, and then he acquired a wardrobe of wigs, one for church, another for golf, and a third for street wear. By then there wasn't much point in pretending he was average anyway, so he lived on into great old age wearing the quaint frock coat and plug hat of Victorian bankers.

Inasmuch as his lifetime spanned three generations and the industrialization of a continent, he had time to play a great many roles. Americans over 50 recall him as the wraithlike citizen of Ormond Beach who was mortified by the local garden club's decision to disqualify him from its annual flower show after the ladies discovered that his butler had arranged his blossoms—logical to the end, John D. argued that the butler was an extension of himself—but at the height of his powers he had been anything but vulnerable. Throughout the last third of the 19th century, he was a powerfully built, rawboned titan with hypnotic eyes who was, in his own words, "all business," and who strode purposefully over the mustard-colored carpets at 26 Broadway, Standard Oil's great keep, swapping refineries, railroads, and mountain ranges glittering with iron ore.

His refusal to abandon cherished objectives reminded James Ford Rhodes of Napoleon and Bertrand Russell of Bismarck, and his passion for facts was much like that of a fictional character, the industrialist Thomas Gradgrind in Dickens's *Hard Times*. Indeed, throughout John D.'s life Dickensian names cropped up in his retinue with extraordinary frequency. They included his ruthless successor as president of Standard Oil (Archbold), the former Baptist clergyman who opened his fortune to a host of charities (Gates), a labor-baiting monopolist (Welborn), the pompous homeopath who enjoyed issuing bulletins about his health at the turn of the century (Biggar), a night nurse (Sly) and the physician who checked him a few days before his death and thought he looked just fine (Merryday). A clergyman who matched John D. stroke for stroke on the golf course was a Bustard.

One character in his life that the tycoon never resembled was his father, William A. (Big Bill) Rockefeller, a celebrated mountebank who roamed the frontier playing a violin on his hip, selling elixir by the bottle and advertising himself at county fairs as a "botanic physician" or "herbal doctor." Big Bill was a cancer quack. He was also a rake. Between hawking fake nostrums and hoodwinking credulous rubes, he spent a lot of time in strange beds, and on one of his infrequent visits to his family in the upstate New York town of Richford, he was indicted by a Cayuga County grand jury on charges of ravishing a working girl.

After this, his appearances in his home became even rarer. His most famous son could evoke a rare pity when, as a lonesome child, he played

pendragon	A supreme head or ruler.
anaconda	A very large tropical serpent that crushes its prey in its folds.
Moloch	A tyrannical power, taken from the wicked god of the Phoenicians.
medicaster	A medical charlatan.

by the road in a homemade suit and waited, month after poignant month, for a glimpse of his absent father.

Big Bill was spectacular when he did come—an immaculately dressed giant with a Stonewall Jackson beard who galloped up behind sleek new horses, never with less than a thousand dollars in his pocket. It would be wrong to picture him as generous, however. To a neighbor he boasted that he cheated his sons "to make 'em sharp." He loaned little John D. $5 gold pieces at 10 percent interest. That seems hard, but few parental lessons have been better learned. At the age of seven the boy was filling a blue china dish on the family mantel with coppers earned from digging potatoes, managing a turkey flock, and—an omen—buying candy by the pound and selling it to his brothers and sisters by the piece.

At 13 he was lending $50 at compound interest. At 14 he was a boarder in Cleveland, a city to which he had moved in order to attend Central High, where Mark Hanna, a fellow student, later recalled that John D. was "sane in every way but one—he was money-mad." To a classmate, the future billionaire confided that the thought of his father supporting him gave him a "cold chill." After a three-month bookkeeping course he went to work for a produce commission merchant, where, he later said, he fell in love with "all the method and system of the office."

He liked everything about it—the smell of the ledgers, the feel of the high desk, the sunlight slanting across his blotter—and after he had opened his own produce commission office at the age of 19, he began working later each evening. At one point he wrote in his private journal that he had "covenanted" with himself not to be seen at his books after 10 P.M. for 30 days. Later he wrote under this, "Don't make any more such covenants." His mother, a chanter of proverbs, had taught him that "willful waste makes woeful want," and he was nagged by the fear that he might squander precious hours.

One day in 1863 he glanced out the window and observed a kerosene scow floating by on the muddy water of the Cuyahoga River. He was making good money selling salt and mess pork to the Union Army, but the war wouldn't last forever, and he reasoned correctly that after it, the moving frontier would leave Cleveland produce behind. Therefore, he invested in a small refinery. By the end of the year he was donning hip boots and toiling in the slime of Pennsylvania's oil regions.

Allan Nevins once called the Rockefeller fortune a historical accident. Certainly John D. looked out his window at the right time. As a child in Richford he had read by candlelight. The only oil business then had been run by the whalers of New England. Petroleum was something that ruined salt wells, or was sold by peddlers like Big Bill to relieve aching joints. Then, while John D. was still in Central High, a Dartmouth professor had found a way to refine it, and the month after the young commission merchant's 20th birthday, the first oil well was sunk near Titusville, Pennsylvania. Gasoline was merely an annoying byproduct in the 1860s, but even so, the possibilities were exciting: kerosene for illumination, paint bases, industrial lubricants.

At the time of John D.'s arrival on the scene the petroleum market was being drowned by overproduction. The price of oil hovered just above that of water. Willful waste was making woeful want, the oil industry needed organizing to curb the cutthroat price war among rival drillers, and nobody could organize like John D. He wasted nothing. Meal stops were short on the trains of those days, so when he traveled he would leap off, cram his cheeks with food, and methodically masticate all the way to the next station. ("I always had a good big mouth," he later explained gravely.) Blotting his signature took valuable energy, so he hired a man to stand by his desk, blotter in hand. Concluding that he needed more rest, he moved a couch into the office and addressed colleagues from his pad.

In his new enterprises little economies mounted. Forty drops of solder were being used to seal each five-gallon can of kerosene; he experimented, found that 39 drops would do as well and rejoiced in the saving. Barrels cost other refiners $2.50 apiece; John D. made them for 96 cents each. Presently he had his own wagons, lighters, warehouses, and railroad tank cars. By 1869 his refinery was the largest in Cleveland, and he was learning that the bigger he became, the more efficient he became. To him the lesson was plain: He would achieve the ultimate in efficiency if he became the only oil man in the world.

John D. wasn't much interested in oil production, in the frowzy oil regions he scornfully called "mining camps." He was after the refineries, which J. A. Hobson, the English economist, has compared to the highway "narrows" that medieval barons seized to tax passing commerce. Control the refineries, seize the narrows, and John D. would dominate the industry. His weapon for reducing competition was similar to what is called today the quantity discount—the more a customer buys, the greater his markdown. His capacity had reached 1,500 barrels a day. Many of his rivals were refining only a barrel or two. He was in a position to drive them to the wall by demanding lower transportation costs than they could get, and that was what he did. First he demanded, and received, a rebate of 15 cents a barrel from the Lake Shore and Southern Michigan Railroad. The principle established, he incorporated the Standard Oil Company of Ohio with $1 million on January 10, 1870.

His rebates grew higher and higher; at one point competing refineries were paying transportation charges five times those of Standard Oil Trust. Even more vicious were his "drawbacks"—fixed rates that the railroads paid him for every barrel of rival oil they carried. They didn't haggle. He was managing their traffic, guaranteeing them huge daily shipments, and absorbing all their credit risks. After the panic of 1873, he began absorbing competitors right and left, and in 1882, when he organized the Standard Oil Trust, altering the meaning of a word whose definition had been benign, he had 14,000 miles of pipeline webbed under U.S. soil and controlled 95 percent of the country's refining capacity.

The Standard was now the largest and richest company in the world. Its undisputed commander was John D. He knew his refineries down to the last pipe and vat. No byproduct escaped him—Vaseline, chewing gum, paraffin, whatever—and if a political campaign was shaping up, he was prepared to fuel the torchlights, even though, as in 1884, the first minority party to assemble was dedicated to putting him in jail. "Rockefeller," said John Archbold, who served for many years as his chief lieutenant, "always sees a little farther than the rest of us—and then he sees around the corner."

It was part of John D.'s genius that he could persuade almost anyone to join him. Archbold was one convert. Another was Roger Sherman, a heroic enemy of monopoly in the courts who switched to become a Standard attorney. A third was Cettie Spelman, who became John D.'s wife. Cettie had been a dedicated Congregationalist, and her graduation essay at Central High had been "I Can Paddle My Own Canoe," but when she married him she quietly followed him into the Baptist Church.

Part of the trouble with fighting him was that you never knew where he was. All important messages were in code—Baltimore was "Droplet," refiners were "douters," the Standard itself was "Doxy." Shadowy men came and went by his front door; shadowy companies used his back door as a mailing address. For a long time the public didn't realize how powerful he was because he kept insisting he was battling firms that he secretly owned outright. John T. Flynn cites the case of a last-ditch Cleveland refiner going to Peru for oil and finding that all available wells had been bought by a company that was a subsidiary of a corporation owned by the Anglo–American Oil Company of England—which belonged to John D.

By then Standard Oil was operating in each of the world's 24 time zones. John D.'s six-hooped, bright blue barrels of Royal Daylight or Atlantic Red kerosene were being borne by elephants in India, by camels on the Sahara, by coolies in Asia. From Manchuria to the sacred fires of Baku on the Caspian, drillers knew that they need only reach the nearest Standard pipeline to get a certificate at least as good as gold. Foreign governments discovered what the vanquished refiners of Cleveland could have told them: There was no stopping John D. They built tariff walls; Standard men climbed them. Sinaean mandarins, at the urging of local vegetable oil guilds, made the use of Standard fuel a capital offense, and their peasants secretly bartered rice and chickens for Royal Daylight to light the lamps of China.

And that was only the beginning. Peering around the corner and into the future, John D. saw the dawning age of the internal combustion engine. He quietly ordered the development of gasoline and machine oils. When Gottlieb Daimler unveiled his automobile on March 4, 1887, Standard Oil was ready. The sequel astonished the world. Unhampered by income taxes, the Rockefeller fortune, which had been $40 million the year the trust was founded, had quintupled by 1896. Despite gifts to charities, it more than quadrupled again by the eve of World War I. "Who," John D. wondered at the end of his life, "would ever have thought that it would grow to such a size?"

Even today the extent of his wealth boggles the mind. Nobody has ever been richer than John D. at his peak. Only the old **pendragon** himself, who had a balance sheet struck to the penny at the end of each day, knew exactly how much he had, and he was among the most discreet men in the history of commerce. It is known, however, that in 1913 his assets were worth over $900 million, and $1 then was worth $6 today. At one point his fortune was growing at the rate of $100 a minute, which amounts to over $50 million a year. The precise extent of his heirs' wealth is unknown even to them, because of interlocking trusts, jointly held estates, fluctuating securities markets, and stocks that have been accumulating capital gains and compound interest for the better part of a century. However, the late Stewart Alsop estimated that the family's combined wealth in the 1970s may run as high as $10 billion.

For as long as they can remember, opulence has been a central fact of the Rockefellers' life. John D., Jr., the tycoon's only son, said that from his birth big money "was there, like air or food or any other element." Bobo Rockefeller, the first wife of one of Nelson's younger brothers, the late Winthrop Rockefeller, who served three years as governor of Arkansas, once observed that if you belong to the family, "you can almost feel the prices rise when you walk into a store." During one of Nelson's campaign autographing sessions in New York, an eager young man actually thrust a blank check toward his wiggling pen, and when the Rev. Frederick T. Gates, John D.'s chief almsgiver, once suggested to him that he ought to try to make more friends on golf courses, the old man replied drily, "I have made experiments, and nearly always the result is the same. Along about the ninth hole out comes some proposition, charitable or financial."

Greedy strangers were the least of the hardships his wealth brought him. From the day Standard Oil emerged as a stifler of competition, John D. was a target of ferocious press attacks. Editorial writers denounced him as the "**Anaconda**" and the "**New Moloch**." Cartoonists depicted him as an octopus with pipelines for tentacles and dollar signs for eyes. For children he replaced the bogeyman; "Rockefeller will get you if you don't watch out," their mothers told them. He was accused of fleecing his friends and dynamiting rival refineries, and attacking him was smart politics.

John D.'s daughter-in-law gave birth to a son, John D. 3d, but his grandfather couldn't see him because the attorney general of Missouri was harrying the old man up and down the roads around New York brandishing a subpoena. When Cettie died, John D. couldn't bury her for fourth months because process servers were preparing to waylay him at the grave; the body had to be kept in a friend's mausoleum while the governor of Ohio straightened things out.

The pattern of harassment had become clear in 1890, when the Sherman Antitrust Act became law. Two years later the attorney general of Ohio announced that John D.'s trust violated the charter of the Standard Oil Company of Ohio. The trust was safe for a while—the New Jersey Holding Company Act rescued it before the bailiffs closed in—but then two calamities doomed it. An assassin made Theodore Roosevelt president, and Mark Hanna, who had been the Standard's best friend in Washington, died. T. R. attacked all "malefactors of great wealth," and everyone knew precisely which malefactor he had in mind.

John D. was golfing when a messenger brought him word that Judge Kenesaw Mountain Landis, with a thump of his gavel, had fined the Standard $29,240,000 for shipping carloads at secret rates. He paused briefly, turned to his companions on the tee, and aid, "Well, shall we go on, gentlemen?" Four

years later, on May 15, 1911, the U.S. Supreme Court ordered the trust dis-
solved within six months. The monopoly was split into 33 giant companies.
John D. formally quit as president, and by 1924 he wasn't even a stockholder in
the key firm, Jersey Standard, though to this day his heirs get unsolicited advice on how to run Exxon, its corporate descendant.

The titan's attitude toward his critics never changed. To him they were all
"spoiled children." "We must be patient," he told his son, and again, "Let the
world wag." Furtive by temperament, he fought extradition and dodged
process servers, while telling his Sunday school class with a straight face, "The
kind of man I like is one that lives for his fellows—the one that lives in the
open." He believed a strong man should "get all the money he honestly can"
and extend charity to the poor. When hecklers gathered outside his door he
mounted a bike and pedaled off to play golf.

Early in the 1880s he had moved to Manhattan. Thereafter most of his middle years were spent within a triangle bounded by the rolltop desks at 26
Broadway, his brownstone house at 4 West 54th Street, and the Baptist church
on Fifth Avenue, though he would venture forth on special occasions—to meet
the trains of new men from Cleveland, for example, introducing them to
guides who would show them to available houses, and always taking his leave
with a cheery, "God bless you, and God bless Standard Oil." Winters he would
have the side yard of his home flooded, and there, not far from the Rockefeller
Center skating rink of today, he would methodically circle the ice each morning before work, with skates clamped to his patent-leather boots, his silk hat
jammed over his pate and his frock coat sailing sedately behind. He also liked
buggy racing. From time to time he would don a yellow duster and goggles,
summon his carriage and pair, and trot over to Seventh Avenue looking for
competition. He would go all out when he got it, winning, on one occasion, by
hot rodding to safety at the last split second and passing so closely by a heavy
dray loaded with scrap iron that he scraped its hubcaps.

Everything John D. did was strategic, even at home. Taking the family
swimming, he wore a straw hat in the water to ward off the sun. On ice-skating expeditions he issued his son a long narrow board to be carried under the
arm in case the ice broke. He liked blindman's bluff, and he played as he
worked, for keeps, trying to trick children with complicated feints and lightning thrusts and huzzaing when he succeeded. Success in everything was important to him; when John D., Jr., became manager of the Brown's football
team, his loyal father attended a game between Brown's and the Carlisle Indians in New York. The old man may have come out of duty, but once he was
there his powerful competitive instincts were aroused. He was out of the
stands before the game was over, prancing along the sidelines in his beaver
and cheering the team wildly. (Brown's won, 24 to 12.)

His opinions on everything of importance had been formed in childhood,
and they never changed. More than any other man he underwrote modern
medical science, yet when he himself was ill he relied on **medicasters** or
smoked mullein leaves in a clay pipe. A true loner, he never needed outside
stimulus—he said he never experienced a craving for tea, coffee, or "for any-

thing." His most extravagant comment was "Pshaw!" He reserved it for extraordinary situations, such as when he was accosted by an enemy of the Standard, or had triumphed in a bitter pipeline war. He absolutely refused to deal with anyone who tried to hurry him, and he declined to honor his membership in the New York Stock Exchange by appearing on the floor because he despised the turmoil there.

Because the popular press regarded him as an ogre, there was little suggestion in it that he was human, let alone virile. Yet his family knew him as a man of considerable physical courage. One evening the house burglar-alarm rang and a frightened maid cried that there was a prowler in one of the upstairs bedrooms. John D. called for his revolver and, without waiting for it, dashed to the back door to intercept the intruder, who escaped him by sliding down a pillar. On another occasion, the dynast insisted on driving his son to Grand Central Station at a time when anarchists were threatening to kill him. John D., Jr., thought it would be prudent to take a bodyguard along, but his father wouldn't hear of it. "I can take care of myself," he said, adding, in a Nick Carter riposte, "If any man were foolish enough to attack me, it would go hard with him."

His privacy became increasingly important to him. If his son wanted to communicate with him, he had to write him a letter, even though they worked in the same building. Later, when the younger Rockefeller visited his father, he was required to stay in a nearby hotel. After acquiring his 4,180-acre estate at Pocantico Hills in Westchester County, John D. built a mighty iron fence around it. John D., Jr., who worked with the architects, was lucky his father would settle for the fence; the old man had wanted to ring the estate with barbed wire. Yet there was no arrogance in him. He wanted to be known as "Neighbor John," and always addressed his grandsons warmly as "Brother."

To the annoyance of the family, he declined to replace clothes until they became shiny, and when his son presented him with a fancy fur coat, he wore it a couple of times, sent it to storage, and finally gave it back. He never mentioned his great wealth at home. There he remained merely the attentive father, obviously well-to-do but still a man of plain tastes. One of his favorite dishes was bread and milk, and he liked to keep a paper bag of apples on the sill outside his bedroom window and eat one each night at bedtime.

The world does not remember him as a wit, but his grandsons do. With mournful gestures and a piteous voice he would start a tragic tale, turning at the end to a grotesquerie. They heard the same jokes again and again and always laughed, especially if there was a guest present who was deceived by the solemn opening. His humor was anything but sophisticated. A typical story described a visitor's call at an insane asylum, where he met an inmate who complained that he had been unjustly confined. In John D.'s tag line the inmate concluded, "If you can't get me out, bring me a piece of dry toast. I'm a poached egg." Nelson recalls how one of his brothers, forgetting where he had heard this one, retold it to John D., winding up, "Bring me a piece of toast. I'm a poached egg."

After a grave silence his grandfather looked up.

"Dry toast, Brother," murmured the old man, who liked to get things right.

"What do the figures show?" he used to ask his grandsons. "It's the figures
that count." Nelson still marvels at his astonishing grasp of detail—how, rousing from a nap, John D. would beckon him over to his Morris chair and ask
searching questions about Rockefeller Center, for which Nelson, then fresh out
of Dartmouth, was leasing office space. In his prime he had always been able
to pinpoint the exact location of Standard tankers on distant seas, and in his
80s he would exasperate golfing partners by interrupting the game to search
painstakingly for lost balls. He just liked to know where things were.

His approach to golf was typical of him. He took up the game at the turn
of the century, after his doctor told him that he needed more recreation. Golf
was then relatively new in this country. One of the few players John D. knew
was Cettie, who was getting to be pretty good. He decided that he would get
to be better on the sly. According to Joe Mitchell, the pro who tutored him, he
proceeded with the same methods he had employed in tackling the oil industry: secrecy, cunning, and resourcefulness.

Rubbers and an umbrella were strapped to his caddie, in case it rained.
Then a watch was maintained by other youths, who would call out if Cettie
drew near, whereupon John D. would vanish into a clump of bushes until she
had passed. Alone once more, he would hammer croquet wickets over his feet
to keep them in position while a boy, hired to stand opposite him, kept repeating, "Hold your head down! Hold your head down!" Next the old man
chalked the face of his club, swung back, and uncoiled. If the ball's mark was
in the center of the club he would cry, "See, see! Method, method!" If it wasn't,
he would bow his head and mutter, "Shame, shame, shame." Finally, he hired
a photographer to make a series of pictures of his stroke. Studying them, he
developed fair distance.

Ready at last, he strolled up to Cettie one day when she was squaring
away on her first tee and remarked casually that it looked like a nice game; he
might try it. To her astonishment he belted the ball 160 yards.

Until he discovered golf, the Baptist church had provided his chief social
life. As a young bookkeeper he had always rung the Sunday bell at Cleveland's Erie Street Baptist Mission. At 17 he was a trustee of the church, sweeping its floors and washing its windows in his spare time; at 19 he saved it from
a $2,000 mortgage; for 30 years he was a Sunday School superintendent, and
when his wife was in childbed he brought foolscap to church, took notes during the sermons, and repreached them to her at home.

During the week, life for the Rockefellers revolved around the morning
Bible readings (with a penny fine for those who were late), the Friday evening
prayer meeting, lantern slides shown by visiting missionaries, and sessions at
which the head of the household would lead the others in chanting: "Five
cents a glass, does anyone think/That is really the price of a drink?"

To this day, a bottle of liquor is the one thing you cannot buy in Rockefeller
Center, though the family's puritan discipline has relaxed a great deal since the
days when ministers came and went in the West 54th Street home, and the
rosewood sliding doors separating rooms on the first floor were thrown open
to accommodate rapt congregations who sat erect on massive furniture be-

tween the dark red brocaded walls while speakers discussed charities, missions, and the evils of booze, or led the group in prayer so solemn that, John D. Jr., noted in an essay written at the age of 11, even the dog "would lie down under a chair and be very quiet until the exercises were over."

On trips John D. always took a minister along to preach at way stations and lead the family in rollicking hymns as their private train thundered across the country. At home Cettie served cold meals Sundays because it was a sin to cook then. Much as John D. loved ice-skating, he wouldn't skate on the Sabbath or even direct workmen to flood his yard until 12:01 Monday morning. It is worth noting that Nelson taught Sunday school through four years at Dartmouth and took his first oath as governor of New York on Cettie's old Bible.

On those rare occasions when reporters managed to corner John D., they would ask him to comment on Luke 18:25: "For it is easier for a camel to go through a needle's eye, than for a rich man to enter into the kingdom of God." He would quote the Scriptures back—"Seest thou a man diligent in his business? He shall stand before kings"—or simply say of his career: "I was right. I knew it as a matter of conscience. It was right between me and my God." Still, reconciling his piety and his great wealth wasn't that easy, and his determination to find another way is the explanation for his extraordinary philanthropies.

He had begun to tithe as a boy. While still a poor bookkeeper he bought a cheap ledger to record his contributions one by one ("Method, method!") and the ledger, which is extant, reveals that his first gift to the poor, wrung from his slender hoard during a winter when he himself was too poor to afford an overcoat was, symbolically, a dime. At the same time, he began contributing to the Underground Railroad. Belief in racial equality was a thread that ran through his entire life. It is significant that at the end of his life, he was the only white parishioner in a Negro church. Nelson points out that Spelman College in Atlanta, founded by John D. in 1881, was almost unique: "It's marvelous now to think of Grandfather giving money to a college for black women when higher education for *either* blacks *or* women was unheard of."

For the most part he gave as he earned, secretly. He liked to sit in church and scan the congregation for needy brethren; before leaving he would furtively press cash into deserving hands. They had to be deserving. He had to be sure that the money would do some good. His idea of bad charity was the annual dinner given for tramps by Cleveland's Five Points House of Industry. He did not want handouts, but results. As long as his largess was limited to the church, he could be sure he was getting them, but checking up became harder as his bounty grew. In 1891 he took the plunge into what Gates called wholesale philanthropy by establishing a big Baptist university in Chicago. Its grateful students sang: "John D. Rockefeller, wonderful man is he/Gives all his spare change to the U. of C."

"The good Lord gave me the money," he said, "and how could I withhold it from the University of Chicago?" That was always his attitude. He called his fortune "God's gold," and once he refused to get out of his car at the dedication of a project he had endowed because, he said, he hadn't had much to do with it; he had just given the money. Altogether he donated $600 million to various causes, and John D., Jr., dispensed another $400 million, which comes to an even billion.

One of the difficulties in appraising John D.'s personality is that he often comes through as a caricature of himself. There is an explanation for this. Essentially a loner, he was hounded, decade after decade, by journalists and politicians who believed that the public had a right to know more about a man possessed of such power than this man was willing to divulge. They had a point, but he was never willing to concede it. Hence his camouflages, disguises, and masquerades. John D.'s approach to public relations was, quite simply, to ignore the public.

Nevertheless, he had two Achilles' heels: his piety and his love of his family. Like many another industrialist, he longed to see his son succeed him in the corridors of power. But John D., Jr., Nelson's father, was cut from a different bolt of cloth. Deeply troubled by the arrogance of his father's lieutenants and sympathetic to the nascent labor movement, the son decided that he wanted a different career. He felt that he could best honor the Christian principles his father had taught him by devoting his life to almsgiving. And John D., always the shrewdest member of the family, understood and approved.

John D.'s influence on John D., Jr.'s, children is more diffuse, largely because the age gap is so great. The oldest of the titan's grandsons, John D. 3d, was five years old when the Supreme Court broke up the Standard Oil trust. Nelson was born on his grandfather's 69th birthday. Understandably, their memories of him are hazy. But they are all firmly convinced that their civic activities are a contemporary expression of his Baptist faith. Like the sons of Joseph P. Kennedy, they were told early that they must justify their wealth by public service. The difference is that Rockefeller wealth is much greater than that of the Kennedys, and Rockefeller eleemosynary activities are consequently far more conspicuous.

The family's philanthropies include the Rockefeller Institute for Medical Research, five national parks, Colonial Williamsburg, and countless other endowments whose beneficiaries are often unaware of where the money came from. Sociologists pore over the Lynds' "Middletown," birth control advocates over the work of Margaret Sanger, and physicists over the studies of Fermi and Oppenheimer, unaware that Rockefeller money was behind each. Few librarians know of Rockefeller gifts to bibliothecas in Geneva and Tokyo, let alone the Library of Congress, and hardly any prostitutes are aware that John D., Jr., established the laboratory of social hygiene at the New York State Reformatory for Women.

At the end of his life the titan was baffled by the Depression. In 1894 he had stopped a panic with a European draft for $10 million. After the 1929 crash, he placed a dramatic bid for a million shares of Jersey Standard at $50, tried to buck up confidence by saying that he and his son were buying common stocks, and gave $2 million for emergency relief in New York. It wasn't enough. In 1932 all he could say was, "God's in His heaven, all's right with the world."

Five years later, he died in Florida at the age of 97, hoarsely whispering to his valet, "Raise me up a little bit." The sexton of the Union Baptist Church tolled its steeple bell and posted the 23d Psalm, a favorite of John D.'s. For five minutes petroleum workers around the world stood in silent tribute to his memory. Everywhere his dimes had been saved and were treasured: One admirer, a ferry tender in Nyack, New York, proudly exhibited four of them to passengers. Bales of unsolicited flowers preceded mourners to the Cleveland cemetery where the family laird was buried between his mother and his wife, and John D., Jr., led his five sons in decorating nearby graves with overflow blossoms.

Yet the image of the New Moloch was not dead. Even as the old man lay in state, squads of state troopers were stalking intruders on the 70 miles of private roads behind the iron fence in Pocantico Hills, and after the family had left Cleveland, two cemetery guards, alert for cranks, began a three-month vigil. The Rockefellers had learned long ago that they could never escape the legend of their wealth.

John D. accepted that, but all his life he was curiously indifferent to the symbols of his affluence. Once when his securities filled a whole suite of safe-deposit rooms, a secretary begged him to come and see them. He went, poked a couple of drawers, and excused himself. He was always more drawn by the rituals of business than by its rewards.

Yet he was always moved by the highlights of his career. Even in old age, a glimpse of the building in which he first went to work as a bookkeeper could bring him to his feet, quivering with emotion. The anniversaries of his first job and his first partnership were red-letter days for him. When they rolled around he always ordered the flag at Pocantico Hills unfurled, to snap over his estate like a festive pennant. It is still hoisted on those days. Yet nobody notices it now. Today the Pocantico flag flies all the time.

AFFIDAVIT OF GEORGE O. BASLINGTON

John D. Rockefeller's philanthropic activities made little impression on the many people he drove out of business. Having experienced firsthand the ruthless tactics used to establish the Standard Oil monopoly, they had little trouble deciding where they stood in the robber baron–captain of industry debate. One of these unfortunate businesspeople was George O. Baslington, the co-owner of Hanna, Baslington & Company, a Cleveland-based oil refinery founded in 1869. In the affidavit that follows, Baslington provided a revealing description of what happened to those entrepreneurs who had something that Rockefeller wanted.

• • • • •

Some time in February, 1872, the firm received a message from the Standard Oil Company requesting said firm to have an interview as to the disposal of

Source: Reprinted with the permission of Simon & Schuster from *The History of the Standard Oil Company* by Ida M. Tarbell (New York: MacMillan, 1933), pp. 290–91.

the refining works of said firm; that they were indisposed to enter into any arrangement for the disposition of said works because the investment of capital in said works had proved abundantly profitable to their satisfaction and they had no disposition whatever to part with the works; but upon investigation they were somewhat surprised to find that the Standard Oil Company had already obtained the substantial control of the different refineries in the City of Cleveland; that it had obtained such rates of transportation of crude and refined oil from the different railroads that it was impossible for them to compete with it, and upon an interview which was had by Mr. Hanna and affiant with Mr. Rockefeller who was at the time president of the Standard Oil Company. Mr. Flagler, the secretary of the company, being present, Mr. Rockefeller in substance declared or said that the Standard Oil Company had such control of the refining business already in the City of Cleveland that he thought said firm of Hanna, Baslington & Company could not make any money; that there was no use for them to attempt to do business in competition with the Standard Oil Company.

Affiant further says that after having had an interview both with Mr. Watson, who was the president of a company called "The South Improvement Company," and Mr. Devereux, who was the general manager of the Lake Shore Road, he became satisfied that no arrangement whatever could be effected through which transportation could at least be obtained on the Lake Shore Road that would enable their firm to compete with the Standard Oil Company, the works of said Hanna, Baslington & Company, being so situated that they could only obtain their crude oil through the line of the Lake Shore Road. And finding that the Standard Oil Company had such special rates of transportation that unless the firm of Hanna, Baslington & Company were enabled to bring as much oil as the Standard Oil Company, that it was impossible for said firm of Hanna, Baslington & Company to obtain a fair competing rate with the Standard Oil Company. They at least came to the conclusion that it was better for them to take what they could get from the Standard Oil Company and let their works go.

And affiant further says that under these circumstances they sold their works to the Standard Oil Company, which were on the day of the sale worth at least $100,000, for $45,000 because that was all they could obtain from them, and works too which in cash cost them no less than $76,000, and which with a fair competition would have paid them an income of no less than 30 percent per annum on the investment.

Affiant further says that at the interviews which he had with Mr. Rockefeller, Mr. Rockefeller told him that the Standard Oil Company already had control of all the large refineries in the City of Cleveland and there was no use for them to undertake to compete against the Standard Oil Company, for it would only ultimate in their being wiped out, or language to that effect.—(November 1, 1880.)

•••••

[handwritten annotation: secluded as a child, didn't learn to compromise.]

QUESTIONS

[handwritten annotation: Con-man / Cheated his sons to make themselves sharp]

1. What influence did Rockefeller's father have on the development of his business views? In what ways did Rockefeller's subsequent business career reflect his internalization of the proverb that "willful waste makes woeful want"?

2. Why, in his efforts to achieve a dominant position in the oil industry, did Rockefeller concentrate on controlling the refineries rather than the oil fields? What additional steps did he take to reduce competition in the oil industry? Why did railroad companies so readily agree to Rockefeller's business terms?

3. What could someone like George Baslington do when confronted by Standard Oil? Were there any organizations or social movements to which he might have turned for support? What does Baslington's dilemma suggest about the state of public affairs in Gilded Age America?

4. What were Rockefeller's most prominent character traits? In what ways did Rockefeller's conduct of his personal life reflect his approach to business affairs?

5. What influence did Rockefeller have on the era in which he lived? Do you think that the robber baron thesis provides an adequate conceptual framework for interpreting Rockefeller's business career? If not, can you suggest a more appropriate descriptive term?

6. What challenges does a biographer who has chosen to write about Rockefeller confront? How well did Manchester meet those challenges?

BIBLIOGRAPHY

The standard biography of Rockefeller is Allan Nevins, *A Study in Power: John D. Rockefeller, Industrialist and Philanthropist* (1953). Although well written, Nevins's account largely overlooks the darker side of Rockefeller's activities and should be supplemented by David Freeman Hawke's briefer but more balanced treatment in *John D.: The Founding Father of the Rockefellers* (1970). There are also a number of works on the Rockefeller family that interested readers might wish to consult. They include Peter Collier and David Horowitz, *The Rockefellers: An American Dynasty* (1976); William Manchester, *A Rockefeller Portrait: From John D. to Nelson* (1959); and John E. Harr and Peter J. Johnson, *The Rockefeller Century: Three Generations of America's Greatest Family* (1989). For more on the Gilded Age business world that Rockefeller did so much to shape, see Glenn Porter, *The Rise of Big Business, 1860–1910* (1973); Edward Kirkland, *Dream and Thought in the Business Community, 1860–1900* (1956); Matthew Josephson, *The Robber Barons: The Great American Capitalists, 1861–1901* (1934); and Alfred D. Chandler, Jr., *The Visible Hand: The Managerial Revolution in America* (1977).

Stephen Crane

As with so much else in American life during the half century following the Civil War, the world of letters underwent enormous change. Moving beyond the socially and grammatically correct protagonists of antebellum literature, Gilded Age writers experimented with new themes, new subjects, and new techniques in an effort to capture the era's social developments in their prose. It was a time when Mark Twain combined humor and craft to create some of the most fascinating characters in American fiction; when Henry James sought to develop a language capable of exploring the psychological roots of human behavior; and when William Dean Howells not only defined and promoted the literary realism of Twain, James, and others, but added his own enduring contribution in novels such as The Rise of Silas Lapham *(1885) and* A Hazard of New Fortunes *(1890).*

In addition to the sometimes bewildering array of social changes taking place in postbellum America, broader intellectual developments also had an influence on Gilded Age writers. Of these, none was more significant than Charles Darwin's writings on evolution. According to Darwin, humans were unique not because they had been created in God's image, but because they were better able than other species to adapt to environmental change. This assault on traditional conceptions of the relationship between man and nature forced those writers who took Darwin seriously to

view human behavior in a new light. One reaction was to adopt a "naturalistic" perspective, which focused attention on the ways social and economic forces conditioned what people did and why they did it. Like Darwin, literary naturalists viewed life as a struggle; and in their work, they attempted to portray that struggle with a blunt frankness that left little to the imagination.

The leading American naturalists included writers such as Frank Norris, Jack London, Kate Chopin, Theodore Dreiser, and Hamlin Garland. There was also Stephen Crane. The son of a Methodist minister, Crane was a restless, driven individual who rejected his father's religion and everything else associated with his middle-class upbringing. His search for an outlet for the creative impulses surging within him ultimately brought Crane to New York City, which served as the backdrop for his first novel, Maggie: A Girl of the Streets *(1893). Although William Dean Howells considered* Maggie *to be Crane's finest work, the book's pessimistic portrayal of urban life held little appeal for most readers. Undeterred, Crane continued to develop his craft, and at the youthful age of 24 he achieved international renown as the author of* The Red Badge of Courage. *Five years later he would be dead. In the essay that follows, Stephen B. Oates examines the process by which Crane came to write* Red Badge. *At the same time, he provides a compelling character study of a gifted writer whose disregard for convention was the main source of the self-destructive behavior that resulted in his early death.*

Stephen Crane

Stephen B. Oates

In a squalid old boarding house on Manhattan's Lower East Side, a pale young man sat in his room, staring at a pad of paper before him. Beyond his window, a blizzard howled in the night, lashing the city with wind and snow. The young man seemed oblivious to the storm, to everything about him, even to the medical student who shared his room. Presently he began writing, slowly and methodically, accentuating every punctuation mark and circling every period. He had yellow fingers and a chronic, hacking cough from excessive smoking. From time to time, he would rise, relight his pipe, and ramble about the room with his toes protruding from his shoes. Lost in thought, coughing, he would pause to stare out the window into the snow-streaked shadows of the night. He was a short, slender youth of 21, somewhat stooped, with dark shaggy hair and large, remarkable eyes, strange eyes, full of luster and changing lights, with a deep, ineradicable sadness in them. As he waited for inspiration to come, he would break into some popular song or bacchanalian ditty, often singing a single bar over and over. When he returned to his writing pad,

Source: This essay originally appeared in the June–July 1988 issue of *Timeline,* a publication of the Ohio Historical Society. Reprinted with permission.

his next sentences would be lined up in his head "all in a row" and would march out of his pen and across the page in such impeccable formation that he scarcely had to erase or change a word.

It was late in 1892, and the young man was writing his first novel, about a slum girl named Maggie, and living hand-to-mouth in what amounted to a voluntary experiment in misery. For him, the nearer a writer got to the hard realities of life, the better he became as an artist. As a consequence, he wore rags and went hungry like the slum-dwellers of his story. He hiked along the Bowery in an old overcoat, studying the jungle of tenements and impoverished humanity on the Lower East Side. He drank beer in its dingy saloons and observed inebriated derelicts; he frequented sleazy music halls and bordellos, and bought love from painted girls of the night, and slept on cots in pungent flophouses, coughing and shivering from the cold. Gone sometimes for days, he would return at last to his work, to transform his impressions and enforced suffering into art. He went at life with a fierce intensity, for he was certain that his destiny was to die young, that his life was only a flash in the black rush of time. His restless mind burned like a furnace, driving his small, frail body until it collapsed from exhaustion or illness. Then some Good Samaritan friend, one of the Bohemian artists he had come to know on the East Side, might take him in until he recovered. Thereupon he would hurry back to his Bowery haunts, back to his curriculum of life in the streets, with a cigarette hanging from his lips and his hair flying with the wind.

A family friend once pointed him out as "the outcast son of a minister," an eccentric wastrel who was throwing his life away. In a sense, the youth would have agreed with that. He had certainly rebelled against his Methodist parents and had thrown away the pious life they had envisioned for him. He had been their 14th and last child, born in 1871 in Newark, New Jersey, and christened Stephen Crane after his colonial and Revolutionary ancestors. As a child, he had sat dutifully in his father's congregations, watching in awe as the Reverend Dr. Crane, an otherwise compassionate, dignified man, inveighed against the Devil's temptations, against dancing and drinking, smoking, gambling, and especially reading novels, which Dr. Crane denounced as one of the filthiest vices of the age. His exhortations about God's wrath and man's impotence, about Satan's legions and the horrors of a godless universe, created terrible fears in his imaginative child. One day, strolling the ocean beach with his mother, little Stephen saw black riders on black horses burst out of the

Flaubert   Brilliant 19th century French novelist.

Balzac   Prolific 19th century French novelist.

George Eliot   The pseudonym used by Mary Anne Evans, a 19th century English writer of Victorian fiction.

William Dean Howells   Late 19th century American novelist influenced by the development of realism.

Henry James   Novelist and great figure in trans-Atlantic culture.

surf brandishing swords and shields, and he had recurring nightmares about those diabolical horsemen and each time woke up screaming.

His mother reinforced the idea of a world menaced with temptation. In truth, she was one of the Lord's most devoted soldiers in the war against wickedness. She wrote religious articles, attended Methodist conferences, and planned campaigns against intemperance like a general marshalling forces for battle. She was so busy, was gone so often, that caring for the boy fell to Agnes, the sister nearest to him in age; all his other brothers and sisters were already grown and gone. Fifteen years older than he, Agnes lavished affection on the boy, nursed him when he was ill, and directed his early education. A temperamental young woman with a zest for life, she aspired to be a writer despite her father's literary proscriptions, and she encouraged "Stevie" to create stories and poems himself. It was Agnes who taught him a love for language, she who instilled in him a hunger for life in all its riddles and complexities, she who implanted the seeds of his subsequent repudiations.

In 1880, when Stephen was eight, the Reverend Dr. Crane died of a heart attack. Three years later Agnes also died. The boy missed her terribly, yet her creative spirit blazed on in him. By age 14, he had a boundless imagination and a prodigious vocabulary that dazzled everyone; in an impromptu class essay, he demonstrated his mastery of words like *impartial, memorial, irascible,* and *pyrotechnic.* At the same time, he developed a passionate interest in war, fueled by the military tales of an older brother whose hobby was the Civil War, especially the campaigns of Chancellorsville and Gettysburg. The youth dreamed of battles, of bloody conflicts that thrilled him with "their sweep and fire." He saw himself, a little man, in desperate and heroic struggles with the demons of the universe.

By then, he had mounted an insurrection against his pious mother and ghostly father, rejecting the inflexible religious dogmas they espoused. To his mother's shock and dismay, he flagrantly violated all her rules of conduct. He smoked cigarettes. He took up poker and dancing. He frequented pool halls. He played baseball with fiendish delight and wanton profanity. To correct his wicked ways, his mother sent him to Pennington Seminary, where he fell in love successively with two redheads and a tall, dark-haired girl from Iowa. From Pennington, he informed his mother that he intended to become a professional baseball player. Later he enrolled in a coed, semi-military boarding school, with an eye on a future career in the army. When an older brother dissuaded him from that, he transferred to Lafayette College in Pennsylvania, but displayed such inaptitude for the classroom that the dean invited him to withdraw after one term. Exasperated, his mother shipped him off to Syracuse University, in hopes that a strict Methodist education might yet save him from his descent into sin. When he wasn't on the baseball diamond, he roamed the slums of Syracuse and hung out at the police court, enthralled by the dramas of human misery that transpired there. He much preferred studying "faces on the streets," he said, than the university's "cut-and-dried curriculum," which he proved by failing algebra, chemistry, physics, elocution, and German and departing Syracuse after a single term. By then he had decided to become a writer, and college had little to do with the kind he intended to be.

During the summer of 1891, he worked on a brother's newspaper in a New York coastal resort named Ocean Grove. People he interviewed saw a small, sallow, serious 19-year-old who puffed energetically on a large German pipe. That same summer he met Hamlin Garland, a self-assured young critic from Boston who reminded Crane of "a nice Jesus Christ." Garland, a disciple of William Dean Howells, the leading proponent of literary realism in America, read and liked Crane's newspaper work and made him a convert to realism as he interpreted it: In its deeper sense, Garland argued, it meant "the statement of one's own individual perception of life and nature, guided by devotion to truth." Crane loved that idea. He applied it to a series of tales he wrote about his hunting and camping adventures in which "a little man" like Crane confronted and overcame what seemed to him the sinister, monstrous spirits of nature. For Crane, realism as Garland taught it had the force of a conversion experience. When a friend complained that he couldn't fathom "the real thing" in a story he was writing, Crane tossed a handful of sand in the air. "Treat your notions like that," he said. "Forget what you think about it and tell how you feel about it . . . That's the big secret of story-telling. Away with literary fads and canons. Be yourself."

Away with clever writing, he believed, and all the other stale conventions of traditional Victorian literature—the romantic subjectivity, the idealized heroes in constant pursuit of some noble end. In recoiling from that, Crane identified himself with **Flaubert** and **Balzac** in France, **George Eliot** in England, and Howells and **Henry James** in the United States, who sought to describe the commonplace conventions of life without romantic embellishments.

The following summer Crane had a love affair with a lovely young married woman named Lily Brandon Munroe, who was visiting Ocean Grove with her sister and mother-in-law. She and Stephen strolled arm-in-arm on the beach; they rode the merry-go-round at the amusement park. He told her that he didn't expect to live long, that all he wanted was a few years of happiness. Lily worried about his bad eating habits, about his smoking and his cough, and she blushed when he said he loved her; yet she refused to leave her husband when Crane begged her to do so. Later he wrote a tender comedy based on their courtship, which nourished a pleasant fantasy: the fictional lovers eloped.

Disappointed in love, he repaired to New York City and plunged into Bohemian life on Manhattan's East Side. There he befriended aesthetic young painters and illustrators, all dedicated to the romantically austere life of the studio and to style above all else; their ideas only reinforced Crane's own natural inclinations. Through them, he became acquainted with the French Impressionists, whose iridescent paintings captured reality in a constant flux of colors; later Crane spoke of their "mental light and shade" and what a revolutionary effect that had on him. But even in a room full of like-minded artists, Crane always felt alone, isolated, "separated from humanity by impassable gulfs." Determined nevertheless to know life as it was, he made repeated pilgrimages to the Bowery and the teeming slums of the Lower East Side. During the winter he embarked on his realistic novel about the slum girl named Maggie and completed it in late February or early March of 1893. The novel was a statement as well as a story, a public renunciation of "the clever school of literature," as Crane phrased it, in favor of the psychological novel that explored both the outer world of its heroine and her inner response to it, that sought to reveal the knower as well as the known.

Crane failed to find a publisher for *Maggie: A Girl of the Streets.* But he remained undaunted. With the financial help of a brother, he published the novel himself under the pseudonym of Johnston Smith. Ablaze with confidence, he expected the book to be a sensation, whereupon he intended to drop "like a trapeze performer from the wire," he said, "and coming forward with all the modest grace of a consumptive nun, say, I am he, friends!"

The book flopped. While Garland liked it, nobody else seemed to notice it or to care. The one bookstore that stocked the novel sold only two copies. The rest lay piled in his room unsold. According to one story, a housemaid used some of them to fire the stove. "Poor Maggie!" Crane mourned. "She was one of my first loves." Depressed and destitute, he plunged into gloom. At one point, he was so poor that he had to clerk for a few unendurable days in a men's clothing store, only to spend his entire earnings of $15 on a single champagne supper.

Meanwhile, he had turned to something else, a Civil War story that had occurred to him while he was writing *Maggie.* He didn't take the story seriously. In fact, he intended it to be "a potboiler," he said, "something that would take the boarding-school element." He knew the general history of the war, of course, but found that he needed specific details of battle for his setting. An artist friend named C. K. Linson had collected back copies of *Century Magazine,* which contained a monumental series of illustrated chronicles called "Battles and Leaders of the Civil War"; the authors had all been officers in the war, save one Warren Lee Goss, who contributed "Recollections of a Private." At Linson's studio, Crane pored avidly over the articles, especially Goss's account. While they yielded valuable information about campaigns and soldiering, the articles irritated him. "I wonder that some of these fellows don't tell how they *felt* in those scraps!" he complained to Linson. "They spout eternally of what they *did,* but they're as emotionless as rocks!"

As the spring of 1893 came on, Crane pondered his story, wondering how it felt to be in battle, what went on in the mind of a private soldier as he responded to external events during an extreme crisis. The more he thought about that, the more the private soldier, whom he named Henry Fleming, took shape in his mind. In truth, Crane strongly identified with young Henry, who was also small in size and given to dreams of glory and heroism in battle. Among his artist friends, Crane often spoke of Fleming. "He's getting to be quite a character now," Crane would say, as if he were a parent speaking of a growing son. But Crane found that his character was more easily imagined than were military circumstances. From a family friend, he borrowed the full four-volume set of *Battles and Leaders of the Civil War,* which had been published in book form, and undertook more strenuous research. In late March he spent 10 straight nights trying to write Henry's story, only to thrust it aside. He told the family friend, "I am not sure that my facts are real and the books won't tell me what I want to know so I must do it all over again, I guess."

But how to do it all over again? By now he had given up the idea of producing a potboiler. The story possessed him. He had a clear sense of what he wanted to do: to "see war from within," to convey what it felt like when war assaulted the depths of the mind. He saw that Henry Fleming, a green volunteer in the Union army, went marching into battle, only to throw down his gun and run, only to return to his regiment and fight again. Crane wanted passionately to understand how Henry could do that. What did he think about, what did he feel, during his test of courage? What did he learn about fear, about war and heroism, about himself in the violent world of battle?

Crane knew he was onto something profound, but he didn't pick up his pen again, not right away. His method was to get away by himself, think over things, let the details of a story filter through his blood, until he knew what he wanted to say and it simply poured out of his pen. For some six months, Crane thought and planned. He reviewed *Battles and Leaders,* consulted maps of northern Virginia, and perhaps reread Tolstoy's *Sebastopol,* which he admired so extravagantly that he had once pronounced Tolstoy the "world's foremost writer." Devoid of traditional heroes, full of irony and unforgettable scenes of chaos and butchery, *Sebastopol* was an example of realism at its best. Yes, this was Crane's model for the kind of Civil War tale he had in mind. His would be no picture-book story of the glory and wonder of war, no romance about heroic generals who unerringly accomplished their ends. No, he was after the reality of war as seen and felt by a common soldier; he was after what it meant to become a man. What if he had never been in a war, had never been shot at in battle, had never seen friends die? He would rely on his prodigious powers of imagination and empathy to bring his research alive and capture the reality of battle. He would also draw on his experiences on the football field. He had often played the game in recent years—he did so again that summer, while staying with a brother—and claimed it gave him insight "into the rage of conflict."

Meanwhile, word came from **William Dean Howells**, who had finally got around to reading *Maggie* and "cared for it immensely." He thought it revealed a promising young artist with a great "literary conscience." This from the leading novelist and critic in the land! Thus encouraged, Crane was more determined than ever to forge ahead with the story of Henry Fleming.

In the fall, he moved in with three artist friends, who shared a studio in the old Art Students League building on East 23rd Street. Crane was so impoverished that he could contribute nothing to the studio's maintenance, but that was all right with his companions; they were delighted to have him. Just turning 22, he was their literary counterpart, a free-spirited artist who believed in narrative simplicity because simplicity was truth. In a studio cluttered with painting paraphernalia, Crane now felt that inexpressible longing, that sorrow "and heart-hunger," he always experienced when a story had worked itself out in his mind and was ready for the telling. Sometime that autumn of 1893, he began writing what he tentatively called "Private Fleming, His Various Battles," forming his letters in a round, legible script: "The cold passed reluctantly from the earth, and the retiring fogs revealed an army stretched out on the hills, resting." He wrote as simply as he could, methodically recording the sentences that marched from his head. His descriptive passages betrayed the influence of French Impressionism and Rudyard Kipling's *The Light That Failed;* they captured a landscape that turned from brown to green, a river "amber-tinted in the shadow of its banks," sunshine that beat upon a tent until it glowed "a light yellow shade." As he described the blue-clad army, Crane introduced Henry and the other characters—a tall soldier named Jim Conklin, whom Henry had known all his life, and a loud soldier named Wilson. Then Crane flashed back into Henry's past, recounting his fantasies about the glory of war, his decision to enlist in the Union army in defiance of his mother (an autobiographical touch here), and his delusions of grandeur that he would perform "mighty deeds of arms."

As he followed Henry's progress, Crane worked with military discipline, writing in the quiet of the night from midnight until four or five in the morning. He would sleep into the afternoon, then rouse himself for a trip to the corner saloon and a "free lunch," his only food for the day. He would spend the late afternoons and evenings reviewing his maps and consulting *Battles and Leaders,* smoking and hacking incessantly. He chose not to name the battle that loomed in his story, lest some Civil War veteran step forward later and claim that "this damned young fellow was not there. I was however. And this is how it happened." Nevertheless, his description of the terrain and choice of detail suggested that it was the Battle of Chancellorsville.

Crane showed portions of his manuscript to his roommates and other friends, using them to measure both the reasonableness of his characterization and the credibility of his plot. When he resumed his composition at midnight, he shut himself off in a creative inner sanctum. One artist said that Crane could write while sitting on a little stool in the middle of the studio floor, impervious to the bustle of people and hum of conversation about him. One of his roommates, David Ericson, remembered him working on his novel while he lay in a hammock; when he completed a passage, he exclaimed, "That is great!" Ericson thought him incredibly conceited until Crane read him the passage; then Ericson realized "how wonderfully real it was."

In Crane's accumulating pages, Henry and his regiment were finally moving forward into battle, and the youth was struggling with a terrible question: What if he threw his gun down and ran? Crane's animistic imagination allowed Henry to see "dark shadows that moved like monsters," columns that resembled "huge crawling reptiles," campfires that glowed like "the orbs of a row of dragons," all of which heightened the tension as Henry pursued his lonely, internal debate. He tried to rationalize his fear, then worked himself into "a fever of impatience," until at last he found himself in battle, with shells screaming overhead and bullets whistling in the branches nearby. As he watched, frozen in silence, "the din in front swelled into a tremendous chorus." A battle flag jerked madly about in the distance, as though struggling to free itself from agony. Then a moblike body of men emerged from the smoke and galloped like wild horses toward him. But the regiment held; as the smoke cleared, Henry saw that the charge had been repulsed. A battery of Union guns, squatting in a row "like savage chiefs," argued violently in "a grim pow-wow." So it was over, the youth thought. "The supreme trial had been passed. The red, formidable difficulties of war had been vanquished." To his horror, though, the rebels regrouped and attacked again, like "an onslaught of re-doubtable dragons," and this time the youth threw down his gun and fled in blind, animal panic. The test of courage and manhood had come, and Henry Fleming had failed . . .

In part, Crane was now writing from firsthand experience—from his own sense of failure with *Maggie,* which had filled him with depression and self-doubt. Indeed, Crane's narrative voice conveyed a remarkable sense of imme-diacy and compassion as it described Henry's forest flight and wild emotional swings. It was as though Crane were with Henry as he stumbled onto the col-umn of wounded men, heard the tattered soldier's dreaded question, wit-nessed Jim Conklin's death as he fell to the ground, and then took off again in spasms of revulsion and shame for his cowardice, yearning desperately for his own wound, his own "red badge of courage."

Thus far, Crane had been grinding chapters out, one building logically and dramatically to the next. The first half of his story, which began with fear and ended with desertion and despair, had been clear to him from the start. But now he had reached an impasse. How was he to get Henry back to his regi-ment so that he could fight again and regain some control? How to invent a se-ries of credible and significant events which did that? Crane opted for a chap-ter of meditative passages about Henry's moral confusion and tragic passion, seeking to let ideas bridge the gap. When he returned to the line of action, Crane understood what to do now; all the pieces fell together for him. When Henry witnessed a heroic column charging to the front, he started toward it too, seeking moral vindication for his fall, knowing that he could not wear "the sore badge of his dishonor through life." In his torment, he wished he were dead. He longed for the defeat of the whole army, only to reject that as useless to consider. He tried to think of a fine tale he might tell his comrades that would ward off "the expected shafts of derision." Then, to his shock, the heroic column came sweeping by him in panic and rout. Henry couldn't bear the sight; he felt the need to cry out, make a rallying speech, sing a battle hymn. But when he clutched a fleeing soldier by the arm, all he could utter was an inarticulate "why—why—." When Henry wouldn't let go, the soldier smashed him across the head with his gun. Henry had his red badge of courage at last. For Crane, it was an exquisite irony.

But the blow was more than a badge; it was a test of Henry's will to live. Struggling to his feet, he staggered forward, fighting his body and pain, trying not to fall and die as Jim Conklin had done, drawing on all his strength to stay erect and alive. With Henry's wound and struggle against death, the cycle of his flight was complete. Crane could send him back to the front now, back to redeem himself.

Now that he could see his way through to the end, Crane apparently stopped for a Christmas break. Then he reworked what he had written thus far, sharpening details and adding touches to what he hoped would be a polished, final version of the manuscript. When he reached the point where he had left off, Crane forged on, telling how Henry rejoined his regiment, fought in a mad frenzy of rage in the next engagements, and became the standard bearer and hero of his peers—"a jimhickey," as the colonel put it in a burst of admiration. In the closing scenes, Henry reflected on his deeds, which marched "in wide purple and gold" in his memory, but found that he despised "the brass and bombast of his earlier gospels." No, the old kind of heroism was not for him; his triumph had come from the inner crucible of torment and suffering brought on by his first encounter with war. Despite his sins, he saw that he was good; he had achieved manhood and with it the ability to find his place in the mad, hellish world of combat. Now he could put all that behind him. "He had rid himself of the red sickness of battle," Crane wrote. "The sultry nightmare was in the past. He had been an animal blistered and sweating in the heat and pain of war. He turned now with a lover's thirst to images of tranquil skies, fresh meadows, cool brooks—an existence of soft and eternal peace."

In the spring of 1894, Crane took his manuscript to Hamlin Garland, who was staying in New York with a brother. Crane said he hadn't been to see Garland for a while "because of various strange conditions"—his shoes had worn out completely, leaving him virtually imprisoned in his room until C. K. Linson had brought him a new pair. As Garland's brother served him a steak for lunch, Garland started reading his manuscript, which was soiled from handling. "The first sentence fairly took me captive," Garland recalled. "It described a vast army camp on one side of a river, confronting with its thousands of eyes a similar monster on the opposite bank. The finality which lay in every word, the epic breadth of vision, the splendor of the pictures presented—all indicated a most powerful and original imagination." As he read rapidly through the first seven or eight chapters, Garland experienced the thrill of an editor "who had fallen unexpectedly upon the work of genius." He studied young Crane as he ate his lunch, unable to associate this small, sallow, yellow-fingered youth with the fabulous manuscript he held in his hand. Had the boy spoken to the spirit of some Civil War veteran? Garland wondered. How else account for his realistic knowledge of war? When Garland mentioned this, Crane, in his "succinct, self-derisive way," confessed that he had acquired all his knowledge of battle on the football field.

Amazing! Well, they must get this published without delay. At Garland's urging, Crane removed excess dialect from the dialogue in his novel and in May took it to S. S. McClure, the restless, excitable man who published *McClure's Magazine* and ran the first U.S. newspaper syndicate. McClure kept the manuscript, giving Crane the impression that he would serialize it in his magazine or distribute it to his newspapers.

As he awaited publication, Crane decided to delete the chapter of fanciful meditative passages and let the action convey Henry's moral confusion. In all likelihood, it was now that he gave the book its ironic final title, *The Red Badge of Courage.* Meanwhile, he arranged for a Boston firm to bring out a group of poems he had written while finishing his war novel; most of them were about his own struggles with religion and God, with the Methodist gospels hurled at him from his father's pulpits. The title poem, *The Black Riders,* which he added now, recalled the demonic, sword-wielding horsemen who had exploded from the sea in his boyhood nightmares.

Six months passed without further word from McClure. By the fall Crane was "near mad" with impatience and bitterness, sure that McClure was simply sitting on the book. What "a beast" the man was; Crane felt as though he had been thrown into a ditch. Finally, he collected himself, retrieved his book in person, and took it to Irving Bacheller, owner of a struggling young newspaper syndicate in need of talented writers. Crane said he didn't know whether his novel was any good or not, but he was desperate for money and tired of praise. That night Bacheller and his wife took turns reading *The Red Badge of Courage* aloud, and the next morning he summoned Crane to his office and bought the serial rights for $90—a small fortune to an impecunious youth, who had recently been too poor to afford a nickel cab fare. But his spirits fell again when Bacheller said the book would have to be cut for serialization, from 55 thousand words down to 18 thousand.

In December 1894 the first installments of the truncated version appeared in the *New York Press* and the *Philadelphia Press* and commanded a great deal of attention. At the urging of his associates in Philadelphia, Bacheller brought the author down on the train, with Crane singing Kipling ballads in his excitement. When they appeared at the *Press,* editors, reporters, proofreaders, and compositors all crowded around Crane to offer their congratulations. Crane was simply amazed.

When he returned to New York, Ripley Hitchcock, an editor at Appleton and Company, one of the largest and most prestigious houses in the city, asked for samples of his work. Unsure of himself, Crane gave him a couple of sketches he had done. Well, these were fine, Hitchcock said, but they were too short. "Haven't you got something we can make a book of?" Crane mentioned *The Red Badge of Courage* and later sent him clippings of the newspaper version, which, Crane pointed out, was "much smaller and to my mind much worse than its original." At Hitchcock's request, Crane brought him the complete manuscript, but he was not hopeful that it would ever be published. If Appleton rejected it, he resolved to throw *The Red Badge of Courage* into the fire.

In January 1895 Crane headed for the Far West as a roving reporter for Bacheller's syndicate. In Lincoln he met a young, part-time reporter named Willa Cather, who had edited installments of Crane's novel for *The Nebraska State Journal* and thought it remarkable. To her, Crane appeared "thin to emaciation," his face gaunt and unshaven, with shaggy dark hair falling across his forehead, a thin moustache straggling on his upper lip, and "a profound melancholy" showing deep in his eyes. In February he was still in Lincoln gathering stories when a letter reached him from Ripley Hitchcock. Appleton and Company wanted to publish *The Red Badge of Courage,* Hitchcock said; Crane wouldn't have to burn it after all. But the terms offered were disappointing. After publishing costs had been met, Crane would receive a flat royalty of 10 percent on domestic sales and no share of foreign sales at all. Crane agreed without enthusiasm. To Willa Cather, he seemed bitter and depressed.

Crane went on to New Orleans, where he filed a colorful report on Mardi Gras and received the typescript of his war novel from Hitchcock. Before sending it back, he made minor corrections and added a final paragraph: "Over the river a golden ray of sun came through the hosts of leaden rain clouds." Then he toured Texas and Mexico by train, and in May 1895, returned to New York tanned "the color of a brick sidewalk." *The Black Riders* had just come out and went on to win Crane considerable acclaim as a radical young poet, but it scarcely prepared him for what happened when *The Red Badge of Courage* appeared in October.

The sensation it created was phenomenal. Newspapers from Boston to Minneapolis hailed it as the most realistic war novel ever written. The *Atlantic Monthly* asserted that it was "great enough to start a new fashion in literature." The *New York Times* called it "a deathless book," "outside all classifications," because Crane had done something unique: he had defined the "actual truth about battle" by projecting it through the eyes of a sensitive participant. As a consequence, *The Red Badge of Courage* was "more vehemently alive and heaving with dramatic human action than every other book of our time." It was so authentic, in fact, that some Civil War veterans felt sure they knew the author. "I served with Crane at Antietam," one said flatly. There were detractors, of course. A Chicago critic condemned Henry Fleming as the product of a "diseased imagination," an ignorant dolt "without a spark of patriotic feeling or soldierly ambition." The *New York Tribune* faulted the book, too, and Howells argued in *Harper's Weekly* that other writers had provided a more realistic sense of battle. But these were isolated voices in a continental chorus of approval.

And that was only the beginning. An English edition came out in November and produced even greater excitement. Joseph Conrad said he would never forget the book's impact on the English literary world. In all directions, it was on the tongue of literary connoisseurs, the talk of statesmen and generals alike. In the *Illustrated London News,* General Sir Evelyn Wood declared it quite the finest book of its kind ever written. The London *Saturday Review* compared it to Zola's *Downfall* and Tolstoy's *War and Peace* and argued that its picture of "the effect of actual fighting on a war regiment is simply unapproached in intimate knowledge and sustained imaginative strength . . . Mr. Crane's extraordinary book will appeal strongly to the insatiable desire, latently developed, to know the psychology of war—how the sights and sounds, the terrible details of the drama of battle, affect the senses and the soul of man."

The English reviews stimulated still more enthusiasm for the book in America, and in 1896 it swept to the best-seller lists across the country. There was good reason for its spectacular popularity at home, for the patriotic fervor of the Civil War generation had dimmed now and reading Americans were ready to accept Crane's stark and lyrical realism, his flouting of received notions about patriotism and heroics. By September 1896 *The Red Badge of Courage* had gone into its ninth printing and soon had readers all over the world. In the story of Henry Fleming, Crane had captured experiences that spoke to people universally.

At first, Crane was elated by his success. But then he had to face a new reality—the cruel reality of fame. At 24, he found himself a venerated public figure, a hero. Everywhere he went admirers hounded him. His friends thought him vain because they did not see him enough. Publishers clamored for more war stories, always more war stories. "Hang all war stories," he cried to a female friend. He took to deprecating the book that had made him famous, calling it the "damned 'Red Badge,'" the "accursed 'Red Badge,'" the "Disgraceful *Red Badge.*" He said that he liked his book of poems better, that it was the more ambitious effort because it contained what he thought about life in general. The war novel was "a mere episode in life, an amplification." He longed for the "happy-go-lucky" days when he had only dreamed of success. He felt worse than "the storm-beaten little robin who has no place to lay his head." He was afraid that success might turn him from the pursuit of truth, afraid that he might lose the resolution that had carried him this far. Now he was fighting for his sense of himself, for work still to come in whatever time he had left. He must, he said, meet the challenge of his fame with "desperate resolution," must remain true to his conception of his life.

While Crane did write other novels and stories without war settings, he could never escape the success of *The Red Badge of Courage* and the road it charted for him. He even wrote a series of Civil War stories, collected as *The Little Regiment,* which included a short sequel to his novel called "The Veteran"; it told how Henry Fleming as an old man gave his life trying to save two colts from a blazing barn. Despite his vow that he was now "positively" finished with stories of war, Crane spent most of his remaining years witnessing and writing about it. In late 1896 he took up with Cora Stewart, the ample, elegant madam of a high-class Florida brothel, whose soldier–husband refused to grant her a divorce; the next year she and Crane sailed for Greece, to cover the Greco–Turkish War for the *New York Journal.* Here, at last, Crane saw combat for the first time and felt that "mysterious force" of war that imperiled soldiers even more than the enemy; later he drew on his war experiences for a novel called *Active Service.* In 1897 he and Cora settled in England, in a damp villa in a London suburb, and lived together in reckless improvidence, telling everyone they were married. Crane became a warm and intimate friend of Joseph Conrad and enjoyed the admiration of the English, but he missed America fiercely and might have returned had he and Cora been able to marry. For the benefit of English intellectuals and literateurs, he assumed a dramatic pose as a western man of action. When Ford Madox Ford and others visited him, Crane loved to sit about in leggings and shirt-sleeves with a huge Colt revolver strapped to his belt. On hot days he impressed Ford with his ability to flick flies off the walls with the Colt's front sight.

In 1898 he hurried off to Cuba to report on the Spanish–American War and displayed coolness under fire in a fight at Guantanamo, which he described in a book of Cuban war stories, *Wounds and the Rain.* Exhausted and sick from the rigors of campaigning, he left for New York with his lungs in terrible shape, his fragile health irreversibly broken. By now, stories of his Bohemian life on the East Side had swollen into ugly rumors that he was a drunk and a dope addict. He returned to England in disgust and lived with Cora in a dilapidated, medieval manor in Sussex. Here, day after day, he sat in an austere workroom over the porch and turned out clever novels and stories with which to pay his mounting debts. By then, his wasted face and body betrayed the ravages of tuberculosis, "Cuban fever," and overwork, and he felt as if he were "a dry twig on the edge of the bonfire." In the spring of 1900, his 29th year, he suffered two massive hemorrhages, and Cora arranged to have him moved to a sanitarium in the Black Forest in Germany, where she remained at his bedside. He lingered until June, crying out in feverish dreams, and then died during his favorite time for writing—in the late stillness of the night.

HOW THE OTHER HALF LIVES

Literary realists like Stephen Crane were not the only writers who attempted to chronicle the underside of late nineteenth-century urban life. A host of reporters also did their part to expose the human costs of social and economic development. The best known of these journalists was Jacob A. Riis, whose most famous work, How the Other Half Lives *(1890), appeared two years before Crane arrived in New York City. The following excerpts from this classic study may well have influenced Crane's choice of topic for his first novel,* Maggie: A Girl of the Streets.

•••••

It is estimated that at least 150 thousand women and girls earn their own living in New York; but there is reason to believe that this estimate falls far short of the truth when sufficient account is taken of the large number who are not wholly dependent upon their own labor, while contributing by it to the family's earnings. These alone constitute a large class of the women wage earners, and it is characteristic of the situation that the very fact that some need not starve on their wages condemns the rest to that fate. The pay they are willing to accept all have to take. What the "everlasting law of supply and demand," that serves as such a convenient gag for public indignation, has to do with it, one learns from observation all along the road of inquiry into these real women's wrongs. To take the case of the saleswomen for illustration: The investigation of the Working Women's Society disclosed the fact that wages averaging from $2 to $4.50 a week were reduced by excessive fines, the employers placing a value upon time lost that is not given to services rendered. A little girl, who received $2 a week, made cash sales amounting to $167 in a single day, while the receipts of a $15 male clerk in the same department footed up

Source: Jacob A. Riis, *How the Other Half Lives: Studies Among the Tenements of New York* (New York: Charles Scribner's Sons, 1890), pp. 235–39.

only $125; yet for some trivial mistake the girl was fined 60 cents out of her $2. The practice prevailed in some stores of dividing the fines between the super-intendent and the timekeeper at the end of the year. In one instance they amounted to $3,000, and "the superintendent was heard to charge the time-keeper with not being strict enough in his duties." One of the causes for fine in a certain large store was sitting down. The law requiring seats for saleswomen, generally ignored, was obeyed faithfully in this establishment. The seats were there, but the girls were fined when found using them.

Cash-girls receiving $1.75 a week for work that at certain seasons length-ened their day to 16 hours were sometimes required to pay for their aprons. A common cause for discharge from stores in which, on account of the oppres-sive heat and lack of ventilation, "girls fainted day after day and came out looking like corpses," was too-long service. No other fault was found with the discharged saleswomen than that they had been long enough in the employ of the firm to justly expect an increase of salary. The reason was even given with brutal frankness in some instances.

•••••

Sixty cents is put as the average day's earnings of the 150,000, but into this computation enters the stylish "cashier's" $2 a day, as well as the 30 cents of the poor little girl who pulls threads in an East Side factory, and, if anything, the average is probably too high. Such as it is, however, it represents board, rent, clothing, and "pleasure" to this army of workers. Here is the case of a woman employed in the manufacturing department of a Broadway house. It stands for a hundred like her own. She averages $3 a week. Pays $1.50 for her room; for breakfast she has a cup of coffee; lunch she cannot afford. One meal a day is her allowance. This woman is young, she is pretty. She has "the world before her." Is it anything less than a miracle if she is guilty of nothing worse than the "early and improvident marriage," against which moralists exclaim as one of the prolific causes of the distress of the poor? Almost any door might seem to offer welcome escape from such slavery as this. "I feel so much healthier since I got three square meals a day," said a lodger in one of the Girls' Homes. Two young sewing-girls came in seeking domestic service, so that they might get enough to eat. They had been only half-fed for some time, and starvation had driven them to the one door at which the pride of the American-born girl will not permit her to knock, though poverty be the price of her independence.

•••••

QUESTIONS

1. What influence did Hamlin Garland have on Crane's development as a writer? Why did Crane find literary realism such an appealing means of expression?
2. Why did Crane adopt the daily routines of an urban slum-dweller while he was writing *Maggie*? To what extent did such behavior represent a rejection of his own background? Why do you think he made the novel's main character a woman?

3. In what ways did Crane's conception of *Red Badge* change during the period when he was writing the book? Why do you think Crane chose to write about a war that had ended six years before he was born? Why did he select an enlisted man rather than an officer as the novel's main character?

4. What was the main theme of *Red Badge?* Why was the novel so popular? Why would a work of this sort probably have been less well received by Americans if it had been written shortly after the war ended?

5. Had Crane adopted John D. Rockefeller as a fictional character, what aspects of the oil tycoon's personality and actions do you think he would have emphasized? In what ways would Crane's portrait most likely have differed from William Manchester's profile in the last chapter?

6. Which of the historical figures profiled in this unit do you find most admirable? If asked to write about that figure, what questions would you ask? What sources would you use to answer those questions?

BIBLIOGRAPHY

The most recent biography of Crane is Christopher Benfy, *The Double Life of Stephen Crane* (1992). Of the various earlier treatments of Crane's life, R. W. Stallman, *Stephen Crane: A Biography,* rev. ed. (1973), is the most comprehensive. Critical examinations of Crane's literary contributions include Donald G. Hoffman, *The Poetry of Stephen Crane* (1957); Milne Hoffman, *Cylinder of Vision: The Fiction and Journalistic Writing of Stephen Crane* (1972); and Donald B. Gibson, *The Red Badge of Courage: Redefining the Hero* (1988). For more on the emergence of naturalism and a closer look at the broader cultural developments that took place during the late nineteenth century, see John J. Conder, *Naturalism in American Fiction: The Classic Phase* (1984); Donald Pizer, *Realism and Naturalism in Nineteenth-Century American Literature,* rev. ed. (1984); and Alan Trachtenberg, *The Incorporation of America: Culture and Society in the Gilded Age* (1982).

Introduction

If the main theme of American life during the first four and a half decades of the twentieth century could be captured in one word, that word would be *struggle*. This was the case both at home and abroad. Not only did the United States play a major role in two international conflicts; on the domestic scene, movements for economic justice, women's rights, and racial equality posed unprecedented challenges to the status quo. Though the nation emerged from the period as the world's leading economic power, it did so only after experiencing the widespread social turmoil of the Great Depression.

One of the more significant political changes of these years was the growth of executive power. The administration of Theodore Roosevelt marked a major turning point. Unlike his Gilded Age counterparts, most of whom were little more than figureheads, Roosevelt brought a penchant for action to the White House that helped lay the foundation for the "Imperial Presidency" of later decades. His willingness to use the federal government as a vehicle for social and economic reform also made Roosevelt a leading figure in the progressive movement. In his essay on Roosevelt, Edmund Morris provides a lively portrait of this "over-engined" man whose expansive personality dominated the first decade of twentieth-century American political life.

The social programs championed by progressive politicians like Roosevelt did not satisfy everyone. Where Roosevelt believed American society was fundamentally sound and needed only minor reform, others called for more sweeping changes. One such person was Eugene V. Debs, the best-known American socialist of the early twentieth century. Outraged by corporate policies that impoverished and demeaned labor, Debs envisioned a world in which working people controlled their own destiny. And as Francis Russell notes in his essay, he possessed the oratorical skills needed to convey that vision to working-class audiences. Despite receiving nearly a million votes for president in 1912, Debs never achieved the state power that he sought for labor. Nevertheless, his tireless exertions on behalf of workers helped move the nation's political agenda to the left during a period of extensive social reform.

The group that benefited least from Progressive Era reforms were African-Americans. In the South, social segregation and political disfranchisement placed sharp limitations on black achievement, while in many parts of the North, racism and discrimination made conditions only marginally better. During the first half of the twentieth century, few people worked harder than W. E. B. Du Bois to remove these barriers to racial equality. Moreover, as Elliott Rudwick relates in his essay, Du Bois did not confine his concerns to black Americans. A leading figure in the Pan-African movement, as well as a founding member of the National Association for the Advancement of Colored People (NAACP), he adopted a broad perspective that addressed the problems and prospects of people of color everywhere.

Whereas the struggle for racial equality faced formidable obstacles during the first half of the twentieth century, the women's movement appeared, for a time at least, to be making significant headway. With ratification of the Nineteenth Amendment in 1920, women finally obtained the voting rights that had long been the movement's primary aim. Though a major accomplishment, some women insisted that much more remained to be done. Margaret Sanger, for example, believed women could hardly be said to have achieved true equality until they controlled their own bodies. Accordingly, she continued her campaign for female reproductive rights into the post–World War II period. In her essay on Sanger, Margaret Forster provides an insightful portrait of the nation's best-known birth control reformer.

Despite passage of the Nineteenth Amendment, it would be decades before large numbers of women would begin to hold elective office. Yet some women did exercise considerable political influence during the earlier period, perhaps none more so than Eleanor Roosevelt, who, in addition to being FDR's wife, was also one of his most trusted and able political advisors. As the conscience of the New Deal, she became a forceful advocate of women's equality, black rights, and a host of other noble causes; and as the leading voice of American liberalism, she remained a powerful presence in the Democratic party for decades afterward. In his essay on Roosevelt, William H. Chafe examines her sometimes troubled private life as well as her public achievements.

The broadranging New Deal reforms of the mid-thirties were not simply the work of compassionate insiders like Eleanor Roosevelt. They were also a response to a growing restiveness among the political left. When FDR's initial programs did little to relieve the widespread suffering of the Great Depression, a variety of individuals and groups proposed initiatives that went well beyond anything the president then had in mind. New Deal officials felt particularly threatened by Huey Long, whose Share Our Wealth plan promised every American a "household estate" of $5,000 and who appeared to have his own designs on the White House. Peter King's portrait of the Louisiana "Kingfish" does much to explain why Franklin Roosevelt considered Long one of the two most dangerous men in America.

In the end, it was not the New Deal but World War II that ended the Great Depression. As government war orders flooded U.S. factories following the Japanese attack at Pearl Harbor, labor shortages replaced unemployment as the nation's most pressing economic problem. Meanwhile, U.S. forces in Europe and Asia did their part to turn back the Axis onslaught. Among their commanding officers, few achieved greater renown than George Patton. In their essay on the colorful and hard-driving West Pointer, Stephen E. Ambrose and Judith D. Ambrose explore the complex personality of one of the war's most controversial generals.

Theodore Roosevelt

The first two decades of the twentieth century are often called the Progressive Era. The term refers to a diverse group of reformers who sought to correct the accumulating social, economic, and political problems of Gilded Age America. The progressives were so diverse, in fact, that some historians have questioned whether they constituted a coherent movement. Not only were their concerns—which ranged from conservation to corporate regulation—as broad and variegated as the nation itself; they often disagreed about the best approach to specific issues. Yet, for all their differences, progressives did share several basic beliefs. These included an abiding faith in progress and a conviction that the laissez-faire attitudes of the previous century were no longer adequate. Government, they felt, could and should play a more positive role in American life.

The progressives operated at all levels of government. In major cities, the administrations of reform mayors such as Hazen S. Pingree of Detroit and Tom Johnson of Cleveland attacked political corruption and instituted a host of measures designed to improve urban life: opening parks and beaches, lowering utility rates, regulating transit systems, and improving various municipal services. At the same time, some progressive governors turned their states into virtual laboratories of reform. The most notable example was Wisconsin, where Robert M. LaFollette often sought the counsel of social scientists in his efforts to reform electoral practices, curb corporate abuses, and protect state forests.

In 1901, when the assassination of William McKinley elevated Theodore Roosevelt to the presidency, progressivism also reached the White House. As president, Roosevelt made his mark in a number of areas important to progressives. In addition to being an ardent conservationist, he did as much as anyone of the period to increase the accountability of large corporations: by establishing the Bureau of Corporations, strengthening the Interstate Commerce Commission, and supporting the enactment of regulatory measures such as the Pure Food and Drug Act of 1906. Though primarily a domestic president, Roosevelt also exhibited a keen interest in international affairs, receiving the Nobel Peace Prize for mediating an end to the Russo–Japanese War of 1904–1905.

Despite all this, Roosevelt is remembered as much for his personality as for his accomplishments in office. An outspoken proponent of "the strenuous life" who projected an exuberant optimism, Roosevelt evoked strong feelings in people—not all of them positive. To some, he was an arrogant windbag; to others, he embodied all that was noble in American life. In the essay that follows, Edmund Morris provides a searching examination of Roosevelt's personality that explains much about the mixed reaction Americans had to this attention-seeking extrovert who restored the chief executive's role as a major player in U.S. government.

Theodore Roosevelt

Edmund Morris

Let us dispose, in short order, with Theodore Roosevelt's faults. He was an incorrigible preacher of platitudes; or to use Elting E. Morison's delicious phrase, he had "a recognition, too frequently and precisely stated, of the less recondite facts of life." He significantly reduced the wildlife population of some three continents. He piled his dessert plate with so many peaches that the cream spilled over the sides. And he used to make rude faces out of the presidential carriage at small boys in the streets of Washington.

Now those last two faults are forgivable if we accept British diplomat Cecil Spring-Rice's advice, "You must always remember the president is about six." The first fault—his preachiness—is excused by the fact that the American electorate dearly loves a moralist. As to the second and most significant fault—Theodore Roosevelt's genuine blood-lust and desire to destroy his adversaries, whether they be rhinoceroses or members of the United States Senate—it is paradoxically so much a part of his virtues, both as a man and a politician, that I will come back to it in more detail later.

One of the minor irritations I have to contend with as a biographer is that whenever I go to the library to look for books about Roosevelt, Theodore, they infallibly are mixed up with books about Roosevelt, Franklin—and I guess

Source: Copyright © 1981 by Edmund Morris. Essay first appeared in *American Heritage.* Reprinted by permission of Georges Borchardt, Inc.

FDR scholars have the same problem in reverse. Time was when the single word "Roosevelt" meant only Theodore; FDR himself frequently had to insist, in the early thirties, that he was not TR's son. He was merely a fifth cousin, and what was even more distant, a Democrat to boot. In time, of course, Franklin succeeded in preempting the early meaning of the word "Roosevelt," to the point that TR's public image, which once loomed as large as Washington's and Lincoln's, began to fade like a Cheshire cat from popular memory. By the time of FDR's own death in 1945, little was left but the ghost of a toothy grin.

Only a few veterans of the earlier Roosevelt era survived to testify that if Franklin was the greater politician, it was only by a hairsbreadth, and as far as sheer personality was concerned, Theodore's superiority could be measured in spades. They pointed out that FDR himself declared, late in life, that his "cousin Ted" was the greatest man he ever knew.

Presently the veterans too died. But that ghostly grin continued to float in the national consciousness, as if to indicate that its owner was meditating a reappearance. I first became aware of the power behind the grin in Washington, in February of 1976. The National Theater was trying out an ill-fated musical by Alan Lerner and Leonard Bernstein, *1600 Pennsylvania Avenue*. For two and a half hours Ken Howard worked his way through a chronological series of impersonations of historic presidents. The audience sat on its hands, stiff with boredom, until the very end, when Mr. Howard clamped on a pair of pince-nez and a false mustache, and bared all his teeth in a grin. The entire theater burst into delighted applause.

What intrigued me was the fact that few people there could have known much about TR beyond the obvious cliches of San Juan Hill and the Big Stick. Yet somehow, subconsciously, they realized that here for once was a positive president, warm and tough and authoritative and funny, who believed in America and who, to quote Owen Wister, "grasped his optimism tight lest it escape him."

In the last year or so Theodore Roosevelt has made his long-promised comeback. He has been the subject of a *Newsweek* cover story on American heroes; Russell Baker has called him a cinch to carry all 50 states if he were running for the White House today; he's starring on Broadway in *Tintypes*, on television in *Bully*, and you'll soon see him on the big screen in *Ragtime*. Every season brings a new crop of reassessments in the university presses, and as for the pulp mills, he figures largely in the latest installment of John Jakes's *Kent Chronicles*. No time like the present, therefore, to study that giant personality in color and fine detail.

When referring to Theodore Roosevelt I do not use the word "giant" loosely. "Every inch of him," said William Allen White, "was over-engined." Lyman Gage likened him, mentally and physically, to two strong men combined; Gifford Pinchot said that his normal appetite was

> **Brownsville Affair**   A 1906 affair in which an African-American army regiment was unjustly accused of crimes which led to dishonorable discharges; these were changed to honorable discharges in 1972.

enough for four people; Charles J. Bonaparte estimated that his mind moved 10 times faster than average; and TR himself, not wanting to get into double figures, modestly remarked, "I have enjoyed as much of life as any nine men I know." John Morley made a famous comparison in 1904 between Theodore Roosevelt and the Niagara Falls, "both great wonders of nature." John Burroughs wrote that TR's mere proximity made him nervous. "There was always something imminent about him, like an avalanche that the sound of your voice might loosen." Ida Tarbell, sitting next to him at a musical, had a sudden hallucination that the president was about to burst. "I felt his clothes might not contain him, he was so steamed up, so ready to go, to attack anything, anywhere."

Reading all these remarks it comes as a surprise to discover that TR's chest measured a normal 42 inches, and that he stood only five feet nine in his size seven shoes. Yet unquestionably his initial impact was physical, and it was overwhelming. I have amused myself over the years with collecting the metaphors that contemporaries used to describe this Rooseveltian "presence." Here's a random selection. Edith Wharton thought him radioactive; Archie Butt and others used phrases to do with electricity, high-voltage wires, generators, and dynamos; Lawrence Abbott compared him to an electromagnetic nimbus; John Burroughs to "a kind of electric bombshell, if there can be such a thing"; James E. Watson was reminded of TNT; and Senator Joseph Foraker, in an excess of imagination, called TR "a steam-engine in trousers." There are countless other steam-engine metaphors, from Henry Adams's "swift and awful Chicago express" to Henry James's "verily, a wonderful little machine: destined to be overstrained, perhaps, but not as yet, truly, betraying the least creak." Lastly we have Owen Wister comparing TR to a solar conflagration that cast no shadow, only radiance.

These metaphors sound fulsome, but they refer only to TR's physical effect, which was felt with equal power by friends and enemies. People actually tingled in his company; there was something sensually stimulating about it. They came out of the presidential office flushed, short-breathed, energized, as if they had been treated to a sniff of white powder. He had, as Oscar Straus once said, "the quality of vitalizing things." His youthfulness (he was not yet 43 at the beginning of his first term, and barely 50 at the end of his second), his air of glossy good health, his powerful handshake—all these things combined to give an impression of irresistible force and personal impetus.

But TR was not just a physical phenomenon. In many ways the quality of his personality was more remarkable than its quantity. Here again, I have discovered recurrences of the same words in contemporary descriptions. One of the more frequent images is that of sweetness. "He was as sweet a man," wrote Henry Watterson, "as ever scuttled a ship or cut a throat." But most comments are kinder than that. "There is a sweetness about him that is very compelling," sighed Woodrow Wilson; "You can't resist the man." Robert Livingstone, a journalist, wrote after TR's death: "He had the double gifts of a sweet nature that came out in every hand-touch and tone . . . and a sincerely powerful personality that left the uneffaceable impression that whatever he said was right. Such a combination was simply irresistible." Livingstone's final verdict was that Theodore Roosevelt had "unquestionably the greatest gift of personal magnetism ever possessed by an American."

That may or may not be true, but certainly there are very few recorded examples of anybody, even TR's bitterest political critics, being able to resist him in person. Brand Whitlock, Mark Twain, John Jay Chapman, William Jennings Bryan, and Henry James were all seduced by his charm, if only temporarily. Peevish little Henry Adams spent much of the period from 1901 to 1909 penning a series of magnificent insults to the president's reputation. But this did not prevent him from accepting frequent invitations to dine at the White House and basking gloomily in TR's effulgence. By the time the Roosevelt era came to an end, Adams was inconsolable. "My last vision of fun and gaiety will vanish when my Theodore goes . . . never can we replace him."

It's a pity that the two men never had a public slanging match over the table, because when it came to personal invective, TR could give as good as he got. There was the rather slow British ambassador whom he accused of having "a mind that functions at six guinea-pig power." There was the state Supreme Court justice he called "an amiable old fuzzy-wuzzy with sweetbread brains." . . . Woodrow Wilson was "a Byzantine logothete" (even Wilson had to go to the dictionary for that one); John Wanamaker was "an ill-constituted creature, oily, with bristles sticking up through the oil"; and poor Senator Warren Pfeffer never quite recovered from being called "a pin-headed anarchistic crank, of hirsute and slabsided aspect." TR did not use bad language—the nearest to it I've found is his description of Charles Evans Hughes as "a psalm-singing son of a bitch," but then Charles Evans Hughes tended to invite such descriptions. Moreover, TR usually took the sting out of his insults by collapsing into laughter as he uttered them. Booth Tarkington detected "an undertone of Homeric chuckling" even when Roosevelt seemed to be seriously castigating someone—"as if, after all, he loved the fun of hating, rather than the hating itself."

Humor, indeed, was always TR's saving grace. A reporter who spent a week with him in the White House calculated that he laughed, on average, a hundred times a day—and what was more, laughed heartily. "He laughs like an irresponsible schoolboy on a lark, his face flushing ruddy, his eyes nearly closed, his utterance choked with merriment, his speech abandoned for a weird falsetto . . . The president is a joker, and (what many jokers are not) a humorist as well."

If there were nothing more to Theodore Roosevelt's personality than physical exuberance, humor, and charm, he would indeed have been what he sometimes is misperceived to be: a simple-minded, amiable bully. Actually he was an exceedingly complex man, a polygon (to use Branden Matthews's word) of so many political, intellectual, and social facets that the closer one gets to him, the less one is able to see him in the round. Consider merely this random list of attributes and achievements:

He graduated magna cum laude from Harvard University. He was the author of a four-volume history of the winning of the West, which was considered definitive in his lifetime, and a history of the naval war of 1812, which remains definitive to this day. He also wrote biographies of Thomas Hart Benton, Gouverneur Morris, and Oliver Cromwell, and some 14 other volumes of history, natural history, literary criticism, autobiography, political philosophy, and military memoirs, not to mention countless articles and approximately 75,000 letters. He spent nearly three years of his life in Europe and the Levant, and had a wide circle of intellectual correspondents on both sides of the Atlantic. He habitually read one to three books a day, on subjects ranging from architecture to zoology, averaging two or three pages a minute and effortlessly memorizing the paragraphs that interested him. He could recite poetry by the hour in English, German, and French. He married two women and fathered six children. He was a boxing championship finalist, a Fifth Avenue socialite, a New York State assemblyman, a Dakota cowboy, a deputy sheriff, a president of the Little Missouri Stockmen's Association, United States civil service commissioner, police commissioner of New York City, assistant secretary of the Navy, colonel of the Rough Riders, governor of New York, vice president, and finally president of the United States. He was a founding member of the National Institute of Arts and Letters and a fellow of the American Historical Society. He was accepted by Washington's scientific community as a skilled ornithologist, paleontologist, and taxidermist (during the White House years, specimens that confused experts at the Smithsonian were occasionally sent to TR for identification), and he was recognized as the world authority on the big-game mammals of North America.

Now all these achievements *predate* his assumption of the presidency—in other words, he packed them into the first 43 years. I will spare you another list of the things he packed into his last 10, after leaving the White House in 1909, except to say that the total of books rose to 38, the total of letters to 150,000, and the catalogue of careers expanded to include world statesman, big-game collector for the Smithsonian, magazine columnist, and South American explorer.

If it were possible to take a cross section of TR's personality, as geologists, say, ponder a chunk of continent, you would be presented with a picture of seismic richness and confusion. The most order I have been able to make of it is to isolate four major character seams. They might be traced back to childhood. Each seam stood out bright and clear in youth and early middle age, but they began to merge about the time he was 40. Indeed the white heat of the presidency soon fused them all into solid metal. But so long as they were distinct they may be identified as aggression, righteousness, pride, and militarism. Before suggesting how they affected his performance as president, I'd like to explain how they originated.

The most fundamental characteristic of Theodore Roosevelt was his aggression—conquest being, to him, synonymous with growth. From the moment he first dragged breath into his asthmatic lungs, the sickly little boy fought for a larger share of the world. He could never get enough air; disease had to be destroyed; he had to fight his way through big, heavy books to gain a man's knowledge. Just as the struggle for wind made him stretch his chest, so did the difficulty of relating to abnormally contrasting parents extend his imagination. Theodore Senior was the epitome of hard, thrusting Northern manhood; Mittie Roosevelt was the quintessence of soft, yielding Southern femininity. The Civil War—the first political phenomenon little Teddie was ever aware of—symbolically opposed one to the other. There was no question as to which side, and which parent, the child preferred. He naughtily prayed God, in Mittie's presence, to "grind the Southern troops to powder," and the victory of Union arms reinforced his belief in the superiority of Strength over Weakness, Right over Wrong, Realism over Romance.

Teddie's youthful "ofserv-a-tions" in natural history gave him further proof of the laws of natural selection, long before he fully understood Darwin and Herbert Spencer. For weeks he watched in fascination while a tiny shrew successively devoured a mass of beetles, then a mouse twice her size, then a snake so large it whipped her from side to side of the cage as she was gnawing through its neck. From then on the rule of tooth and claw, aided by superior intelligence, was a persistent theme in Theodore Roosevelt's writings.

Blood sports, which he took up as a result of his shooting for specimens, enabled him to feel the "strong eager pleasure" of the shrew in vanquishing ever larger foes; his exuberant dancing and whooping after killing a particularly dangerous animal struck more than one observer as macabre. From among his own kind, at college, he selected the fairest and most unobtainable mate—"See that girl? I'm going to marry her. She won't have me, but I am going to have *her!*"—and he ferociously hunted her down. That was Alice Lee Roosevelt, mother of the late Alice Longworth.

During his first years in politics, in the New York State Assembly, he won power through constant attack. The death of Alice Lee, coming as it did just after the birth of his first child—at the moment of fruition of his manhood—only intensified his will to fight. He hurried West, to where the battle for life was fiercest. The West did not welcome him; it had to be won, like everything else he lusted for. Win it he did, by dint of the greatest physical and mental stretchings-out he had yet made. In doing so he built up the magnificent body that became such an inspiration to the American people (one frail little boy who vowed to follow the president's example was the future world heavyweight champion, Gene Tunney). And by living on equal terms with the likes of Hashknife Simpson, Bat Masterson, Modesty Carter, Bronco Charlie Miller, and Hell-Roaring Bill Jones, he added another mental frontier to those he already had inherited at birth. Theodore Roosevelt, Eastern son of a Northern father and a Southern mother, could now call himself a Westerner also.

TR's second governing impulse was his personal righteousness. As one reviewer of his books remarked, "He seems to have been born with his mind made up." No violent shocks disturbed his tranquil, prosperous childhood in New York City. Privately educated, he suffered none of the traumas of school. Thanks to the security of his home, the strong leadership of his father, and the adoration of his brother and sisters, Teddie entered adolescence with no sexual or psychological doubts whatsoever. Or if he had any, he simply reasoned them out, according to the Judeo-Christian principles Theodore Senior had taught him, reached the proper moral decision, and that was that. "Thank heaven!" he wrote in his diary after falling in love with Alice Lee, "I am perfectly pure."

His three great bereavements (the death of his father in 1878, and the deaths of his mother and wife in the same house and on the same day in 1884) came too late in his development to do him any permanent emotional damage. They only served to convince him more that he must be strong, honest, clean-living, and industrious. "At least I can live," he wrote, "so as not to dishonor the memory of the dead whom I so loved," and never was a cliché more heart-felt. Experiment after experiment proved the correctness of his instincts—in graduating magna cum laude from Harvard, in marrying successfully, in defying the doctors who ordered him to live a sedentary life, in winning international acclaim as writer and politician long before he was 30. (He received his first nomination for the presidency, by the Baltimore *American,* when he was only 28; it had to be pointed out to the newspaper's editors that he was constitutionally debarred from that honor for the next seven years.)

In wild Dakota Territory, he proceeded to knock down insolent cowboys, establish the foundations of federal government, pursue boat thieves in the name of the law, and preach the gospel of responsible citizenship. One of the first things he did after Benjamin Harrison appointed him civil service commissioner was call for the prosecution of Postmaster General William Wallace of Indianapolis—who just happened to be the president's best friend. "That young man," Harrison growled, "wants to put the whole world right between sunrise and sunset."

TR's egotistic moralizing as a reform police commissioner of New York City was so insufferable that the *Herald* published a transcript of one of his speeches with the personal pronoun emphasized in heavy type. The effect, in a column of gray newsprint, was of buckshot at close range. This did not stop TR from using the personal pronoun 13 times in the first four sentences of his account of the Spanish-American War. In fact, a story went around that halfway through the typesetting, Scribner's had to send for an extra supply of capital I's.

The third characteristic of Theodore Roosevelt's personality was his sense of pride, both as an aristocrat and as an American. From birth, servants and tradespeople deferred to him. Men and women of high quality came to visit his parents and treated him as one of their number. He accepted his status without question, as he did the charitable responsibilities it entailed. At a very early age he was required to accompany his father on Sunday excursions to a lodging house for Irish newsboys and a night school for little Italians . . .

· · · · ·

TR knew the value of an ethnic vote as well as the next man. There is a famous—alas, probably apocryphal—story of his appointment of Oscar Straus as the first Jewish cabinet officer in American history. At a banquet to celebrate the appointment, TR made a passionate speech full of phrases like "regardless of race, color, or creed" and then turned to Jacob Schiff, the New York Jewish leader, and said, "Isn't that so, Mr. Schiff?" But Schiff, who was very deaf and had heard little of the speech, replied, "Dot's right, Mr. President, you came to me and said, 'Chake, who is der best Choo I can put in de Cabinet?'"

TR realized, of course, that the gap between himself and Joe Murray—the Irish ward-heeler who got him into the New York Assembly—was unbridgeable outside of politics. But in America a low-born man had the opportunity—the *duty*—to fight his way up from the gutter, as Joe had done. He might then merit an invitation to lunch at Sagamore Hill, or at least tea, assuming he wore a clean shirt and observed decent proprieties.

Here I must emphasize that TR was not a snob in the trivial sense. He had nothing but contempt for the Newport set and the more languid members of the Four Hundred. When he said, at 21, that he wanted to be a member of "the governing class," he was aware that it was socially beneath his own. At Albany, and in the Bad Lands, and as colonel of the Rough Riders, he preferred to work with men who were coarse but efficient, rather than those who were polished and weak. He believed, he said, in "the aristocracy of worth," and cherished the revolution that had allowed such an elite to rise to the top in government. On the other hand (to use his favorite phrase), the historian John Blum has noted that he rarely appointed impoverished or unlettered men to responsible positions. He made great political capital, as president, of the fact that his sons attended the village school at Oyster Bay, along with the sons of his servants, of whom at least one was black; but as soon as the boys reached puberty he whisked them off to Groton.

Only the very young or very old dared call him "Teddie" to his face. Roosevelt was a patrician to the tips of his tapering fingers, yet he maintained till death what one correspondent called an "almost unnatural" identity with the masses. "I don't see how you understand the common people so well, Theodore," complained Henry Cabot Lodge. "No, Cabot, you never will," said TR, grinning triumphantly, "because I am one of them, and you are not." TR deluded himself. His plebian strength was due to understanding, not empathy.

[handwritten margin note: teddie was also upper class, but he could talk to anyone]

The fourth and final major trait of Theodore Roosevelt's character was his militarism. I will not deal with it in much detail because it is a familiar aspect of him, and in any case did not manifest itself much during his presidency. There is no doubt that in youth, and again in old age, he was in love with war; but oddly enough, of all our great presidents, he remains the only one not primarily associated with war (indeed, he won the Nobel Peace Prize in 1906).

He did not lack for military influences as a child; four of his Georgian ancestors had been military men, and stories of their exploits were told him by his mother. Two of his uncles served with distinction in the Confederate navy—a fact of which he proudly boasts in his *Autobiography,* while making no reference to his father's civilian status. (The *Autobiography,* by the way, is one of history's great examples of literary amnesia. You would not guess, from its pages, that Theodore Senior ever hired a substitute soldier, that Alice Lee ever lived or died, that TR was blind in one eye as president, that anything called the **Brownsville Affair** ever occurred, or that Elihu Root ever sat at his cabinet table. As James Bryce once said, "Roosevelt wouldn't always *look* at a thing, you know.")

When TR learned to read, he reveled in stories "about the soldiers of Valley Forge, and Morgan's riflemen," and confessed, "I had a great desire to be like them." In his senior year at Harvard, he suddenly developed an interest in strategy and tactics and began to write *The Naval War of 1812;* within 18 months he was the world expert on that subject. As soon as he left college he joined the National Guard and quickly became a captain, which stood him in good stead when he was called upon to lead a cavalry regiment in 1898. Throughout his literary years he made a study of classical and modern campaigns, and he would wage the great battles of history with knives and forks and spoons on his tablecloth. No doubt much of this fascination with things military related to his natural aggression, but there was an intellectual attraction too: He read abstract tomes on armaments, navigation, ballistics, strategy, and service administration as greedily as swashbuckling memoirs. Nothing is more remarkable about *The Naval War of 1812* than its cold impartiality, its use of figures and diagrams to destroy patriotic myths. Roosevelt understood that great battles are fought by thinking men, that mental courage is superior to physical bravado. Nobody thrilled more to the tramp of marching boots than he, but he believed that men must march for honorable reasons, in obedience to the written orders of a democratically elected commander in chief. In that respect, at least, the pen was mightier than the sword.

Now how much did these four character traits—aggression, righteousness, pride, and militarism—affect TR's performance as president of the United States? The answer is, strongly, as befits a strong character and a strong chief executive. The way he arrived at this "personal equation" is interesting, because he was actually in a weak position at the beginning of his first administration.

When TR took the oath of office on September 14, 1901, he was the youngest man ever to do so—a vice president, elevated by assassination, confronted by a nervous cabinet and a hostile Senate. Yet from the moment he raised his hand in that little parlor in Buffalo, it was apparent that he intended to translate his personal power into presidential power. The hand did not stop at the shoulder; he raised it high above his head, and held it there, "steady as if carved out of marble." His right foot pawed the floor. *Aggression.* He repeated the words of the oath confidently, adding an extra phrase, not called for in the Constitution, at the end: "And so I swear." *Righteousness.* His two senior cabinet officers, John Hay and Lyman Gage, were not present at the ceremony, but TR announced that they had telegraphed promises of loyalty to him. Actually they had not; they were both considering resignation, but TR knew any such resignations would be construed as votes of no confidence in him, and he was determined to forestall them. By announcing that Hay and Gage would stay, out of loyalty to the memory of the dead president, he made it morally impossible for them to quit. *Pride.*

As for *militarism,* TR was seen much in the company of the New York State adjutant general the next few days, and an armed escort of cavalrymen accompanied him wherever he went. This was perhaps understandable, in view of the fact that a president had just been assassinated, but it is a matter of record that more and more uniforms were seen glittering around TR as the months and years went on. Toward the end of his second administration, *Harper's Weekly* complained that "there has been witnessed under President Roosevelt an exclusiveness, a rigor of etiquette, and a display of swords and gold braid such as none of his predecessors ever dreamed of."

As the theatrical gestures at TR's inauguration make plain, he was one of the most flagrant showmen ever to tread the Washington boards. He had a genius for dramatic entrances—and always was sure the spotlight was trained his way before he made one. The first thing he asked at Buffalo was, "Where are all the newspapermen?" Only three reporters were present. His secretary explained that there was no room for more. Ignoring him, TR sent out for the rest of the press corps. Two dozen scribes came joyfully crowding in, and the subsequent proceedings were reported to the nation with a wealth of detail.

Here again we see a pattern of presidential performance developing. The exaggerated concern for the rights of reporters, the carefully staged gestures (so easy to write up, such fun to read about!)—it was as if he sensed right away that a tame press, and an infatuated public, were his surest guarantees of political security. To win election in his own right in 1904—his overriding ambition for the next three years—he would have to awake these two sleeping giants and enlist their aid in moral warfare against his political opponents, notably Senator Mark Hanna. (Hanna was chairman of the Republican National Committee and the obvious choice to take over McKinley's government after "that damned cowboy," as he called TR, had filled in as interim caretaker.)

The new president accordingly took his case straight to the press and the public. Both instantly fell in love with him. Neither seemed to notice that administratively and legislatively he accomplished virtually nothing in his first year in office. As David S. Barry of the *Sun* wrote, "Roosevelt's personality was so fascinating, so appealing to the popular fancy, so overpowering, so alive, and altogether so unique that . . . it overshadowed his public acts; that is, the public was more interested in him, and the way he did things . . . than they were about what he did."

This does not mean that TR managed, or even tried, to please all the people all the time. He was quite ready to antagonize a large minority in order to win the approval of a small majority. The sods had hardly stopped rattling on the top of McKinley's coffin when the following press release was issued: "Mr. Booker T. Washington of Tuskegee, Alabama, dined with the president last evening." Now this release, arguably the shortest and most explosive ever put out by the White House, has always been assumed to be a reluctant confirmation of the discovery of a reporter combing TR's guest book. Actually the president himself issued it, at two o'clock in the morning—that is, just in time for maximum exposure in the first edition of the newspapers. By breakfast time white supremacists all over the South were gagging over their grits at such headlines as ROOSEVELT DINES A NIGGER, and PRESIDENT PROPOSES TO CODDLE THE SONS OF HAM. This was the first time that a president had ever entertained a black man in the first house of the land. The public outcry was deafening—horror in the South, acclamation in the North—but overnight

nine million Negroes, hitherto loyal to Senator Hanna, trooped into the Rooseveltian camp. TR never felt the need to dine a black man again.

Although we may have no doubt he had the redistribution of Southern patronage in mind when he sent his invitation to Washington, another motive
was simply to stamp a bright, clear, first impression of himself upon the public
imagination. "I," he seemed to be saying, "am a man *aggressive* enough to challenge a 100-year prejudice, *righteous* enough to do so for moral reasons, and
proud enough to advertise the fact."

Again and again during the next seven years, he reinforced these perceptions of his personality. He aggressively prosecuted J. P. Morgan, Edward H.
Harriman, and John D. Rockefeller (the holy trinity of American capitalism) in
the Northern Securities antitrust case, threw the Monroe Doctrine at Kaiser
Wilhelm's feet like a token of war in the Caribbean, rooted out corruption in
his own administration, and crushed Hanna's 1904 presidential challenge by
publicly humiliating the senator when he was running for reelection in 1903.
He righteously took the side of the American worker and the American consumer against big business in the great anthracite strike, proclaimed the vanity
of muckrake journalists, forced higher ethical standards upon the food and
drug industry, ordered the dishonorable discharge of 160 Negro soldiers after
the Brownsville Affair (on his own willful reading of the evidence, or lack
thereof), and to quote Mark Twain, "dug so many tunnels under the Constitution that the transportation facilities enjoyed by that document are rivalled
only by the City of New York."

For example, when the anthracite strike began to drag into the freezing fall
of 1902, TR's obvious sympathy for the miners, and for millions of Americans
who could not afford the rise in fuel prices, began to worry conservative members of Congress. One day Representative James E. Watson was horrified to
hear that the president had decided to send federal troops in to reopen the anthracite mines on grounds of general hardship. Watson rushed round to the
White House. "What about the Constitution of the United States?" he pleaded.
"What about seizing private property for public purposes without the due
processes of law?"

TR wheeled around, shook Watson by the shoulder, and roared, "*To hell
with the Constitution when the people want coal!*" Remarks like that caused old Joe
Cannon to sigh, "Roosevelt's got no more respect for the Constitution than a
tomcat has for a marriage license."

Pride, both in himself and his office, was particularly noticeable in TR's
second term, the so-called imperial years, when Henry James complained,
"Theodore Rex is distinctly tending—or trying to make a court." But this accusation was not true. Although the Roosevelts entertained much more elabo-
rately than any of their predecessors, they confined their pomp and protocol to
occasions of state. At times, indeed, they were remarkable for the all-American
variety of their guests. On any given day one might find a Rough Rider, a poet,
a British viscount, a wolf hunter, and a Roman Catholic cardinal at the White
House table, each being treated with the gentlemanly naturalness which was

one of TR's most endearing traits. His pride manifested itself in things like his refusal to address foreign monarchs as "Your Majesty," in his offer to mediate the Russo–Japanese War (no American president had yet had such global presumptions), and, when he won the Nobel Peace Prize for successfully bringing the war to a conclusion, in refusing to keep a penny of the $40,000 prize money. This was by no means an easy decision, because TR could have used the funds: He spent all his presidential salary on official functions and was not himself a wealthy man. He confessed he was tempted to put the Nobel money into a trust for his children, but decided it belonged to the United States.

Pride and patriotism were inseparable in Theodore Roosevelt's character; indeed, if we accept Lord Morely's axiom that he "was" America, they may be considered as complementary characteristics. And neither of them was false. Just as he was always willing to lose a political battle in order to win a political war, so in diplomatic negotiations was he sedulous to allow his opponents the chance to save face—take all the glory of settlement if need be—as long as the essential victory was his.

As I have noted earlier, TR's militarism did not loom large during his presidency. The organizational structure of the U.S. Army was revamped in such a way as to strengthen the powers of the commander in chief, but Secretary of War Elihu Root takes credit for that. TR can certainly take the credit for expanding the American navy from fifth to second place in the world during his seven and a half years of power—an amazing achievement, but quite in keeping with his policy, inherited from Washington, that "to be prepared for war is the most effectual means to promote peace." The gunboat TR sent to Panama in 1903 was the only example of him shaking a naked mailed fist in the face of a weaker power; for the rest of the time he kept that fist sheathed in a velvet glove. The metaphor of velvet on iron, incidentally, was TR's own; it makes a refreshing change from the Big Stick.

If I may be permitted a final metaphor of my own, I would like to quote one from *The Rise of Theodore Roosevelt* in an attempt to explain why, on the whole, TR's character shows to better advantage as president than in his years out of power. "The man's personality was cyclonic, in that he tended to become unstable in times of low pressure. The slightest rise in the barometer outside, and his turbulence smoothed into a whir of coordinated activity, while a core of stillness developed within. Under maximum pressure Roosevelt was sunny, calm, and unnaturally clear." This explains why the first Roosevelt era was a period of fair weather. Power became Theodore Roosevelt, and absolute power became him best of all. He loved being president and was so good at his job that the American people loved him for loving it. TR genuinely dreaded having to leave the White House, and let us remember that a third term was his for the asking in 1908. But his knowledge that power corrupts even the man who most deserves it, his reverence for the Washingtonian principle that power must punctually revert to those whose gift it is, persuaded him to make this supreme sacrifice in his prime. The time would come, not many years hence, when fatal insolence tempted him to renege on his decision. That is another story. . . .

CORPORATE REGULATION

Theodore Roosevelt assumed the presidency during the midst of one of the greatest corporate merger movements in American history. Unlike some progressives, who feared all forms of concentrated economic power, Roosevelt thought corporate consolidation was preferable to the cutthroat competition of the late nineteenth-century business world. Though often reluctant to dissolve major trusts, he strongly advocated corporate regulation, and federal oversight of economic affairs expanded markedly during his administration. In the following selection, taken from a 1910 speech, Roosevelt explains why he believed the federal government needed to take the lead in such matters.

•••••

One of the most important Conservation questions of the moment relates to the control of the water power monopoly in the public interest. There is apparent to the judicious observer a distinct tendency on the part of our opponents to cloud the issue by raising the question of state as against federal jurisdiction. We are ready to meet this issue, if it is forced upon us. But there is no hope for the plain people in such conflicts of jurisdictions. The essential question is not one of hairsplitting legal technicalities. It is not really a question of state against nation. It is really a question of special corporate interests against the popular interests of this nation. If it were not for those special corporate interests, you never would have heard of the question of state as against the nation. The question is simply this: Who can best regulate the special interests for the public good? Most of the great corporations, and almost all of those that can be legitimately called the great predatory corporations, have interstate affiliations. Therefore, they are out of reach of effective state control, and fall of necessity within the federal jurisdiction. One of the prime objects of those among them that are grasping and greedy is to avoid any effective control, either by state or nation; and they advocate at this time state control simply because they believe it to be the least effective. If it should prove effective, many of those now advocating it would themselves turn round and say that such control was unconstitutional.

•••••

I want you to understand my position. I do not think that you will misunderstand it. I will do my utmost to secure the rights of every corporation. If a corporation is improperly attacked, I will stand up for it to the best of my ability. I would stand up for it even though I were sure that the bulk of the people were misguided enough for the moment to take the wrong side and be against

Source: Theodore Roosevelt, "Natural Resources," Speech at St. Paul, Minnesota, September 6, 1910, in *The New Nationalism*, ed. William E. Leuchtenburg (Englewood Cliffs, NJ: Prentice Hall, 1961), pp. 78–81.

it. I should fight hard to see that the people, through the national government, did full justice to the corporations; but I do not want the national government to depend upon their good will to get justice for the people. Most of these great corporations are in a large part financed and owned in the Atlantic states, and it is rather a comic fact that many of the chief and most serious upholders of states' rights in the present controversy are big business men who live in other states. The most effective weapon is federal laws and the federal executive. That is why I so strongly oppose the demand to turn these matters over to the states. It is fundamentally a demand against the interest of the plain people, of the people of small means, against the interest of our children and our children's children; and it is primarily in the interest of the great corporations which desire to escape effective government control.

•••••

QUESTIONS

1. Which of the four personality traits discussed in the essay do you think most influenced Roosevelt's behavior? Do you think Roosevelt would have exhibited the same lifelong preoccupation with "manliness" if he had enjoyed better health as a youth?
2. What influence did Roosevelt's class background have on the development of his personality? How was he able to get along so well with people from backgrounds different from his own?
3. What do the omissions in Roosevelt's autobiography tell us about his personality? What does the Booker T. Washington incident suggest about Roosevelt's character and approach to politics?
4. In light of the views expressed by Roosevelt in his speech on corporate regulation, how do you think he felt about John D. Rockefeller's Standard Oil Company? How would he have reacted to George O. Baslington's account of the way Rockefeller conducted business?
5. In the essay, Morris states that Roosevelt "intended to translate his personal power into presidential power." What evidence does Morris provide to support this observation? How effective a president do you think Roosevelt would be today?
6. What challenges does a biographer who has chosen to write about Roosevelt confront? Based on what you know about Roosevelt, would your assessment of him be positive or negative?

BIBLIOGRAPHY

Those wishing to learn more about Roosevelt have a broad range of works from which to choose. Major biographies include Nathan Miller, *Theodore Roosevelt: A Life* (1992); Edmund Morris, *The Rise of Theodore Roosevelt* (1979); David McCullough, *Mornings on Horseback* (1981); and William H. Harbaugh, *Power and Responsibility: The Life and Times of Theodore Roosevelt* (1961). Studies that focus more narrowly on his political career include: Lewis L. Gould, *The Presidency of Theodore Roosevelt* (1991); John Morton Blum,

The Republican Roosevelt (1977); and George Mowry, *The Era of Theodore Roosevelt, 1900–1912* (1958). For a comparative analysis of Roosevelt and the leading Democratic politician of the Progressive Era, see John Milton Cooper, Jr., *The Warrior and the Priest: Woodrow Wilson and Theodore Roosevelt* (1983). On Roosevelt's approach to foreign affairs, Howard K. Beale, *Theodore Roosevelt and the Rise of America to World Power* (1956), remains required reading four decades after its publication.

Eugene V. Debs

During the late nineteenth century, the rise of massive corporations employing thousands of workers presented the American labor movement with both new opportunities and new problems. On one hand, the concentration of large numbers of people in a single workplace made organization potentially easier; moreover, the long hours, low wages, and substandard working conditions that most industrial workers endured gave them ample incentive to join unions. On the other hand, huge, multidivisional corporations were formidable adversaries, all too capable of mobilizing their vast material resources to crush labor's organizational campaigns. During strikes, manufacturers also could expect assistance from the government, as friendly judges issued injunctions that restricted picket-line activity and state authorities called out the National Guard to protect corporate property. On some occasions, as at

Pullman in 1894, striking workers had to contend with federal troops as well.

Given the hostile, antilabor climate of the period, some union leaders opted for a defensive strategy. This was the tack taken by Samuel Gompers and the American Federation of Labor (AFL). Rather than openly confronting the new corporations, where semiskilled operatives comprised the bulk of the work force, the AFL chose instead to focus on the organization of skilled craftsmen, many of whom still labored in small shops. This same cautiousness can be seen in the AFL's reluctance to become

actively involved in politics. Federation leaders believed labor could expect lit-
tle aid from the capitalist-dominated major parties. They also wished to avoid
the political controversies that long had been a source of factionalism among
unionists.

Not all labor leaders accepted the AFL approach. Some continued to es-
pouse a much broader vision of labor's role in American society. One of them
was Eugene V. Debs, the founder of the American Railway Union and a lead-
ing figure in socialist politics for more than two decades. Although Debs had
largely withdrawn from active trade union work by the late 1890s, he re-
mained a staunch advocate of industrial unions that protected all workers,
not simply skilled craftsmen. Debs further believed labor had to achieve state
power in its own right. Only then could workers successfully challenge capi-
talist–government collusion and claim their fair share of America's expanding
economic surplus.

Although Debs never realized his dream of a labor commonwealth, the
first two decades of the twentieth century were a heady time when anything
seemed possible for American socialists. And as Francis Russell contends in
the essay that follows, party successes during the period owed much to the
lanky railroad unionist from Terre Haute. With his manifest sincerity, extra-
ordinary oratorical powers, and ability to cut through Marxist abstractions,
Debs captivated American audiences in ways unmatched by any other major
figure of the political left.

Eugene V. Debs

Francis Russell

In the decades before the First World War he was the most dynamic, persuasive, and at the same time the most lovable figure that American socialism had
produced. He hated capitalism but could hate no man. Hoosier-born, he combined in his gangling person a rural nativist populism and the class-conscious
zeal of the urban foreign-born worker. Now that the American Socialist movement, shattered by World War I and disintegrated by the Russian Revolution,
has faded and the other Socialist leaders of that era are forgotten or all but forgotten, Eugene Debs remains a vital memory. His Indiana friend James Whitcomb Riley wrote of him:

And there's 'Gene Debs—a man 'at stands
And jes' holds out in his two hands
As warm a heart as ever beat
Betwixt here and the Jedgement Seat.

Source: Reprinted by permission of *American Heritage* magazine, a division of Forbes, Inc. © Forbes,
Inc., 1975.

On the platform, with his gymnastic delivery, he was the very **Billy Sunday** of socialism, carrying his audience along as much by his personality as by what he said. Once, facing a crowd of hostile Poles in Chicago, he completely captivated them by his presence, his voice, and the animation of his gestures, even though most of them could not understand his words. He was a man it was impossible to dislike. When, after his leadership in the great Pullman strike of 1894, he was sent to the McHenry County jail for six months for violating a court injunction, he formed a friendship with the sheriff and his family that lasted the rest of his life. Twenty-five years later he was sentenced to 10 years in prison under Wilson's Espionage Act for an antiwar speech he made at Canton, Ohio, in the summer of 1918. The first few months he spent in the West Virginia state prison at Moundsville. When he was transferred to the federal penitentiary at Atlanta, the Moundsville warden wrote to the Atlanta warden: "I never in my life met a kinder man. He is forever thinking of others, trying to serve them, and never thinking of himself." At Atlanta he charmed everyone he came in contact with, prisoners and guards alike. "While there is a lower-class, I am in it," he had written earlier. "While there is a criminal class, I am of it. While there is a soul in prison I am not free." He took pains to seek out the dregs among the prisoners, to encourage them by letting them know that he cared about them. Prisoners of all sorts came to him for advice. Whenever the men were allowed outside their cells, Debs always formed the center of a group, radiating warmth and fellowship. The warden came to feel deeply obligated to him for his tremendous influence in calming and often rehabilitating other prisoners. During his penitentiary term the Socialists in 1920 nominated him for the fifth time as their presidential candidate, and over 900,000 Americans voted for him. President Wilson, always relentless against anyone who opposed him, refused even to consider reducing Debs's sentence. It took the easygoing Harding, after his inaugural in March 1921, to release the Socialist leader as soon as it seemed politically propitious. Three weeks after the inauguration Debs was allowed to go on the train to Washington alone and unguarded for a three-hour interview with Harding's attorney general, Harry Daugherty. That scarred and cynical politician was, against all his instincts, captivated by his visitor. "He spent a large part of the day in my office," Daugherty later confided to Clarence Darrow, "and I never met a man I liked better."

On December 23 the White House announced that Debs and 23 other political prisoners would be released on Christmas Day. He could not go

Billy Sunday   An evangelical preacher with a sensational style who preached a fundamentalist theology.

dialectical materialist   A person who believes in the theory and practice of weighing and reconciling contradictory arguments for the purpose of arriving at the truth, especially through discussion and debate.

Das Kapital   A monumental political-economic study written by Karl Marx that serves as the theoretical basis of Communism.

Juno the Divine   An ancient Roman goddess of womanhood.

directly to his home in Terre Haute, Indiana, however, for Harding had asked him to call at the White House in passing. As he walked through the penitentiary gates for the last time 2,300 convicts crowded against the prison's front wall—the warden having in his honor suspended the usual rules—to wave and cheer him on his way. Just outside the gates Debs turned to face them, the tears running down his cheeks.

Free after two years and eight months, he arrived at the White House to find the genial Harding his most genial self. "Well," said the president, bounding out of his chair to shake hands, "I have heard so damned much about you, Mr. Debs, that I am now very glad to meet you personally." What the two men discussed in their private interview they never said. But afterward Debs told the waiting reporters: "Mr. Harding appears to me to be a kind gentleman, one whom I believe possesses humane impulses. We understand each other perfectly."

When Eugene Victor Debs was born in Terre Haute in 1855, that roistering frontier town on the Wabash River had a population of 6,000. His bookish father, Daniel, an Alsatian millowner's son, had named his own son after his two literary heroes, Eugène Sue and Victor Hugo. Daniel had left Alsace in 1848 for what he considered the freer life of America, but bad luck had dogged him from the outset. On the 71-day voyage over he was fleeced of all his money by an American con man and arrived in New York penniless. Supporting himself by odd jobs, he nevertheless managed to save enough to send for his fiancée, Daisy Bettrich, one of his father's mill hands, whom he would have married in Alsace if his class-conscious family had not been so opposed. Marriage in New York did not change his luck. He found no permanent work, and Daisy's first child, a daughter, died a few days after birth. In their sadness and isolation the young couple struck out for the West, ending up in Terre Haute, where they heard there was a French colony. All their small possessions were accidentally shipped down the river to New Orleans and lost for good.

In Terre Haute, Daniel worked 14 hours a day in the fetid dampness of a packinghouse until his health gave out. Then he drifted from one casual job to another. Daisy gave birth to a second daughter, who did not live long enough to be named. But when life seemed at its lowest ebb for the Debses, the tide slowly shifted. Two more daughters were born, and both lived. The determined and practical-minded Daisy took $40 that she had somehow managed to save, bought a stock of groceries, and opened a store in the front room of their little frame house. The Debses were well liked, and against Daniel's gloomy predictions the store soon brought them a modest living.

The two Debs daughters had been baptized, but by the time Eugene Victor was born, the Protestant Daniel and the Catholic Daisy had drifted away from the church. Daniel became a freethinker. Whenever he could save a little money, he ordered books, filling his shelves with the French and German classics and even buying small busts of Rousseau and Voltaire for the mantel. At home the parents spoke French and German, and the children picked up a smattering of both languages.

Eugene was five when the Civil War broke out. Almost his first memories were of marching men, of troop trains moving slowly through the town. More garish were his memories of the frontier town itself on a Saturday night, the flaring lights of Wabash Street just west of the canal, with its saloons and gambling joints and sporting houses. But he found the most permanent fascination of his boyhood in the railroads: trains and the men who ran them.

School with its prosaic, didactic curriculum bored the growing boy. High school bored him still more. In 1870, when he was 14, thin, angular, and six feet tall, he quit. Gravitating to the railroad, he found his first job with the Vandalia line, cleaning grease from the trucks of freight engines at 50 cents a day. At the end of the long workday his hands would be raw and his knuckles bleeding from the potash he used to loosen the grease. The youngest and least in the roundhouse, he had to take orders from everyone. Railroading soon lost much of its glamour for the weary boy. Yet he stayed on, proud at least to bring home his pay on a Saturday night. The grocery business continued to prosper. Daniel moved to a larger house. There were five children in the family now.

Gene's shop torment ended when he was sent with a crew to paint switches on the 70-mile stretch of track between Terre Haute and Indianapolis. He soon showed himself deft at painting. Later he was assigned to paint stripes on car bodies, then to lettering locomotives. In his spare time he made signs for his friends. Always he showed a friendly readiness to do small favors for anyone, without any thought of ulterior reward. Children loved him. He made kites for them and brought them pocketfuls of candy from his father's store.

In December 1871, when a drunken fireman failed to show up for work, the gangling boy was pressed into service as a night fireman. There he remained, on the run between Terre Haute and Indianapolis. "As a locomotive fireman," Debs wrote in reminiscent bitterness, "I learned of the hardships of the rail in snow, sleet, and hail, of the ceaseless danger that lurks along the iron highway, the uncertainty of employment, scant wages, and altogether trying lot of the workingman, so that from my very boyhood I was made to feel the wrongs of labor . . ." That feeling actually came later. For the present he was contentedly earning more than a dollar a night. With the extra money he went to business college every afternoon but found himself too drugged from lack of sleep to learn much. The scantiness of his education now began to trouble him, and he tried with only modest success to study at home. On the day his former high-school class graduated in 1873, he crept to his attic bed and cried.

The panic of that same year threw him out of a job, along with thousands of others. Since there was nothing for him in Terre Haute, he rode a freight to Evansville, where he found the prospects as bleak as at home. He moved on to St. Louis, and he was lucky enough to be hired as a fireman. But in St. Louis, for the first time in his life, he encountered large-scale urban misery: unemployed derelicts, homeless, wandering families, others living in shacks by the Mississippi, a world of desolation he had known before only in the pages of Victor Hugo's *Les Misérables*. What he as an individual could do about such conditions he did not know, but he burned with unfocused indignation.

Railroading was then a very hazardous trade, with accidents frequent and most of the lines callously indifferent to even elementary safety measures. Late in 1874, after one of Gene's friends slipped under a locomotive and was killed, his mother begged him to come home. At her insistence he gave up railroading and returned to Terre Haute to become a billing clerk with the wholesale grocers Hulman & Cox, the largest firm in the Midwest. Yet for all its hardships and dangers, railroad life continued to fascinate him. The wholesale grocery business did not. "There are too many things in business that I cannot tolerate," he wrote. "Business means grabbing for yourself." Evenings he used to like to walk down the tracks and watch the engines back and switch. Often he would drop in at one of the bars near the station to pass an hour or two with the trainmen. On one such evening he learned that Joshua Leach, the grand master of the Brotherhood of Locomotive Firemen, as he was entitled with Masonic grandeur, was coming to Terre Haute to organize a lodge. The idea of fraternal unity in a common cause, a railroad cause, appealed vastly and at once to the young billing clerk. He attended the meeting and at the end pushed forward and asked to join the newly founded Vigo Lodge. Leach—whose organizing efforts over two years had met only scanty success—concealed his surprise and asked the eager young man if he felt he could do his duty on being admitted. With no real idea as to what his duty might be, Debs answered, "Yes sir!"

In his enthusiasm Debs soon took over as secretary of Vigo Lodge No. 16. It was a job no one else would take. The brotherhood itself was a weak, benevolent organization concerned chiefly with group insurance plans at a time when the real issues for the railroad workers were pay, safety measures, and hours. Membership in the new lodge declined. Sometimes the young secretary would be the only one present at the fortnightly meeting. Undiscouraged, he turned to other town affairs, helping to found the Occidental Literary Club, a weekly debating society to which he invited such well-known speakers as Robert G. Ingersoll, Wendell Phillips, the women's-rights crusader Susan B. Anthony, and the then almost unknown rhymester James Whitcomb Riley. Everybody in Terre Haute had come to know and like the lanky, friendly Gene Debs by this time. In 1879, as a Democrat, he was elected city clerk. Two years later, in spite of a general Republican comeback, he was reelected.

In 1880, with the firemen's brotherhood almost bankrupt, the grand master persuaded the reluctant Debs to become secretary–treasurer of the moribund organization and editor of its paper, *The Magazine*. To accommodate Debs, union headquarters were moved to Terre Haute. The young secretary's determination and abounding effort soon brought an astonishing reversal in the brotherhood's fortunes. When he took over, assisted by his younger brother Theodore, he found himself working 18 hours a day on the firemen's problems. Suddenly the organization was alive. New members flooded in. The sprightly *Magazine* circulated far beyond the membership.

This success, however, hardly foreshadowed Debs's later career. Wrapped up as he was in his benevolent-association union, he did not think of himself as a socialist. The railroad brotherhoods were nonstriking unions, and in those early years Debs found even Samuel Gompers's American Federation of Labor too radical. The closed shop he considered an infringement on liberty, and he could even refer to the rapacious William H. Vanderbilt as "the great railroad president." In 1884, thinking he could help his union as a lawmaker, he ran successfully as a Democratic candidate for the state legislature. But after he saw a railroad safety bill that he had sponsored buried in the upper house, he lost faith in the two-party parliamentary system, with its inevitable jobbery; he did not run again.

With his customary drive and enthusiasm he now went on to organize the neglected brakemen, a task he found challenging but physically and financially exhausting. Coming back to Terre Haute from week-long travels for the new Brotherhood of Railroad Brakemen, often with scanty results, he turned for consolation and encouragement to his sister's solemnly handsome friend Kate Metzel, stepdaughter of the town's most prominent druggist. Debs's social life had been confined more to saloons than to the dances and polite evenings of the increasingly prim upper-class Terre Haute, and until he met Kate, he had paid little attention to women. But she, drawn to him from the beginning, listened to him gravely, as women do when they are in love, her interest in him masking her basic lack of interest in his concerns. What she herself cared about most deeply was material success: elegance, a large house, membership in Terre Haute's emergent society. Why she chose him she probably later wondered herself. They were married a few months before his 30th birthday in a formal wedding at Saint Stephen's Episcopal Church, of which Kate was a devout member. After a brief honeymoon they returned to housekeeping rooms. Kate found herself much alone in her rented quarters while her husband traveled from state to state drumming up membership for his union. Whatever his salary might be, money had a way of slipping through his fingers. Railroad men in their need habitually turned to him. Once when he learned that a fireman could not be promoted for lack of a good watch, he gave the man his own. At least once he gave away his overcoat. His wife never suffered actual want, but such casualness, such a hit-or-miss life, was not what she had dreamed of in her girlhood. She loved her husband and would continue to love him, but she could not give her heart to his activities. On the death of an aunt she inherited enough money to build her dream house, a towered and gabled affair of her own design on an upper-class street.

The panic year 1893 marked Debs's break with his conservative past. Up until then he could still write that "we indulge in none of the current vagaries about a conflict between capital and labor." But after Chicago's 1886 Haymarket bombing he edged toward a more militant stance. The bombing was basic for him. There, in Haymarket Square during a prolonged strike for an eight-hour day, a police captain advanced with a squad of bluecoats as a local anarchist was addressing a small but orderly crowd and ordered the meeting dispersed. When the police closed in, some unknown person threw a bomb. Seven policemen died. In the aftermath eight anarchists and union leaders were arrested and tried, and four of them were hanged for the crime—although only two of the convicted men had even been near the square. The outraged Debs, like many other labor leaders, came to regard the executed men as martyrs to the cause of industrial freedom. Following Haymarket, after Henry Frick of the Carnegie Steel Company had brutally broken the Homestead steelworkers' strike in 1892 and after federal troops had at about the same time put down a silver miners' strike in Coeur d'Alene, Idaho, Debs turned permanently to the radical left. During the depression of 1893 he denounced capitalists furiously in his *Magazine*, comparing them to tentacled devilfish dragging the workers down to degradation.

Such grim times, with over three million unemployed walking the streets, made Debs increasingly unhappy with the self-centered unionism of the railroad brotherhoods, who could not even be counted on to support one another in a strike. Engineers and conductors, the aristocrats of labor, held themselves aloof. Carmen, firemen, switchmen, raided each other's membership at will. Debs now set out to organize an American railway union that would take in *all* railroad employees, from engineer to engine wiper.

Even Debs was astonished at the immediate and overwhelming response to his union. Within three weeks 34 locals had been organized. Not only the unskilled and the unorganized joined, but many carmen, firemen, and even some of the engineers and conductors transferred their lodges *in toto*, braving the surly resentment of the brotherhood officers. The new union's first test of strength came when it launched a strike against James Hill's Great Northern Railroad. The autocratic Hill, who regarded unionism as an infringement on his God-given right to do as he pleased, had already cut wages twice on his line in that depression year. When, from his office in St. Paul, he announced a third cut, Debs called the strike. Within days the Great Northern was brought to a standstill. Seeking a solution to the impasse, the St. Paul Chamber of Commerce asked Debs to state his case. Generally Debs spoke in the florid McKinley-baroque manner of his day, but this time, facing a group of essentially hostile businessmen, he muted his rhetoric to tell them simply and directly what it was like to be a section hand or a brakeman, what it meant to raise a family on a dollar a day. So persuasive was he that he completely won over his audience. A delegation of chamber leaders visited Hill and told him he would have to arbitrate. The arbitrators granted the union almost all its demands. It was a handsome victory for Debs. When his train left St. Paul, after Hill had signed the agreement, the section men stood along the tracks at attention, bareheaded, shovels in hand.

On the heels of his victory over Hill, Debs found himself in an even more formidable confrontation with George M. Pullman, the president of the Pullman Palace Car Company, maker of dining and chair cars as well as the celebrated sleepers. Just outside Chicago, Pullman had built what he considered a model town. So it appeared, in green contrast to the industrial grime of Chicago, with neat brick homes, shaded streets, grassy yards, and even an artificial lake beside which the Pullman band gave summer concerts. But it was Pullman's town—houses, schools, churches, the luxurious new library, even the cemetery. With the onset of the depression Pullman discharged over a third of his workers and cut the wages of the others by up to half while refusing to lower rents at all. During the bleak and bitter winter of 1893–1894 destitution spread along Pullman's well-planned streets. Many of the tenants all but starved even as the company's dividends increased. Children lacked shoes to wear to school; some stayed in bed all day to keep warm in the heatless houses.

Because of a few miles of track operated by the Pullman company its workers were eligible for the American Railway Union. In the late spring of 1894 they rushed to join. Their first act was to call a strike, even before Debs had put in an appearance. Debs arrived in Pullman knowing little about conditions there. He was appalled at what he discovered. Yet he was at the same time cautious. His victory over Hill was the only success any union had scored that year. Strike after strike had been broken. Labor was in retreat. Debs knew he could expect little help from the railroad brotherhoods. Rather than risk defeat he preferred to arbitrate. But Pullman refused to sit down at any discussion table. "Nothing to arbitrate," was his stock reply. Pushed along by the indignation of the American Railway Union members and the Pullman workers, Debs finally proposed that switchmen refuse to switch Pullman cars onto trains. At the same time he warned against violence. In response to this the General Managers' Association, representing the 24 railroads running out of Chicago, announced that switchmen who balked at switching Pullman cars would be discharged.

Nevertheless, the boycott began on June 26, 1894, spreading quickly to 27 states and territories in the most extensive strike the country had yet known. More than a hundred thousand men walked out; 20 railroads were shut down. United States Attorney General Richard Olney, a former railroad lawyer and member of the General Managers' Association, then obtained an injunction against the union and the strikers that was one of the most sweeping and drastic ever issued. Workers who quit interstate jobs were to be considered criminals. Union leaders were forbidden to take part in or even to talk about the boycott.

For Debs to obey the injunction would be for him to lose the strike by default and probably destroy his union. To disregard it might send him and other leaders to jail. He felt he had no choice but to disregard it. Olney, by a process of maneuvering and misinformation, persuaded President Cleveland that the safety of the mails was endangered by the chaos in Chicago. The president, believing the situation critical, dispatched infantry, cavalry, and artillery. In spite of Debs's warning against violence, turbulent crowds had begun to hold up trains and detach the Pullman cars. With the arrival of the troops at Chicago—aided by over 3,000 floaters hastily sworn in as deputy federal marshals—violence exploded. Mobs smashed switches, halted trains, and burned hundreds of railroads cars. A mob finally attacked the troops. They in turn opened fire, and seven men lay dead in the street. The soldiers now took over the city. Two days later Debs and three colleagues were arrested, then tried and sentenced for contempt and for obstructing the mails. The strike was broken, and Debs was on his way to jail.

The Pullman strike became known as Debs's strike. On his release from jail six months later he was the most famous labor leader in the United States. While in jail he had been visited by Victor Berger and other Socialist leaders, who hoped to enlist him in their cause. Yet for all his increased radicalism Debs remained unconvinced. Populism attracted him more than socialism. In 1896 the Populists even considered running him as their presidential candidate, and a third of the delegates to their convention were pledged to him. He urged them instead to support the silver-tongued, silver-minded William Jennings Bryan. Bryan became the nominee of both the Populists and the Democrats. McKinley's defeat of Bryan was the weight thrown in the balance that finally convinced Debs that the old system of capitalism was not enough, that it must be superseded by a system of public ownership and public use. On New Year's 1897, in a lead article in the *Railway Times,* the journal of his now faltering American Railway Union, he announced that he was a Socialist.

Debs was a Socialist more of the heart than of the head, a utopian rather than a **dialectical materialist**. Though he later kept a framed picture of Karl Marx in his office, it is doubtful that he ever read *Das Kapital*. While in the Atlanta penitentiary he tacked on the wall of his cell a picture of Jesus Christ, whom he liked to consider the first socialist. To the small Socialist Labor party, founded in 1877 and appealing mostly to the eastern foreign-born, he brought a western nativism as homespun as that of his friend James Whitcomb Riley. Debs Americanized the Socialist party. In turn it became his final vision. "Promising indeed is the outlook for socialism in the United States," he wrote at the beginning of the new century. "The very contemplation of the prospect is a wellspring of inspiration."

In 1900 the Socialists looked to Debs as their logical and their most inspiring presidential candidate. At first he refused. But at the party convention the leaders finally persuaded him to put aside his personal reluctance for the sake of the cause. "With your united voices ringing in my ears, with your impassioned appeals burning and glowing in my breast," he told the delegates in his Sunday-best rhetoric, "I am brought to realize that in your voice is a supreme command of duty."

Renaming themselves the Social Democratic party, the Socialists put forward a socialist–reformist platform that they hoped would appeal to the Populists and draw many of the disaffected from Bryan. Debs proved himself a spectacular campaigner. An actor by instinct, he found that he loved the applause of crowds, the open platform, the tense moment of anticipation as men waited for his words. Yet for all his zeal and enthusiasm he polled fewer than a hundred thousand votes, while McKinley was reelected comfortably with 7,218,491 votes to 6,356,734 for Bryan. Swallowing his chagrin, Debs bravely predicted that "the next four years will witness the development of socialism to continental power and proportions."

During those four years Debs became a permanent propagandist for the Socialist cause, lecturing, speaking, organizing, exhausting his none-too-robust body on journeys up and down the land. Rarely did he get enough sleep; rarely did he eat properly. Though only in his mid-40s he looked much older: bald, gaunt, hollow-eyed. His evenings of speeches and discussions were often followed by drinking bouts that exhausted him still further. But socialism as a force was taking hold. He could see that in the crowds he met, in the tumultuous welcome he got from western logging camps and mining towns. The Socialist press was growing too. The party had high hopes in 1904 when the Social Democratic Convention chose him by acclamation as its presidential candidate. "I shall be heard in the coming campaign," he told the delegates, "as often, and as decidedly, and as emphatically, as revolutionarily, as uncompromisingly as my ability, my strength, and my fidelity to the movement will allow."

Under the dual banners of the Red Flag and the Stars and Stripes, the Socialists waged a presidential campaign with the customary paraphernalia of badges, buttons, ribbons, lithographs, and lantern slides, plus thousands of "little red stickers" and a catchy song, "The Dawning Day." Theodore Roosevelt, president by inheritance, easily defeated the conservative Democrat, Judge Alton B. Parker, by over two and a half million votes. But Debs's vote increased fourfold, to 402, 895. One voter in 36 had voted for the Socialists, establishing them as a third party that, they were convinced, would in a decade or so become America's first party.

In 1901 the Social Democrats united with dissident socialists to form the Socialist party of the United States. During the next four years the party doubled its membership. Farmers of the West and Midwest, workers, scholars, intellectuals, liberal clergymen, suffragists, and social workers were drawn by their different roads to the Red Flag. Every state in the Union now had its Socialist locals. There were a hundred Socialist newspapers; there was the Rand School of Social Science in New York; there was the Intercollegiate Socialist Society, supported by Jack London's lusty presence. Debs was now recognized across America as the popular spokesman for socialism. In 1905 he helped "Big Bill" Haywood organize the lumberjacks and miners and other revolutionary-minded Westerners into the Industrial Workers of the World. Though himself inclined to the radicals, he managed to hold the radical and conservative wings of the party together. In 1908 he was nominated for the third time as presidential candidate, but not by acclamation and not unanimously. Conservative Socialists like Victor Berger—"Slowcialists," as some called them—were beginning to have reservations.

The Socialist campaign was made both widespread and spectacular by the Red Special, a train that Debs rented as his mobile headquarters. Decked out with red flags and banners, carrying a brass band, the Red Special's three cars started from Chicago at the end of August on a two-months' journey that would take Debs across the West to California and back to Boston and New York to end with a 10-mile-long triumphant parade in Chicago. Crowds packed Boston's Faneuil Hall and New York's Hippodrome to hear him. Crowds lined the tracks at whistle stops to watch him pass. In sections of Wisconsin the schools were closed to let the children see the Red Special. Debs spoke until his throat was raw. Sometimes his voice failed him completely, and his younger brother Theodore, who much resembled him, took over in his place. "The 'Red Special' is a trump," Debs wrote halfway across America. "The people are wild about it and the road will be lined with the cheering hosts of the proletarian revolution."

But for all the Red Special's sensational passage and the warm welcomes Debs received, the election results were coldly disillusioning. The Socialists increased their total of four years earlier by a mere 18,000 votes. Yet even as they were debating the discouraging results, in the months that followed they benefited from a sharp upturn in popular favor as a result of the Taft–Roosevelt split and the rise of progressivism. In 1910 the Socialists even elected a mayor of Milwaukee, and Victor Berger became the first Socialist congressman, representing the same bumptious city. By 1911 some 435 Socialists had been elected to office in various parts of the country. Yet the party's 1912 convention was marked by increasing dissent between the "Slowcialists" and the radicals. The conservatives finally forced through an amendment excluding those who, like Haywood's IWW Wobblies, favored industrial sabotage and violence over mere political agitation. Debs was in an anomalous position. He disliked any form of violence, and yet when he called for revolution he did not mean evolution. Never wholly trusting him, the conservatives put forward several other candidates to oppose him. Still, there could be no doubt about the outcome. Debs, like no other leader, had captured the imagination and the hearts of the rank-and-file party members. He was the inevitable candidate.

That election of 1912 was the most frenzied, the most viciously contested, since Bryan had run against McKinley in 1896. With Roosevelt and his Bull Moose party moving head-on against Taft and the embattled party regulars, the election of New Jersey's Governor Woodrow Wilson was predictable. As Debs admitted to Lincoln Steffens, he himself campaigned for Socialist propaganda purposes, with never the remotest hope of winning. His campaign was as lively as ever, though it lacked the flamboyance of the Red Special this time. Again he toured the country, and again he brought the crowds to their feet with his electrifying delivery, his evangelistic denunciations of capitalism. The more optimistic Socialists had predicted he would gather in at least two million votes. Though this was wide of the mark, Debs did manage to more than double his 1908 vote. Almost 1 voter in 16 had given the Socialists his allegiance. They seemed now a permanent force in American politics.

Kate Debs did not accompany her husband on his tours. His brother and his parents had followed him enthusiastically into socialism, but there was a rumor that Kate had fainted when he announced his conversion. Socialism was alien to her bourgeois heart. She remained nevertheless a loyal wife. In a short article, "How My Wife Has Helped Me," Debs wrote in 1922:

> She trudged through the snow to a cold office when I was on the road, lighted the fire, emptied the ashes, cleaned the office, answered the mail, shipped bundles of literature to me and to others, and then returned to cook her meals, set the house in order, and attend to the wants of the home.

But even at the time when he wrote this, Debs, from a health sanitarium, was writing perfervid letters to another woman.

Debs was never a philanderer. He cared deeply for his wife, who represented home for him, with all the connotations of the word. But passion, unstinted affection, and emotional release he found in a Terre Haute neighbor, Mabel Curry, the wife of a professor of literature at Indiana State Normal College. She and Debs first became intimate two decades after his marriage. A blond and rather buxom housewife, mother of three daughters, she was for Debs "**Juno the Divine**," without whom, he told her over and over, he could not have endured his loneliness. During the Red Special's tour she sometimes traveled aboard or met him secretly at one of the cities where he stopped off. Although not a formal Socialist, she was much more sympathetic to socialist doctrine than Kate was. She was for him beautiful, lovable, irresistible, he repeats in letters cloying in their repetitiveness. At the same time a strong streak of religiosity runs through the letters. Though Debs adhered to no formal religion, he tells Mabel that he believes with all his heart and soul in a future life and is convinced that she will have her place in it with him. Love, he insists, defies reason and the limitations of the human senses because it is itself divine and akin to the creative soul of the universe. God still reigns, he assures her, and love holds the planets in their orbits and the stars in their courses.

The bright day that seemed to dawn for American socialism in 1912 soon clouded over. As Wilson captured the popular imagination with his New Freedom, interest in socialism waned. Then the fateful August of 1914 arrived. Debs and his American comrades were thunderstruck as the European Socialists declared for war and nationalism. "I am opposed to every war but one," Debs wrote; "I am for that war heart and soul, and that is the worldwide revolution." As American sentiment swung from neutrality to the side of the Allies, and even after the entry of the United States into the war, Debs never moved an inch from that early statement. He was certain that peace could come only by the destruction of capitalism, not by the victory of the Allies. All his innate anger had been aroused by Wilson's dispatch of American troops to Mexico in 1914 for what Debs maintained was merely a defense of Standard Oil interests. At the outbreak of the European war he called for unconditional neutrality; and when, after the sinking of the *Lusitania*, the preparedness tide rose higher, so that even Socialists like Upton Sinclair were carried along, Debs joined Bryan, Jane Addams, and Senator LaFollette in stern opposition to militarism in any form.

In 1916 he refused to consider running again for president, and the Socialists named a competent but relatively obscure newspaperman as their candidate. Nevertheless, over Debs's protests, the Indiana comrades nominated him for Congress. Into this more limited role he put his best efforts, touring his district in a Model T and concluding the campaign with a boisterous torchlight parade through Terre Haute. Kate, nettled by reports and rumors that she was at odds with her husband, marched arm in arm with him at the parade's head.

Wilson won only narrowly over the Republicans' more war-minded Charles Evans Hughes. The Socialist vote dropped to almost half that of 1912. Debs ran ahead of the Democratic congressman, but the Republican candidate won easily. The United States war declaration, following on the heels of Wilson's second inauguration, split the Socialist party. Debs, aging and in ill health, remained as adamant as ever in his attitude toward the war. But much of the spark seemed to have gone out of him. Although the wartime hysteria of patriotism and the violations of civil liberties stirred him to angry protest, he did not publicly denounce the conscription act, the Liberty Loan drives, or the subsidies to the Allies.

Socialists proved themselves scarcely more immune to the war fever than the rest of the country. Some 100,000 of them made a public declaration of their support of the war. A bare 20,000 refused. Debs saw his own wife carried away in the surge of conforming patriotism. Kate became chairman of the women's division of the Liberty Bond drive, was active in the Red Cross, and knitted socks for our boys "over there."

Russia's October Revolution came as a breath of life to the more intransigent American radicals and Socialists. For the great majority of Americans, carried away by their war sentiments, it seemed a betrayal. All who were not for America were against America. To speak out against the war became dangerous. Pressure for conformity culminated in the Espionage Act, a law so draconian that one could be sent to jail merely for commenting adversely on a soldier's uniform or using language judged to aid the enemy's cause. That act reactivated Debs, and he determined to defy it. On June 16, 1918, at Nimisilla Park in Canton, on a platform bare of flags, he made a defiant two-hour speech that became a Socialist legend and that he knew would bring him to jail. "I would a thousand times rather be a free soul in jail than a sycophant and a coward in the streets," he told a crowd of 1,200. Government agents took down every word he spoke. A fortnight later he was arrested.

He had expected no other outcome. On leaving for prison he threw a kiss to Kate from the train, and he told a friend en route that "she has stood shoulder to shoulder with me through every storm that has beat upon us and she is still standing firm now." Yet in all the months he spent at the Atlanta penitentiary she never once visited him. Nor had she attended his trial. The reasons given by his biographers—her own ill health, the care of her aged mother, and the burden of running her Terre Haute house—seem hardly adequate. Debs's one constant visitor was Mabel Curry, who gave up her own homelife for months to see and be near him. She visited him daily, smuggled notes past the guards for him, and even took charge of the large correspondence that came to him from all over the world. He was 64 when he entered the penitentiary, an old man in failing health. Yet the letters he wrote her in those years are those of a young lover—eager, idealistic, and, it must be admitted, somewhat florid and sentimental. There are few actual letters from prison, partly because Mabel was there much of the time to see him, partly because the one letter a week he was allowed to send he generally wrote to Kate.

In 1920 the battered Socialist party, from which the Left Socialists had seceded the year before to form the Communist and the Communist Labor parties, met in convention in New York to choose a presidential candidate. After a ritual singing of the "Marseillaise" and the "Internationale" the delegates piled red roses around a portrait of the absent Debs, and he, Convict No. 9653, was nominated by acclaim. A delegation arrived at Atlanta to notify him formally, and he received them in his prison denims. He was allowed to issue statements of 500 words a week, and that was the extent of his campaigning. In the year that had expanded the electorate to include women, he received 919,977 votes, 3.5 percent of the total and about half his percentage of 1912. The victorious Harding had 16,152,200 votes. A few Socialists tried to take heart at almost a million votes, but the old-time Socialist leader Morris Hillquit sensed the election rightly as "the last flicker of the dying candle." Over the decades the two major parties would borrow much from the Socialist program as the United States stumbled toward the welfare state. But socialism as a third-party alternative was gone.

Following his release from Atlanta, Debs spent a half year with Kate in Terre Haute. At 67 his health was broken. He was suffering from heart trouble, kidney trouble, arthritis, and blinding headaches, and his digestion had still not recovered from his prison diet. After six months in Terre Haute he went to the Lindlahr Sanitarium, a "nature" health resort near Chicago.

There in his room night after night the faded Socialist leader bent his head over his desk—he claimed to have had only three hairs left—writing to his Juno with all the fervor of an adolescent. Rarely did he mention politics or his Socialist activities. But he let her see the underlying sadness beneath the equanimity of his painfully assumed cheerful exterior. Most of his life, he admitted, had been spent in the depths and very little on peaks.

Debs lived on for six more years in increasingly poor health and reduced activity. When he had entered the penitentiary, he was so sympathetic to Soviet Russia that he had declared himself a Bolshevik from the top of his head to the soles of his feet. Now, when fellow travelers like Lincoln Steffens and Communist stalwarts like Ella Reeve Bloor urged him to show his allegiance to the Soviet state, he replied that "when the people of Russia aspire toward freedom I'm all for them, but I detest the terror which the Bolsheviks imposed to wrest and hold power. I still have, and always will have, a profound faith in the efficacy of the ballot." Nor did he have any more sympathy for the American Communists, with their tactics of violence and underground activity. In 1923 he tried to resuscitate his dying party by a speaking tour of the major cities. Huge crowds came to listen to him, more out of curiosity and respect than conviction. Finally he collapsed and had to return to the sanitarium. He had stated that he would never run for president again. Nor, as 1924 approached, would his physical condition have allowed it. In that year the Socialists ran no candidate, but instead endorsed the candidate of the new Progressive party, Wisconsin's Senator Robert LaFollette.

In 1925 Debs was able to attend the banquet that the Socialist party of New York gave him on his 70th birthday. Yet it was almost beyond his strength. To the chance remark that socialism was dead he could still respond with the old fire. But he was a dying man. Some time in the spring of 1926 he went with Kate on a cruise to Bermuda and after a singularly rough return voyage came home worse than when he had started. Although he had hoped to attend a Socialist national convention in Pittsburgh on May 1, he was too ill to leave his bed. There he managed to write an appeal for Sacco and Vanzetti, his last published work. On September 20 he went back to the Lindlahr Sanitarium for another cure and died there three weeks later, with Kate and Theodore at his bedside.

Debs is remembered as the brightest star of American socialism, yet more for his character and kindly spirit than for his doctrinaire beliefs. That man was naturally good was his simplistic conviction. In his own case it happened to be true.

CHILD LABOR

The working people who listened most intently to Eugene Debs had no greater concern than their children's welfare. All too often, however, poverty-level wages placed sharp limitations on what they could do for their offspring. This was particularly so among the semiskilled, foreign-born machine tenders who formed the largest group in most early twentieth-century factories. The children of these workers frequently left school and filed into the mills alongside their parents shortly after their 14th birthday. As the youths interviewed below make clear, many had no alternative.

Statement of Charles Vasiersky, Fifteen-year-old Doffer at the Everett Mills, Lawrence, Massachusetts, 1912

MR. LENROOT: How much have you been to school?

Master VASIERSKY: I have been to school until I was 14 years old.

MR. LENROOT: What grade were you in when you left?

Master VASIERSKY: I was in the seventh grade when I left.

MR. LENROOT: Would you have liked to keep on there if you could?

Master VASIERSKY: I would have kept on, but we did not have anything to eat, and so I had to go to work.

MR. LENROOT: Do you go hungry sometimes?

Master VASIERSKY: Not all the time; but when I come home we do not have much to eat; just a piece of bread; instead of butter we have molasses.

Statement of John Boldelar, Fourteen-year-old Bobbin Boy at the Arlington Mill, Lawrence, Massachusetts, 1912

MR. CAMPBELL: What school did you attend?

Master BOLDELAR: I went to Arlington school.

MR. CAMPBELL: What grade were you in when you quit?

Master BOLDELAR: I was in the fourth grade, naval, when I quit.

MR. CAMPBELL: Were you glad when you quit school?

Master BOLDELAR: No, sir.

MR. CAMPBELL: You would have been glad if the law had not permitted you to go to work until you were 16?

Master BOLDELAR: If we had had enough money, I would not have quit it.

MR. CAMPBELL: But you would like to have the law changed so that boys could not go into the mill until they were 16?

Master BOLDELAR: I would; but what would we eat if I go to school? We should live on bread and water all the time.

Source: U.S. Congress, House of Representatives, *The Strike at Lawrence: Hearings before the Committee on Rules of the House of Representatives on Resolutions 409 and 433,* 62nd Cong., 2d sess. (Washington, D.C.: Government Printing Office, 1912), pp. 145, 153.

QUESTIONS

1. Why did Debs decide to form the American Railway Union? How would you assess his leadership of the Pullman strike? What influence did the strike have on the development of Debs's political beliefs?
2. Why did Debs give up active trade-union work to become a Socialist orator and politician? In what ways did Debs "Americanize" the Socialist movement?
3. What factors were most responsible for the electoral successes of the Socialist party during the early twentieth century? Do you think the general reform sentiment of the period increased or diminished the Socialist appeal? What effect did World War I have on the American Socialist movement?
4. How do you think Debs felt about Theodore Roosevelt? Would their views regarding child labor have been appreciably different? Can you think of any other issues on which Debs and Roosevelt might have adopted similar positions?
5. How did Debs respond to the growing factionalism within the Socialist movement during the 1910s? What was his reaction to the Russian Revolution and the rise of an American Communist movement?- not in support   in support
6. What influence did Debs have on the times in which he lived? Would he have been any more successful if he had chosen to work within the mainstream of the labor movement?

BIBLIOGRAPHY

The best biography of the Socialist leader is Nick Salvatore, *Eugene V. Debs: Citizen and Socialist* (1982), although Ray Ginger, *The Bending Cross: A Biography of Eugene Victor Debs* (1949), is still worth consulting. Studies of the Socialist movement include Howard H. Quint, *The Forging of American Socialism: Origins of the Modern Movement* (1953); David A. Shannon, *The Socialist Party of America: A History* (1955); James Weinstein, *The Decline of Socialism in America, 1912–1925* (1967); and William M. Dick, *Labor and Socialism in America: The Gompers Era* (1972). Two important analyses of major developments in the world of labor during Debs's lifetime are David Montgomery, *The Fall of the House of Labor: The Workplace, the State, and American Labor Activism, 1865–1925* (1987), and the relevant chapters in Bruce Laurie, *Artisans into Workers: Labor in Nineteenth-Century America* (1989).

W. E. B. Du Bois

During the late nineteenth century, assaults on the liberties and the well-being of nonwhite peoples increased everywhere. In the western world, it was an era of imperialism and scientific racism—a time when major European powers, marching beneath the banner of a Social Darwinism that decreed "superior races" had a right and duty to dominate the world's "lesser peoples," acquired colonies throughout the globe. By century's end, the United States also had entered the competition, staking its claim to possessions in both the Pacific and the Caribbean.

Meanwhile, the condition of African-Americans continued to deteriorate. This was especially so in the South, where social segregation and political disfranchisement became the order of the day. To make matters worse, most northerners had by this time lost interest in what they euphemistically referred to as the "Southern Question," and regional blacks had limited means of resisting these developments. No one considered open rebellion a serious option, as this was the heyday of southern lynching, a period when white mobs needed little incitement to shoot, hang, or mutilate African-Americans who violated regional racial norms. It was against this grim backdrop that the founder and president of the Tuskegee Institute in Alabama, Booker T. Washington, formulated an accommodationist program that urged southern blacks to forgo political action, accept the con-

straints of segregation, and focus their energies on constructing an economic base within the South.

Washington's message found a ready audience among both southern whites and northern conservatives. By the early twentieth century, extensive contacts in business and government had made the "Wizard of Tuskegee" the nation's most powerful black leader. But not everyone believed African Americans should follow his counsel. The most outspoken dissenter was a young college professor named W. E. B. Du Bois. Although Du Bois fully understood the oppression most blacks faced, it was not in his nature to submit. Addressing Washington in his 1903 classic, The Souls of Black Folk, *Du Bois could barely conceal his contempt: "In the history of nearly all other races and peoples the doctrine preached at such crises has been that manly self-respect is worth more than lands and houses, and that a people who voluntarily surrender such respect, or cease striving for it, are not worth civilizing." For Du Bois, this was only the beginning. During the next half century, no American—black or white—would write so eloquently or so discerningly about what he called "the problem of the color line."*

For all his militancy, Du Bois was not one of those activists who unreservedly embraced a given policy and refused to adapt to changing conditions. A keen observer of world affairs, he knew that history does not stand still; and as the times changed, so did he. In the essay that follows, Elliott Rudwick examines the evolution of Du Bois's thought and explores the inner forces that drove this proud, contentious black leader who unfailingly exhibited the courage of his convictions.

W. E. B. Du Bois

Elliott Rudwick

During the nineteenth century and the early decades of the twentieth, when blacks were virtually powerless, propagandists like Frederick Douglass, Booker T. Washington, and W. E. B. Du Bois naturally loomed large in the **pantheon** of black leaders. The term propagandist—used here in its neutral meaning as denoting one who employs symbols to influence the feelings and behavior of an audience—is a particularly apt description of the role played by Du Bois, the leading black intellectual and the most important black protest spokesman in the first half of the twentieth century. As platform lecturer and particularly as editor of several publications, Du Bois was a caustic and prophetic voice, telling whites that racist social institutions oppressed blacks and telling blacks that change in their subordinate status was impossible unless they demanded it insistently and continuously. Du Bois himself in his

Source: From edited by John Hope Franklin and August Meier. *Black Leaders of the Twentieth Century* Copyright © 1982 by the Board of Trustees of the University of Illinois. Used with permission of the University of Illinois Press.

noted autobiographical work, *Dusk of Dawn,* aptly evaluated his principal contribution when he wrote of "my role as a master of propaganda."

Central to Du Bois's role as a propagandist were the ideologies that he articulated. And Du Bois's ideas reflected most of the diverse themes in black thinking about how to assault the bastions of prejudice and discrimination. Most important, he articulated the blacks' desire for full participation in the larger American society and demanded "the abolition of all caste distinctions based simply on race and color." On the other hand, he also exhibited a nationalist side—a strong sense of group pride, advocacy of racial unity, and a profound identification with blacks in other parts of the world. As he said in one of his oft-quoted statements,

> One ever feels his twoness—an American, a Negro; two souls, two thoughts, two unreconciled strivings; two warring ideals in one dark body, whose dogged strength alone keeps it from being torn asunder. The history of the American Negro is the history of this strife—this longing to attain self-conscious manhood, to merge his double self into a better and truer self. In this merging he wishes neither of the older selves to be lost. . . . He simply wishes to make it possible for a man to be both a Negro and an American, without being cursed and spit upon by his fellows, without having the doors of opportunity closed roughly in his face.

In addition Du Bois was both a pioneering advocate of black capitalism, and later was one of the country's most prominent black Marxists. Essentially a protest leader he was also criticized at times for enunciating tactics of accommodation. An elitist who stressed the leadership role of a college-educated Talented Tenth, he articulated a fervent commitment to the welfare of the black masses.

Given the persistent and intransigent nature of the American race system, which proved quite impervious to black attacks, Du Bois in his speeches and writings moved from one proposed solution to another, and the salience of various parts of his philosophy changed as his perceptions of the needs and strategies of black America shifted over time. Aloof and autonomous in his personality, Du Bois did not hesitate to depart markedly from whatever was the current mainstream of black thinking when he perceived that the conventional wisdom being enunciated by black spokesmen was proving inadequate to the task of advancing the race. His willingness to seek different solutions often placed him well in advance of his contemporaries, and this, combined with a strong-willed, even arrogant personality made his career as black leader essentially a series of stormy conflicts.

---

pantheon   A collective reference to the gods of a people.

negrophobic   Fear or hatred of black people.

aphoristic   A concise, pointed statement of a principle.

Marcus Garvey   Black nationalist leader of the 1910s and 1920s, who advocated racial separatism and founded the Universal Negro Improvement Association.

proselytize   To make converts.

Thus Du Bois first achieved his role as a major black leader in the controversy that arose over the program of Booker T. Washington, the most prominent and influential black leader at the opening of the twentieth century. Amidst the wave of lynchings, disfranchisement, and segregation laws, Washington, seeking the good will of powerful whites, taught blacks not to protest against discrimination, but to elevate themselves through industrial education, hard work, and property accumulation; then, they would ultimately obtain recognition of their citizenship rights. At first Du Bois agreed with this gradualist strategy, but in 1903 with the publication of his most influential book, *Souls of Black Folk*, he became the chief leader of the onslaught against Washington that polarized the black community into two wings—the "conservative" supporters of Washington and his "radical" critics. For Du Bois, the blacks' only effective way to open the doors of opportunity was to adopt tactics of militant protest and agitation; by employing this style of propaganda, he made a key contribution to the evolution of black protest in the twentieth century—and to the civil rights movement.

Du Bois's background helps explain his divergence from the Washingtonian philosophy. From a young age, Du Bois saw himself as a future race leader, part of an elite corps of black college graduates dedicated to advancing the welfare of black people. The Tuskegean deprecated Du Bois's perspective, and although other factors were involved in the disagreement between the two men, a central issue in what became a titanic leadership struggle was Washington's denigration of the Du Boisian commitment to higher education.

Du Bois was born in Great Barrington, Massachusetts in 1868, and his sense of special mission to free black America had appeared even before his graduation at twenty from Fisk University, one of the leading black institutions of higher education. Committed to a platform of racial unity, Du Bois, while still an undergraduate, was earnestly lecturing fellow students that as "destined leaders of a noble people," they must dedicate themselves to the black masses. He declared to his classmates: "I am a Negro; and I glory in the name! . . . From all the recollections dear to my boyhood have I come here [to Fisk], . . . to join hands with this, my people." Du Bois felt that a college degree was important because it equipped black youth with knowledge and wisdom essential to serve the race.

The first application of Du Bois's ideas about the role of an educated elite took the form of scientific investigations that were intended to advance the cause of social reform. In 1895 Du Bois became the first black to receive a Ph.D. from Harvard University, and utilizing his broad training in the social sciences, he published *The Philadelphia Negro* in 1899, the first in-depth case study of a black community in the United States. By then as a professor at Atlanta University, he had begun to publish annual sociological investigations about living conditions among blacks. Du Bois at this point in his career passionately believed that social science would provide white America's leaders with the knowledge necessary to eliminate discrimination and solve the race problem. At the same time he had seen much value in Washington's program. But with his sociological publications virtually ignored by influential reformers, and with the Negroes' status deteriorating under Washington's ascendancy, Du Bois gradually came to the conclusion that only through agitation and protest could social change ever come.

The unbridgeable differences that thus appeared between Washington's accommodating stance and Du Bois's advocacy of militant protest were rooted in personality incompatibility as well as irreconcilable emphases regarding the solution of the race problem. Du Bois felt awkward and uneasy with Washington, who, in turn, considered him haughty and arrogant and who appeared jealous of highly educated blacks with Ivy League degrees and cultural advantages. But the more serious barrier to a trusting relationship lay beyond personality. Where the heart of Du Bois's solution to the race problem lay in the hopes for the Talented Tenth—the college-trained leadership cadre responsible for elevating blacks economically and culturally—Washington was the preeminent black advocate of industrial education. Beyond this and other ideological concerns lay certain very practical conflicts: that the popularity of industrial education the needy black colleges were slighted by the philanthropists, and that the Tuskegean—while decrying black political participation—acted as a White House broker for black appointees. Increasingly, Du Bois became incensed that Washington was using connections with the powerful to build up his own Tuskegee Machine while doing little to disturb the caste barriers that were causing devastating problems for blacks.

In 1903 Du Bois took the crucial step that led to his command of a movement dedicated to reducing Washington's influence and to raising black consciousness against the caste system. For the very first time, the Atlanta professor publicly denounced the Tuskegean for condoning white racism and for shifting to blacks the major blame for their deprivation. Charging that the accommodationist Tuskegean had brought together the South, the North, and the blacks in a monumental compromise that "practically accepted the alleged inferiority of the Negro," Du Bois declared that social justice could not be achieved through flattering racist whites; that blacks could not gain their rights by voluntarily tossing them away or by constantly belittling themselves; and that what was needed was a clamorous protest against oppression. Du Bois's critical analysis of Washington's leadership was later credited by James Weldon Johnson with effecting "a coalescence of the more radical elements . . . thereby creating a split of the race into two contending camps." Yet the camps were not evenly matched; Washington had the support of most articulate blacks and among most of those whites who displayed any interest in black advancement, and in successive battles the Du Bois forces were outmaneuvered by the wily Tuskegean.

Nevertheless Du Bois initiated a frontal assault on this Tuskegee Machine in 1905, publicly charging that Washington was imposing thought control inside black America through payments of "hush money" to certain editors. More important, Du Bois was already meeting privately with fellow "radicals" in several cities, exploring the extent of potential support for a militant anti-Washington movement dedicated to protesting this accommodation to white supremacy and segregation. Yet Du Bois had to ponder the chances of survival for an organization that challenged Washington. Could it accomplish anything constructive if nearly all influential whites and the most powerful among the blacks opposed its ideas? Might a militant protest prove counterproductive by arousing a white backlash? And could Du Bois answer Washington's charge that black intellectuals were merely status-hungry elitists far removed from the black masses?

Responding to Du Bois's call, twenty-nine delegates, who had been carefully screened to eliminate "bought" and "hidebound" Washingtonians, met on the Canadian side of Niagara Falls in July 1905. The Niagara Movement, whose tiny membership was drawn chiefly from the ranks of northern college-educated professional men, held annual meetings for the next five years. The chief function of these gatherings was to issue declarations of protest to white America. On every basic issue the Niagara men stood in direct contrast to Washington—denouncing the inequities of the separate-but-equal doctrine, the unfairness of the disfranchisement laws, and the notion that blacks were contentedly climbing from slavery by "natural and gradual processes." Niagara platforms—in whose formulation Du Bois played the most prominent role—were sharp and vigorous, clearly telling whites that they had caused the "Negro problem" and insisting that blacks should unequivocally protest. The Niagara men declared in 1905: "We repudiate the monstrous doctrine that the oppressor should be the sole authority as to the rights of the oppressed. . . . The Negro race in America, stolen, ravished, and degraded, struggling up through difficulties and oppression, needs sympathy and receives criticism, needs help and is given hindrance, needs protection and is given mob-violence, needs justice and is given charity, needs leadership and is given cowardice and apology, needs bread and is given a stone. . . . We do not hesitate to complain and to complain loudly and insistently. To ignore, overlook, or apologize for these wrongs is to prove ourselves unworthy of freedom. Persistent manly agitation is the way to liberty."

While articulating the anger of a small group of black intellectuals, the leaders of the Niagara Movement like Du Bois said they wanted to be "in close touch with the people and with intimate knowledge of their thoughts and feelings." Clearly the Atlanta professor hoped that his propaganda would both raise the consciousness of the black millions and awaken the complacent whites. And in view of the Tuskegee Machine's influence with the mass media, both black and white, not surprisingly two basic Niagara principles were "freedom of speech and criticism" and "an unfettered and unsubsidized press." As it turned out, Du Bois was very proficient at composing annual Addresses to the Nation, but powerless at removing the barriers that prevented the messages from being widely heard.

From the day of its inception Washington plotted the destruction of the Niagara Movement. He and his associates used political patronage to strengthen their hand, and they even considered the idea of having leading Niagara men fired from their federal jobs. The public speeches of key Niagara people like

Du Bois were regularly monitored, and Washington, acting through his private secretary Emmett Scott, even planted spies to report what was transpiring at the organization's conventions. Yet these cloak-and-dagger operations could hardly have produced enough significant information to justify all the trouble, and the Washingtonians were far more effective in stymying the movement through their influence over the black press. Usually black editors were counseled to ignore Niagara, but for a period Scott decided that it would be more damaging if the race press would "hammer" the movement. The Tuskegean himself justified these maneuvers on the grounds that Niagara's leaders were not honest "gentlemen," and he even went so far as to subsidize key black journals in cities where his opponents were especially active.

In the large northern centers Washington had considerable contacts among white editors who easily concluded that the Niagara Movement was potentially damaging to harmonious race relations. Thus they followed the strong suggestions of Washington and his agents to ignore the activities of Du Bois and his group. Since the Tuskegean was assumed to be the blacks' only "real leader," white editors found nothing incongruous about giving the Niagara Movement the silent treatment. Indeed with the saintly image that Washington cultivated in the white media, the Niagara Movement's anti-Washington stance was beyond their comprehension. In 1906 the editor of the prominent white weekly, the *Outlook*, contrasted the pronouncements of the Tuskegean's National Negro Business League with the recent Niagara manifesto, and Washington's "pacific" group was praised because it demanded more of blacks themselves, while Du Bois's "assertive" group unreasonably demanded more of whites on behalf of blacks—to the latter's moral detriment. The Business League was lauded for focusing on achieving an "inch of progress" rather than strangling itself in a "yard of faultfinding" as the Niagara Movement was doing. Washington's supporters in the black press made even more invidious contrasts. Thus the New York *Age* asserted that blacks needed "something cheerful," which the Tuskegean offered the masses, rather than the "lugubrious" and "bitter" commentary of Niagara's jealous "aggregation of soreheads."

Despite these highly personal attacks, the Tuskegeans were correct about the lack of accomplishments of the Niagara Movement, whose local branches were usually inactive or ineffective. The Illinois unit futilely tried to mobilize when the **Negrophobic** *Clansman* opened at a Chicago theater, while the Massachusetts branch lobbied unsuccessfully to prevent the state legislature from appropriating tax dollars for Virginia's segregated exposition celebrating the three hundredth anniversary of the founding of Jamestown. The Niagara Movement's weakness existed less because of its leaders than because of the nation's racist social climate. Epitomizing the steady deterioration in race relations and the Niagara Movement's inability to do anything about it were the eruption in 1906 of a race riot in Atlanta, the city where Du Bois lived and worked, and later in the same year the serious miscarriage of justice at Brownsville, Texas, where despite inadequate evidence, three companies of black soldiers were dishonorably discharged on unproven charges of "shooting up" the Texas town. Helplessly the Niagara Movement issued an "Address to the World" attacking President Theodore Roosevelt (to whom enfranchised blacks had long given political allegiance) for his unfair treatment of the soldiers.

The 1907 Niagara conference was very depressing, with Du Bois himself conceding his own "inexperience" as a leader and admitting that the movement was now operating with "less momentum" and with considerable "internal strain." Indeed during the conclave he had a serious falling-out with Boston *Guardian* editor William Monroe Trotter, one of the earliest and most prominent critics of Washington. With this controversy further damaging the Movement's morale, the organization limped along; most of its 400 members even declined to pay the modest annual dues. When the fourth annual conference opened in 1908 soon after the Springfield, Illinois, race riot, the small band of black militants faced its own impotence and the powerlessness of a race that could not count on the authorities for protection even in the North. The leaders could only curse the "Negro haters of America" and remind blacks that they possessed the right to use guns against white mobs.

While the Niagara Movement was thus falling apart, Du Bois, undoubtedly to compensate for the organization's inability to obtain publicity, managed to implement his long-held dream of editing a militant "national Negro magazine" that would be a vehicle for his agitation. Although an earlier effort to publish a periodical of "new race consciousness," the *Moon,* had failed after a brief existence, Du Bois and two associates (F. H. M. Murray and L. M. Hershaw, both civil servants in Washington) had in 1907 started publishing *Horizon,* the niagara Movement's unofficial organ. As Du Bois informed the *Horizon's* early subscribers, "We need a journal, not as a matter of business, but as a matter of spiritual life and death." The journal enunciated the Niagara Movement's philosophy and sought to convert the slight voting power of northern Negroes into a racial asset. Preaching that blacks owed nothing to the Republicans, it condemned the GOP and hammered away at the theme that Secretary of War William Howard Taft (associated with Roosevelt in the Brownsville injustice and a veteran apologist for the southern caste system as well as a denigrator of higher education for blacks) had to be prevented from reaching the White House in 1908 as Roosevelt's successor. But the Tuskegee Machine, operating on the Republicans' behalf, flailed away at Du Bois's political defection to the Democrats; to the disappointment of the editors of *Horizon,* on election day most black voters made Washington's choice their own. Not surprisingly, Du Bois's two colleagues on the *Horizon* had placed their government jobs in jeopardy because of their service to the race. Charles W. Anderson, who as collector of Internal Revenue in New York was a prominent Republican politician in the Tuskegee Machine, tried to persuade the president to fire the pair.

With the Niagara Movement hovering near death, it was clear that the resources to make the black protest movement viable would have to be found elsewhere. Du Bois and other leading "radicals" had been in touch with the small number of prominent whites who were becoming disillusioned with Washington's accommodationist platform. Du Bois concluded that an interracial protest movement was essential, considering the devastating problems that his black movement had experienced and the increased resources and legitimization that prominent whites could provide. It was the mob violence at Springfield in 1908 that finally convinced this group of whites of the absolute necessity of forming an interracial protest organization possessing the aims or goals of the Niagara Movement. Through publicity directed at the whole nation, through litigation in the courts and lobbying in the legislature, this new organization called the National Association for the Advancement of Colored People hoped to topple the walls of race discrimination. Du Bois became the principal black founder and the most prominent Niagara veteran connected with the NAACP.

Although the membership was overwhelmingly black, for nearly a decade the NAACP was largely white-funded and white-dominated, and Du Bois was the only black in its inner circle. He performed a very significant role in the organization—serving as the embodiment of militant protest, the link to the small band of black "radicals," and the symbol to the public of demonstrably successful interracial cooperation. Beyond these contributions lay his more significant asset to the NAACP as its chief propagandist. As director of Publicity and Research, he founded the *Crisis* in 1910 and edited this influential NAACP official organ for a quarter-century.

In many ways Du Bois was all that the white founders had hoped for. It is true that he was not intimately involved in the administrative work of the NAACP, and only on rare occasions did he even attempt to influence policy. He quite consciously confined himself to his work as *Crisis* editor and saw his role as being a molder of public opinion—chiefly among blacks. As *Crisis* editor he recorded and supported the NAACP program for constitutional rights; he stirred up intellectual controversies, commented on current events related to the race problem, and provided arguments for racial equalitarianism. His expressions of protest were clearly, sharply, and often dramatically written, in sentences sometimes so **aphoristic** that black readers cherished them: *"I am resolved to be quiet and law abiding, but to refuse to cringe in body or in soul, to resent deliberate insult, and to assert my just rights in the face of wanton aggression."* Oppression costs the oppressor too much if the oppressed stand up and protest." "Agitate, then, brother; protest, reveal the truth and refuse to be silenced." "A moment's let up, a moment's acquiescence, means a chance for the wolves of prejudice to get at our necks." The reverence that many blacks families had for the magazine was described by the writer, J. Saunders Redding, who recollected that in his boyhood home the only periodical that the children could not touch was the *Crisis,* which "was strictly inviolate until my father himself had unwrapped and read it—often . . . aloud" to the family.

At last Du Bois had fulfilled the vision that had inspired him for so many years. The *Crisis* was his opportunity to edit a national black journal of opinion to which people would listen. As early as 1913, when the NAACP could scarcely attract 3,000 members, the circulation of the *Crisis*—chiefly among blacks—reached 30,000. Clearly Du Bois was making a considerable impact. Yet given his personality and his deep-seated desire for autonomy, the public image of harmony within the NAACP was belied by the battling that erupted between Du Bois and certain key board members.

The basic problem involved how much independence Du Bois as the only board member who was also a paid NAACP executive would have in operating the organization's official magazine, and what contributions to other NAACP activities were required of him. Du Bois, who was frequently unavailable for organizational chores like writing pamphlets, regarded the *Crisis* as "the only work" in the NAACP "which attracts me." In fact, he believed that the *Crisis*, rather than serving the NAACP as its interpreter to the public, was the one vehicle—through raising the consciousness of thousands of blacks— that could "make the NAACP *possible*." Demanding "independence of action" in running the *Crisis*, Du Bois was determined "to prove the possibilities of a Negro magazine," and he clashed with two successive white board chairmen—Oswald Garrison Villard (who was dictatorial and seemed at times subtly prejudiced) and Joel Spingarn (whom Du Bois described as a "knight" untarnished by any racist tendencies). To these board chairmen, faced with the problem of stretching limited funds to cover such vital activities as branch development and legal redress, the *Crisis* did not have the same priority that it had for Du Bois. And when the Crisis editor published materials that the other NAACP leaders felt were tactically ill advised and even harmful to the organization, open conflict resulted.

Villard was determined that the *Crisis* editor like other paid executives should be subordinated to the board chairman. Moreover, he resented that although the magazine was the property of the NAACP, and despite its large circulation not self-supporting, Du Bois wanted to "carry it around in his pocket." In protest Villard resigned as chairman in late 1913, being replaced by Spingarn—but the board struggle with the editor continued. Spingarn was more understanding than Villard and wanted to see a black editor like Du Bois exercise maximum influence, but he also believed that Du Bois's difficult personality produced situations that damaged the organization. Indeed there were even times when the NAACP, in its drive for black support, was acutely embarrassed by the editor's attacks on black ministers, journalists, and educators. For example, in 1912 Du Bois had indicted the Negro churches: "the paths and the higher places are choked with pretentious ill-trained men . . . in far too many cases with men dishonest and otherwise immoral." Two years later at a time when the NAACP desperately needed support from the black press, Du Bois fired a volley against these weeklies, claiming that many were not "worth reprinting or even reading" because their editors were venal, empty-headed, or ungrammatical. The barrage did not go unanswered, and Du Bois created a serious public relations problem for the NAACP.

Du Bois's original indiscretion had been precipitated by his acute sensitivity to a black newspaper's comment that the *Crisis* was financially dependent on an NAACP subsidy. Moreover the subsidy was one that the NAACP found it hard to afford, especially with a recent recession sharply reducing the organization's income. Nonetheless, Spingarn and the board reluctantly acceded to Du Bois's demands for more staff and office space—at a time when the national administrative office with fund-raising responsibilities shouldered by a small staff was forced to accept budgetary cuts. Because of such incidents, Spingarn, although having the highest respect for Du Bois, like Villard, eventually concluded that the *Crisis* editor was exercising too much autonomy and reluctantly announced his own intention to resign as chairman. Yet in the end Spingarn had too much admiration for Du Bois's contributions to make more than a gentle rebuke. In 1916 he and the board agreed that the *Crisis* under Du Bois could not simply be a house organ and that its editorials must be permitted to represent Du Bois's opinions within the framework of broad NAACP policy.

By 1916 in the wake of Washington's death, Du Bois became the nation's most prominent black leader, freed now from the heavy burden of competing with the Tuskegean. To the end, the *Crisis* editor had remained Washington's most implacable foe among NAACP leaders. Even before Washington's death, a noticeable shift in sentiment had begun among leading blacks, which was reflected in the successful attempts to organize NAACP branches. This shift reflected not only the growing stature of Du Bois and the NAACP, but changing social conditions as well. With increasing urbanization and educational attainment and with more migration to the North, growing numbers of blacks by World War I were embracing Du Bois's doctrine of agitation and protest.

Ironically, with the passing of Washington from the scene and the decline of Tuskegee's influence, Du Bois and the NAACP now occupied a centrist rather than a "radical" role in the black community, and the editor of the *Crisis* even found himself on occasion attacked for conservatism and lack of militancy. To some extent Du Bois made himself vulnerable on this score, since during World War I he muted his criticism. Hopeful that the return of peace blacks would be rewarded for their contributions to the war that was supposed "to make the world safe for democracy," he had urged blacks to "forget our special grievances" and "close ranks" with fellow white Americans in the battle against the country's European enemies. Not only did a number of black editors openly criticize Du Bois for this stand, but during the war and postwar years the young socialist A. Philip Randolph stridently condemned the NAACP spokesman as a "hand-picked, me-too-boss, hat-in-hand, sycophant, lick spittling" Negro.

For his part, Du Bois, disillusioned by the new spurt in racism and the resurgence of mob violence that followed the war, composed some of the most ringingly militant editorials of his career. Enraged when he discovered evidence that black soldiers who had risked their lives in Europe were discriminated against by the American military establishment there, Du Bois documented these facts in a special *Crisis* issue that also featured an editorial, "Returning Soldiers": "By the God of Heaven, we are cowards and jackasses if now that the war is over, we do not marshal every ounce of our brain and brawn to fight a sterner, longer, more unbending battle against the forces of hell in our own land. *We return. We return from fighting. We return fighting.* Make way for Democracy! We saved it in France, and by the Great Jehovah, we will save it in the United States of America, or know the reason why."

This particular number of the *Crisis,* which sold 100,000 copies, was not only widely discussed among blacks but created a furor outside the race. To say that certain U.S. government officials were alarmed is putting it mildly. The Post Office Department held up the copies while debating whether to allow them through the mails. Representative James Byrnes of South Carolina, epitomizing the sentiment of many in Congress, delivered a speech charging that Du Bois and other black newsmen had precipitated the postwar rioting. Although white mobs had caused most of the bloodshed, Byrnes singled out "Returning Soldiers" as the inspiration for black violence, holding that Du Bois should be indicted for having encouraged resistance to the government. Du Bois's fury continued unabated, and he warned blacks again to arm themselves against white mobs. The Justice Department, also anxious about "Returning Soldiers," investigated the *Crisis,* Randolph's *Messenger,* and other black periodicals. Noting that blacks like Du Bois had counseled retaliatory violence against white attackers, the department reported that black newsmen were actually "antagonistic to the white race and openly defiantly assertive of [their] own equality and even superiority."

As noted earlier, there had always been a strong nationalist strain in Du Bois's thinking, and in the postwar era this aspect of his propaganda became the focus of another controversy—his acrimonious struggle with the famous black separatist leader, **Marcus Garvey**. The most influential aspect of Du Bois's nationalism had been his pioneering advocacy of Pan-Africanism, the belief that all people of African descent had common interests and should unite in the struggle for their freedom. Moreover, he articulated both a cultural nationalism encouraging the development of black literature and art and an economic nationalism urging blacks to create a separate "group economy."

All of these themes had been expressed much earlier. Thus in an 1897 paper aptly entitled "The Conservation of Races," Du Bois enunciated the doctrine of "Pan-Negroism"—that regardless of what nation they lived in, Africans and their descendants had a common identity and should feel an emotional commitment to one another. American blacks, the vanguard of blacks the world over, should have a special attachment to Africa as the race's "greater fatherland." Arguing that "the Negro people as a race have a contribution to make to civilization and humanity, which no other race can make," he maintained that blacks possessed "a distinct mission as a race . . . to soften the whiteness" of an uninspiring materialistic Teutonic culture that seemed to dominate the world. Accordingly, Du Bois argued that Afro-Americans should maintain their group identity and institutions; for them salvation would come only from an educated elite who would chart the way to cultural and economic elevation, teaching the doctrine that blacks "MUST DO FOR THEMSELVES," by developing their own businesses, newspapers, schools, and welfare institutions.

Later Du Bois used the *Crisis* as a vehicle for cultural nationalism. Calling for the systematic cultivation of all kings of black art forms, he proudly presented works by young black novelists, essayists, painters, and poets, and in the early 1920s he proposed an Institute of Negro Literature and Art. Determined to harness the race's creative strivings, he told defeatists, "Off with these thought-chains and inchoate soul-shrinkings, and let us train ourselves to see beauty in black." Blacks were "a different kind" of people, possessing the spirit and power to build a "new and great Negro ethos." The race, armed with "group ideals," could bring forth a flood of artistic and literary creation based on themes in black life and black history. *Above all, blacks could enrich themselves and America only by defining their own standards of beauty, rather than permitting whites to define them.*

The *Crisis* also taught lessons in *economic nationalism.* Early in his life Du Bois had made bourgeois pleas for black capitalist enterprises based on the Negro market, but after coming under Socialist influences during his leadership of the Niagara Movement, he began advocating black consumers' and producers' cooperatives as a basic weapon for fighting discrimination and poverty. Du Bois devoted considerable space in the *Crisis* to stimulate readers to open cooperative stores, and in 1918 he helped form the Negro Cooperative Guild, which hoped to set up retail stores, cooperative warehouses, and even banks. Du Bois believed that white racism, by reducing the range of black incomes, had unintentionally made a socialized black economy feasible. *Blacks, rather than aspiring to be rapacious millionaires, would find it satisfying to be "consecrated" workers devoted to "social service" for the race.* Du Bois saw no reason why this "closed economic circle" could not encompass a complex racial manufacturing-distributive system, with profits reinvested in useful race projects like large housing developments. Moreover, a black cooperative system could be extended to race members in far off places like Africa.

Du Bois's cultural nationalism was intimately related to the stirrings among black intellectuals and artists known as the Harlem Renaissance, but his quasi-socialistic brand of economic nationalism was never widely accepted. Even his more influential Pan-Africanism was really not a central element in Afro-American thinking at that period. Du Bois had probably been the first black American to develop explicitly the concept of Pan-Africanism; certainly of all the black American intellectuals, he was the one most deeply identified with Africa itself—at a time when most Afro-Americans were embarrassed by the "primitiveness" of their ancestral societies. In 1900 Du Bois had been a leader in the first Pan-African Conference, and as chairman of its "Committee on the Address to the Nations of the World," he called for the creation of "a great central Negro State of the World" in Africa, which would raise the status of blacks wherever they lived. No sooner had World War I ended when, amidst the discussion of European imperialism and the disposition of the German colonies in Africa, Du Bois again took up the Pan-African theme and convened four Pan-African congresses in Europe and the United States between 1919 and 1927. *Urging the recognition of the "absolute equality of races" and the end of imperialist exploitation of blacks everywhere, these conclaves focused on racial developments in Africa and were, in fact, a concrete application of his notion that black intellectuals should lead the race into the future.*

His nationalist Pan-African Movement shared several parallels with the integrationist Niagara Movement: it was dominated by Du Bois's towering personality; it attracted only a very small segment of the Talented Tenth; it suffered from serious internal schisms; it exemplified his strength as a propagandist leader and his weakness as an organizational leader; it clashed sharply with a popular black spokesman of the period; and yet it was important as an ideological forerunner of very significant future developments among Afro-Americans.

When Du Bois revived the Pan-African Movement in 1919, he had hoped that the NAACP would be a base of grass-roots support. But neither the black middle and upper classes who were the readers of the *Crisis* and the backbone of the NAACP's supporters nor the masses of the black poor rallied to it. The NAACP contributed only token funds and considered the movement incompatible with its basic thrust. Since Du Bois largely isolated himself from the machinery of the NAACP and was not essentially an organizational leader, he did almost nothing to convince the board to adopt his cause as their own. Certainly Du Bois did not try to alter the thinking of the leadership in conferences with key officials or in board meetings. Nor did he seek to organize NAACP branch officials behind the Pan-African Movement. Characteristically, he attempted to **proselytize** through *Crisis* editorials and seemed satisfied to persuade the NAACP to make occasional official statements (which he wrote) supporting his views on Africa.

Regardless of his differences with the NAACP on Pan-Africa and other matters, Du Bois usually could be counted upon to defend the organization publicly. Thus in 1921 when the *Crisis* exonerated the board of charges of undemocratic domination, its editor declared, "It is foolish for us to give up this practical program." But behind the scenes, however, the potential for serious disruption was inherent in the ongoing problem of competition for scarce resources. Money difficulties became even more acute during the 1920s because the circulation of the *Crisis* fell drastically, from over 100,000 in 1919 to about 30,000 in 1930. Du Bois expected the board to cover the deficit, and the board did so, although his colleagues would undoubtedly have been more agreeable to providing additional money had Du Bois been willing to make the *Crisis* more decidedly the house organ of the NAACP and to devote more pages to the organization's national projects as well as branch activities. But Du Bois found that route unpalatable—he still insisted that he must "blaze a trail" and perform "a work of education and ideal beyond the practical steps of the NAACP."

At the end of the 1920s the financial crunch facing the *Crisis* set the stage for a serious, in one sense fatal, conflict between Du Bois and new NAACP Executive Secretary Walter White. White disliked Du Bois intensely and believed that the *Crisis* had become the NAACP's rather superfluous tail; for Du Bois, of course, it was still the other way around. In 1929, White protested that Du Bois's requests for ever-larger subsidies were being granted only at the expense of a weakened administrative office and were becoming a luxury that could be afforded no longer. But the board managed to find the money until the Great Depression set in, when its members paid more attention to White's admonitions that scarce dollars could be better spent on anti-lynching campaigns, court cases, and legislative lobbying.

Du Bois's problem was that as the Depression deepened, White's powers grew not only in the administrative office but also in matters directly affecting the *Crisis*. Thus in 1931, after the magazine lost another several thousand dollars (although the NAACP was paying Du Bois's entire salary), the Crisis Publishing

Company was organized (with White on the board of directors) as a legal maneuver to limit the NAACP's liability for the obligations of the *Crisis.* Du Bois fought back, ostensibly to overhaul the NAACP's structure but actually to strip White of much of his power. First the *Crisis* editor informed the board that its members were undemocratically chosen since the rank-and-file throughout the country had no voice in the selection process. Then in 1932 he went public with his charges and called for transferring the central office's power to the branches; simultaneously he urged that the NAACP adopt a program that would replace the "mere negative attempt to avoid segregation and discrimination." In his solution to the many problems posed by the Depression, Du Bois went beyond the NAACP's official program of protecting constitutional rights and revived his old dream for systematic "voluntary segregation" in the form of a separate black cooperative economy. "That race pride and race loyalty, Negro ideals and Negro unity have a place and function today, the NAACP never has denied and never can deny!" Refusing to accept Du Bois's distinction between enforced and voluntary separation, White and Spingarn challenged the *Crisis* editor, contending that he was undermining the decades-long struggle against segregation. White declared that blacks "must, without yielding, continue the grim struggle *for* integration" and stop the damage that Du Bois was inflicting on the organization. The whole debate degenerated into bitter personal recriminations between White and the *Crisis* editor. Defeated, Du Bois resigned in 1934 and returned to his old professorship at Atlanta University.

Neither inside nor outside the NAACP had there been any groundswell of support for Du Bois's position. The Talented Tenth by and large was marching to a different drummer. Black intellectuals like the sociologist E. Franklin Frazier, the political scientist Ralph Bunche, and the former NAACP Executive Secretary James Weldon Johnson all repudiated his separatism, arguing that an all-black economy in an era of black powerlessness could easily be destroyed by "the legal and police force's of the state [which] would inevitably be aligned against them." Most critics actually viewed Du Bois's call as retrogression, a return to Washington's accommodationist apologia for segregation.

This Du Bois had created serious problems for himself. His "voluntary segregation" campaign put him outside the mainstream of the civil rights movement in the mid-1930's, and in severing his *Crisis* ties he had given up the platform that was essential for his role as propagandist. Although he remained a venerated symbol, he had lost his position of effective leadership. No longer was he the molder and shaper of Negro opinion that he had been since the early part of the century.

During the 1940s Du Bois downplayed the plan for a separate economy, but he gradually identified himself with pro-Russian causes, thus drifting further from the main currents of black thinking at the time. In 1951 he was tried in federal court on charges of being an unregistered agent of a foreign power, and although the judge directed an acquittal, Du Bois became so thoroughly disillusioned about the United States that in 1961 the officially joined the Communist party and moved to Ghana.

Du Bois continued to write and lecture until the end of his life, but the output of his last three decades had slight impact among his black American contemporaries. Then, ironically, shortly after his departure from the United States, Du Bois's reputation soared, and he was transformed into a prophet. In the early 1960s the militant integrationist phase of the black direct-action protest movement was building toward its climax, and his enormous contributions became widely recognized and revered among young activists. Du Bois died on the very day that one-quarter of a million people gathered at the March on Washington—August 27, 1963. Moments before the mammoth march departed from the Washington Monument, the vast assemblage stood bowed in silent tribute at the announcement of his death. Later at the Lincoln Memorial Roy Wilkins, now executive secretary of the NAACP, referred to Du Bois's vast contributions to the long struggle for black freedom. Then a few years afterward, with the decline of militant integrationism and the ascendancy of the Black Power Era with its separatist thrust, the relevance of his nationalist writings became widely appreciated.

W. E. B. Du Bois, the propagandist, had now become symbol and prophet, and events both in the United States and abroad vindicated the celebrated words he had used in *Souls of Black Folk* in 1903: "The problem of the Twentieth Century is the problem of the color line."

BOOKER T. WASHINGTON

During the early part of his career, Du Bois's main ideological adversary within black America was the politically powerful president of Tuskegee Institute, Booker T. Washington. A complex man who surreptitiously aided efforts to achieve full racial equality, Washington publicly counseled black southerners to accept segregationist policies and concentrate on achieving the kinds of economic advances that would win the approval of regional whites. The most famous expression of this accommodationist philosophy was Washington's Atlanta Compromise address of 1895, from which experts appear below.

Atlanta Compromise Address, September, 1895

• • • • •

Our greatest danger is that in the great leap from slavery to freedom we may overlook the fact that the masses of us are to live by the productions of our hands, and fail to keep in mind that we shall prosper in proportion as we learn to dignify and glorify common labour, and put brains and skill into the common occupations of life; shall prosper in proportion as we learn to draw the line between the superficial and the substantial, the ornamental gewgaws of life and the useful. No race can prosper till it learns that there is as much dignity in tilling a field as in writing a poem. It is at the bottom of life we must

Source: Louis R. Harlan, Stuart B. Kaufman, and Raymond W. Smock, eds., *The Booker T. Washington Papers: Volume 3, 1889–1895* (Urbana: University of Illinois Press, 1974), pp. 584–86.

begin, and not at the top. Nor should we permit our grievances to overshadow our opportunities.

To those of the white race who look to the incoming of those of foreign birth and strange tongue and habits for the prosperity of the South, were I permitted I would repeat what I say to my own race, "Cast down your bucket where you are." Cast it down among the eight millions of Negroes whose habits you know, whose fidelity and love you have tested in days when to have proved treacherous meant the ruin of your firesides. Cast down your bucket among these people who have, without strikes and labour wars, tilled your fields, cleared your forests, builded your railroads and cities, and brought forth treasures from the bowels of the earth, and helped make possible this magnificent representation of the progress of the South. Casting down your bucket among my people, helping and encouraging them as you are doing on these grounds, and to education of head, hand, and heart, you will find that they will buy your surplus land, make blossom the waste places in your fields, and run your factories. While doing this, you can be sure in the future, as in the past, that you and your families will be surrounded by the most patient, faithful, law-abiding, and unresentful people that the world has seen. As we have proved our loyalty to you in the past, in nursing your children, watching by the sick-bed of your mothers and fathers, and often following them with tear-dimmed eyes to their graves, so in the future, in our humble way, we shall stand by you with a devotion that no foreigner can approach, ready to lay down our lives, if need be, in defense of yours, interlacing our industrial, commercial, civil, and religious life with yours in a way that shall make the interests of both races one. In all things that are purely social we can be as separate as the fingers, yet one as the hand in all things essential to mutual progress.

· · · · ·

The wisest among my race understand that the agitation of questions of social equality is the extremest folly, and that progress in the enjoyment of all the privileges that will come to us must be the result of severe and constant struggle rather than of artificial forcing. No race that has anything to contribute to the markets of the world is long in any degree ostracized. It is important and right that all privileges of the law be ours, but it is vastly more important that we be prepared for the exercise of these privileges. The opportunity to earn a dollar in a factory just now is worth infinitely more than the opportunity to spend a dollar in an opera-house.

· · · · ·

QUESTIONS

1. What were the practical and philosophical differences between Du Bois and Booker T. Washington? Are there any parts of Washington's Atlanta compromise speech with which Du Bois might have agreed? Why did white editors side with Washing-

ton in his struggle with the Niagara Movement? Why, as editor of the *Horizon*, did Du Bois single out Republicans for criticism?

2. Why did Du Bois believe an organization like the NAACP was necessary? Why was he constantly at odds with prominent NAACP board members? Do you think the *Crisis* was as indispensable to the struggle for black rights as Du Bois believed?

3. In what ways did Du Bois's later views on the race question differ from the approach he had championed during the early twentiety century? Why did Du Bois identify so closely with Africa and Africans? What do you think Du Bois meant when he said that black people ahd a mission to "soften the whiteness" of Teutonic culture? Why did so few African Americans support his Pan-African campaign of the 1920s?

4. Why did Du Bois sever his longtime relationship with the NAACP during the 1930s? In what ways did the civil rights movement of the 1960s reflect Du Bois's thinking on racial matters?

5. Do you see any similarities between Du Bois and Henry McNeal Turner? What were they? In what ways did Du Bois differ from Turner? In what ways did Du Bois's writings and organizational initiatives parallel the activism of Ida Wells-Barnett?

6. Which aspects of Du Bois's life do you find most interesting? If asked to write about Du Bois, in what ways would your profile differ from Bennett's portrait?

BIBLIOGRAPHY

When completed, David Levering Lewis's two-volume treatment should be the standard biography of Du Bois for decades to come. To date, Lewis has finished only the first volume, *W. E. B. Du Bois: Biography of a Race, 1868–1919* (1993). Older studies include Elliott M. Rudwick, *W. E. B. Du Bois: Propagandist of the Negro Protest* (1960), and Francis L. Broderick, *W. E. B. Du Bois: Negro Leader in a Time of Crisis* (1959). Du Bois provided his own account of major episodes in his life in *Dusk of Dawn: An Essay Toward an Autobiography of a Race Concept,* intro. by Martin Luther King, Jr. (1968). For more on the NAACP during the Du Bois era, see Charles F. Kellogg, *NAACP: A History of the National Association for the Advancement of Colored People* (1970). The best biography of Du Bois's main African-American adversary is Louis R. Harlan's excellent two-volume work: *Booker T. Washington: The Making of a Black Leader, 1856–1901* (1972) and *Booker T. Washington: The Wizard of Tuskegee, 1901–1915* (1983). August Meier, *Negro Thought in America, 1880–1920: Racial Ideologies in the Age of Booker T. Washington* (1970), is an able examination of African-American social thought during an important period of Du Bois's life.

Margaret Sanger

Among the more significant social developments in nineteenth-century America was a dramatic drop in the national birth rate. Where married women bore an average of seven children in 1800, that figure had declined by half a century later. Despite this drop, women concerned about family limitation still faced major obstacles. One was the limited knowledge available. Not only did most women know little about the process of conception, but most members of the medical profession refused to aid them. Many doctors believed that, as one prominent Gilded Age physician put it, females had a special "aptitude for impregnation." Where women could expect little help from physicians of this sort, those doctors who did provide counsel on birth control frequently offered conflicting advice.

When women sought other sources of assistance, they confronted additional barriers. Beginning in 1868, a series of states passed laws forbidding

the dissemination of birth-control information; and in 1873 Congress enacted a statute providing for the "suppression of trade in and circulation of obscene literature and articles of immoral use"—a ban that included materials related to family limitation. To enforce the measure, postal authorities hired the New York vice crusader Anthony Comstock as a special agent, and for the next half-century he would carry out his duties with a zealousness that bordered on fanaticism.

The feminist response to these developments was mixed. On one hand, sexual radicals such as Victoria Woodhull openly denounced the moral tyranny of Comstock. Believing that women would never achieve full independence until they separated sexuality from reproduction, Woodhull viewed all restrictions on the distribution of birth-control information as an assault on women's autonomy. But the sexual radicals were a distinct minority. Most feminists adopted a more cautious stance. Unlike Woodhull, who equated birth control with sexual freedom, the majority of women's rights activists called for "voluntary motherhood." This emphasis on family limitation rather than sexual autonomy both reflected their concerns about preserving women's respectability and underscored their main objective: the attainment of female self-control within the marriage relationship.

These legal restraints and ideological differences provided the context for Margaret Sanger's efforts on behalf of birth control. Like Victoria Woodhull, Sanger equated reproductive control with the free expression of women's sexuality. And as Margaret Forster shows in the essay that follows, her crusade encountered opposition from conservative feminists as well as Anthony Comstock and other Victorian moralists. In relating Sanger's story, Forster provides a fascinating portrait of a headstrong individual who had a well-earned reputation for outspoken aggressiveness.

Margaret Sanger

Margaret Forster

Margaret Higgins was one of the few feminist activist leaders to come from a working-class background. She was born on September 14th, 1879 (a date carefully concealed as she always made herself four years younger), in Corning, a factory town near New York. She was the 6th of 11 children and realized very early what being part of a large, poor family meant: going without. Yet, in spite of the material deprivation she suffered, she valued the love she had been given by her parents and remembered with gratitude the closeness of her family. There was respect and affection among them in the midst of all the hardship. The family was dominated by the father, Michael Higgins, born in Ireland and once a drummer boy in Lincoln's army. He was a large, red-headed, free-thinking man, a stonemason by trade, and his one rule in life was that people should "say what they mean." He was a member of the **Knights of Labour** and organized visits from other free-thinkers which often ended in fights. Margaret was, she said, neither ashamed nor frightened on these occasions and was in fact quite proud of being called, with her brothers and sisters, "children of the devil." Her father represented power to her. Her mother, Anne (also of Irish descent), worked hard to keep the family and the house clean and tidy even

Source: Margaret Forster, *Significant Sisters: The Grassroots of Active Feminism, 1839–1939* (Knopf, 1985).

though she was not physically strong. She always had a cough and was always recovering from or about to undergo childbirth. But there was no friction between these parents—"no quarreling or bickering"—and they each idolized the other. Michael Higgins was a great believer in women's rights, supporting female suffrage and even the wearing of the bloomer costume, but this "never evidenced itself in practical ways." He would sit "when he had nothing on hand" laughing and joking while Anne worked incessantly around him.

Outsider her home, the young Margaret was conscious of different lives going on. Corning was an unattractive place and the poor, like the Higgins family, lived in the most unattractive part, on the crowded river banks near the factories. The rich lived literally above them, on the hill tops above all the noise, dirt, and overcrowding. Margaret envied them. She noticed in particular the contrast between her mother's way of life and that of the women who lived up there: "mothers . . . played croquet and tennis with their husbands in the evening . . . (they were) young looking . . . with pretty, clean dresses and they smelled of perfume." Margaret's own mother usually smelled of milk as she produced and fed baby after baby, all delivered by Michael Higgins himself. He would never allow a doctor anywhere near his wife, not even to attend to her cough. After every birth she was weaker and coughed more but he dosed her with whisky and eventually she would be on her feet again. None of this put Margaret off childbirth. She loved the babies and looked forward to having her own. She liked to look at pictures of the Virgin Mary and fantasized herself looking like that after she had had a baby. "Sex knowledge," she wrote, "was a natural part of my life." She always knew how babies were made and how they arrived and there seemed nothing repugnant or scarring about either process. Babies were always welcome in the overcrowded Higgins household and if one died the grief was real. Margaret remembered vividly the death of Henry, aged four, and her mother's inconsolable distress which her father tried to soothe. He took Margaret with him in the night to the cemetery where he dug up Henry's coffin, opened it,

Knights of Labour   An industrial union founded in Philadelphia in 1869 and headed by a general assembly to which workers belonged regardless of sex or race.

coitus interruptus   Sexual intercourse which is purposely interrupted in order to prevent the ejaculation of semen into the vagina.

Matisse   Brilliant French painter of the era.

pessary   An instrument or device worn in the vagina to prevent conception.

Havelock Ellis   A British physician noted for his investigation of human sexual behavior and author of the seven volume *Studies in the Psychology of Sex.*

Mary Ware Dennet   Suffragist, pacifist, and birth control and sex education advocate of the early 20th century.

nolle prosequi   An entry on the records of a legal action denoting that the prosecutor or plaintiff will proceed no further in his or her actions or suit.

took a plaster cast of his face and next day made a bust of the dead child for his wife. She was greatly comforted.

But if she loved her family, Margaret hated Corning. She wanted to get out. Her two older sisters, Mary and Nan, recognizing that she had talent and ambition deserving something better than they had had, saved up to send her away to school. Both of them had worked from the age of 14 as companions and maids to supplement the family income and they wanted Margaret to escape this likely fate. Entirely through their self-sacrifice, Margaret was sent to Claverack, one of the first coeducational schools in the East, at the age of 13, supplementing her board by helping as a domestic assistant. At home, she had had no background of learning although her father was an intelligent man and a great reader of political tracts . . . She had a great deal of background to make up but did well, although causing some problems as the ringleader in various escapades.

When her schooldays ended, she found a job in a new public school in southern Jersey as a student teacher but she was called home after a few months. Her mother was dying. The TB from which she had clearly suffered for a decade at least, even if it did go undiagnosed, had flared up after the birth of her 11th child and not even Michael Higgins's all-purpose whisky cure worked. Her death was a long drawn out affair during which she tried desperately to protect her children from witnessing the full horror of it. One by one they were sent off on "holidays" to stay with friends and relatives in the surrounding area while she battled to prepare her husband for the inevitable end. But he remained willfully blind and unprepared. When Anne Higgins died, aged only 48, Michael Higgins became an embittered, unpleasant, belligerent man. Grief made him violent and tyrannical. Margaret began to hate him. She was expected to look after the smaller children and require no life of her own. If she went out with her sister Ethel to a dance they were quite likely to come back and find the door bolted against them. Margaret stood this for a year but then she had had enough. She managed to find a place for herself at White Plains Hospital, near New York, where she could train as a nurse. It was not what she wanted, which was to be a doctor so that she could save people like her mother, but it was the best escape route she could find.

White Plains, which she entered in 1898 aged 18, was not a modern hospital run on any kind of Nightingale lines. The building was old, a three-story manor house set in overgrown grounds which gave it a "spooky" air to the young nurses. There was no resident intern. The probationers not only made and fixed dressings but also did a great deal of heavy domestic work. They also assisted at operations and Margaret was pleased to find she could do so without feeling squeamish. The hardest part of her job was night-duty which she hated. All sorts of emergencies, with which she was not equipped to deal, tended to happen at night and she found it frightening to have to cope with them . . .

Most of these were maternity cases. They would arrive to find neither qualified midwife nor doctor present and would just have to go ahead and deliver the baby themselves. Naturally, this gave Margaret valuable practical obstetric experience, which she found exciting, but it also plunged her into a world she had never encountered before. Most of the mothers were not ecstatic with joy at giving birth and new babies were not greeted with the rapture which had awaited them in the Higgins household. The circumstances in which they arrived were often not just poor but desperate. The most common question Margaret was asked by the mothers whose confinements she attended was "Miss, what should I do not to have another baby straight away?" She did not know. When she referred the question to the doctor on the case, if there was one, he would brush it aside and remonstrate with the mother for asking it of a young nurse. She grew used to seeing not just women but men, too, driven nearly insane with worry about having more children. Something, clearly, was wrong . . .

The last six months of Margaret's three-year training were spent at the Manhattan Eye and Ear Hospital. While there, she met a young architect called William Sanger at one of the hospital dances. He was eight years older than Margaret and the first serious suitor she had had. His mother was German and his father had been a wealthy sheep farmer in Australia. He was, wrote Margaret, "a dark young man with intense, fiery eyes" who was very romantic and ardent. He proposed marriage very quickly but Margaret says she was adamant she did not want to marry. It was, she said, "a kind of suicide." But Bill Sanger was "impatient of conventionalities, intense in his new love" and she was deeply attracted to him. He admired her tremendously, writing that he thought her "really heroic" for putting up with the hours she did and he didn't know how she could stand it—"I must have at least six hours sleep," he wrote, "and you have none at all at night!" He wanted her to "give up this strenuous life" and promised he would soon be able to provide her with "a real home . . . a little house nestling under the trees—we shall build it, of course we shall . . ."

In the last week of her training she capitulated and married him. Bill whisked her off to a secret wedding ceremony. "That beast of a man William," she wrote to her sister Mary, "took me for a drive last Monday and drove me to a minister's residence and married me. I wept with anger and wouldn't look at him for it was so unexpected . . . I had on an old blue dress and looked horrid . . . He was afraid this precious article would be lost to him . . . I am very, very sorry to have the thing occur but yet I am very, very happy." To her sister Nan she gave a simpler explanation. Bill was, she wrote, "beastly, insanely jealous." He insisted on marriage and, since she did not want to lose him and he would not wait, she married him. But even then Margaret was a strong character. She would never have married Bill Sanger if she had not thought she loved him and certainly not out of fear of losing him alone. The fact was, she was not just attracted to him but irresistibly drawn to the way of life he could offer her.

The marriage was at first happy, in spite of Margaret's poor health. She had been ill off and on throughout her nurse's training with "gland trouble" and when she became pregnant soon after her marriage this flared into TB. She was sent to a sanatorium outside New York where she was acutely miserable and determined to leave. In November 1903 she returned home to her apartment in New York and gave birth to her first son, Stuart. It was, she commented, "agonizing" and made worse by the inexperience of the doctor who attended her. She was sent back to the hated sanatorium but quickly rebelled against the régime imposed there. Deciding that if she was going to die she'd rather do it at home she discharged herself and once more returned to New York. There she doctored herself and against all expectations the outbreak of TB began to subside (although she was never free from such outbreaks for the rest of her long life). Meanwhile, intent on fulfilling his wife's dream and also moving her to somewhere healthier, Bill had designed and begun to build a house at Hastings-on-Hudson, a pleasant suburb outside New York. It took a long time to complete but in 1907 the Sangers moved in and early the next year Margaret gave birth to her second son, Grant. She then found herself happily in the position she had always wanted to be . . . In 1910, when a daughter, Peggy, was born, everything seemed perfect.

But it was not. Margaret was far too honest to pretend her dream life satisfied her. She became restless and critical not just of the life she was living but of the people among whom she was living it. She saw that "this quiet withdrawal into the tame domesticity of the pretty hillside suburb was bordering on stagnation." It bored her. She had no great love for cooking or dressmaking or any of the other hobbies with which her neighbors filled their time and although she maintained she had "a passion for motherhood" it did not prove an all-consuming one. If Bill was disappointed he did not show it. He said he did not particularly like Hastings-on-Hudson either and was perfectly agreeable to moving. So the Sangers sold their dream house and moved back into New York, into Greenwich Village. There, they joined the local Socialist party, Labour Five, and instantly became involved in recruiting new members from the clubs of working women in the area. It beat genteel games of tennis any day . . . Among the wives of Hastings-on-Hudson careers were rare and frowned upon but in Greenwich Village any self-respecting Socialist wife wished to justify her existence. Bill's mother came to stay to look after Peggy and Grant while Stuart was enrolled in a progressive local school and Margaret took on obstetric cases (because these were short term).

Her work took her more and more frequently to the lower East Side of New York where she came across misery far worse than any she had found during her training. She was called to cases in tenements where families were living 10 to a small room, where women had neither the food nor the money to support the babies she was delivering, where both men and women alike were prematurely aged by the struggle to survive. But what was even more of a shock to her was her involvement in botched abortions. She would be called out to what she thought was a birth and arrive to find some terrified woman bleeding to death. She passed queues on Saturday nights outside well-known (but not to the authorities) abortionists and found herself the next morning dealing with the effects of what the women had been given to take. What disturbed her most was that the women who tried to abort their babies were so very often "good" mothers. They were not the feckless or wanton type, nor were their husbands blackguards or brutes. It was simply cause and effect. Marriage meant sex, sex meant babies, babies meant increased poverty. The

only solution was abstinence but even having sexual intercourse only once a
year produced a baby a year. To Margaret's disgust she heard doctors tell one
distraught husband to "go and sleep on the roof" if he wanted to avoid his
wife becoming pregnant again. It was this brutal indifference to genuine suffering that made Margaret determined to do something to help.

She was by this time not the inexperienced young girl of the White Plains
days. As a married woman, who after the birth of her third child had been advised not to have any more children, she had practiced contraception herself.
But when she came to pass on to her patients the "secret"of not having any
more babies she found that her wonderful information was virtually useless to
them. "I resolved," she wrote, ". . . to do something to change the destiny of
the mothers whose miseries were as vast as the sky." She discovered that explaining about *coitus interruptus* and condoms changed no destinies among
the mothers of the lower East Side. What they needed was *female* contraception
which was efficient and above all easy to use. They wanted the responsibility
in their own hands. They also wanted to understand more about the workings
of their own bodies and it was this demand for knowledge that led Margaret to
give health talks for the Women's Commission of the Socialist party and to
write short articles on health matters for the New York paper *Call*. Out of all
this came a series of articles in 1912 originally entitled *What Every Mother
Should Know* then changed to *What Every Girl Should Know*. These at first simply gave information about sex and facts about reproduction which mothers
were advised to tell their daughters, but then the articles became bolder, including more detailed notes on human physiology and also trying to stress
that the sex act was normal and healthy and not something to be feared or
shunned by women. Finally, the last article touched on venereal disease, its
causes and effects, and how to avoid it. The Post Office immediately banned
Call under the 1873 Comstock Law which made it illegal to send obscene matter through the U.S. mail.

As far as Margaret Sanger was concerned this was flinging down the
gauntlet. She determined to pick it up. Bill encouraged her, urging her to write
up her articles into a pamphlet for distribution by hand. "You go ahead and
finish your writing," she quotes him as saying, "and I'll get the dinner and
wash the dishes." This he would then do "drawing the shades so no one
would see him." The children were not so cooperative. She describes her sons
hating to come home and find her writing. But a sense of mission had begun to
inspire her and she began trying to find out all she could about every form of
contraception available. Her quest took her to various libraries, where she
missed a lot of valuable information apparently through not knowing how to
look for it, and to talk with Socialists like Bill Haywood who had a great interest in the subject of limiting families through judicious use of contraception.
Emma Goldman, whom Margaret also met, had already included the subject in
her lectures. But as she went about her enquiries, interrupted by helping to organize picket lines during the Paterson silk-workers' strike of February 1913,
Margaret began to doubt whether even those advocating contraception were
doing so for the reasons which inspired her. Were any of them really thinking

about the women, or were they just influenced by political and economic considerations? "I was enough of a feminist," she wrote, "to resent the fact that woman and her requirements were not being taken into account in reconstructing this new world about which all were talking. They were failing to consider the quality of life itself." This, she became convinced, was for women intimately bound up with being able not only to *choose* to have babies but also to enjoy the act which produced them. But where was the simple, safe contraceptive which even an illiterate woman could use? She might find it, Bill Haywood said, in France.

There was really no sense in going to France in person (and perhaps no real need at all if only Margaret could have tapped existing American sources) but both the Sangers became wildly enthusiastic about such a venture . . . They ended up on the Left Bank in Paris. Bill immediately plunged himself into the art world, where he met **Matisse** and was "aglow" with pleasure, while Margaret followed up Bill Haywood's introductions to people who would help her find out about contraception. What she discovered was that although there was no actual movement there was a large body of individual knowledge about family limitation in existence. "I went into shops and bookstalls," she wrote, "and purchased all the devices of contraception available." She was shown pamphlets which were in circulation and talked to women who possessed "recipes" for suppositories passed down from generation to generation. It amazed her that in a Catholic country it should prove easier to learn about contraception for women than in New York, where the Comstock Law had made the circulation of information impossible.

When the three-month trip was at an end it was Margaret and not Bill Sanger who was ready to go home. She was full of enthusiasm for her cause, eager to return to New York with samples of all kinds of contraceptives and ready to put into practice what she had learned. Beside the thought of this mission the fun of being in Paris was nothing. But Bill did not agree. He loved Paris, felt he was making progress as an artist, and had no desire at all to return. Far from causing conflict in the Sanger marriage this difference of opinion was faced by both Bill and Margaret with equanimity. He would stay, she would go. In fact, Margaret was glad to go back just with the children. She wanted a return to America "to stir up a national campaign" and Bill would just get in the way. But of course there was more to it than that. After 12 years of marriage Margaret was beginning once more to view the institution as "a kind of suicide." She felt stifled by being married. Although Bill was the most understanding and accommodating of husbands she still wanted to be on her own and free of the emotional obligation under which he placed her. Nobody mentioned the phrase "trial separation" but it is clear Margaret thought that was what she was embarking on when in December 1913 she sailed for home.

As soon as she arrived she rented an apartment in upper Manhattan and set about planning the production of her own newspaper in order to spread contraceptive advice. At once she came up against those laws with which she was already familiar, the Comstock laws. These proved far more all-embracing and obstructive than she had ever realized, especially since Anthony Comstock himself was still in office as special inspector of the Post Office. He had been responsible personally for 700 arrests, 333 sentences, and the seizure of 34,836 articles classed as "for immoral use." Margaret raged against him—"his stunted, neurotic nature and savage methods of attack had ruined thousands of women's lives"—but she was not quite so silly as to doubt that any direct challenge to Comstock would invite certain prosecution and probable imprisonment.

For a while, she cast about trying to find ways of getting round the Comstock laws, as many had done before her, and seeking help for her general mission. Naturally, she approached influential feminists, among them Charlotte Perkins Gilman. They advised her (so she said) to join them in helping to win the vote and then all would be well—women would vote for the right to information on contraception. Margaret did not believe them, nor did she have any intention of waiting until the millennium dawned. It made her angry that the avowed feminists were not giving priority to the release of woman from her biological subservience which in her opinion was a far greater obstacle to progress than not having the vote. The Socialists were of more use to her (and of course a great many of them were also feminists) because they gave her hints on how to set about publishing a clandestine newspaper, which they had great experience in doing. But Margaret was determined to accept only advice from her political friends and nothing more: Her newspaper would not be part of any general political propaganda but specifically feminist in purpose. She said she wished to make it "as red and flaming as possible" in order to bring to everyone's notice the problems affecting women.

She called her newspaper *The Woman Rebel.* The first issue, on eight pages of cheap paper, came out in March 1914 and was a very serious-looking publication. Bill Sanger had sent over some cartoons to enliven the pages but Margaret scorned them—she *was* serious and was not going to dress up what she had to offer. The whole tone of her paper was strident and belligerent, full of startling statements like "The marriage bed is the most degenerating influence of the social order." It was sent by mail to a list of 2,000 subscribers obtained from Socialist friends. There was no precise contraceptive advice given but it was made clear that contraception was approved of and known about. Meanwhile, Margaret was working hard to provide this very information. A pamphlet she was writing called *Family Limitation* was going to be absolutely explicit.

Family Limitation was written in plain, strong, fearless language. It was outspokenly feminist, stating women's right to enjoy sex as much as men and even asserting that if they did not it was usually because men were "clumsy fools." It tried to rouse women to help themselves, speaking scornfully of women who were lazy or sentimental—"of course it is troublesome to get up to douche, it is also a nuisance to have to trouble about the date of the menstrual period . . . it seems inartistic and sordid to insert a **pessary** or a suppository . . . but it is far more sordid to find yourself several years later burdened down with half-a-dozen unwanted children . . . yourself a dragged out shadow of a woman . . ." What to do to prevent yourself becoming a shadow was starkly set out. The importance of keeping a calendar of monthly periods was stressed, the existence of any "safe" period emphatically denied, *coitus interruptus* condemned as well as all douches labeled as cleansing but no preventative in themselves. Advice on condoms was thorough (what they were made of, which were best, where to buy them, how to make sure they were used properly) but the real emphasis was on female contraceptives.

Crude, and rather alarming, diagrams (Marie Stopes found them "prurient") illustrated how to use a pessary and fears about the use of it were banished—it was "silly" to think this object might "go up too far" and mysteriously get lost—"It cannot get into the womb nor can it get lost." Nor was there any need to worry about it spoiling a man's pleasure (though the pamphlet made it quite clear what it thought on *that* subject). Sponges, if used with the right chemical solution, were recommended and if all else failed suppositories were better than nothing. A recipe was given for a vaginal suppository for those quite unable to get them—"take 1 ounce of cocoa butter, 60 grains quinine, melt the cocoa butter, mix the quinine with it, form it into suppositories by letting the mixture harden into a cake and then cutting it up into ten pieces—insert one into the vagina 3 minutes before the act." An address was given for mail-order goods in case anybody lived far from a chemist. At the end of the pamphlet 14 of the most common queries about contraception were printed (e.g., "Does nursing a baby prevent pregnancy?") and dealt with. Women were urged to tell other women how to avoid pregnancy—"spread this important knowledge!"—and to help the movement towards birth control (a term she had coined and now used for the first time) which it was prophesied "will shortly win full acceptance and sanction by public morality as well."

Naturally, once Margaret finished her pamphlet she then found it difficult to get it printed. She touted it round various Socialist printers, who all "turned deadly pale" and told her the risks were too great, until she found Russian-born Bill Shatoff who was prepared to do the job on his own after hours so that it could be kept completely secret and nobody else would risk imprisonment. But, as soon as the printing of 100,000 copies had been arranged in the summer of 1914, events began to move too fast. Within days of the first issue of *Woman Rebel* coming out in March letters started to arrive asking for specific information, but by that time the Post Office had sent word to say the newspaper was breaking the Comstock Law. Margaret ignored the communication and went ahead with the April issue. There were no objections to that one. In May, July, August, other issues appeared and then at the end of August Margaret received a visit from two officials. They told her the last three issues broke the law on nine counts. They refused to say how but announced they had orders to arrest her. She received the news calmly, but was instantly aware that she must move very fast to exploit her arrest as much as possible.

Margaret was told she would have plenty of time to prepare her case but in October she was "suddenly informed" that it would be in two days' time. Considering she had had six weeks since August 25th when she was told a trial would take place she was perhaps unreasonable to find this "sudden" but she seems to have been genuinely startled. In any case, although thrilled at the thought of hearing the words "The People vs. Margaret Sanger," and longing to stand up to open court and proclaim her beliefs, she had no intention of going to battle over the *Woman Rebel*. She wanted to do so over *Family Limitation*. It seemed to her foolish to risk losing the chance to fight over this much more important document so she decided to take the drastic step of leaving the country, having *Family Limitation* released as soon as she was safely away, then returning after an interval with a case prepared specifically on the birth control issue. In one way, this made obvious sense, but it was fraught with problems. The most important one was the fate of her children. Stuart, then 10, was at camp and could stay there until he returned to his boarding school where he had been for some years but Grant was only five and Peggy three. . .

What Margaret then decided to do is very difficult to understand. Grant and Peggy were sent on holiday to the Catskills with a friend and extremely precarious arrangements made for their return . . . She seems to have convinced herself that she had made the "supreme sacrifice" a mother could make. She claimed to be "passionately maternal" and yet thought sending children away, to school or anywhere else, "the most unselfish act . . . because it shows a selfless consideration for the child's good rather than an egoistic self-indulgence in sentimentality." Any consideration for her own children's good seems nevertheless to have been entirely lacking when she decided, the day before she was due to appear in court, to take the train for Montreal. This can either be seen as heroic or as incomprehensible but either way it puts Margaret Sanger's attitude to motherhood in a different category from most women's.

In Montreal, Margaret was put up by some friends until a place was found for her on the RMS *Virginian*, sailing for Liverpool on November 1st, 1914. She selected the pseudonym "Bertha Watson," which she said was a name so "atrociously ugly" that it robbed her of her femininity every time she answered to it. Unable to produce a passport she had no idea how she would get herself into England, especially in wartime conditions, but she says she made friends with an official on board who managed to arrange her entry. She stayed in Liverpool for a few "dreadful bleak weeks" suddenly feeling not quite so brave and noble and miserably conscious that her children, especially Peggy whom she had left with a sore leg, might be missing her as much as she was missing them. Then she went to London where she rented a room in Torrington Square. From there, she went every day to the British Museum to do research on birth control methods.

She was not friendless, arriving in London with several useful introductions to leading exponents of birth control in England. The Drysdales asked her to tea and through them she received an invitation to visit **Havelock Ellis** whose books she had just read and admired. She took a bus to Dover Mansions in Brixton and had tea and toast with him in front of the fire. Afterwards, they met in the British Museum where Ellis showed himself keen to direct the studies of this young and attractive student. Very soon they were close friends, though never lovers technically if Ellis is to be relied upon. "On me this first meeting simply left a pleasant impression," he wrote, "aided by sympathy with her lonely situation in a strange city," and after the second he found himself brought into "a relationship of friendship, I may say of affectionate friendship . . ." Within two weeks they were on kissing terms which for Ellis, says his biographer, counted as "near rape by anyone else." Even if, as Ellis maintained, the friendship with Margaret merely had a touch of "sweet intimacy" about it he records himself, after a kiss on New Year's Eve, as "like a drunken man . . . all of a rapture . . . I was aching and beaten and sore." Perhaps in kissing as in all else Margaret Sanger was a powerful lady. But for her part, although pleased with Ellis's attention, she was hardly swept off her feet. Her relationship with her husband she now regarded as finished and was about to write him "an epoch making letter" telling him so. Starting another such relationship was no part of her plan. She had work to do.

It was Ellis who suggested to her a visit to Holland where, he had been told, birth control clinics were in existence teaching the use of the comparatively newly invented diaphragm. England was of course at war and the idea of going to Holland a dangerous one but Margaret set off in January 1915 with introductions to Dr. Rutgers of The Hague. Dr. Rutgers was elderly and harassed and his English was poor but he was very welcoming. He took Margaret to his clinic, showed her the Mensinga diaphragm and demonstrated with several of his patients how to use it . . . The diaphragm was *not* a cervical cap of the type Margaret Sanger and others had publicized but a much simpler and more efficient cap which fitted longitudinally in the vagina, secured by the pubic bone. It amounted to the greatest advance since the condom and had the additional advantage of being for women. At his clinic Dr. Rutgers showed his fascinated visitors 14 different sizes of the German diaphragm which, since its use in Holland, had become known as the Dutch cap, and he emphasized that accurate fitting was vital. It was, he stressed, a medical matter and decidedly not something women could do for themselves although once fitted and taught they could certainly manage to use it much more easily than a pessary. Margaret was at first disappointed. Her vision had been of women taking matters into their own hands and helping each other until a chain of self-help existed everywhere. But she accepted Dr. Rutgers's verdict quickly and turned to examining how his clinics worked.

A network of birth control clinics was already in existence in Holland under the direction of Dr. Aletta Jacobs, a great feminist as well as the country's first qualified woman doctor. Unfortunately, Dr. Jacobs was not as friendly or helpful as Dr. Rutgers. She was deeply suspicious of this young, nonmedical American woman and refused either to meet her or to take her round her clinics. Brusquely, she said birth control was not a matter for laypeople. Offended and annoyed, Margaret had to make do with visiting other doctors. She also discovered that, in spite of the insistence by them that this was a medical matter, women could actually go into shops throughout Holland and be fitted up. She went into several herself and found ". . . there was a small, adjoining room, containing a reclining chair and a wash basin. The woman, if she so desired, was taken into this room, examined, and fitted by the shop attendant." It seemed to her that this being so there must be room for some sort of compromise. Nurses, for example, like herself, were surely medical—perhaps it would be possible to run clinics with specially trained nurses in charge. What she wanted was a system whereby women went to places specifically designed for this one purpose and where they would find other women specifically catering for this purpose without doctors necessarily being in control as Dr. Jacobs insisted they must be. Beside that, pamphlets paled into insignificance. What she wanted to do now was return to New York, face her trial, then put her energies into opening clinics . . . For a while, she hesitated. In her autobiography she goes over the alternatives: Should she bring Grant and Peggy over to join her, leaving Stuart at school, and take them to Paris to write a book? But that was as risky as returning herself. Which risk ought she to take?

While all this agonizing was going on Bill Sanger, back in New York, had been arrested by Comstock's agents for possessing one of Margaret's *Family Limitation* pamphlets. He wrote telling her what had happened and assuring her that he was proud to be standing trial for her sake. Offered a free pardon by Comstock if he revealed where his wife was Bill boasted that he had replied he would "Let hell freeze over first." If he expected Margaret to be impressed or touched he was greatly mistaken. She was extremely angry, commenting "Bill had to get mixed up in my work after all and of course it made it harder for me." She saw his stand as showing off and an attempt to ingratiate himself with her. But at least it brought her to a rapid decision: She must return at once before Bill grabbed any more of the limelight. In September 1915 she sailed, via Bordeaux, through the torpedo-threatened Atlantic to New York, arriving safely only to find Bill had already been released after serving a nominal jail sentence and that, ironically, his trial had been the occasion of Anthony Comstock catching a chill which had killed him. She also found that in other ways the birth control scene had significantly changed. Other people were now interested and trying to take control of a movement she had regarded as hers to head and lead. One of these "other people" was **Mary Ware Dennet** who infuriated Margaret by explaining that she envisaged, now that Comstock was dead, an orderly campaign staying strictly within the law aimed at repealing those statutes blocking the advance of birth control. This Margaret rejected. What *she* wanted was direct action, challenging the law flamboyantly, and starting with her own deferred court case for which she desired maximum publicity. As far as she was concerned ". . . the whole issue is not one of a mistake, whereby getting into jail or keeping out of jail is important, but the issue is to raise . . . birth control out of the gutter of obscenity and into the light of understanding." To attract even more "light" she intended to conduct her own defense at her trial.

Before this was to take place, Margaret Sanger had a trial of a different sort to go through. On November 6th, 1915, five-year-old Peggy died of pneumonia. Margaret was never able to write about it, as Josephine Butler later managed to, nor was this normally expressive woman able to express her grief. "The joy in the fullness of life went out of it on that morning," she wrote, "and has never returned." As well as grief there was also guilt to confront—guilt that of Peggy's short life she had robbed herself of almost a quarter by leaving her to go to England and that during the remainder she had very often indeed put her second to work. But there was no breakdown. The horror of Peggy's death seemed to freeze all emotion in her. Her only way of dealing with it was to block it out by redoubling her efforts for the birth control cause. She longed passionately for her trial to begin and was bitterly upset when told that instead the case against her was to be dropped. She *needed* that trial, needed to make it the focus of her damaged life, needed to stand up and show she had left Peggy for something that mattered. But pressure had been brought to bear upon the government to prevent it making a fool of itself. As George Bernard Shaw put it, "Comstockery is a world joke at the expense of the U.S." and the laughter was growing uncomfortably loud. The New York *Sun* commented accurately, "The Sanger case presents the anomaly of a prosecutor loath to prosecute and a defendant anxious to be tried." But on February 18th, 1916, the government finally entered a *nolle prosequi.*

Margaret's immediate reaction was to go off on a speaking tour for three months. She made the same speech 119 times, first practicing it from the roof of her hotel in Lexington Avenue. In it, she went over seven sets of circumstances in which birth control should be used, including the first two years of any young couple's marriage "to give them a chance to grow together." She began in New Rochelle by reading her speech but by Pittsburgh she had memorized it and become less nervous. She presented a curious spectacle wherever she went because of her apparent fragility. For a while, conscious that she might not look "serious," she wore "severe suits" but soon gave up because they made her feel constrained and uncomfortable. In any case, she quickly realized that there was in fact an advantage in looking frail and feminine—it made audiences protective and that was an asset . . . Wherever she went she was a great success. People packed the halls in which she spoke and supporters marched the streets with banners proclaiming such slogans as "Poverty and large families go hand-in-hand." The atmosphere everywhere on this issue was highly charged and Margaret delighted in inflaming passions. She wrote that "my flaming Feminist speeches . . . scared some . . . out of their wits." When the opposition took action by arresting her or locking her out of halls she was pleased and said, "I see immense advantages in being gagged. It silences me but it makes millions of others talk about me and the cause in which I live."

But Margaret Sanger's avowed purpose in returning to America had been to open clinics and once her tour was over she began to consider how and where she could start. She had already been quoted in [the] *Tribune* as saying, "I have the word of four prominent physicians that they will support me in the work . . . There will be nurses in attendance at the clinic and doctors who will instruct women in the things they need to know. All married women, or women about to be married, will be assisted free and without question." As she herself added, "A splendid promise but difficult to fulfill." For a start, which "prominent physician" when it came to the bit would put his professional head on the legal block? The answer, as she found, was not one of them. Carefully, she went over and over the two sections of the 1873 Comstock Law, under which she would be prosecuted if she opened a clinic, looking for a loophole. Section 1142, the one most often cited, said *no one* could give information to prevent conception to *anyone* for *any* reason, but Section 1145 did say that doctors could give advice "to cure or prevent" sexual diseases. This had been squeezed in to cover venereal disease but Margaret saw how it might be used if the prevention of disease was interpreted as covering lives endangered through too many pregnancies. But she did not, of course, really imagine that such a specious line of argument would be accepted. Obviously, as soon as she opened a clinic it would be closed and she would then face arrest and trial. She knew this, and accepted her fate not just with resignation but with positive relish.

This decided, she set about finding premises and helpers. "I preferred a Jewish landlord," she wrote later, "and a Mr. Rabinowitz was the answer." The point of him being Jewish was that she had the idea Rabinowitz lived in Brownsville, a poor but perfectly respectable immigrant district of New York. "He was willing to let us have No. 46, Amboy St. at $50 a month, a reduction from the regular rent because he realized what we were trying to do." He spent hours cleaning the rooms they were going to use and even insisted on white-washing the walls so that the atmosphere would be "more hospital looking."

•••••

On the morning the clinic was due to open, October 16th, 1916, there was a long queue outside—"halfway to the corner they were standing in line, at least 150, some shawled, some hatless, their red hands clasping the cold, chapped, smaller ones of their children." It was a pathetic and moving sight. By seven in the evening, they were still arriving, standing patiently and hopefully in line, many of them accompanied by men. It was impossible to see them all. When the doors were regretfully closed at the end of that first exhausting day a hundred women had been seen—but not one by a doctor. Margaret had failed to recruit a single qualified doctor. She had to run the clinic herself with the help of her sister Ethel, also a nurse. Another friend, Fania Mindell, helped by keeping the records and looking after the children while Ethel and Margaret lectured batches of 7 to 10 women each, in separate rooms, on contraception in general. It had not escaped Margaret's notice that in Holland no records were kept. She had rightly concluded that if there had been records, which could be collated and published, they might be of great value for research purposes and so she was determined from the beginning to adopt this businesslike approach—it was all part of her greater design and indicated the scope of her ambition. She knew quite well that her Brownsville clinic would in itself be insignificant but that was not the point. The point was to make a positive beginning from which all else would flow.

And it did, remarkably rapidly. The clinic was only open nine days, packed to bursting all the time, before it was raided in a gratifyingly spectacular fashion. Black Marias, screeching sirens, fully armed policemen, and all to herd three perfectly willing women to the local police station. If the authorities had been trying to attract sympathy for Margaret Sanger and publicity for her cause they could not have managed it better. By the time the first case was called, against Ethel, a committee of a hundred prominent women had been formed to work for the reform of the Comstock Law. On the day of Ethel's trial, 50 of them took Margaret to breakfast at the Vanderbilt Hotel before proceeding with her to the courtroom. Ethel, sentenced under Section 1142, as expected, was given 30 days' imprisonment. She went on hunger strike, refusing liquid as well as food. Margaret, still awaiting her own trial, was genuinely concerned for her sister's health but determined to exploit the situation, as indeed Ethel wished her to do. She kept Ethel's suffering in the public eye, in spite of attempts by the authorities first to keep it secret and then to play it down. By the time she herself went on trial, a month later, public opinion was widely alerted to what was going on. When she took the stand, she was impressive. Every allegation the prosecution made was fiercely contested, especially that of wishing "to do away" with Jewish people by preventing them breeding. Birth control, she said, was nothing to do with doing away of any sort, nor was it a way of making money as was also alleged. She itemized the cost of her clinic and invited those in court to do their own sums.

After half of the 50 Brownsville mothers who had attended the clinic had given evidence, Judge Freschi said, "I can't stand this any longer," and adjourned the court—he was overwhelmed by the endless recitation of miscarriages, illnesses, and childbirths. When it met again, a compromise was quickly offered: If Mrs. Sanger would promise to agree not to break the law again she would get a free pardon this time. She refused, standing up and saying, "I cannot respect the law as it stands today." She was sentenced to 30 days, like Ethel. This was more of a shock than she had thought. Whenever she had thought of going to prison she said she had somehow always imagined that at the last minute she would be saved—"I believed fully and firmly that some miracle would happen and that I should not go to jail." But no miracle happened, and she went to jail, quite amazed to find the indignities of which she had heard actually coming to pass. Even so, she was given preferential treatment (not, for example, being strip-searched) and knew she had an easy time compared to others. Nobody stopped her giving birth control talks to the other prisoners and she enjoyed herself. What she enjoyed even more was coming out to the strains of the Marseillaise being sung at the gates by a crowd of her friends. "No other experience in my life has been more thrilling," she wrote triumphantly.

Yet when she took stock of what opening a clinic and going to prison had gained her she was depressed to conclude very little indeed. She was particularly disappointed at the response from the women of New York whom she described as sitting "with folded hands" and keeping "aloof from the struggle for women's freedom." She had, she felt, sounded the call to action but "American women were not going to use direct action." The next few years, 1917 to 1921, were "leaden years." She had resolved, after prison, on a four-part campaign: agitation, education, organization, and legislation, but it was hard to be the driving force behind all four. Most of her energies went into launching a magazine again, the *Birth Control Review,* which she herself helped to sell on street corners. "Street selling was torture for me," she said, "but I sometimes did it for self-discipline and because only in this way could I have complete knowl-edge of what I was asking others to do." She soon found that selling the maga-zine was an unsatisfactory business anyway. Those who bought it were ag-grieved and disappointed when they found it contained no practical contraceptive advice. However hard she tried, it seemed impossible to give people what they undoubtedly wanted without promptly landing back in prison again and again. Not only did her work make her unhappy at this time but so did her personal life. She had been a woman on her own since her return in 1915. Her two sons were at boarding school, and she was lonely. She had al-ways thought she liked to be on her own but the reality of "not a cat, dog, or bird to greet this homecoming, the fire dead in the grate" was too much. Work was not, after all, enough. Her health was poor again in the winter of 1917–18 so she went to California, uprooting Grant and taking him with her for com-pany. There, she spent three months recuperating and writing a book.

The book was *Woman and the New Race,* finally published in 1920. In it, Margaret Sanger expounded with great fervour and passion her belief that the most important force in the remaking of the world was "a free motherhood." Legal and suffrage rights were utterly unimportant beside birth control be-cause "these don't affect the most vital factors of her existence." But "free motherhood" was not going to be given to women—she stressed repeatedly it was something they had to claim for themselves. Women had to stop accepting their inferior status. They had to realize they had power of their own because it was only through them that the future generations could be born. The "new women" so in vogue thought the ability to earn her own living a great victory and perhaps it was but "it is of little account beside the untramelled choice of mating or not mating." Only by using contraception could women make the most of this "untramelled choice." The "new woman" must look after herself and not be stupid enough to leave it to men. As for any idea that using birth control was immoral—that was absurd. All that was immoral was having un-wanted babies, or leading oneself to believe that governments were right to en-courage large families. This was "the most serious evil of our times" especially as the modern woman was not as suited as other generations to motherhood because of the tension of modern life . . .

When she returned from California (and put Grant back into school as quickly as she had snatched him out) she felt rejuvenated. She had also de-cided to try new tactics to get clinics opened. Aware that certain prominent medical men, such as Dr. Robert Dickinson (who was one of America's most eminent gynecologists), were beginning to feel uneasy about their profession's attitude to birth control, Margaret Sanger decided to set about suggesting her movement could be put into the hands of doctors. In 1923 she opened a Clini-cal Research Bureau on Fifth Avenue in New York and then asked Dickinson if he and his newly formed Committee on Maternal Health (composed of New York obstetricians and gynecologists and privately financed) would like to take the bureau over and develop it. She herself, of course, would still control it but she would be more than happy to involve Dickinson and his colleagues in the running of it. If they wanted to, they could man it completely. For seven years of constant argument Dickinson tried to get doctors to do this but he failed. The stumbling block was always Mrs. Sanger herself. The doctors neither liked nor trusted her. They suspected her motives, doubted her competence, and feared her interference. Yet in spite of this setback, Margaret was more hopeful and buoyant than she had been since her imprisonment. She had failed to get any "doctors only" legislation through state legislatures and failed to get medical cooperation for her research bureau but everywhere she saw her movement making headway.

•••••

It seemed, in the twenties and thirties, that Margaret Sanger was everywhere, endlessly traveling and lecturing and preaching for her cause. Her personal life was also happier. In 1920 she had been quietly divorced from Bill Sanger for whom she still felt affection but nothing more. He irritated her, he was in the way. In the way of what she did not quite know, and when she got her official freedom she describes in her autobiography how she went through a period of slight panic during which she attempted to form closer relationships with her sons, then 17 and 12. Grant, the younger one, was easier for her to woo. He was always the more original and still young enough for her to dominate. In 1921 she once more took him out of school, against the advice of the headmaster who strenuously objected on the grounds that Grant's studies were continually interrupted to serve as his mother's companion, and took him with her to Japan. He was "a tall, dark, rather gawky youth," very affectionate and demonstrative. Margaret was extremely proud of him, referring to him as "Exhibit A." She was rather hurt when, during the last part of this Far Eastern tour, he announced he was fed up and wished he could get to see some decent tennis. She let him go home ahead of her but missed him dreadfully.

When she arrived home herself she amazed her friends by marrying again, in 1922. Noah Slee, her new husband, was a businessman 20 years older than she who had courted her with presents of filing cabinets and date stamps. Hearing that although she was a formidable career lady she was frivolous enough to enjoy dancing he had also taken 10 lessons at Arthur Murray's Dancing School so that he could partner her. Once again, Margaret succumbed to the prospect of a way of life put before her. Noah Slee was a rich widower. He was only too willing to put considerable amounts of money and his business organization at the service of birth control. So, at the age of 43, Margaret married him, on the understanding that she would not be tied down by the marriage . . .

The same year that she married Noah Slee, Margaret had also published another book—*The Pivot of Civilization*. In it she had a great deal to say about the importance of sex. "Woman," she wrote, "must elevate sex into another sphere." To do so, she must reject the present teaching that sex was merely a means of procreating children. This was "a superficial and shameful view of the sexual instinct." Birth control carried with it, she argued, "a thorough training in bodily cleanliness and physiology, and a definitive knowledge of

the physiology and function of sex." She attacked the Catholic church for saying birth control was "unnatural" when what was in fact unnatural was being
forced to thwart or subdue the sexual instinct. Mankind had gone forward to
"capture and control the forces of nature" and this should be a matter of re-
joicing. No longer need fear inhibit women—"women can attain freedom only
by concrete, definite knowledge of themselves, a knowledge based on biology,
physiology, and psychology." Using birth control was the means to all this,
she claimed. Margaret Sanger called this book her "head" book, full of reasoned argument she hoped, while her earlier one, *Woman and the New Race*,
was her "heart" book, full of passion and emotion. In fact, they were both similar, setting out the same arguments and only differing in the emphasis on sex
and in the examples she chose to illustrate her points. They both sold well and
established her more firmly as a figure on the international birth control scene.
But she was not a secure figure in her own country. From the day she founded
the American Birth Control League (in 1921) Margaret Sanger was involved in
internal power struggles and in 1928 she resigned as its president. She also
gave up the *Birth Control Review,* and Noah withdrew his financial support.
From then onwards, she confined herself to the research bureau and to a new
organization she set up, the National Committee on Federal Legislation for
Birth Control.

In 1937, the Committee on Contraception of the American Medical Association agreed that physicians now had the right to give contraceptive advice
and that the subject should be taught in medical schools. By then, the anticon-
traception laws had been side-stepped for nearly a decade anyway and the
birth control movement had become respectable. But Margaret Sanger saw this
victory as only the first official one of the many more needed. The next battle
was to get the government to make birth control a public health program.
"Birth control must seep down until it reaches the strata where the need is
greatest; until it has been democratized there can be no rest." A visit to India in
1936 had made her see the true evils of overpopulation and she was haunted
by the sight of the "unspeakable poverty . . . the poorest women of Bombay,
sober faced and dull looking . . . lived in the grubby and deadly 'chawls,' huts
of corrugated iron, no windows, no lights, no lamps, just three walls and
sometimes old pieces of rag or paper hung up in front in a pitiful attempt at
privacy." It made her determined not just to establish a whole, worldwide system of birth control clinics but to continue to seek a better, simpler, cheaper female contraceptive. The rest of her life remained devoted to this quest. From
her winter home in Tucson, Arizona, and her New York estate, Willow Lake in
Dutchess County, she sallied forth agitating for more money to spend on research and contributing a good share of her own from the inheritance Noah
left her on his death in 1943. It was her research bureau which financed Dr.
Ernst Graefenberg, pioneer of the IUD [intrauterine device], and began work
on hormonal contraceptives which led to the development of the Pill. In 1959,
Dr. Gregory Pincus inscribed the report on oral contraceptives: "To Margaret
Sanger with affectionate greetings—this product of her pioneering resolute-
ness." By then, she was living full-time in Arizona, on her own, feeling very

much out of contact with what was going on in the movement to which she had dedicated her life. "I would hesitate to go anywhere to speak on birth control these days," she said. There was no need to do so. By the time she died in 1966, it looked as though the Pill had solved the whole birth control problem, at least in the Western world, and with it many of the problems feminism had been unable to overcome.

●●●●●

LETTERS TO MARGARET SANGER

Although middle-class women dominated the leadership ranks of the campaign to distribute birth control information, the movement also drew support from working-class mothers. For many of the latter, reproductive control often meant the difference between destitution and making ends meet. As the letters below indicate, these women were deeply appreciative of Sanger's efforts.

●●●●●

I am the mother of four little ones, the oldest only six years old. They are all puny little things, and need so much care and I am not strong enough to care for them, although I try, as we are not able to hire help. The baby is five weeks old. I am so nervous and weak I can hardly stand, yet I have all the care of the children, cooking, washing to do. My husband is a hired man on a farm. His pay is $50.00 per month. What can we do for our children? We can't even dress them comfortably and feed them as they should be fed, although we try so hard. My man goes to work at six in the morning and comes back at seven in the evening so he can't help me any. He isn't strong, only weighs 125 pounds, while I weigh 100 pounds. It is an awful thing for us to bring more children, little weak things like ourselves, with no way to make a living only their two hands, into the world to be knocked and brow-beat all their lives. I cry and pray and be careful and it all does no good. I have one of your books and don't see why there isn't more people like you in this world. I am only 26 years old, my husband the same, so we have a long time yet ahead, although we both have lots of gray hair already, we are old at 26. What a burning shame when I think of how rearing children has brought us down from what we were. I can't see why I should be denied the information I ask for.

●●●●●

I am 35. In 17 years of married life have brought eight children into the world and went down in the grave after three I failed to get. We bought us a little home to start with and oh, the struggle! Have both worked like slaves, I with

Source: From Margaret Sanger, *Motherhood in Bondage.* Copyright © 1928. Reprinted by permission of Alexander C. Sanger, Executive of the Estate of Margaret Sanger.

my own efforts have kept the family in what we had to buy, have sold $300.00 worth of butter, eggs, and chickens. He raises what he can for us to eat and saves a little and in this way we have managed to pay for our little home, but have no conveniences whatever. Sometimes I've had only my husband to wait on me when the children came and in every instance have been on the job, slinging pots and pans when my baby was two weeks old and strange to say am still well. I have six children in school and two under my feet, am milking five cows, sell from 75 to 100 pounds of butter a month, fit a package for parcel post every day.

I have milked six cows at six o'clock and brought a baby into the world at nine.

My baby is nine months old and the thoughts of another almost kills me.

Oh! tell me how to keep from having another. Don't open the door of heaven to me and then shut it in my face.

Oh! please tell me, I feel like it's more important to raise what I have than to bring more.

QUESTIONS

1. In what ways, if any, did Sanger's childhood and adolescent experiences shape her later activities as a birth control reformer? What influence did working as a nurse have on Sanger's developing views about family limitation?
2. What did Sanger mean when she described marriage as "a kind of suicide"? How would you characterize her attitudes toward motherhood? Did her first husband help or hinder her work?
3. Why do you think someone like Anthony Comstock was able to acquire the power that he did? What does this suggest about popular attitudes toward women and sexuality during the late nineteenth and early twentieth centuries?
4. Why did Sanger have such a negative opinion of physicians? Why were doctors so reluctant to cooperate with her?
5. What advice do you think Sanger offered to working-class mothers who wrote to her? How would you have responded to these letters?
6. Why was Sanger so often at odds with most voting-rights feminists? Do you think Sanger's personality traits strengthened or weakened her campaign for birth control reform? In what ways did Sanger's achievements influence the development of the contemporary women's rights movement?

BIBLIOGRAPHY

The most recent biography of Sanger is Ellen Chesler, *Woman of Valor: Margaret Sanger and the Birth Control Movement in America* (1992), though readers also might consult *An Autobiography* (1938), in which the famous reformer relates her own story. All major examinations of the birth control movement provide additional information on Sanger. Three especially noteworthy works are Linda Gordon, *Woman's Body, Woman's Right: A Social History of Birth Control in America* (1977); James Reed, *From Private Vice to Public*

Virtue: The Birth Control Movement in America Since 1830 (1978); and David M. Kennedy, *Birth Control in America: The Career of Margaret Sanger* (1970). For a comprehensive historical overview of American attitudes toward sexuality, see John D'Emilio and Estelle Freedman, *Intimate Matters: A History of Sexuality in America* (1988). A more specialized study of the subject is G. J. Barker–Benfield, *Horrors of the Half-Known Life: Male Attitudes Toward Women and Sexuality in Nineteenth Century America* (1976), which focuses on the opinions and activities of physicians.

Eleanor Roosevelt

As the man who led the country through the Great Depression and World War II, Franklin D. Roosevelt (FDR) is one of the most esteemed figures in American political history. This was especially so among working people, one of whom remarked that FDR was "the first man in the White House to understand that my boss is a son of a bitch." Yet little in Roosevelt's background suggested that he would become a champion of the common man. Born into one of the nation's most famous families, he grew up on the family's vast estate in Hyde Park, New York. Mindful of his quasi-aristocratic origins, historians later referred to him as the Lord of the Manor and the Squire of Hyde Park.

How, then, did FDR manage to achieve such rapport with America's working masses? According to one interpretation, a major turning point occurred during the early 1920s when he was paralyzed with polio. Never able to walk again without support, Roosevelt struggled desperately to come to grips with this awful disease, so that he could resume his political career. It was during this period, some have suggested, that FDR developed those qualities that as president enabled him to win the love and admiration of the nation's dispossessed. This is all speculation, though there is no reason to doubt that Roosevelt's battle against polio made him better able to sympathize with the personal misfortune of others.

More certain is the influence that his wife Eleanor (ER) had on both FDR and his presidency.

Although she came from a background just as privileged as that of her husband, ER exhibited a lifelong concern with the plight of those less fortunate than herself. After FDR was stricken with polio, she also demonstrated a political acumen that made her indispensable to her ailing husband during this critical period of his career. By 1928, when FDR won election as governor of New York, ER had become a major player in state politics; and when FDR secured the presidency four years later, ER became a powerful national advocate for a broad range of liberal causes. She would remain so for the last three decades of her life.

In the public sphere, that life was one of enormous self-fulfillment. But in other areas, it contained a good deal of disappointment. Though ER and her husband functioned well together as political partners, their marital relationship often left much to be desired. In the essay that follows, William H. Chafe not only discusses her influence on Democratic party politics during the New Deal years and beyond; he also examines her efforts to compensate for a marriage that had lost much of its lustre while she was still a young woman. The result is a compelling portrait of a compassionate but tough-minded individual who never stopped believing that the world could be made a better place in which to live.

Eleanor Roosevelt

William H. Chafe

Anna Eleanor Roosevelt was born in New York City on October 11, 1884, the first child and only daughter of Elliott Roosevelt and Anna (Hall) Roosevelt. Descended on both sides from distinguished colonial families active in commerce, banking, and politics, she seemed destined to enjoy all the benefits of class and privilege. Yet by the time she was 10, both her parents had died, as had a younger brother Elliott, leaving her and her second brother Hall as the only survivors.

As a youngster, Eleanor experienced emotional rejection almost from the time she could remember. "I was a solemn child," she recalled, "without beauty. I seemed like a little old woman entirely lacking in the spontaneous joy and mirth of youth." Her mother called her "Granny" and, at least in Eleanor's memory, treated her daughter differently than her son, warmly embracing the boy while being only "kindly and indifferent" to her little girl. From most of her family, young Eleanor received the message that she was "very plain," almost ugly, and certainly "old fashioned." When her parents died, she went to live with her grandmother, who was equally without warmth. As Eleanor's cousin Corinne later remarked, "it was the grimmest childhood I had ever known. Who did she have? Nobody."

Source: From *Without Precedent: The Life and Career of Eleanor Roosevelt,* edited by Joan Hoff Wilson. Reprinted by permission of the publisher, Indiana University Press.

In fact, Eleanor had one person—her father. "He was the one great love of my life as a child," she later wrote, "and . . . like many children, I have lived a dream life with him." Described by his friends as "charming, impetuous, high-spirited, big-hearted, generous, [and] friendly," Elliott exhibited ease and grace in his social interactions. With Eleanor, he developed an intimacy that seemed almost magical. "As soon as I could talk," she recalled, "I went into his dressing room every morning and chattered to him . . . I even danced with him, intoxicated by the pure joy of motion . . . until he would pick me up and throw me into the air." She dreamed of the time when they would go off together—"always he and I . . . and someday [we] would have a life of our own together."

But Elliott's capacity for ebullient play and love also contained the seeds of self-destruction—alcoholism, irresponsibility, cruelty. He never found an anchor, either in public life or business, to provide stability for himself and his family. Elliott's emotional imbalance quickly produced problems in his marriage and banishment from the household. The last four years of his life were like a roller coaster. Elliott nourished the emotional relationship with Eleanor through letters to "father's own little Nell," writing of "the wonderful long rides . . . through the grand snow-clad forests, over the white hills" that he wanted them to enjoy together. But when his long-awaited visits occurred, they often ended in disaster, as when Elliott left Eleanor with the doorman at New York's Knickerbocker Club, promising to return but going off on a drunken spree instead. The pain of betrayal was exceeded only by Eleanor's depth of love for the man she believed was "the only person who really cared." Looking back later in life for an explanation of her inability to express emotions spontaneously, she concluded that the trauma of her childhood was the main cause. "Something locked me up," she wrote.

After her father's death, an emotional void pervaded Eleanor's life until, at age 14, she enrolled in Allenswood, a girls' school outside London presided over by Marie Souvestre, daughter of a well-known French philosopher and radical. At Allenswood, the girl found a circle of warmth and support. "She was beloved by everybody," her cousin remarked. "Saturdays we were allowed a sortie in Putney which has stores where you could buy books, [and] flowers. Young girls had crushes and you left [gifts] in the room with the girl you were idolizing. Eleanor's room every Saturday would be full of flowers because she was so admired." Allenswood also provided educational inspiration. Souvestre passion-

---

Dreyfus   French army officer of Jewish descent who was convicted of treason in 1894, sentenced to life imprisonment, and ultimately acquitted when the evidence against him was shown to have been forged.

Junior League   A voluntary organization in which members are engaged in volunteer charity or civic affairs.

anti-Tammany forces   Opponents of the often corrupt political machine of New York City.

je t'aime et je t'adore   I love and adore you.

ately embraced unpopular causes, staunchly defending **Dreyfus** in France and the cause of the Boers in South Africa. "I consider the three years which I spent with her as the beginning of an entirely new outlook on life," Eleanor wrote. Marie Souvestre toured the continent with the girl, confiding in her and expressing the affection that made it possible for Eleanor to flower. Describing her stay at Allenswood as "the happiest years of my life," Eleanor noted that "whatever I have become since had its seeds in those three years of contact with a liberal mind and strong personality." The love and admiration were mutual. "I miss you every day of my life," Souvestre wrote her in 1902.

The imprint of Marie Souvestre was not lost when Eleanor returned to the United States at age 17 to "come out" in New York society. Even in the rush of parties and dances, she kept her eye on the more serious world of ideas and social service. Souvestre had written her in 1901: "Even when success comes, as I'm sure it will, bear in mind that there are more quiet and enviable joys than to be among the most sought-after women at a ball." Heeding the injunction, Eleanor plunged into settlement-house work and social activism.

Much of Eleanor Roosevelt's subsequent political life can be traced to this early involvement with social reform. At age 18 she joined the National Consumers' League, headed by Florence Kelley. The league was committed to securing health and safety for workers—especially women—in clothing factories and sweatshops. On visits to these workplaces, Eleanor learned firsthand the misery of the working poor and developed a lifelong commitment to their needs. At the same time, she joined the **Junior League** and commenced work at the Rivington Street Settlement House, where she taught calisthenics and dancing and witnessed both the deprivation of the poor and the courage of slum dwellers who sought to improve their lot. Eleanor discovered that she preferred social work to debutante parties. More and more, she came to be recognized as a key member of a network of social reformers in New York City.

At the same time, however, Eleanor was secretly planning to marry her cousin Franklin Roosevelt, an event that would be followed by a a 15-year hiatus in her public activities. Like his godfather (Eleanor's father), Franklin was "a gay cavalier," spontaneous, warm, and gregarious. But unlike Elliott, Franklin also possessed good sense and singleness of purpose. Eleanor saw in him the spark of life that she remembered from her father. After their engagement, she even sent to Franklin a letter signed "little Nell," her father's favorite name for her. Franklin, in turn, saw in Eleanor the discipline that would curb his own instincts toward excess.

After their marriage on March 17, 1905, the young Roosevelts settled in New York City while Franklin finished his law studies at Columbia. Franklin's mother Sara had warned Eleanor that she should not continue her work at the settlement house because she might bring home the diseases of the slum, but soon Eleanor was preoccupied with other concerns. Within a year, Anna was born (1906), then the next year James (1907), and two years later Franklin. Although Eleanor cherished her children, it was not a happy time. Sara dominated the household and imposed her will on almost all issues, including the raising of the children. As Eleanor later recalled, her mother-in-law "wanted . . .

to hold onto Franklin and his children; she wanted them to grow up as she wished. As it turned out, Franklin's children were more my mother-in-law's children than they were mine." Nor was Sara's possessiveness limited to the children. At the family estate at Hyde Park, she was in total control. At dinner, Franklin sat at one end of the table, his mother at the other, and Eleanor in the middle. Before the fireplace there were two wing chairs, one for the mother, the other for the son. Eleanor was like an uninvited guest.

Fearing that she would hurt Franklin and lose his affection, Eleanor did not rebel. But she did experience a profound sense of inadequacy about her abilities as a wife and mother. Daughter Anna described her mother as unpredictable and inconsistent with the children, sweet one moment, critical and demanding the next. "Mother was always stiff, never relaxed enough to romp . . . Mother loved all mankind, but she did not know how to let her children love her." Eleanor herself recognized the problem. "It did not come naturally to me to understand little children or to enjoy them," she later said. "Playing with children was difficult for me because play had not been an important part of my own childhood." Instead of comforting the children when they experienced pain, she urged upon them an attitude of stoicism and endurance, as if to say that expressing emotion was a sign of bad character. The death of her third child, Franklin, a few months after his birth only reinforced Eleanor's unhappiness and feeling of inadequacy. Three additional children were born in the next six years—Elliott in 1910, Franklin in 1914, and John in 1916. Eleanor was devoted to each, yet motherhood could not be fulfilling in a household ruled by a grandmother who referred to the children as "my children . . . your mother only bore you."

In the years between 1910 and the beginning of World War I, Eleanor Roosevelt's activities revolved more and more around Franklin's growing political career. Elected as the Democratic assemblyman from Dutchess County in 1910, he rapidly became a leader of insurgent **anti-Tammany forces** in Albany. In 1913 Franklin was appointed assistant secretary of the Navy, and Eleanor, in addition to managing a large household, became expert at hosting the multiple social events required of a subcabinet member, as well as moving the entire household at least twice each year—to Campobello in New Brunswick during the summer, then to Hyde Park and back to Washington. During these years, she fulfilled the many traditionally female social activities expected of her.

America's entry into World War I in 1917 provided the occasion for Eleanor to reassert the public side of her personality. As her biographer Joseph Lash has noted, "the war gave her a reason acceptable to her conscience to free herself of the social duties that she hated, to concentrate less on her household, and to plunge into work that fitted her aptitude." She rose at 5 A.M. to coordinate activities at the Union Station canteen for soldiers on their way to training camps, took charge of Red Cross activities, supervised the knitting rooms at the Navy department, and spoke at patriotic rallies. Her interest in social welfare led to her drive to improve conditions at St. Elizabeth's mental hospital, while her sensitivity to suffering came forth in the visits she paid to wounded soldiers. "[My son] always loved to see you come in," one mother wrote. "You always brought a ray of sunshine."

The war served as a transition for Eleanor's reemergence as a public personality during the 1920s. After Franklin's unsuccessful campaign for the vice presidency on James Cox's ticket in 1920, the Roosevelts returned to New York where Eleanor became active in the League of Women Voters. At the time of her marriage, she had opposed suffrage, thinking it inconsistent with women's proper role; now, as coordinator of the league's legislative program, she kept track of bills that came before the Albany legislature, drafted laws providing for equal representation for men and women, and worked with Esther Lape and Elizabeth Read on the league's lobbying activities. In 1921 she also joined the Women's Trade Union League—then viewed as "left-leaning"—and found friends there as well as political allies. In addition to working for programs such as the regulation of maximum hours and minimum wages for women, Eleanor helped raise funds for the WTUL headquarters in New York City. Her warm ties to first- and second-generation immigrants like Rose Schneiderman and Maud Swartz highlighted how far Eleanor had moved from the upper-class provincialism of her early years.

When Franklin was paralyzed by polio in 1922, Eleanor's public life expanded still further: She now became her husband's personal representative in the political arena. With the aid of Louis Howe, Franklin's political mentor and her own close friend, Eleanor first mobilized Dutchess County women, then moved on to the state Democratic party, organizing all but five counties by 1924. "Organization," she noted, "is something to which [the men] are always ready to take off their hats." No one did the job better. Leading a delegation to the Democratic convention in 1924, she fought (unsuccessfully) for equal pay legislation, the child labor amendment, and other planks endorsed by women reformers.

By 1928, Eleanor Roosevelt had clearly become a political leader in her own right. Once just a "political wife," she gradually extended that role and used it as a vehicle for asserting her own personality and agenda. In 1928, as head of the national women's campaign for the Democratic party, she made sure that the party appealed to independent voters, to minorities, and to women. She was also instrumental in securing the appointment of Frances Perkins as commissioner of industrial relations in New York after Franklin had been elected governor there. Dictating as many as one hundred letters a day, speaking to countless groups, acting as an advocate of social reform and women's issues, she had become a political personality of the first rank.

Eleanor Roosevelt's talent for combining partisan political activity with devotion to social welfare causes made her the center of an ever-growing female reform network. Her associates included Marion Dickerman and Nancy Cook, former suffragists and Democratic party loyalists; Mary (Molly) Dewson, a longtime research secretary of the National Consumers' League; and Mary Dreier of the Women's Trade Union League. She walked on picket lines with Rose Schneiderman, edited the *Women's Democratic News,* and advised the League of Women Voters on political tactics. Her political sophistication grew. "To many women, and I am one of them," she noted, "it is difficult to care enough [about an issue] to cause disagreement or unpleasant feelings, but I have come to the conclusion that this must be done for a time so we can prove our strength and demand respect for our wishes." By standing up for women in politics, ER provided a model for others to follow. In the process, she also earned the admiring, if grudging, respect of men who recognized a superb organizer when they saw one.

During the 1932 campaign, which led to Franklin's election to the presidency, Eleanor coordinated the activities of the Women's Division of the Democratic National Committee. Working with Mary (Molly) W. Dewson, she mobilized thousands of women precinct workers to carry the party's program to local voters; for example, the women distributed hundreds of thousands of "rainbow fliers," colorful sheets containing facts on the party's approach to various issues. After the election, Mary (Molly) W. Dewson took charge of the Women's Division, corresponding daily with Eleanor both about appointing women to office and securing action on issues that would appeal to minorities, women, and such professional groups as educators and social workers. The two friends were instrumental in bringing to Washington an unprecedented number of dynamic women activists. Ellen Woodward, Hilda Worthington Smith, and Florence Kerr all held executive offices in the Works Progress Administration, while Lorena Hickok acted as eyes and ears for WPA Director Harry Hopkins as she traveled across the country to observe the impact of the New Deal's relief program. Mary Anderson, director of the Women's Bureau, recalled that women government officials had formerly dined together in a small university club. "Now," she said, "there are so many of them that we need a hall."

Eleanor Roosevelt not only provided the impetus for appointing these women but also offered a forum for transmitting their views and concerns across the country. Soon after she entered the White House, she began a series of regular press conferences to which *only* women reporters were admitted, and where the first lady insisted on making "hard" news as well as providing social tidbits for the "women's page." She introduced such women as Mary McLeod Bethune and Hilda Worthington Smith to talk about their work with the New Deal. These sessions provided new status and prestige for the female press corps and they also underlined the importance of women's issues to the first lady. Her efforts helped create a community of women reporters and government workers. When the all-male Gridiron Club held its annual dinner to spoof the president and his male colleagues, the first lady initiated a Gridiron Widows' Club where the women in Washington could engage in their own satire.

Largely as a result of ER's activities, women achieved a strong voice in the New Deal. The proportion of women appointed as postmasters shot up from 17.6 percent in 1930 to 26 percent between 1932 and 1938. More important, the social welfare policies of the administration reflected a reform perspective that women like Ellen Woodward and Florence Kerr shared with men like Harry Hopkins and Aubrey Williams. When a particularly difficult issue involving women came up, the first lady would invite Mary (Molly) Dewson to the White House and seat her next to the president, where she could persuade him of her point of view. ER's own political role appears most clearly in her work on the reelection drive of 1936, when she coordinated the efforts of both men and women and used the "educational" approach developed by the Women's Division in 1932 as a major campaign weapon. More than 60,000 women precinct workers canvassed the electorate, handing out "rainbow fliers" as the party's principal literature. For the first time women received equal representation on the Democratic Platform Committee, an event described by the *New York Times* as "the biggest coup for women in years."

Eleanor Roosevelt's fear that she would have no active role as a presidential wife had been unfounded. She toured the country repeatedly, surveying conditions in the coal mines, visiting relief projects, and speaking out for the human rights of the disadvantaged. Through her newspaper column, "My Day," she entered the homes of millions. Her radio programs, her lectures, and her writings communicated to the country her deep compassion for those who suffered. At the White House, in turn, she acted as advocate of the poor and disenfranchised. "No one who ever saw Eleanor Roosevelt sit down facing her husband," Rexford Tugwell wrote, "and holding his eyes firmly, [and saying] to him 'Franklin, I think you should' . . . or, 'Franklin surely you will not' . . . will ever forget the experience . . . It would be impossible to say how often and to what extent American governmental processes have been turned in a new direction because of her determination." She had become, in the words of columnist Raymond Clapper, a "cabinet minister without portfolio—the most influential woman of our times."

But if Eleanor had achieved an unparalleled measure of political influence, it was in place of, rather than because of, an intimate personal relationship with Franklin. In 1932 Eleanor described a perfect couple as one where two people did not even need to tell each other how they felt, but cared so much that a look and the sound of a voice would tell all. Probably at no time after their first few years together did Franklin and Eleanor achieve that degree of intimacy. Not only was Sara still a dominant presence, but Franklin had embarked on his own interests and enthusiasms, often different from Eleanor's. The differences in their temperaments became a permanent barrier that tormented their relationship. He loved to party; she held back and frowned on his willingness to "let go" . . .

During the years he was assistant secretary of the Navy, Franklin acted more frequently on his fun-loving instincts. "He deserved a good time," Eleanor's cousin Alice Roosevelt acidly noted, "he was married to Eleanor." A frequent companion on Franklin's pleasurable excursions was Lucy Mercer, Eleanor's social secretary. Over time, the relationship between Lucy and Franklin became intimate, particularly during the summers when Eleanor was absent at Campobello. After Franklin was stricken with pneumonia in the fall of 1918, Eleanor discovered the letters between Franklin and Lucy describing their affair. Although Franklin refused Eleanor's offer of divorce, and Sara engineered an agreement for them to stay together if Franklin stopped seeing Lucy, their marriage would never again achieve the magical possibility of being "for life, for death," one where a word or look would communicate everything. In the wake of the Mercer affair, James Roosevelt later wrote, his parents "agreed to go on for the sake of appearances, the children and the future, but as business partners, not as husband and wife . . . After that, father and mother had an armed truce that endured until the day he died."

In the eyes of some, Eleanor Roosevelt's emergence as a public figure seemed a direct consequence of profound anger at her husband's betrayal. Yet Eleanor's activism predated her discovery of the Mercer affair. World War I provided the occasion for expressing long-suppressed talents and energies that could be traced back to her early involvement with the National Consumers' League and the settlement house and were rooted, ultimately, in her relationship with Marie Souvestre. The Lucy Mercer affair, like Franklin's polio, reinforced the move toward public self-assertion, but did not itself cause a transformation.

What the Mercer affair did cause was a gradual reallocation of emotional energy away from Franklin and toward others. Through the polio episode and afterward, Eleanor remained devoted to Franklin's care and career. During the 1920s a warmth of tone and feeling continued in her letters to and about him. Yet gradually their lives became separate. Franklin went off on his houseboat in Florida or to Warm Springs, Georgia, with his secretary Missy LeHand. Eleanor stayed away, as if intentionally ceding to others any emotional involvement with her husband . . .

Increasingly, Eleanor appeared to draw on her own family experience when offering advice to others. When a woman wrote her in 1930 about a marital problem, Eleanor replied: "All men who make successes of their work go through exactly the same kind of thing which you describe, and their wives, one way or another, have to adjust themselves. If it is possible to enter into his work in some way, that is the ideal solution. If not, they must develop something of their own and if possible make it such a success they will have something to interest their husbands." In a poignant piece entitled "On Being Forty-five," which she wrote for *Vogue* in 1930, Eleanor elaborated

> Life is a school in which we live all our days, and by middle-age, we should know that happiness . . . is never ours by right, but we earn it through giving of ourselves. You must have learned self-control. No matter how much you care, how much you may feel that if you knew certain things you could help, you must not ask questions or offer help, you must wait until the confidence is freely given, and you must learn to love without criticism . . . If you have learned these things by 45, if you have ceased to consider yourself as in any-way important, but understand well the place that must be filled in the family, the role will be easy.

Above all, Eleanor concluded, the 45-year-old woman must

> keep an open and speculative mind . . . and [then] she will be ready to go out and try new adventures, create new work for others as well as herself, and strike deep roots in some community where her presence will make a difference in the lives of others . . . One can no longer be interested in one's self, but one is thereby freed for greater interest in others and the lives of others become as engrossing as a fairy story of our childhood days.

Taking her own advice, Eleanor increasingly transferred the emotional focus of her life away from Franklin. The political network of women reformers of which she was the center provided intimate friendship as well as political camaraderie. During the 1920s she spent one night a week with Esther Lape and Elizabeth Read, reading books together and talking about common interests. She also became close friends with Women's Trade Union League women like Rose Schneiderman, inviting them to Hyde Park for picnics. Mary (Molly) Dewson became an especially close friend, and Eleanor wrote in 1932 that "the nicest thing about politics is lunching with you on Mondays." In a revealing comment made in 1927, Eleanor observed that "more than anything else, politics may serve to guard against the emptiness and loneliness that enter some women's lives after their children have grown."

Many of Eleanor's friendships during the 1920s and 1930s were with women who lived with other women. She had become particularly close to Nancy Cook and Marion Dickerman, who lived together in New York City. In 1926 she moved with them into Val-Kill, a newly constructed cottage at Hyde Park, an event that accurately symbolized her growing detachment from Franklin and his mother. Although she returned to the "Big House" at Hyde Park when Franklin was present, it was never without resentment and regret. She and Dickerman purchased Todhundter, a private school in New York, where Eleanor taught three days a week even after Franklin was elected governor of New York. The three women also jointly managed a furniture crafts factory at Val-Kill. The linen and towels at Val-Kill were monogrammed "EMN," and the three women together constituted as much a "family" for Eleanor during those years as Franklin and her children.

There were always "special" relationships, however, and during the 1930s these acquired an intensity and depth that were new to Eleanor's life. One of these was with her daughter Anna and Anna's new love, John Boettiger, a reporter whom Anna had met during the 1932 presidential campaign. Eleanor shared a special bond with her daughter, different from the one she had with her sons. Although the two women had had a difficult relationship during Anna's adolescence and early adulthood, caused partly by Anna's resentment of her mother's "distance" and preference for other, competing personalities like Louis Howe, the two women rekindled their affection during Anna's romance with John. Eleanor seemed to be reliving her early days with Franklin by investing enormous energy and love in Anna and wanting her daughter to find the kind of happiness she felt she had lost forever with her own husband . . .

Perhaps Eleanor's most carefree relationship during these years occurred with Earl Miller, a former state trooper who had been Governor Al Smith's bodyguard and who subsequently provided the same service to the Roosevelt family. He encouraged Eleanor to drive her own car, take up horseback riding again, and develop confidence in her own personality. He was strikingly different from her other friends—tall, handsome, a "man's man." Although they talked about ideas and politics, the relationship was more that of "boon companions." With Earl Miller, Eleanor found a way to escape the pressures of her political and social status. She went frequently to his home for visits, had him stay at Val-Kill or her New York apartment, and accompanied him whenever possible for long walks and late-evening suppers. Although some of her friends disliked his tendency to "manhandle" Eleanor, all understood the importance of the relationship, and Marion Dickerman even said that "Eleanor played with the idea of marriage with Earl." Miller himself denied that the subject had ever been raised. "You don't sleep with someone you call Mrs. Roosevelt," he said. But without question, the two had an extraordinarily close relationship, and James Roosevelt later observed that his mother's tie to Miller "may have been the one real romance in [her] life outside of marriage . . . She seemed to draw strength from him when he was by her side, and she came to rely on him . . . Above all, he made her feel like she was a woman."

It was Eleanor Roosevelt's relationship with Lorena Hickok, however, that proved most intense during the 1930s and that subsequently has caused the most controversy. The two women became close during the 1932 campaign, when Hickok was covering the prospective first lady in her role as a reporter for the Associated Press. "That woman is unhappy about something," Hickok noted. Eleanor had not wanted Franklin to become president and feared that life in the White House would destroy her independence and cast her in an empty role as hostess and figurehead. As the two women talked about their respective lives, they developed an intimacy and affection so close that Hickok felt compelled to resign her position as a reporter because she no longer could write "objectively" about the Roosevelts.

Within a short time, the two women were exchanging daily letters and phone calls, the contents of which suggested that each woman was deeply infatuated with the other. "Hick darling," Eleanor wrote on March 6, "how good it was to hear your voice. It was so inadequate to try to tell you what it meant. Jimmy was near and I could not say, **je t'aime et je t'adore** as I long to do but always remember I am saying it and I go to sleep thinking of you and repeating our little saying." The next night, Eleanor was writing again. "All day," she said, "I thought of you, and another birthday I *will* be with you and yet tonight you sounded so far away and formal. Oh! I want to put my arms around you. I ache to hold you close. Your ring is a great comfort. I look at it and think she does love me, or I wouldn't be wearing it!" The two women plotted ways to be together, to steal a few days in the country, to bridge the gap of physical separation that so often stood between them.

> Only eight more days [Hickok wrote]. Twenty-four hours from now it will be only seven more—just a week! I've been trying today to bring back your face—to remember just *how* you looked . . . Most clearly I remember your eyes, with the kind of teasing smile in them, and the feeling of that soft spot just northeast of the corner of your mouth against my lips. I wonder what we will do when we meet—what we will say when we meet. Well—I'm rather proud of us, aren't you? I think we have done rather well.

Over time, the relationship cooled somewhat under the pressure of Hickok's demands on Eleanor's time and Eleanor's reluctance to give herself totally to her new friend. Hickok was jealous of Eleanor's other friends, even her children. "Darling," Eleanor wrote, "the love one has for one's children is different, and not even Anna could be to me what you are." From Eleanor's point of view, the two were like a married couple whose relationship had to "flower." "Dearest," she wrote, "strong relationships have to grow deep roots. We are growing them now, partly because we are separated. The foliage and the flowers will come somehow, I'm sure of it . . ." But an impatient Hickok was jealous of Eleanor's other friends and unable to limit the ardor of her affection.

In time, the situation became too much for Eleanor. In an attempt to explain herself to Hickok, she wrote: "I know you often have a feeling for me which for one reason or another I may not return in kind, but I feel I love you just the same and so often we entirely satisfy each other that I feel there is a fundamental basis on which our relationship stands." "Hick" had to understand, Eleanor wrote, "that I love other people the same way or differently, but each one has their place and one cannot compare them." But in the end, Eleanor could not explain herself sufficiently to satisfy Hickok and concluded that she had failed her friend . . .

Many observers have speculated on the sexual significance of Roosevelt's relationship with Hickok. Hickok herself appears to have had numerous lesbian involvements, and the intimacy of her correspondence with Roosevelt has suggested to some that the love the two women shared must, inevitably, have had a sexual component as well. Many of Eleanor's other women friends lived together in what were called, at the time, "Boston marriages," and some of these associates undoubtedly found fulfillment through sexual relationships with other women. In all likelihood, Marie Souvestre was one of these. Nor has speculation about Eleanor's sexual life been limited to women. Her son James believed that she had an affair with Earl Miller, and later in her life some believed that she had sexual relationships with other men.

Although the accuracy of such speculation may ultimately be irrelevant, the preponderance of evidence suggests that Eleanor Roosevelt was unable to express her deep emotional needs in a sexual manner. Her friend Esther Lape has recalled the distaste and repugnance with which Eleanor responded to the issue of homosexuality when they discussed a French novel dealing with the topic in the 1920s. Eleanor herself told her daughter that sex was something to be "borne," not enjoyed. Eleanor's own reference to Hickok having "a feeling for me which for one reason or another I may not return in kind" may be an allusion to a sexual component of Hickok's desire that Roosevelt could not reciprocate. Earl Miller, and other men with whom Eleanor was rumored to have had a sexual relationship, have all denied—persuasively—the truth of such conjecture. Moreover, we must never forget that Eleanor was raised in a Victorian culture that attempted to repress the sexual drive. She tied her daughter's hands to the top bars of her crib in order to prevent her from masturbating. "The indication was clearly," Anna recalled, "that I had had a bad habit which had to be cured and about which one didn't talk!"

All of this conforms to Eleanor's own repeated declarations that she could never "let herself go" or express freely and spontaneously her full emotions. A person who had been raised to believe that self-control was all-important was unlikely to consider sexual expression of love—especially outside of mar-

riage—a real option. She might sublimate her sexual drives and seek fulfillment of them through a series of deeply committed, even passionate, ties to a
variety of people. But it is unlikely that she was ever able to fulfill these drives
through actual sexual intimacy with those she cared most about. She was imprisoned in the cage of her culture, and her own bitter experiences through
childhood and marriage reinforced her impulse toward self-control and repres-
sion . . .

In this context, it is not surprising that Eleanor Roosevelt derived some of
her emotional gratification from public life and by giving herself emotionally
even to distant correspondents who somehow sensed her willingness to listen
to their needs. Such expression of concern constituted the intersection of her
public and private lives. Over and over again she answered pleas for help with
either a sensitive letter, an admonition to a federal agency to take action, or
even a personal check. When a policeman she knew suffered a paralyzing injury, she helped pay for his treatment, visited him repeatedly and, to encourage his rehabilitation, even asked him to help type a book she was composing
about her father. The indigent wrote to her because they knew she cared, and
in caring she found an outlet for her own powerful emotional needs.

The same compassion was manifested in Eleanor Roosevelt's advocacy of
the oppressed. It was almost as though she could fully express her feelings
only through externalizing them on political issues. Visiting the poverty-
stricken countryside of West Virginia and hearing about the struggle of Ap-
palachian farmers to reclaim land, she became a champion of the Arthurdale
Resettlement Administration Project, devoting her lecture fees as well as influence to help the community regain autonomy. Poor textile workers in the
South and garment union members in the North found her equally willing to
embrace their cause. She invited their representatives to the White House and
seated them next to the president at dinner so that he might hear of their
plight. She and Franklin had worked out a tacit understanding that permitted
her to bring the cause of the oppressed to his attention and allowed him, in
turn, to use her activism as a means of building alliances with groups to his
left. The game had clear rules: Franklin was the politician, Eleanor the agitator,
and frequently he refused to act as she wished. But at least the dispossessed
had someone advocating their interests.

Largely because of Eleanor Roosevelt, the issue of civil rights for black
Americans received a hearing at the White House. Although Roosevelt, like
most white Americans, grew up in an environment suffused with racist and
nativist attitudes, by the time she reached the White House she was one of the
few voices in the administration insisting that racial discrimination had no
place in American life. As always, she led by example. At a 1939 Birmingham
meeting inaugurating the Southern Conference on Human Welfare, she insisted on placing her chair so that it straddled both the black and white sides of
the aisle, thereby confounding local authorities who insisted that segregation
must prevail. Her civil-rights sympathies became most famous when in 1939
she resigned from the Daughters of the American Revolution after the organization denied Marian Anderson permission to perform at Constitution Hall.

Instead, the great black artist sang to 75,000 people from the Lincoln Memorial—an idea moved toward reality owing to support from the first lady.

Roosevelt also acted as behind-the-scenes lobbyist for civil rights legislation. She had an extensive correspondence with Walter White, executive secretary of the NAACP [National Association for the Advancement of Colored People], who wished to secure her support for legislation defining lynching as a federal crime. She immediately accepted the role of intermediary and argued that the president should make such a bill an urgent national priority. She served as the primary advocate for the anti-lynching bill within the White House, and she and White became fast friends as they worked toward a common objective. When the NAACP sponsored a New York City exhibit of paintings and drawings dealing with lynching, Roosevelt agreed to be a patron and attended the showing along with her secretary. After White House Press Secretary Steve Early protested about White, she responded: "If I were colored, I think I should have about the same obsession [with lynching] that he has." To the president ER communicated her anger that "one could get nothing done." "I'm deeply troubled," she wrote, "by the whole situation, as it seems to me a terrible thing to stand by and let it continue and feel that one cannot speak out as to his feelings."

Although Eleanor lost out in her campaign for Franklin's strong endorsement of an anti-lynching bill, she continued to speak forthrightly for the cause of civil rights. In June 1939, in an address before the NAACP's annual meeting, she presented the organization's Spingarn Medal to Marian Anderson. A few weeks later, she formally joined the black protest organization.

As the threat of war increased, Roosevelt joined her black friends in arguing that America could not fight racism abroad yet tolerate it at home. Together with Walter White, Aubrey Williams, and others, she pressed the administration to act vigorously to eliminate discrimination in the Armed Forces and defense employment. Although civil-rights forces were not satisfied with the administration's actions, especially the enforcement proceedings of the Fair Employment Practices Commission created to forestall A. Philip Randolph's 1941 March on Washington, the positive changes that did occur arose from the alliance of the first lady and civil-rights forces. She would not give up the battle, nor would they, despite the national administration's evident reluctance to act.

Roosevelt brought the same fervor to her identification with young people. Fearing that democracy might lose a whole generation because of the Depression, she reached out to make contact with the young. Despite warnings from White House aides that her young friends could not be trusted, between 1936 and 1940 she became deeply involved in the activities of the American Student Union and the American Youth Congress, groups committed to a democratic socialist program of massively expanded social-welfare programs. She advanced their point of view in White House circles and invited them to meet the president so that they might have the opportunity to persuade him of their point of view. To those who criticized her naiveté, she responded: "I wonder if it does us much harm. There is nothing as harmful as the knowledge in our

hearts that we are afraid to face any group of young people." She was later betrayed by some of her young allies, who insisted on following the Communist
party line and denouncing the European war as imperialistic after the Nazi-So-
viet Non-Aggression Pact in 1940. Nonetheless, Roosevelt continued to believe
in the importance of remaining open to dissent . . .

With the onset of World War II, the first lady persisted in her efforts for
the disadvantaged. When it appeared that women would be left out of the
planning and staffing of wartime operations, she insisted that administration
officials consult women activists and incorporate roles for women as a major
part of their planning. Over and over again, she intervened with war-produc-
tion agencies as well as the military to advocate fairer treatment for black
Americans. After it seemed that many New Deal social-welfare programs
would be threatened by war, she acted to protect and preserve measures directed at the young, tenant farmers, and blacks. Increasingly, she devoted herself to the dream of international cooperation, perceiving, more than most, the
revolution rising in Africa and Asia, and the dangers posed by the threat of
postwar conflict.

When Jewish refugees seeking a haven from Nazi persecution received
less than an enthusiastic response from the state department, it was Eleanor
Roosevelt who intervened repeatedly, trying to improve the situation. Parents,
wives, or children separated from loved ones always found an ally when they
sought help from the first lady. Nowhere was Roosevelt's concern more
poignantly expressed than in her visits to wounded veterans in army hospitals
overseas. When the world of hot dogs and baseball seemed millions of miles
away, suddenly Eleanor Roosevelt would appear, spending time at each bedside, taking names and addresses to write letters to home, bringing the cherished message that someone cared.

Perhaps inevitably, given the stresses of the times, the worlds of Franklin
and Eleanor became ever more separate in these years. As early as the 1936 reelection campaign, she confessed to feeling "indifferent" about Franklin's
chances. "I realize more and more," she wrote Hickok, "that FDR's a great
man, and he is nice, but as a person, I'm a stranger, and I don't want to be anything else!" As the war proceeded, Eleanor and Franklin more often became
adversaries. He was less able to tolerate Eleanor's advocacy of unpopular
causes, or her insistence on calling attention to areas of conflict within the administration. "She was invariably frank in her criticism of him," one of his
speechwriters recalled, "[and] sometimes I thought she picked inappropriate
times . . . perhaps a social and entertaining dinner." In search of release from
the unbearable pressures of the war, Franklin came more and more to rely on
the gaiety and laughter of his daughter Anna and other women companions.
One of these was Lucy Mercer Rutherfurd, who began to come to White House
dinners when Eleanor was away (with Anna's complicity) and who, unbe-
knownst to Eleanor, was with the president in Warm Springs when he was
stricken by a cerebral hemorrhage and died in April 1945.

With great discipline and dignity, Eleanor bore both the pain of Franklin's
death and the circumstances surrounding it. Her first concern was to carry for-

ward the policies that she and Franklin had believed in and worked for despite their disagreements. Writing later about her relationship with Franklin, she said: "He might have been happier with a wife who had been completely uncritical. That I was never able to be and he had to find it in some other people. Nevertheless, I think that I sometimes acted as a spur, even though the spurring was not always wanted nor welcome. I was one of those who served his purposes." What she did not say was that Franklin had served her purposes as well. Though the two never retrieved the intimacy of their early relationship, they had created an unparalleled partnership to respond to the needs of a nation in crisis.

Not long after her husband's death, she told an inquiring reporter, "The story is over." But no one who cared so much for so many causes, and was so effective as a leader, could long remain on the sidelines. Twenty years earlier, ER had told her students at Todhunter: "Don't dry up by inaction, but go out and do new things. Learn new things and see new things with your own eyes." Her own instincts, as well as the demands of others, reaffirmed that advice. Over the next decade and a half, Roosevelt remained the most effective woman in American politics. She felt a responsibility not only to carry forward the politics of the New Deal, but also to further causes that frequently had gone beyond New Deal liberalism. In long letters to President Truman, she implored the administration to push forward with civil rights, maintain the Fair Employment Practices Committee, develop a foreign policy able to cope with the needs of other nations, and work toward a world system where atom bombs would cease to be negotiating chips in international relations.

Appropriately, President Truman nominated the former first lady to be one of America's delegates to the United Nations. At the UN, her name became synonymous with the effort to compose a declaration of human rights embodying standards that civilized humankind would accept as sacred and inalienable. For three years, she argued, debated, lobbied, and compromised until finally on December 10, 1948, the document she had fundamentally shaped passed the General Assembly. Delegates rose in a standing ovation to the woman who more than anyone else had come to symbolize the cause of human rights throughout the world. Even those in the United States who had most opposed her nomination to the delegation applauded her efforts.

●●●●●

Although Roosevelt disagreed profoundly with some of the military aspects of U.S. foreign policy, she supported the broad outlines of America's response to Russia in the developing Cold War. In debates at the UN, she learned quickly that Soviet delegates could be hypocritical, and on more than one occasion she responded to Russian charges of injustice in America by proposing that each country submit to investigation of its social conditions—a suggestion the Soviets refused. When Henry Wallace and other liberal Americans formed the Progressive party in 1947 with a platform of accommodation toward the Soviet Union, Roosevelt demurred. Instead, she spearheaded the drive by other liberals to build Americans for Democratic Action, a group that espoused social reform at home and support of Truman's stance toward Russia.

Through public speeches and her newspaper column, as well as her position at the UN, Roosevelt remained a singular public figure, able to galvanize the attention of millions by her statements. She became one of the staunchest advocates of a Jewish nation in Israel, argued vigorously for civil rights, and spoke forcefully against the witch-hunts of McCarthyism, attacking General Dwight Eisenhower when he failed to defend his friend George Marshall from Senator McCarthy's smears. Although Eisenhower did not reappoint her to the United Nations when he became president in 1953, she continued to work tirelessly through the American Association for the United Nations to mobilize public support for international cooperation. She also gave unstintingly of her time to the election campaigns in 1952 and 1956 of her dear friend Adlai Stevenson, a man who brought to politics a wit and sophistication Roosevelt always admired.

• • • • •

As she entered her eighth decade, Eleanor Roosevelt was applauded as the first lady of the world. Traveling to India, Japan, and the Soviet Union, she spoke for the best that was in America. Although she did not initially approve of John Kennedy and would have much preferred to see Adlai Stevenson nominated again, she lived to see the spirit of impatience and reform return to Washington. As if to prove that the fire of protest was still alive in herself, in 1962 Roosevelt sponsored hearings in Washington, D.C., where young civil-rights workers testified about the judicial and police harassment of black protestors in the South.

It was fitting that Eleanor Roosevelt's last major official office should be to chair President Kennedy's Commission on the Status of Women. More than anyone else of her generation, her life came to exemplify the political expertise and personal autonomy that were abiding themes of the first women's rights movement. Eleanor Roosevelt had not been a militant feminist. Like most social reformers, she publicly rejected the Equal Rights Amendment of the National Woman's Party until the early 1950s, believing that it would jeopardize protective labor legislation for women then on the statute books. Never an enthusiastic supporter of the ERA, neither she nor JFK's commission recommended the amendment. In addition, she accepted the popular argument during the Great Depression that, at least temporarily, some married women would have to leave the labor force in order to give the unemployed a better chance. At times, she also accepted male-oriented definitions of fulfillment. "You are successful," she wrote in a 1931 article, "when your husband feels that he has been a success and that life has been worthwhile."

But on the issue of women's equality, as in so many other areas, Eleanor Roosevelt most often affirmed the inalienable right of the human spirit to grow and seek fulfillment. Brought up amid anti-Semitic and antiblack attitudes, she had transcended her past to become one of the strongest champions of minority rights. Once opposed to suffrage, she grew to exemplify women's aspirations for a full life in politics. Throughout, she demonstrated a capacity for change grounded in a compassion for those who were victims.

There was, in fact, a direct line from Marie Souvestre's advocacy of intellectual independence to Eleanor Roosevelt's involvement in the settlement house, to her subsequent embrace of women's political activism in the 1920s and 1930s, and to her final role as leader of the Commission on the Status of Women. She had personified not only the right of women to act as equals with men in the political sphere, but the passion of social activists to ease pain, alleviate suffering, and affirm solidarity with the unequal and disenfranchised of the world.

On November 7, 1962, Eleanor Roosevelt died at home from a rare form of bone-marrow tuberculosis. Just 20 years earlier, she had written that all individuals must discover for themselves who they are and what they want from life. "You can never really live anyone else's life," she wrote, "not even your child's. The influence you exert is through your own life and what you've become yourself." Despite disappointment and tragedy, Eleanor Roosevelt had followed her own advice and because of it had affected the lives of millions. Although her daughter Anna concluded that Eleanor, throughout her life, suffered from depression, she had surely tried—and often succeeded—through her public advocacy of the oppressed and her private relationships with friends to find some measure of fulfillment and satisfaction.

"What other single human being," Adlai Stevenson asked at Eleanor Roosevelt's memorial service, "has touched and transformed the existence of so many? . . . She walked in the slums and ghettos of the world, not on a tour of inspection . . . but as one who could not feel contentment when others were hungry." Because of her life, millions of others experienced a new sense of possibility. It would be difficult to envision a more enduring or important legacy.

AFRICAN-AMERICANS AND THE NEW DEAL

Although African-Americans overwhelmingly supported Franklin Roosevelt, his administration's record on racial issues was decidedly mixed. Blacks certainly benefited from New Deal policies, but never to the degree that they might have. Where some programs were segregated, others functioned in ways that harmed African Americans. Black leaders had no illusions about what was happening. They also knew that, more so than most administration figures, Eleanor Roosevelt shared their concerns. In the letter below, Roy Wilkins informs ER that her attendance at the NAACP annual convention would do much to allay black misgivings about the New Deal.

Source: Roy Wilkins to Eleanor Roosevelt, May 20, 1935, reel 19, Papers of Eleanor Roosevelt, Microfilm Edition (Frederick, MD: University Publications of America, 1986).

Roy Wilkins to Eleanor Roosevelt, May 20, 1935

I want to add a personal note to the official invitation extended to you, and say what had better be left unsaid in our official letter.

There is great restlessness, doubt, and even some hostility among the colored people because of some things which the administration has, or has not, done. I think it extremely important that at this conference, which comes just prior to the election year, that the administration have a good will spokesman . . .

There is hardly a phase of the New Deal program which has not brought some hardship and disillusionment to colored people. The N[ational] R[ecovery] A[dministration] benefited them little, if at all; from the P[ublic] W[orks] A[dministration] they secured a very small amount of employment; from the A[gricultural] A[djustment] A[ct] the black tenants and sharecroppers have thus far received little consideration; the F[ederal] E[mergency] R[elief] A[ct] has benefited them some, but there has been a great deal of discrimination in its administration. Now that the new $5 billion work relief program is announced, colored people are viewing their prospects with greater and greater cynicism.

It has not helped any of these matters that the anti-lynching bill, despite all the support it had, was not able to get a hearing and a vote in the Senate.

It is my feeling that it would be good strategy from the administration's standpoint, and good Americanism from the standpoint of our people, for some emissary to give a sincere word of reassurance to the colored population through their oldest civil rights organization. We hope that you will consent to be that ambassador.

QUESTIONS

1. In what ways did ER's later activities reflect the influence of Marie Souvestre? In what ways did World War I mark a period of transition in ER's life?

2. How did ER's life change after her husband was paralyzed by polio in 1921? How would you characterize her personal relationship with FDR? How did ER attempt to compensate for the emotional barrenness of the relationship?

3. What were ER's greatest strengths as a political activist? In what policy areas did ER have the greatest influence on her husband? Why was she increasingly at odds with FDR over political matters during World War II? In what ways would the New Deal have been different if she had not attempted to influence her husband's actions?

4. What does Roy Wilkins's letter tell us about ER's role as a political operative? Why did Wilkins communicate his misgivings to ER personally rather than include them in the NAACP's official letter? Would he have been better advised to make a public statement? What would W. E. B. Du Bois have done in this situation?

5. Do you see any similarities between ER and Margaret Sanger? In what ways did the two women differ? Do you think they would have worked well together?

6. What was ER's greatest contribution to the struggle for women's equality? Of the first ladies who have since followed her in the White House, which one do you think has been most similar to ER?

BIBLIOGRAPHY

The most recent biography of Eleanor Roosevelt is Blanche Wiesen Cook, *Eleanor Roosevelt, 1884–1933: A Life: Mysteries of the Heart* (1992), though interested readers also should consult Joseph Lash's excellent two-volume treatment: *Eleanor and Franklin: The Story of Their Relationship Based on Eleanor Roosevelt's Private Papers* (1971) and *Eleanor: The Years Alone* (1972). Other studies include Lois Scharf, *Eleanor Roosevelt: First Lady of American Liberalism* (1987); Doris Kearns Goodwin, *No Ordinary Time: Franklin and Eleanor Roosevelt: The Home Front in World War II* (1994); and the collection of articles from which this chapter's essay is taken: Joan Hoff-Wilson and Marjorie Lightman, eds., *Without Precedent: The Life and Career of Eleanor Roosevelt* (1984). For more on the New Deal women's network, see two works by Susan Ware: *Beyond Suffrage: Women in the New Deal* (1981) and *Partner and I: Molly Dewson, Feminism, and New Deal Politics* (1987). Ware also has written a fine survey of women in the Great Depression, *Holding Their Own: American Women in the 1930s* (1982).

Huey Long

By late 1934 Franklin Roosevelt's New Deal appeared to have lost its way. Despite the unprecedented wave of reform legislation that had marked Roosevelt's first 18 months in office, unemployment remained unacceptably high. Meanwhile, there was growing criticism of the president's policies. Some of it came from the Right—from groups like the Liberty League, an organization of conservative Democrats backed by some of the nation's wealthiest businesspeople and dedicated to laissez-faire principles of government. Because so many Americans were then living in poverty or worse, Roosevelt could safely ignore these attacks. In fact, he soon found that such criticism added to his popularity. After five years of depression, many people believed that corporate remedies would more likely worsen than cure the country's economic ills.

More worrisome was the growing restiveness on the Left. In Minnesota,

the Farmer-Labor party had drafted a platform that was considerably more progressive than that of the national Democrats. And in California, Upton Sinclair had recently received nearly a million votes for governor in a campaign that proposed doing away with the profit system: by establishing land colonies that would produce food to feed the jobless and creating state-run factories to meet their remaining needs.

Because they were state-based, these developments did not pose an immediate threat to Roosevelt. Of much greater concern were three other move-

ments: Dr. Francis E. Townsend's campaign for old-age security; Father Charles Coughlin's radio crusade for monetary reform; and Huey Long's Share Our Wealth initiative, which promised every American family a "household estate" of $5,000. All three movements had national followings, and if they had ever joined forces—as it appeared for a time they might—the Roosevelt administration would have been in for the fight of its life.

New Deal strategists particularly feared Huey Long. To Franklin Roosevelt, he was one of the two most dangerous men in America. (General Douglas McArthur was the other.) The president had good reason to feel as he did. In addition to being one of the most talented politicians of the period, Long was also one of the most ruthless. During the 1930s, he established a virtual dictatorship in Louisiana, and by the time of his assassination in 1935, he had become a viable contender for the presidency. Although Peter J. King focuses on Long's Louisiana exploits in the essay that follows, his portrait of the "Kingfish" tells us much about why national leaders considered Long to be such a formidable political foe.

Huey Long

Peter J. King

On September 8, 1935, a young doctor stepped from behind a pillar in the state capitol at Baton Rouge and fired one shot from his revolver. Two days later his victim, Senator Huey Pierce Long of Louisiana, died, and his death caused countless Americans, from President Roosevelt downward, to breathe a sigh of relief, while the poor farmers of Louisiana lamented the passing of their hero. Within his short career, Huey Long had wrought a revolution in his own state and threatened to extend it to the whole of the country. Long is a controversial figure who has aroused fervent enthusiasm and almost complete hatred. He had been hailed as the savior of the poor and the oppressed, but more often denounced as a dictator, the harbinger of American fascism, and even as the potential Mussolini of America. Long was certainly a demagogue and, to a large extent, a dictator; but he was no alien or un-American phenomenon. His régime was rooted firmly in the social and political soil of Louisiana, which furnished him with both his opportunity and his raw material. Yet there is also much truth in his own claim to be ***sui generis;*** for many of the distinguishing characteristics of his régime were the product of the vicissitudes of his career and his own peculiar personality.

Huey Long was born in 1893, the eighth of nine children, in the parish of Winn in north central Louisiana. The son of a subsistence farmer, he grew up in an atmosphere of poverty and dissent. Although the circumstances of his

Source: "Huey Long" by Peter J. King. First appeared in *History Today,* March 1964. Reprinted by permission.

own family were not of extreme poverty—his father farmed 340 acres—they were far from being comfortable, and Long was unable to have the college education he desired. Winn was a parish with radical traditions that "produced only one crop—dissent." It had been a center of Populist activity in the 1890s and had voted for Eugene Debs, the Socialist candidate for the presidency in 1912. The people from among whom Huey sprang were very much the forgotten men of Louisiana, poor, often illiterate, and almost completely ignored by the state government in Baton Rouge. Huey Long was a "hillbilly" raised among hillbillies, who knew their plight and sympathized with their aspirations. In his teens, as a shortening salesmen, he traveled the whole region of the northern parishes and came to know and understand the people there, as no other Louisiana politician had ever done.

As an individual, Long was ambitious, self-centered, and domineering. His private life was uneventful and devoid of any marked excess or significant moral lapses. His opponents, always eager for ammunition, found little in it worthy of note. Before his election, married to a girl he had met in his days as a salesman, he lived as any prosperous citizen in his elegant house at Shreveport built from the profits of his law practice. Long's private life, however, was small. He chose to live very much in the public eye and there his true character came to light. His humble origins and scanty education revealed themselves in his uncouth manners and coarse profanity. His behavior was often boorish and arrogant as on the occasion when he tossed a dish of oysters not fried to his liking on to the floor in a fashionable hotel. In the Senate, where freshmen senators are expected to be seen and not heard, he outraged his colleagues by breaking all that club's hallowed traditions and, as a result of his habit of conducting business in bed, he touched off a diplomatic incident by receiving German dignitaries in his green silk pajamas. The struggles of his youth, of course, left an enormous chip on his shoulder and bred a bitter resentment that proved a strong spur to his ambitions. Yet Long also seemed to suffer from a deep sense of personal insecurity which fanned the already roaring flames of his ambition and lay at the root of the vindictiveness that was so dominant a trait of his character. "Once disappointed in a political undertaking," he confessed, "I could never cast it from my mind." Always seeking to dominate, he found it hard to converse and always tended to orate and, like many a bully, he seemed to have been a coward, afraid of physical hurt. Not that he lacked moral courage: He was a political gambler who played the high stakes, although he took care to stack the deck whenever possible.

---

sui generis   The only example of its kind; unique.

John Law   A financier involved in an early 18th century speculation of Louisiana development that ultimately collapsed as he fled the country in ruin.

Long is often charged with destroying democracy in Louisiana; but it is worth recalling what that "democracy" consisted of. Louisiana had been conceived and born in corruption, at the time of **John Law** in the 18th century; it had lived in it ever since. As a mayor of New Orleans once said, "you can make corruption illegal in Louisiana but you can't make it unpopular." For over 50 years after the collapse of the Reconstruction government, the state had been ruled by an oligarchy of the dominant economic interests, the planters, and lumber and sugar producers, the railroads and the utilities; and by the 1920s Standard Oil was the major economic and political force in the state. While not always corrupt in the strict sense of the word, the oligarchy pursued its own interests of low corporation taxes and modest expenditure, neglecting the poorer sections of the state, who received next to nothing for the taxes they paid. Nor did it attempt to broaden the base of its support by catering to the needs of the rural communities, of which it seemed largely unaware. In 1928 Riley J. Wilson, one of the candidates for the governorship, found Long's scheme for paving all the state's roads utterly ridiculous; he could not conceive how the money could be found under the existing pattern of state finance. The oligarchy was stronger than that in any other southern state; and it had maintained its undisputed control by an alliance with the Old Regulars of the Choctaw Club, the city machine of New Orleans. By means of padded registration rolls, paid-up poll-tax receipts and police pressure, the machine could swing the city to any candidate willing to give it a free hand with the state patronage in the city. There was no regular state machine; power tended to rest in the hands of the local sheriffs; and little campaigning was done. Indeed, when running for governor, Long was often the first gubernatorial candidate the up-country parishes had ever seen. By exploiting the differences between the Baptists of the North and the Catholics of the Delta, the oligarchy had smothered Populism and left no safety valve for discontent. When the explosion came, therefore, it was of greater proportions than elsewhere in the South.

The catalyst that produced the upheaval was Long's ambition and political genius, wedded to his understanding of the poor white farmers. Their aspirations provided him with an opportunity he had the skill to exploit. For all his apparent coarseness, Long was a very able man—a first-class lawyer with a brilliant mind, who had crammed a three-year law course into 12 months and been admitted to the bar at 21. His ability for hard work, mastery of detail, and knowledge of the intricacies of the law were powerful aids in the creation of his dictatorship. He understood where power lay and knew how to use it: Even at the tender age of 15, he organized his schoolmates to get the high school principal dismissed. As an orator, he was extraordinarily gifted. Appealing to the people in language they could understand, he knew how to capture their sympathy and imagination, and his Baptist background and knowledge of the Bible were great assets. The much-quoted "Evangeline" speech demonstrates his skill:

> And it is here that Evangeline waited for her lover Gabriel who never came . . . But Evangeline is not the only one who has waited here in disappointment. Where are the schools that you have waited for your children to have that have never come? Where are the roads and highways that you spent your money to build, that are no nearer now than ever before? Where are the institutions to care for the sick and the disabled? Evangeline wept bitter tears in her disappointment. But they lasted through only one lifetime. Your tears in

this country, around this oak, have lasted for generations. Give me the chance to dry the tears of those who still weep here.

He also knew the value of a sense of humor in winning support and disarming criticism. To the delight of the crowd, he would play the buffoon, whether by ridiculing his opponents, adopting his sobriquet of "Kingfish" from a popular radio show, or personally leading the band at state university football games.

The poor whites might have found a leader sooner or later; but the emergence of Long as that leader had profound consequences. The rural voters elected him a railroad commissioner at 25—this was the one post he found that had no minimum age qualification. Later, he became chairman of the Public Service Commission. In these positions he began to wage war on the interests, especially on Standard Oil and the utility companies. Through his efforts, Standard's pipeline was declared a common carrier, and reductions were forced in telephone and electricity rates. But, even here, he was already fighting his own personal battles as well as those of his supporters. He bore a grudge against the utilities for thwarting his appointment as a United States attorney; and, as a holder of independent oil stock, he had been hurt financially when Standard tried to freeze the independents out. Politics were always a highly personal matter for Huey. He had no deep ideological convictions, and many of his later excesses, and successes, can be ascribed to his great capacity for hatred and revenge.

By supporting John W. Parker for the governorship in 1920, he broadened his knowledge of politics and his contacts with the people. After Parker had sold out to the interests, he ran for the governor's chair himself in 1924, losing narrowly after rain had kept his rural supporters from the polls. Although strong in the northern part of the state, he lacked support in the urban areas; and in the Catholic south he was unknown, except as a northern Baptist and a possible supporter of the Ku Klux Klan. The essence of his program, however, was already in being—concrete and asphalt roads, more bridges and free bridges, free schoolbooks, and college education for the boys. It was a program to repair the neglect of decades and end the geographic, economic, and mental isolation of the up-country farmers who supported him at the polls.

The near miss of 1924 was transformed into the triumph of 1928, once he had managed to close the most glaring gap in the ranks of his supporters. By campaigning for Ed Broussard in the senatorial election of 1926, he taught the creoles and cajuns of the southern part of the state to know and trust him. In 1928, by preaching his message of "Everyman a King," by crusading against the interests, offering roads and education, and lower utility rates, he not only appealed to the rural population's material needs, but also presented them with a figure they could recognize, and with which they could identify themselves. He was an easy victor when the sun shone on election day.

The hillbilly was now in office. It had happened in the South, if not in Louisiana, before. But Long was a triumphant demagogue with a difference. He had not fought the existing forces to bring them to terms; he was out to destroy them. He intended to satisfy his followers and realize his program. To this end, he began to build up his own machine by using state patronage to the full. He laid hands on as many state offices as he could and installed his own men. When the supply of jobs ran out, he brought municipal jobs under state control. This was essential. To complete his own program, he needed his own machine. The existing political forces could not be the agents of a hillbilly revolution. The control and extension of state patronage was the linchpin of his system.

Yet it is doubtful whether, in 1928, he intended to create the fully fledged dictatorship that eventually emerged. This was the result of forces beyond his immediate control, forces that reacted with his own personal ambition and highly sensitive nature. For, although elected governor in 1928, he still did not control the legislature. The days when he could push bills through, one every two minutes, were yet to come. The old interests had lost a battle, but not as yet the war. Long's program meant money; and money meant taxes, and taxes on the wealthy, not on the poor farmer. The legislative session of 1928–1929 was a bitter fight. Intimidation and corruption were common on both sides. In the circumstances Long had little choice. "They say they don't like my methods. Well, I don't like them either . . . I'd much rather get up before a legislature and say: 'Now this is a good law; it's for the benefit of the people, and I'd like you to vote for it in the interests of public welfare.' Only I know laws aren't made that way. You've got to fight fire with fire."

The crisis came to a head with the governor's plan to impose a five-cent occupational tax on oil: thus the greatest of the interests would pay for his vast public works scheme and pay off their personal debt to Huey Long. Standard Oil and the interests fought virtually to the death on the issue. They exerted as much pressure on the legislature as they could bring to bear, not only to kill the tax, but Long himself, by inducing the lower house to impeach the governor. Huey was fighting for his political life and survived only because 15 senators announced their intention of voting for acquittal regardless of the evidence since they believed the charges were invalid.

It is impossible to overestimate the effect produced by this narrow escape. Long was almost destroyed by a ruthless, venal, and selfish opposition. He was determined to ensure that it could not happen again. He was a great hater, and his desire for revenge was implacable. He needed to increase his power, not only to save himself, but to secure the passage of his program. Although he made tactical concessions, the 1930 session of the legislature still balked at his $60 million road bond issue. State financial appropriations were reduced in a stalemate of legislative rejection and gubernatorial veto. Lacking majorities in the legislature, he needed his own party; and, to create that, he had to build his own machine.

Out of this deadlock came his campaign for the United States Senate in 1930. With two years still to run as governor, by offering himself for election he could appeal directly to the people and receive their endorsement for his program. After a campaign that proved extremely dirty on both sides, he emerged victorious, collecting 57.3 percent of the vote in the primary, as against the 43.9 percent that put him in the governor's chair. While his strength still lay outside the urban areas and the Delta, he almost carried New Orleans. Overwhelmed by the victory, the legislature at last endorsed his highway program. But, to reinforce his position, by a masterpiece of political maneuver he managed to bring the Old Regulars of the New Orleans machine over to his side. This ensured his domination of the legislature. In return for their support, he agreed to let the state liquidate the port debt, build and repair the roads of the city, and bridge the Mississippi. A mere alliance of convenience to secure the passage of his own program, it was repudiated when Long felt strong enough to take on his former big city foes. Although outmaneuvered and small, the opposition to Long lost nothing of its venom.

In 1932 Long's eyes first began seriously to look beyond Louisiana. It was not merely that going to Washington had broadened his horizons—he did not actually take his seat in the Senate until that year. He had played no small part at the Democratic Convention in securing the nomination of Franklin Roosevelt. The Depression was at its height; and, observing the desperation of the country, he saw in the Share Our Wealth movement, which was beginning to spread throughout the nation, a means of putting himself into the White House. He soon broke with Roosevelt and the New Deal, on the grounds that they did not go far enough to meet the needs of the people. His own program, Share Our Wealth, evoked a hillbilly's paradise. A mixture of contorted economics and a shrewd appeal to human cupidity, it seemed an easy solution to the woes of the unemployed. The essence of the program was simplicity itself. "Everyman a king but where no one wears a crown" was the basic slogan. "Redistribute your wealth," the freshman senator exhorted his colleagues, "it's all in God's book. Follow the Lord . . . but we don't seem to be doing it." All fortunes over $3 million were to be confiscated and, from the proceeds, every American family would receive $4,000 or $5,000 to purchase a home, an automobile, and a radio. All citizens over 65 (or 60) would receive a pension of $30 a month (or more). The actual details varied considerably. There would be a minimum wage of $2,500 a year; hours of labor would be limited to balance production and demand; and the government would take over all agricultural surpluses. The veterans bonus, then a live issue in American politics, would be paid at once; and what was left of the loot would finance a college education for bright young men. The program was a demagogue's masterpiece. Based upon the simple principle of "soak the rich," it appealed to virtually every segment of the lower and most numerous orders of society.

Long had no real expectation of being nominated in 1936; he was pinning his hopes on 1940. Yet, through the mushrooming national organization of Share Our Wealth clubs, in 1935 he already posed a serious threat to Roosevelt. Not that he could have denied the president the Democratic nomination; but he could have split the radical vote and let the Republicans in. Long was certainly one of the forces that drove Roosevelt leftward into the Second New Deal. James Farley, FDR's political chief of staff, reckoned him to be worth several million votes.

Whether Long broke with Roosevelt, or vice versa, it is impossible to say. Long's ambition would not have kept him in Roosevelt's shadow for long. His national ambitions, however, led to further developments at home. He needed a stronger grip on his state to provide a secure base of operations, especially as his relations with the administration soured. Federal patronage began to flow, not to the senator, but to his opponents; and the burgeoning New Deal agencies provided much sustenance to offset the Long interests. This had to be neutralized, and reliance on the Old Regulars who maintained friendly relations with the Democratic National Committee and administration had to be ended.

During 1933 and 1934, unfortunately, Huey appeared to be in trouble. The opposition seemed to be making some headway. Besides the attacks from Washington, he saw his own candidate rejected in a virtual counterrevolution in the sixth congressional district. Some of his closest aides were indicted for fraud; and there was strong evidence to suggest that virtually every contract let by the state was graft-ridden. The income tax investigations into Long's own income were reopened on the president's orders. They had begun under Hoover, when Harold Irey, head of the income-tax department, had received the report: "Chief, Louisiana is crawling. Long and his gang are stealing everything in the state . . . and they're not paying taxes on the loot." Even the weapon of ridicule rebounded on his own head, after an incident in the lavatory of a fashionable club where the senator was seen to have had his nose bloodied.

The newspapers, in the spring of 1934, demoted the Kingfish to "Crawfish," and eagerly awaited his nemesis in the elections of the fall; but they reckoned without the sheer drive and ability of the senior senator from Louisiana. He fought back by making his rule in Louisiana virtually absolute; his dictatorship bloomed into full flower. He consolidated his electoral support among the up-country farmers. Through the reduction or removal of tax assessments on small properties, the burden of taxation was transferred to the interests and corporations from the shoulders of the poor . . . , whose gratitude he was able to harvest in full at the polls by the abolition of the poll-tax qualification for the vote. By making his own state-appointed assessors responsible for all tax assessments, and by a flexible policy of giving rebates, as in the case of the 5¢-a-barrel oil tax, he was able to whip the interests into line. The Public Service Commission provided him with an additional lever over the utilities and helped circumscribe what remained of municipal powers. Control over virtually every local government job in the state was assured by the creation of the Civil Service Commission.

With his eyes firmly fixed on the coming elections, he rammed 44 acts through the legislature in seven special sessions. He completed his patronage control and gained a free hand in running elections through the appointment of election commissioners and registration agents to supervise and count the ballots, thus getting around the local sheriffs whom he did not always control. The courts were specifically denied the right to intervene in elections. If there was to be any election stealing, henceforward Long alone would do it. St. Bernard and Jefferson counties testified to his success by casting more votes for Long and his supporters than the total adult population, both white and black. The law-enforcement agencies were also subdued. Earlier elections had given him the Supreme Court. Now he seized control of all the police in the state, from chiefs to patrolmen; sheriff's deputies were placed under the control of the state police; and he was authorized to call out the militia free from judicial restraint. He had complete control of militia and state police and never hesitated to use force where required. The attorney general was empowered to supersede local attorneys in all criminal cases, and even to control their staffs. Recalcitrant judges could be gerrymandered out of their districts; and, by extending the governor's pardon to cover contempt cases, he was able to outflank the opposition's favorite weapon—the judicial injunction.

The larger newspapers he tried to tax into silence, while the smaller ones were brought into line by their dependence on state printing contracts. His own newspaper, *Progress*, had the full facilities of the State Highway Department and state police to speed it on its way, and they regularly acted as messenger boys for all Long's leaflets and handouts. All state employees had to contribute to his war chest, and all major state employees were expected to hand over undated resignations. His puppet governor, O. K. Allen, signed anything and everything required of him.

The secret of Long's success was twofold: He gave his supporters what they wanted, and he controlled his machine by meticulous attention to detail. There was no better illustration of his political skill than his destruction of the New Orleans machine. Long had never carried the city, and he could never feel secure until it was brought under his sway. In the political context of 1934, his alliance with the Choctaws was more likely to prove a source of weakness than one of strength. As governor, he caused uproar by sending the state troopers to clean up the vice of New Orleans, allegedly because the "payoffs" were not coming in with their accustomed regularity. He now played a variation on the theme. The "vice vote"—those who earned their living from gambling and prostitution—had been a pillar of machine support. Playing up the vice issue, he secured the appointment of a legislative committee to conduct an investigation. Then, using the hearings as a pretext, he gave the "vice vote" the choice of supporting him or seeing the state police reappear. He induced the legislature to transfer city patronage and financial control to the state government, and so drafted the office holders and job hunters into his ranks; and, by appointing special tax assessors for the city, he was able to blackmail the rich into reluctantly supporting him. Thus the Old Regulars found themselves cut off from their usual sources of nourishment; and, with their padded election registers cleansed and the supervisory powers halved, as a result of other legislation, their usual electoral chicanery was thwarted. In the 1934 elections the Kingfish's followers carried the city. At the time of his death, Huey Long was at the peak of his power. Only the grubbing of the federal income tax authorities seemed to threaten his position.

Long's dictatorship was certainly corrupt, violent, and extensive. Even in the boss-ridden South, it is doubtful if one man ever wielded such power. Yet, despite his humiliation of the Old Regulars and the smashing victories of 1934, his power was not absolute. The 44 acts, and his need to smash the New Orleans machine, indicate his sense of insecurity. He never dominated the urban centers like Shreveport and Baton Rouge. The greater part of the state's congressional delegation was hostile to him, and it survived at the polls. Although he had managed to get Hattie Caraway elected to the U.S. Senate from Arkansas, his writ did not run beyond Louisiana; his attempts at meddling in Mississippi and Georgia had been a fiasco. All the newspapers were not silenced. The opposition was small, but vocal and violent. Indeed, their very violence and militancy seemed to drive him on.

Never forgetting 1929, he was perhaps prone to overestimate their strength; his extreme sensitivity and fear blinded him to their real weakness. A collection of ousted politicians, vested interests, and disgruntled liberals, they were leaderless and devoid of any constructive program. A common hatred of Long and his works was their sole unifying factor. They had no popular support; Long's corrupt régime was probably the nearest thing Louisiana had ever had to a popular government. The majority of the state seemed to prefer a corrupt government, that took some notice of their needs, to a corrupt, or even an honest one, that collected their taxes but left them in ignorance, squalor, and isolation. They suffered from no illusions. They knew that the elections were corrupt—they always had been. In 1939, after the full extent of the corruption of Huey's heirs was known, 55 percent of the people thought Long's influence had been good, and only 22 percent found it wholly bad.

Huey Long may have been the nearest thing to a dictator that the United States has yet produced; but he was neither a prototype American Hitler nor the fascist that nervous liberals in the 1930s thought they saw. He was an American plant, nurtured in American soil. There is little trace of fascism in Share Our Wealth. Long claimed he derived it from the Bible—"The Great American Nostrum, ingredients guaranteed by the Bible." "Everyman a King" was a slogan picked up from William Jennings Bryan; and the Populist and Socialist background of Winn parish account for most of his program. If there was any other influence, it came from the Reconstruction period, with which Long was quite familiar. Long stands very much in the tradition of other southern agrarian insurgents, like Tom Watson, Ben Tillman, and Gene Talmadge, not in that of European fascism. Like them, he was a southern boss, but a different type of boss. The sheer extent of his power, and the use he made of it for reform, account for part of the difference, but not all. He faced the present, not the past. He did not dwell on the glories of the Confederacy nor stoop to "nigger-baiting"—the stock-in-trade of the southern demagogue. In fact, one of the charges leveled against him was the accusation of being a "nigger-lover." Nor did he exploit the religious issue—precluded, incidentally, by the large Catholic element in the state. His outburst on Hitler is instructive: "Don't compare me with that so and so. Anybody that let's his public policies be mixed up with religious prejudices is a plain goddam fool."

Although ultimately hypnotized by the exercise of power for power's sake, Long could point to positive and constructive achievements. The roads and bridges were built; there were more and better hospitals and a great expansion of educational facilities. Thousands of the state's quarter of a million illiterates first received instruction. Utility rates were reduced; and the burden of taxation was made more equitable, with the corporations now paying their share. The state's first income tax was introduced. Nor must it be forgotten that, despite the lavish spending and high taxation, his program was soundly financed and the state's credit good.

But his achievements go deeper. He injected a much needed note of realism into Louisiana and southern politics. He tried to bring Louisiana into the twentieth century; to make the government work for the poor farmer as well as for the corporate interests. He brought politics back into touch with the needs of the people. The old multifactional nature of state politics, quite irrelevant to the times, was destroyed. Since 1928 there have been generally two factions, Longites and their opponents, each standing for something more or less tangible. Above all, he involved in politics a hitherto neglected class; in Louisiana he appealed to precisely the same kind of men as Roosevelt appealed to throughout the nation. He, too, discovered the forgotten man.

It is true, of course, that Long's greatest achievements consisted of public works, a notorious and lavish source of patronage; and it is also true that there was much he did not tackle. Little was done to set up welfare and labor standards. Women and child labor laws did not interest him; and minimum wage provisions and unemployment relief were neglected. In context, this is understandable. Long was the representative of the up-country farmers, not the apostle of urban democracy; he stood in the Populist, not the Progressive tradition. Even so, he showed no readiness to come to grips with the basic agricultural problems of sharecropping and tenant farming.

Whatever the benefits conferred by Long's régime, the price was high. Although the extent of Long's own venality is debatable, there is no doubt that his régime was more corrupt and dictatorial than the strength of the opposition excused; and, after his death, it degenerated into an orgy of corruption. But the régime was produced by more than Long's vaulting ambition and paranoic personality, by more than the cupidity of his followers; its nature was determined by the soil and climate in which it flourished. After all, politics is the art of the possible. To achieve results, Long had to build his own machine or see his program and power destroyed. Faced with an opposition that was neither honest nor scrupulous, he had little choice but to fight fire with fire. The majority of the voters, even allowing for electoral chicanery, seemed content to endorse this. Long's administration and methods were far from perfect; but for many, Long's brand of "caesarean democracy" seemed preferable to what had existed before it.

ADDRESS BY FATHER CHARLES E. COUGHLIN, 1936

After Huey Long's assassination in 1935, Father Charles E. Coughlin replaced the Louisiana "Kingfish" as the main threat from the Left. Known as the "Radio Priest," Coughlin was the Canadian-born pastor of a Roman

Source: From Charles E. Coughlin, "A Third Party," *Vital Speeches of the Day*, 2 (July 1, 1936), pp. 614–15. Reprinted by permission of Vital Speeches of the Day.

Catholic parish in Royal Oak, Michigan, whose radio sermons reached an es-
timated 30 to 40 million people by the mid-1930s, and whose small army of
secretaries and clerks answered about 80,000 letters each week. Although
Coughlin's message initially drew on Catholic social teachings, as the Depres-
sion deepened it became increasingly radical; and as it did, his relations with
Roosevelt soured. By late 1934 he was charging that the administration was
"wedded basically to the philosophy of the money changers." The following
excerpt is from a 1936 speech condemning New Deal policy in which Cough-
lin announced the creation of a Union party to challenge Roosevelt—a party
that Huey Long may well have headed had he lived.

A Third Party

March 4, 1933! I shall never forget the inaugural address, which seemed to re-
echo the very words employed by Christ Himself as He actually drove the
money changers from the temple.

The thrill that was mine was yours. Through dim clouds of the Depression
this man Roosevelt was, as it were, a new savior of the people!

Oh, just a little longer shall there be needless poverty! Just another year
shall there be naked backs! Just another moment shall there be thoughts of revolution! Never again will the chains of economic poverty bite into the hearts of
simple folks, as they did in the past days of the Old Deal!

Such were our hopes in the springtime of 1933.

My friends, what have we witnessed as the finger of time turned the pages
of the calendar? 1933 and the National Recovery Act which multiplied profits
for the monopolists; and 1934 and the A[gricultural] A[djustment] A[ct] which
raised the price of foodstuffs by throwing back God's best gifts into His face;
1935 and the Banking Act which rewarded the exploiters of the poor, the Federal Reserve bankers and their associates, by handing over to them the temple
from which they were to have been cast!

• • • • •

Neither Old Dealer nor New Dealer, it appears, has courage to assail the international bankers, the Federal Reserve bankers. In common, both the leaders of
the Republicans and the Democrats uphold the old money philosophy. Today
in America there is only one political party—the banker's party. In common,
both old parties are determined to sham battle their way through this November election with the hope that millions of American citizens will be driven
into the no-man's land of financial bondage.

My friends, there is a way out, a way to freedom! There is an escape from
the dole standard of Roosevelt, the gold standard of Landon. No longer need
you be targets in no-man's land for the financial crossfire of the sham-battlers!

Six hours ago the birth of "the Union party" was officially announced to
the newspapers of the nation, thereby confirming information which hitherto
was mine officially. The new candidate for president, together with his spon-

sors, formally requested my support, as they handed to me his platform. I have studied it carefully. I find that it is in harmony substantially with the principles of social justice.

QUESTIONS

1. What were the sources of Long's reform proposals? To what extent was he motivated by a genuine desire to improve the lives of the common people?
2. What actions did Long take to create a political machine in Louisiana? Why was he generally more popular in rural areas than in urban centers?
3. Given the extent of corruption in state government during the Long era, why was Long such a popular political figure in Louisiana? Do you think his programs had a positive or negative effect on the state?
4. What does the popularity of Long's Share Our Wealth program tell us about the American political scene in the mid-1930s? Do you agree with Roosevelt's remark that Long was one of the most dangerous men in America? Give reasons for your answer.
5. How do you think Roosevelt reacted to Father Coughlin's speech on the New Deal? Do you think Coughlin and Long would have been able to work together as leaders of the same political party?
6. If Long had lived and been elected president, what kind of chief executive do you think he would have been?

BIBLIOGRAPHY

The most balanced biography of Long is William Ivy Hair, *The Kingfish and His Realm: The Life and Times of Huey P. Long* (1991). For a less critical but immensely readable treatment, see T. Harry Williams, *Huey Long* (1969). Long's place in Depression-era politics is ably examined in Alan Brinkley, *Voices of Protest: Huey Long, Father Coughlin and the Great Depression* (1982). For more on Louisiana politics during the Long era, see Allen P. Sindler, *Huey Long's Louisiana: State Politics, 1920–1952* (1956). The most comprehensive survey of the South during the period is George Brown Tindall, *The Emergence of the New South, 1913–1945* (1967). Major studies of the New Deal and the Great Depression include Anthony Badger, *The New Deal: The Depression Years, 1933–1940* (1989); Robert S. McElvaine, *The Great Depression: America, 1929–1941* (1984), and William E. Leuchtenberg's still valuable older work, *Franklin D. Roosevelt and the New Deal, 1932–1940* (1963).

George Patton

On December 7, 1941, Japanese planes attacked the U.S. naval base at Pearl Harbor. Although the assault caught American forces in Hawaii by surprise, Washington responded immediately and in the week that followed events moved quickly both there and in other parts of the world. On December 8, the United States and Britain declared war on Japan. Three days later, Hitler recognized his obligations to the Japanese under the Tripartite Pact and declared war on the United States. Meanwhile, Japanese armies invaded Thailand, Malaysia, the Philippines, and Java. The Second World War had truly become a global conflict.

American troops contributed much to the fighting of that war, in Europe as well as the Pacific. In fact, U.S. policymakers had decided months earlier that if the nation did go to war, its first aim would be to defeat Hitler. They had several reasons for doing so. One was geographical: Access to the Atlantic made Germany a more direct threat to the Western Hemisphere, particularly if it knocked Britain out of the war. American planners further felt that Germany was more likely than Japan to achieve some revolutionary breakthrough in military technology. Lastly, Great Britain and Russia had already made a full commitment to stopping the Axis powers (Germany, Italy, and Japan). By contrast, Chinese resistance to Japan was considerably less active; and given China's internal political problems, no informed observer looked for much improvement anytime soon.

In its initial deployment of U.S. forces, Washington followed Britain's lead and adopted a Mediterranean strategy. This entailed pushing the Axis armies out of North Africa, invading Sicily, and moving up the boot of Italy. In June 1944, American and British armies finally crossed the English Channel and stormed the beaches of Normandy. Although this was a chancy operation—in that the Germans knew an invasion was coming—the Allies held on and established a second front in Europe. Hitler's days were now numbered. He did launch a major counteroffensive that winter, but it proved to be too little, too late. In the Battle of the Bulge, Allied forces not only managed to maintain several key positions; they afterwards regrouped, closed the gap in their lines, and on January 3, 1945, retook the offensive. Although several months of hard fighting lay ahead, the war in Europe was effectively over.

From the invasion of North Africa in November 1942 to the Battle of the Bulge and beyond, George Patton seldom ventured far from the action. A strong proponent of mobility, Patton had, in Dwight Eisenhower's words, "more 'drive' on the battlefield than any other man I know." At the same time, Patton's arbitrary actions and undiplomatic assertions made him one of the most controversial generals of the war. In the essay that follows, Stephen E. Ambrose and Judith D. Ambrose analyze Patton's complex personality and sometimes contradictory behavior, examine his relations with Eisenhower, and assess his strengths and weaknesses as a military leader.

George Patton

Stephen E. Ambrose and Judith D. Ambrose

Shortly after the end of World War II elements of the U.S. Seventh Army were in a little village in Czechoslovakia west of Prague. It was a hot spring day, and the men and officers were concerned with the usual problems of occupation duty, enlivened only by the possibility of conflict with the nearby Russians. Suddenly the quiet of the main street gave way to a blast of noise. Armored cars, jeeps, and wagons began to pour into the village. Horns blared and flags waved from all the cars. There was even a soldier blowing a trumpet. A cloud of dust rose everywhere. As it settled, the Seventh Army men saw sitting in a jeep in the middle of the convoy a general of the United States Army, wearing high, brightly polished boots, two ivory-handled revolvers, and a huge grin. George Patton had arrived.

The members of the Seventh Army were not happy with this development. In the first place, Patton usually meant trouble. More important, they did not like him. His Third Army had stolen the headlines since the preceding August;

Source: This article is reprinted from the July 1996 issue of *American History Illustrated* with the permission of Cowles History Group, Inc. Copyright *American History Illustrated* magazine.

Patton's men felt they were something special, and they let everyone know it. As Patton bounded out of his jeep he was greeted with formal handshakes and cold stares.

Patton just smiled and asked the local commander to call his men together for a review in the village square. When they were all assembled, he went up on a bandstand, looked them over, and said, "So this is the Seventh Army! By God, I've heard a lot about you men. I'm sorry as hell I didn't have a chance to lead you in battle." Patton had a notorious reputation for saying what he thought and the men accepted his flattery as sincerely as he had apparently given it. When he stepped down from the stand, they cheered madly.

That night the officers arranged a banquet. The mayor and other local officials and dignitaries attended. Patton spent the evening talking to the Czechs in French about opera, central European history and geography, and philosophy. As the general left, his caravan again stirring up a cloud of dust, an English-speaking Czech turned to one of the Seventh Army officers and said, "But, monsieur, you did not tell us he was a man of culture."

They had just seen one aspect of the most complicated man of World War II. George Patton was many things, not only to others but to himself. He was a consummate actor always conscious of the role he was playing. Blond and brawny, he carried himself with dignity and poise, usually dressed to the hilt. He saw people as individuals and reacted accordingly. When he wanted to pull out the stops and impress a bunch of tough GIs, he would curse with some of the foulest language ever heard in any army. When he wanted to stir his staff to greater activity he would throw fits of rage that outdid **Caligula.** Then, as the chastised staff left his office, he would turn to his orderly, smile, and say softly, "That ought to get them going." If he were among intellectuals, he would draw on his amazing knowledge of history to impress them. But always, in these and other situations, he was conscious of playing a role, and he kept the real man submerged.

Patton was a man of diverse and often contradictory moods. He was ambivalent in his attitude toward the Germans, extending them grudging respect for their technical abilities while being utterly contemptuous of their strategical mistakes and horrified at their criminal actions. When the Third Army liberated a Nazi concentration camp Patton called the supreme commander, Dwight D. Eisenhower, and insisted that he bring a touring congressional delegation, plus all the attached reporters, to the camp immediately. Patton did not want anyone saying after this war that the German atrocities were all propaganda. As the group toured the camp Patton had to excuse himself and go to a bathroom where he was violently ill. Yet a couple of months later he could tell reporters that "this Nazi business" was just like the Republicans and Democrats back home.

Caligula Emperor of Rome whose ruthlessness, extravagance, and megalomania led to his assassination.

Vichy The capital of unoccupied France during the Second World War.

SHAEF Supreme Headquarters Allied Expeditionary Forces led by Dwight Eisenhower.

He was also capable of making contradictory statements and sticking with them in the face of all logic. During the summer campaign in Sicily in 1943, Patton paid a visit to some combat-zone hospitals. He saw a great many seriously wounded men and tried to say a kind word to each of them. As he was about to leave the tent he saw a boy in his mid-twenties sitting on a box near the dressing station. There was nothing obviously wrong with the soldier, Private Charles H. Kuhl, so Patton went over and asked what was the matter. Kuhl gave Patton a fearful look, then muttered, "I guess I can't take it."

Patton completely lost his temper, slapped Kuhl, kicked him in the pants, swore at him, called him a loathsome coward, and told the doctor, "Don't admit this sonuvabitch. I don't want yellow-bellied bastards like him hiding in their lousy cowardice around here, stinking up this place of honor." Turning again to Kuhl, he shrieked, "You gutless bastard, you're going back to the front, *at once!*"

Later that day, August 10, 1943, Patton visited another hospital and repeated the scene, this time knocking the patient's helmet off. When the shell-shocked soldier told Patton it was his nerves and began to sob, the general screamed at him, "Your nerves, hell, you are just a goddamn coward, you yellow son of a bitch." He again slapped the man, shouting, "Shut up that goddamned crying," and again ordered the doctors not to admit the soldier. On the same day, incidentally, Patton had had a long argument with one division commander, another with Omar Bradley, and relieved General Terry Allen of 1st Division. The war in Sicily was not going well at the time.

The story of the slapping, despite Eisenhower's best efforts, leaked, and Patton had a lot of explaining to do. His cause was weak because it was learned that Kuhl suffered from chronic diarrhea, had a temperature of 102.2°, and had malaria. The second soldier also had a high fever. Patton gave out two separate and distinct explanations, sometimes simultaneously. The first was that he was so upset by seeing apparently healthy men in a hospital with the seriously wounded that he simply lost his temper. He did not believe there was such a thing as shell-shock; it was simply cowardice. The second was that he had had a friend in World War I who suffered from shell-shock and eventually committed suicide. Patton maintained that if someone had slapped his friend at the beginning, he would have been all right. In short, Patton felt he was playing psychiatrist and that his treatment would cure the soldiers. He stuck with both stories until the day he died.

In contrast to the slapping incidents, but illuminating the emotional nature of Patton, there is the story of another visit he made to a hospital shortly after VE-Day. During the war his daughter had gone to Walter Reed Hospital in Washington and asked to be assigned as a nurse's aide in the multiple amputee ward. The superintendent of nurses agreed, not knowing who she was. When her father came to Washington for a short visit, Ruth Ellen asked him to visit her ward. Patton was greatly affected. He tried to make a little speech to the soldier patients but broke down and wept. Finally he gained control of himself and said, "If I had been a better general you wouldn't be here."

There were contradictions in his relationships with his friends, too, most notably with Dwight Eisenhower. Patton and Eisenhower knew each other well, since both had been in armor in World War I. Eisenhower looked up to Patton, who was his senior both in years and in combat experience, and shortly before America entered World War II told Patton he would like to fight under him, perhaps as commander of a regimental combat team. When Eisenhower began his climb Patton adjusted to it easily and was delighted to have a role to play under his old friend in the November 1942 invasion of North Africa. For his part Eisenhower, well aware of Patton's reputation as a trouble-maker and generally embarrassing person to have around, believed that the U.S. Army had available no finer leader of troops in battle and was willing to put up with almost anything to keep Patton in the field.

From the first Patton put Eisenhower's faith to the test. In North Africa he hobnobbed with **Vichy** Frenchmen and various sultans. In Sicily he slapped soldiers. He frequently muttered threats about resigning and going home to tell the "real truth" unless he was given this or that assignment. Withal, Eisenhower stuck with him, absorbing a volume of criticism that Patton never knew about. And for his part Patton too delivered, as in his lightning campaign through Sicily, where he ran the Germans and Italians ragged and showed his heels to Bernard Montgomery and the British Eighth Army.

When Franklin Roosevelt designated Eisenhower as the supreme commander for operation OVERLORD, the invasion of France, Chief of Staff George Marshall gave Eisenhower a free hand in picking his subordinates. Eisenhower's first choice was Omar Bradley. His second was George Patton. At the time, December of 1943, Patton was under tremendous criticism in the United States for the slapping incidents, and Eisenhower along with him for shielding him. The easy thing would have been to pick Mark Clark. But Eisenhower wanted Patton and got him. He told Patton he would have to behave, and Patton was grateful for the opportunity—but resentful because of the lecture. Later, in England training for the invasion, Patton made some ill-considered remarks in a public gathering about how England, the United States, and Russia would have to run the world after the war. Again Eisenhower lectured him but refused to consider dropping him. Again Patton was both grateful and resentful.

In preparing the Third Army for the invasion Patton used many personal touches. Most of his men had not yet participated in combat and he had a favorite story he liked to tell them. Later, like most Patton stories, it became famous. "There is a hill in Sicily," he said, "where several score of soldiers lay down to sleep under the olive trees. They had had a lot of fighting during the day, and were tired and sleepy. They put out a few sentries. But the sentries, too, went to sleep. The corporals didn't make the rounds to see that the sentries were awake, and the sergeants didn't check on the corporals. No officer inspected the sentries, either. Late that night the enemy crept into that olive grove and silently cut the throats of all the sleeping men, who today are buried on that hillside."

Patton had made his point. But then he grinned wolfishly, and added, "There is only one good thing about it. The men whose throats were cut were

Germans. The enemy who did the cutting were our men." The men of Third Army had unbounded confidence in their commander from then on.

On the eve of Third Army's crossing of the Channel, Patton delivered to the assembled throng his greatest speech. Unfortunately, to my knowledge, no verbatim copy exists. It was by all odds the most stirring and the most scurrilous, the most inspiring and the most indecent, eve-of-battle talk ever given. Dwight MacDonald reprinted parts of it in an article called "My Favorite General," but no chopped-up version can do it justice and no complete version could go through the U.S. mails.

The deterioration of the Patton–Eisenhower relationship continued after the invasion. Third Army was not in on the initial landings and did not become operational until the breakout from the beachhead, early in August 1944. Patton and his staff began to feel that Eisenhower and **SHAEF** [Supreme Headquarters Allied Expeditionary Forces] were against them. When Third Army was unleashed, SHAEF tried to keep its presence on the battlefield a secret, so Patton's boys did not get the credit they deserved. It was in those first weeks of August that Third Army did its best work, overrunning France in a campaign unmatched in all history. Patton's staff began to feed him the idea that SHAEF—and Eisenhower—were jealous and would not give him the credit he deserved. The situation became worse in September, as the Allied armies outstripped their supplies, and there was not enough for anyone. Patton was convinced he could go right through the German West Wall and into Berlin if only SHAEF would give his tanks the gas they needed. Montgomery, to the north, was equally convinced that his 21st Army Group could do the same thing. Eisenhower could not satisfy either one, but he did tend to favor Montgomery, since the port of Antwerp was within Montgomery's boundary and its capture would ease the supply problem. Patton began to mutter that Eisenhower was the best general the British had.

Other incidents piled up. They got worse after the war, when Patton assumed the duties of military governor of Bavaria. He refused to follow Eisenhower's—really, the Allied—policy of a hard line toward the Germans and consistently employed or refused to fire former SS men and Nazis. A climax came at a press conference when Patton asserted that the military government "would get better results if it employed more former members of the Nazi party in administrative jobs and as skilled workmen." He then made his statement that joining the Nazi party was just like joining the Republicans or the Democrats back home. Eisenhower was furious. He ordered Patton to call another press conference and take back everything he had said. Patton called the conference, read Eisenhower's general orders on de-Nazification, and then claimed that he had been carrying out the official policy and would continue to act as he had in the past. Eisenhower was dissatisfied. He made Patton come to his headquarters, where he relieved him of his duties. Even at this moment Eisenhower tried to ease the blow, allowing Patton to select his successor. Patton, however, left the meeting murmuring that he now saw the truth of Henry Adams's phrase that a friend in power is a friend lost.

But ingratitude, if that is what it was, was only one of the many facets of

Patton's personality. He came from a very rich family that had roots in Boston, old Virginia, and California. Until he entered West Point he followed no formalized schooling program, and was in fact a spoiled boy who did about what he wanted to. His three great loves were horses, history, and shocking people. He cultivated swearing with such a persistence that he soon became a recognized expert, and he employed his profanity whenever and wherever he felt like it. As it happened, he often felt like it. He liked to show off his ability to carry out his favorite maxim, which was that any true gentleman should be able to curse for two minutes steady without repeating a single word. However, a long-time cavalry friend of his said recently, "Sure, he was an *artiste* with profanity but I was never conscious of his being obnoxious around ladies. After all, he was brought up to be a gentleman, and he was one."

Only "Georgie's" love of horses and history exceeded his fondness for profanity. He could ride with the best, was an outstanding polo player, and probably would have been happiest as a cavalry officer under J. E. B. Stuart. He had authentic connections, through his ancestors, with the Army of Northern Virginia, and studied thoroughly the campaigns of the Civil War. He spent most of the twenties and thirties in the cavalry, which he recognized as a defunct branch of the army—he had been in armor in World War I and was enthusiastic about its possibilities—but which allowed him to ride, socialize, and study history. Unlike most army officers of the period, however, his knowledge went far beyond the American Civil War. He was well versed in all branches of military history, from Alexander the Great to the present. When his troops captured a historic fortress in World War II, such as Metz, he could recount not only how many times Metz had fallen before, not only to whom, but exactly how it had happened. He was also well, if not thoroughly, acquainted with all aspects of European and American history in general.

"He had the damnedest library you ever saw," said the contemporary quoted above. "I remember commenting on this and he told me he had every book obtainable on Napoleon."

Patton was a warm and compassionate family man. To his children he seemed a god, but a god who often descended to earth to play with them. His wife, Beatrice Ayer Patton, of a wealthy Boston family, was a lovely woman whom he loved deeply and who shared and enjoyed his life fully. Because her husband liked horses, she became an avid horsewoman; because he was a deep ocean yachtsman, she became an accomplished sailorwoman, winning many championships in small racing sloops. Her husband liked history, so she, too, studied it. One thing she did not do: she refused to adopt her husband's practice of spelling the same word in several different ways.

Patton could be fatherly to his enlisted men, too. Before the war he was commanding officer at Fort Myer, Virginia, across the river from Washington, D.C. One Sunday a practical joker among the soldiers on the post told two recruits, "You men go at once to call on the post commander. It is the custom in the army." Never suspecting that the custom applied only to officers and their ladies, the recruits put on their ill-fitting blouses, brushed their hair, and presented themselves at the door of the commanding officer's quarters. Those who knew Patton, as the practical joker did, expected that when the recruits told him what they had come for he would make an immediate and noisy ascension.

Instead, Patton politely invited them in, ushered them into the drawing room, presented them to Mrs. Patton, and began a pleasant and amiable chat. Mrs. Patton served tea. The men back at the barracks never believed this story, but Patton loved to tell it on himself.

Enlisted men did not always fare so well with Patton. During the war he began to take violent objection to the characters in Bill Mauldin's cartoons, especially Willie and Joe. Patton thought Mauldin was disrespectful toward the army and under no circumstances did he want his men looking like, or admiring, soldiers who were as sloppy as Willie and Joe. By 1944 Patton could stand it no longer, and he ordered that the *Stars and Stripes,* the enlisted men's newspaper in which Mauldin's cartoons appeared, should no longer circulate in the Third Army.

Eisenhower felt at least as strongly about censorship as Patton did about sloppy soldiers, and he immediately ordered Patton to back down. Patton refused. Eisenhower's personal aide, Harry Butcher, then arranged for a meeting between Patton and Mauldin. Mauldin, who wore three stripes on his arm as compared to the three stars on Patton's shoulders, was scared to death, but at Butcher's urging he went. Patton gave Mauldin the full treatment, appealing to his patriotism and his pride in the army. It didn't work—Mauldin defended his rights as an artist. Patton went into a rage, but although his profanity turned Mauldin's face white it didn't change his mind.

A few weeks later Butcher saw Patton and showed him a *Time* magazine story on the meeting, a story which concluded with a statement from Mauldin to the effect that Patton had not convinced him and he was fairly sure he had not convinced Patton. Patton, in his high-pitched voice, said to Butcher, "Why, if that little s.o.b. ever comes in the Third Army area again, I'll throw him in jail." But Eisenhower overruled Patton, the *Stars and Stripes* did circulate in the Third Army, and the sergeant won the battle with the three-star general.

Yet none of these facets of Patton's personality—the polo playboy, the spewer of profanity, the historian, the psychiatrist, the family man, or the actor—represented the true Patton. At heart he was a man with a fierce inner compulsion to excel at whatever he did. It did not much matter if it was at cursing, making war, or studying history—Patton had to be the best. It was the compulsion that helped create the near-eccentric personality; it was also the compulsion that helped create America's greatest combat soldier.

What George Patton did best of all, better than anyone else, was make a certain type of war. He was not a brilliant strategist nor was he exceptional in launching an attack. But in the pursuit he was the best America or anyone else ever had. His theory of war was simple: "Go like hell." In Sicily he told his men, "We must retain this advantage [the initiative] by always attacking rapidly, ruthlessly, viciously, without rest. However tired and hungry you may be, the enemy will be more tired, more hungry." Once Patton got the enemy started, he never let him stop. If his own superiors began to worry and tried to slow him down, he just cut his communications with the rear and drove right on. He pushed, pulled, cajoled, threatened, screamed at his men, in order to get superhuman efforts out of them, to keep them moving, to grind down and destroy the enemy before he had a chance to rest and regroup and rearm. Like Ulysses Grant he thought not about what the enemy might do to him, but about what he might do to the enemy. In the pursuit he never worried about his flanks, for he was sure—and events proved him right—that an off-balance enemy could never mount a serious counterattack. He used his tanks with audacity and intelligence, and he showed the world mobile armored warfare that no one had previously dreamed possible.

Patton's Third Army went across France in August and September of 1944 faster than the Germans had come through in their much more famous blitzkrieg of 1940, and Patton did it against a stronger and better led opponent. He beat the Germans worse than the Russians, or anyone else, ever did. And they knew it. Hitler and his generals feared Patton more than any other opposing general, as both Heinz Guderian and Gerd von Rundstedt told American officers after the war. Patton moved so fast the Germans simply could not believe it.

Neither could anyone else. No supply service in the world could have kept up with Patton's tanks, much less one depending on a couple of small, damaged ports and required to serve two entire army groups. Patton, in turn, could never understand why they could not keep up, and harbored thoughts of persecution. He did what he could to keep the advance going—hoarding captured gasoline and oil and not telling SHAEF about the capture, so that he received his pittance from supply headquarters in addition to the German materials—but it was not enough. And so he ran out of gas, and a war which he firmly believed he could have ended before Christmas of 1944 dragged on until May of 1945.

No one really knows if Patton could have fought on the defensive. He never had the test, as he never fought a truly set battle—Montgomery's favorite kind—and he quickly turned every defensive-looking situation into a counteroffensive. On December 16, 1944, the Germans began the Battle of the Bulge. On December 19 Eisenhower held a meeting at Verdun. Bradley, Patton, and others were present. Everyone was gloomy, for none had believed that the Germans were capable of launching an attack of this size and scope. Eisenhower looked at his subordinates and declared, "There will only be cheerful faces at this conference table." Patton looked at him, grinned, and said, "Hell, let's have the guts to let the—go all the way to Paris. Then we'll really cut 'em off and chew 'em up." Eisenhower then asked Patton, in the middle of planning an offensive of his own, how long it would take him to change direction and hit the southern flank of the German breakthrough. It was a difficult request. To change direction in the middle of an operation involving a half-dozen divisions, with all the administrative, supply, organizational, and human problems involved, is extremely difficult. Montgomery would have taken three months or a month.

Patton said he would do it in four days. He did it in three.

Patton's abilities, according to his most ardent admirers, were never fully tested. According to them he should have been given at least an army group to command. Actually, he had probably reached his limit with the Third Army. He lacked the tact and breadth of vision to command an army group, with its huge staff system and personality problems with army, corps, and division commanders. Similarly, his tactical maxims do not reveal a particularly brilliant or original mind. Rather, they point up his one-sidedness, a one-sidedness that showed to tremendous advantage with the Third Army but might not have done so elsewhere.

Some of Patton's combat principles, as he called them, were: "There is no approved solution to any tactical situation." "In battle, casualties vary directly with the time you are exposed to effective fire. Your own fire reduces the effectiveness and volume of the enemy's fire, while rapidity of attack shortens the time of exposure. A pint of sweat will save a gallon of blood!" "Battles are won by frightening the enemy. Fear is induced by inflicting death and wounds on him. Death and wounds are produced by fire. Fire from the rear is more deadly and three times more effective than fire from the front, but to get fire behind the enemy, you must hold him by frontal fire and move rapidly around his flank." "Catch the enemy by the nose with fire and kick him in the pants with fire emplaced through movement." "Use roads to march on, fields to fight on." "Troops should not deploy into line until forced to do so by enemy fire." "The larger the force and the more violence you use in the attack, whether it be men, tanks, or ammunition, the smaller will be your proportional losses."

It was not long after World War I that Lawrence of Arabia decided that he had played out his role on the world stage. For himself, he had done what he wanted to do, and after a disastrous venture into occupation politics in the areas he had liberated he actively sought oblivion. He found it first as an enlisted man in the air force, then in death.

George Patton blazed his way through World War II and onto the world stage in much the same way as Lawrence had done earlier. And like Lawrence, his role ended when the shooting stopped. He did not actively seek death, but when it came, in a senseless and minor automobile accident in December 1945, it reminded some observers of Lawrence's death on his motorcycle years earlier. Both men had located and climbed their mountains; there was nothing left for them to conquer.

D-DAY

At daybreak on June 6, 1944, an Allied invasion of nearly 200,000 troops began hitting the beaches along the Normandy coast of France. It was the largest amphibious landing in history. Despite heavy aerial and naval bombardment of German defensive positions, Axis forces put up a fierce resistance

Source: From Ernie Pyle, *Brave Men,* p. 248. Copyright © 1944. Reprinted by permission of Scripps Howard Foundation.

and it was not immediately clear whether the operation would succeed. One of the men who went ashore that morning was Ernie Pyle, a combat journalist famous for his firsthand reporting on the lives of frontline soldiers. In the selection that follows, Pyle provides a gripping account of what it was like during those first critical days in Normandy.

•••••

Our men simply could not get past the beach. They were pinned down right on the water's edge by an inhuman wall of fire from the bluff. Our first waves were on that beach for hours, instead of a few minutes, before they could begin working inland.

The foxholes were still there—dug at the very edge of the water, in the sand and the small jumbled rocks that formed parts of the beach.

Medical corpsmen attended the wounded as best they could. Men were killed as they stepped out of landing craft. An officer whom I knew got a bullet through the head just as the door of his landing craft was let down. Some men were drowned.

The first crack in the beach defenses was finally accomplished by terrific and wonderful naval gunfire, which knocked out the big emplacements. Epic stories have been told of destroyers that ran right up into shallow water and had it out point-blank with the big guns in those concrete emplacements ashore.

When the heavy fire stopped, our men were organized by their officers and pushed on inland, circling machine-gun nests and taking them from the rear.

As one officer said, the only way to take a beach is to face it and keep going. It is costly at first, but it's the only way. If the men are pinned down on the beach, dug in and out of action, they might as well not be there at all. They hold up the waves behind them, and nothing is being gained.

Our men were pinned down for a while, but finally they stood up and went through, and so we took that beach and accomplished our landing. In the light of a couple of days of retrospection, we sat and talked and called it a miracle that our men ever got on at all or were able to stay on.

They suffered casualties. And yet considering the entire beachhead assault, including other units that had a much easier time, our total casualties in driving that wedge into the Continent of Europe were remarkably low—only a fraction, in fact, of what our commanders had been prepared to accept.

And those units that were so battered and went through such hell pushed on inland without rest, their spirits high, their egotism in victory almost reaching the smart-alecky stage.

Their tails were up. "We've done it again," they said. They figured that the rest of the army wasn't needed at all. Which proves that, while their judgment in this respect was bad, they certainly had the spirit that wins battles, and eventually wars.

•••••

QUESTIONS

1. In what ways did Patton's study of history contribute to his development as a military leader? What influence did Patton's experience as a cavalry officer have on the tactics he later employed in World War II?
2. As a former cavalry officer, Patton had much in common with Philip Sheridan. Do you see any similarities between the two men? How do you think Sheridan would have responded to the challenges of World War II? How do you think Patton would have conducted the Indian wars of the late nineteenth century?
3. How would you characterize Patton's relationship with Eisenhower? In that Patton was a more experienced field commander than Eisenhower, why was the latter chosen as the supreme commander for the invasion of France? Do you think Patton could have followed Eisenhower's example and made a successful transition to political life after the war?
4. What do the Mauldin incident and Patton's abuse of shell-shocked soldiers tell us about the general's personality? How was Patton able to command such loyalty from his own troops?
5. What were Patton's greatest strengths as a military leader? What were his shortcomings? Do you agree with the authors' observation that Patton had probably reached his limit as commander of the Third Army?
6. Which of the historical figures profiled in this unit would you most like to write about? What questions would you ask in a study of that person? What types of sources would you consult to answer those questions?

BIBLIOGRAPHY

The two best biographies of the colorful general are Ladislas Farago, *Patton: Ordeal and Triumph* (1963), and Martin Blumenson, *Patton: The Man and the Legend, 1884–1945* (1985). Blumenson has also edited *The Patton Papers*, 2 vols. (1972–1974). The military career of Patton's wartime commander in Europe is examined in Stephen E. Ambrose, *Eisenhower: Soldier, General of the Army, President-Elect, 1890–1952* (1983). For more on the broader context in which Patton operated during the war, see Geoffrey Perret, *There's a War to Be Won: The United States Army in World War II* (1991); Robert Leckie, *Delivered from Evil: A Saga of World War II* (1987); and B. H. Liddell Hart, *History of the Second World War* (1970). Domestic as well as military developments during the period are ably surveyed in William L. O'Neill, *A Democracy at War: America's Fight at Home and Abroad in World War II* (1993).

Introduction

The quarter century after World War II was a period of unprecedented prosperity in the United States. It all began with the release of personal savings accumulated during the war. As consumer goods became increasingly available, Americans went on an incredible spending spree. They later benefited from the sorry condition of the world's leading industrial nations immediately after the war. Of the major combatants, only the United States came out of the conflict with its manufacturing base intact. By contrast, major production centers in the Soviet Union, Japan, Germany, and other parts of Europe had been devastated by wartime bombing. Because recovery took time, most U.S. corporations faced no serious foreign competition for years afterward. Meanwhile, steady increases in real income made American wage earners the world's most affluent working people.

Although the postwar economy performed better than anyone reasonably could have expected, there were a few dark spots on the horizon, none more ominous than the growing estrangement between the United States and its wartime ally, the Soviet Union. The resulting Cold War, during which the United States assumed the unaccustomed role of world policeman, had its domestic counterpart in the investigations of Red-hunting politicians who believed Communist subversives were undermining major national institutions. The best known and most feared of these politicians was Joseph R. McCarthy. In his essay on the Wisconsin senator, Fred Cook examines the events that made McCarthy's name a byword for the public slandering of innocent citizens.

Although the postwar economic boom touched nearly all Americans, not everyone benefited equally. In most parts of the nation, particularly the South, discrimination and segregation still placed sharp limits on what African Americans could do. Throughout the first half of the century, the struggle for black rights had focused on the courts, where National Association for the Advancement of Colored People (NAACP) lawyers had obtained a series of favorable rulings. The most notable of these was *Brown v. Board of Education of Topeka*, a 1954 decision in which the Supreme Court cleared the way for school integration by overturning the "separate but equal" doctrine that it had earlier enunciated in *Plessy v. Ferguson* (1896). Although *Brown* remains the NAACP's greatest triumph, the massive resistance provoked by the ruling revealed the limits of legalism. With the subsequent rise of mass action, the civil rights movement entered a new phase that increasingly centered on the streets rather than the courts. In his essay on Martin Luther King, Jr., Stephen Oates profiles the individual who best personified this phase of the movement.

The postwar period also witnessed the rebirth of the women's movement. There had been an earlier movement, whose most enduring legacy was the woman's suffrage amendment. But the movement itself did not survive the 1920s, and the postwar "cult of domesticity" that decreed woman's place was in the home had erased most memories of those earlier initiatives. Few people did more to revive the struggle for women's rights than Betty Friedan, who authored *The Feminine Mystique* (1963), a pathbreaking work that prompted countless women to begin searching outside the household for a sense of fulfillment their domestic lives too often denied them. In his essay on Friedan, David Halberstam examines the developments that made *The Feminine Mystique* so important to the modern women's movement.

The campaign for gender equality that Friedan helped set in motion was one of several 1960s movements that drew inspiration from the achievements of civil rights activists. Another was Cesar Chavez's effort to organize California's Mexican–American farmworkers. The latter had long been among the nation's most exploited wage earners, and as Cletus Daniel notes in his essay, Chavez confronted formidable obstacles then unknown to most labor leaders. Daniel further relates how, in the course of overcoming them, the charismatic organizer established a union that reflected his own dual personality as a social activist and a trade unionist.

By the 1970s, there were growing signs that the postwar economic boom had run its course. With the industrial revival of Japan, Germany, and other European nations, U.S. corporations lost their earlier competitive advantage; and with the emergence of an integrated world economy, American producers faced unprecedented competitive challenges. As they struggled to adjust, many large employers adopted cost-cutting strategies that depressed wages and eliminated jobs. To illustrate the effects of these changes, the volume's final essay abandons the biographical format of previous chapters and instead presents a group portrait of American wage earners. In it, Katherine Newman explores how displaced managers, unemployed blue-collar workers, and other people who have had an increasingly difficult time matching the economic achievements of their parents' generation have tried to come to grips with life in a period of growing economic instability.

Joseph R. McCarthy

During the immediate postwar period, as tensions between the United States and the Soviet Union escalated, the two superpowers became locked in a Cold War that would last for more than 40 years. Internationally, the conflict involved struggles for dominance in such farflung locales as Poland, Czechoslovakia, China, Korea, and Vietnam. There also was a domestic Cold War. It took the form of security checks, congressional investigations of Communist subversion, and the harassment of dissident political groups. This domestic Cold War affected a broad range of American institutions: schools, unions, and the media, as well as the federal government, which was the initial target of Red-hunting politicians. Before it ended, the crusade destroyed the careers of numerous individuals in both the private and public sectors.

The 1948 presidential contest marked a major turning point in the emergence of the domestic Cold War. Republicans had not held the White House since Herbert Hoover's administration, and nearly everyone believed that this was their year. When Thomas Dewey unexpectedly lost the election, disappointed party leaders began looking for an issue with which to bring down the Truman presidency. A series of events the following year seemed to provide it. The first occurred in September, when Soviet officials announced the successful detonation of an atomic bomb. Coming a half-dozen years sooner than most people expected, the Soviet

breakthrough prompted assertions that the activities of spies operating within the United States had made the Soviet accomplishment possible. The second event was the fall of China a month later, which Republican leaders blamed on the actions of administration critics of Chiang K'ai-shek's nationalist government. Meanwhile, month after month throughout the year, an attentive national audience raptly followed the various twists and turns of the Alger Hiss espionage case. A former State Department official, Hiss had played a secondary but important role in a number of diplomatic initiatives during the Roosevelt era. He also was the walking embodiment of the eastern establishment: a cultured, well-educated, Ivy-league type whom conservative Republicans from the nation's heartland instinctively distrusted and hated.

With these developments, the stage was set for the appearance of one of the most extraordinary demagogues in American history, Joseph R. McCarthy. The Wisconsin senator's public career as a Red hunter began on February 9, 1950, when he told startled members of the Women's Republican Club of West Virginia: "I have here in my hands a list of 205 [employees] made known to the secretary of state as being members of the Communist party and who nonetheless are still working and shaping policy." McCarthy never showed this list to anyone; indeed, he later forgot how many names were supposed to be on it. But this didn't matter to McCarthy, for he had accomplished his primary aim: to capture the country's attention. He remained in the national limelight for another four years.

During this period, McCarthy became the most feared politician in America. In the end, though, he overplayed his hand by deciding to take on the U.S. Army. This foolhardy act placed him at odds with President Eisenhower, the nation's most revered military figure. It was a serious mistake. Over the years McCarthy had made numerous enemies. When Ike turned on him, rival politicians and media critics sensed that it was open season and began firing from all sides. In the essay that follows, Fred Cook reviews significant features of the Wisconsin senator's colorful and destructive career, while providing a thorough examination of the Army–McCarthy hearings.

Joseph R. McCarthy

Fred Cook

• • • • •

Joe McCarthy, as he became known to millions of Americans, was a contradictory figure, two men in one. The first was a likable, backslapping boon com-

Source: Reprinted with the permission of Simon & Schuster Books for Young Readers, an imprint of Simon & Schuster Children's Publishing Division from *The Demagogues* by Fred J. Cook. Copyright © 1972 Fred J. Cook.

panion who wanted to be loved by everyone. The second—the man who emerged under opposition or threat—was a savage, scowling battler who stopped at nothing.

McCarthy was born November 14, 1908, on a worn-out farm in upper Wisconsin about a hundred miles north of Milwaukee. He worked his way through college and law school. In college, he was an amateur boxer, a crude and unskilled one who threw all science to the winds and charged headlong, with swinging, wild, windmill blows. As a young lawyer, his earnings were small, and he played poker more than he worked at the law. He became known as a poker player who would bluff outrageously on every hand. Opponents never knew quite how to figure him. Just when they thought he must be bluffing again, he would come up with a pat hand and rake in a huge pot. These traits told much about Joe McCarthy; he was to remain all his life the reckless headlong battler—and master of the art of the colossal bluff.

In 1939 when he was 31 McCarthy joined the Republican party in Wisconsin and got himself elected as a circuit court judge. Just two years later the United States became involved in World War II, and he enlisted in the marines, was commissioned a lieutenant, and went off to the South Pacific. He was an intelligence officer, assigned to secure rear bases, but sometimes, just for the fun of it, he rode in the tail-gunner's seat of a bomber on routine missions and blasted away at coconut trees. Ever a master at publicizing himself, he had his picture taken in combat uniform; copies flooded the Wisconsin newspapers and, almost overnight, he became "Tail Gunner Joe"—a war hero.

The legend helped in 1946 when he ran for the U.S. Senate seat long held by Robert M. La Follette, Jr. La Follette was the son of Wisconsin's most famous politician, "Fighting Bob" La Follette. The La Follette name was a household word in the state, and few gave upstart young Joe McCarthy a fighting chance.

But times were changing. Even so soon after the war, the jitters were setting in. Russia had become a menace. Things had obviously gone wrong. Republicans throughout the 1946 campaign raised a great hue and cry against Communists and fellow travelers in the Democratic administration in Washington. La Follette, though running in the Republican primary in Wisconsin, had a liberal voting record, having sided on critical issues with the Democratic administration. The result was that La Follette found he had enemies on all sides. Conservative Republicans detested him for his liberalism. And Communists, then strong in some of Wisconsin's labor unions, hated him even more viciously because he had delivered one of the first Cold War speeches in the Senate, denouncing Russia as a menace to world peace. The situation was tailor-made for Joe McCarthy. He attacked La Follette sometimes as a pro-Fascist type; at other times, in utter contradiction, as a Communist fellow traveler. Enough of the wild charges stuck so that La Follette lost his usual strong backing in the big-city labor wards; and brash Joe McCarthy, scoring an upset of upsets, went to Washington as the new U.S. senator from Wisconsin.

As a freshman senator, McCarthy built a record of dubious value. He became known as the lobbyists' best friend. He accepted a $10,000 check from a manufacturer of prefabricated homes for trumpeting the virtues of such housing at the same time he was supposed, in his official capacity, to be investigating housing. He developed a close relationship with a Pepsi-Cola lobbyist who signed a $20,000 note for him—and he battled in the Senate to get postwar sugar rationing relaxed so that Pepsi-Cola could get more sugar. Even worse, he injected himself into a Senate investigation of the World War II Malmedy massacre. It was at Christmastime 1944 that Nazi storm troopers machine-gunned 100 helpless Belgian civilians and 150 captured American soldiers in the little crossroads Belgian town of Malmedy. After the war, several of the Nazi murderers were arrested, tried, and convicted. Then a publicity campaign began in Germany in an effort to save their lives. Back home in Wisconsin, McCarthy had had heavy backing among neo-Nazi elements; and so, though he was not a member of the Senate committee investigating the Malmedy atrocity, he took an active hand in the probe. And he wound up attacking American army officers, contending they had tortured the Nazis to obtain forced confessions. His tactics disrupted the hearings; and, in Germany, the Communist press had a field day slandering America and Americans. The death sentences of the condemned Nazis were finally commuted.

Up to 1950, then, the McCarthy record was hardly admirable. He had become the bosom pal of lobbyists. He had defended the Nazi murderers of Malmedy—and played into the hands of German Communists in doing so. It was not a record with which a politician could go back before his constituents, seeking reelection in 1952. McCarthy needed an issue.

He was hunting for one that would put his name in headlines. And in January 1950, at dinner with some friends in Washington's swank Colony Restaurant, several ideas were batted around unenthusiastically until finally someone suggested the Communist issue. McCarthy seized upon the idea at once and asked the Republican National Committee to arrange some speaking dates for him during the annual Lincoln Day party rallies taking place across the nation.

McCarthy was not well enough known at the time to rate major speaking engagements, and so the committee sent him off to Wheeling, West Virginia. It was there on February 9, 1950, at a Republican rally, that he delivered the speech that was to make him known in every household in America. One paragraph, one gesture stood out. McCarthy was quoted as saying:

> While I cannot take time to name all the men in the State Department who have been named as members of the Communist party and members of a spy ring, *I have here in my hand* a list of 205 that were known to the secretary of state as being members of the Communist party and who, nevertheless, are still working and shaping policy in the State Department.

It was a statement that touched off a frenzy. It was the charge that launched the worst witch-hunt this nation has ever known.

Why should those few lines of type, why should that gesture of a paper waved aloft in clenched hand, have sent an entire nation down the road of a kind of mass insanity, hunting for Communists under every bed? The timing of the charge helps to explain the mass explosion.

Republicans had been trying for years to tar the liberal regimes of Presidents Franklin D. Roosevelt and Harry S. Truman with a Communist affiliation. They had struggled desperately to make the propaganda stick in the presidential campaign of 1948—and had failed by an eyelash. They had concentrated most of their fire on Alger Hiss, a brilliant young aide in the State Department; Whittaker Chambers, a confessed former Communist, charged that Hiss had passed him official papers to send to Russia. It was an infinitely complicated, mysterious case; but, finally, after two trials, Alger Hiss had been convicted of perjury on January 25, 1950, just 15 days before McCarthy spoke at Wheeling. And this was not all.

Even as McCarthy was speaking, the British press was announcing the arrest of Klaus Fuchs. Fuchs, a refugee scientist who had been cleared by British security, had been sent here during wartime to work on the development of the atom bomb. And now Fuchs confessed that he had been spying for Russia and had passed along information through a Communist spy ring operating in this country. Spies. Subversion. The "secret" of the atom bomb gone to Russia. Here was tinder waiting to set off a conflagration; and, at exactly the right minute, Joe McCarthy came along and applied the torch.

He did not realize at once what a good thing he had. There are even some indications he may have been a bit scared himself at first, for as he continued West on his Lincoln Day tour, reporters began to ask him about that 205 figure he had used at Wheeling, and McCarthy at first tried to back off. He didn't think he had used such a figure, he said, but it didn't matter really, he was certain there were enough Communists in the State Department to betray the nation.

In Salt Lake City two days after Wheeling, the 205 Communists had shrunk to 57, a figure that was still startling enough. And McCarthy was positive—oh, so positive—about these. He told a radio interviewer (his words were preserved on tape) that, if Secretary of State Dean Acheson "wants to call me tonight at the Utah Hotel, I will be glad to give him the names of those 57 card-carrying Communists." He added: "I don't want to indicate there are only 57, I say I have the names of 57."

As it became more and more evident that he had touched a quaking nerve in the nation, he became incredibly brash. He fired off a telegram to President Truman, challenging him to a duel of truth about those 57 Communists he said were making policy in the State Department. And, on his return to Washington, he took the Senate floor late in the afternoon of February 20, 1950, and in a long, rambling speech, he indicted the Truman administration for having permitted wholesale penetration and subversion of executive departments by Communists. But the figures had changed again. The number of Communists boring from within was no longer 205 or 57; it was now 81.

Even this new and revised tally would not stand close examination. Although McCarthy claimed to be citing specific cases, an analysis of the speech shows that McCarthy couldn't add. He didn't have 81 cases. He skipped some case numbers completely. He dragged in others even though he admitted himself that they did *not* involve Communist activities. Sometimes he duplicated, and once he even caught himself in the act, confessing: "I believe I have covered this case before, and what I have just said seems to be a repetition . . ."

When McCarthy had finished, even Senator Robert A. Taft, the conserva-

tive "Mr. Republican" of his party, admitted: "It was a perfectly reckless performance." But the Democrats, amazingly, had sat on their hands throughout
those long hours while McCarthy ranted and raved and exposed himself as a
perfect target for their fire. They badgered him about the 205 figure he had
used at Wheeling, but they made no serious attack on his shot-full-of-holes
recital. Why? Political observers speculated then and later that the Democrats'
faith in themselves and their party had been destroyed by the Hiss case—a
case which McCarthy and Republican orators repeatedly cited as the proof of
everything—and so they hesitated to challenge McCarthy's thesis that there
were any number of other Hisses running loose in the State Department.

• • • • •

The presidential election of 1952 saw Joe McCarthy reaching a pinnacle of
power. He had aroused such passions, he had gathered such a following that
he became his party's ultimate weapon. General-hero Dwight D. Eisenhower
was running for the presidency on the high road, bathed in the sunshine of
popular adoration—and there on the low road was Joe McCarthy, the unri-
valed hatchetman, slashing away at the Democratic nominee, Governor Adlai
Stevenson, of Illinois.

In speech after speech, McCarthy referred to Stevenson as "little Ad-lie."
He suggested sometimes that he could "teach patriotism to little Ad-lie" if
someone would only smuggle him aboard the Democratic campaign special
with a baseball bat in his hands. Sometimes he would pretend to have made a
slip, referring to Governor Stevenson as "Alger—I mean Ad-lie," his coy way
of reminding his audiences of the Alger Hiss case.

In his attacks on various candidates that year he always flourished aloft
his trademark—a sheaf of paper—and proclaimed that "I have here in my
hand" proof of one kind or another. The "proof" might consist simply of the
charge that the candidate he was attacking had belonged during the 1930s, in
an entirely different era with entirely different problems, to some organization
that had been adjudged some 10 or 15 years later to have been a "Communist
front." Sometimes it wasn't even necessary for a man to have belonged himself; he might just have been a friend of someone who had belonged, or was
said to have belonged—and so he was considered guilty by this association.
However remote the tie might be, it was enough to give McCarthy the chance
to flourish aloft his papers and rave about his proof that the candidate was a
traitor or, at least, a tainted fellow traveler.

When Eisenhower was elected in a landslide, Joe McCarthy bestrode Capitol Hill, a figure of menace, the author of a nightmare. Before the election,
many had reasoned that Eisenhower would be able to contain and restrain Mc-
Carthy as the Democrats could not. But it soon became obvious that the very
opposite was true. McCarthy had been reelected to the Senate in Wisconsin in
the Eisenhower landslide; and when the Republicans took control of Congress,
McCarthy was given power such as he had never had before. He was made
chairman of the Senate Committee on Government Operations, with broad
powers to investigate and with the command of an investigative staff.

•••••

Some of President Eisenhower's supporters advised him repeatedly to confront McCarthy, to put an end to the frenzy and the witch-hunt. But the president refused, insisting: "I just will not—*I refuse*—to get into the gutter with that
guy." It was clear that Eisenhower did not want to fight, and it was just as clear
that McCarthy was on a collision course, that a battle to the political death
would be inevitable in the end.

The showdown came suddenly at a time when McCarthy seemed to be
riding the crest of the wave of suspicion and frenzy he had created. It was
largely the result of the antics of two young assistants on McCarthy's staff—
Roy M. Cohn, whom McCarthy had named counsel of his investigating committee, and G. David Schine, a staff investigator and close friend of Cohn.
These two brought McCarthy into direct conflict with one of the true power
complexes of the nation—the U.S. Army.

Cohn and Schine were both 26. Cohn was so brilliant he had whipped
through college and Columbia University Law School by the time he was 19,
and he had to wait two years to become of age before he could take his bar examination. He was then appointed an assistant U.S. attorney in New York, and
he began to investigate narcotics traffickers, counterfeiters, and, finally, spies.

Schine was a tall, sleepily handsome young man, the heir to a great hotel
fortune. He had written a sketchy treatise on communism, which he had
placed beside the Bibles in his family's hotels; and so he had come to the attention of Cohn and McCarthy and had been made a specialist in Communist
investigations.

These two young men touched off the first wave of unfavorable publicity
McCarthy had encountered. They toured Europe together at Easter time, 1953.
Their purpose was to investigate the contents of U.S. overseas libraries, and
they went to the kind of extremes that reminded many of the book purges in
Germany during Hitler's time.

•••••

The European tour of Cohn and Schine was followed by events that disgraced the United States as had nothing yet. Books that might offend the Mc-
Carthy witch-hunters, including the detective stories of Dashiell Hammett,
were removed from overseas library shelves. And in some cases books were
actually burned. The number of volumes consigned to bonfires was minute,
only a half-dozen or so, but it was the symbolism of the act that counted. Here
were official agents of this supposedly great and free democracy doing just
what the Nazis had done—destroying the works of authors they hated. Even
President Eisenhower, who had gone to extremes to avoid a break with Mc-
Carthy, felt compelled to denounce book-burning as un-American, and Hammett's harmless detective stories and some other volumes that had been
banned were brought out again into the light of day.

For the moment, it seemed, the showdown had been avoided; but all the
time, behind the scenes, another drama was being enacted. In mid-July 1953,

the U.S. Army began threatening G. David Schine with induction into military service. Roy Cohn, according to the army, began a series of frantic maneuvers designed to get his friend favored treatment. Not only the army but every other branch of the armed services was badgered to obtain a commission for Schine, but none would give him officer status. Cohn, according to the army, was wildly furious, and on one occasion threatened to "get" the army.

Dovetailing with this secret struggle was a succession of public events. There would be much dispute later about whether the Cohn–Schine rumpus was to blame, but the fact remained that it was just at this time that McCarthy began a series of attacks on the army. His first target was the great Signal Corps laboratory complex at Fort Monmouth, New Jersey, where much of the advanced radar for World War II had been developed.

McCarthy bellowed his way into headlines day after day, charging that the Fort Monmouth installations were riddled with spies. He conducted a series of secret hearings in New York, beginning on October 3, 1953; and, after each hearing, he would come out and tell reporters what he had discovered. Since the press could not know what had actually taken place behind the closed doors of the hearing room, it had to take McCarthy's word for it—and McCarthy's words were always alarming and sometimes horrifying. Over and over again, he claimed that he had uncovered evidence of spy rings that were still active at Fort Monmouth.

None of it was true. It took months—in some cases, years—for his charges to be sifted, but in the end they collapsed utterly, every one of them. The commanding general of Fort Monmouth, looking back in 1969, reported that only seven employees had been suspended as "security risks," a designation that is much broader than a charge of espionage. A man may be a security risk if he is a drunk or a homosexual, or if he is chronically head-over-heels in debt. What was truly startling in the Fort Monmouth case, however, was that not even the security risk firings could be sustained. According to Maj. Gen. William B. Latta in 1969, all seven employees suspended as security risks "were reinstated eventually"—and this under a system in which the government needed only to establish that there was enough evidence against a man to create "a doubt" about the advisability of his continued employment. Even under these one-sided circumstances, with all the dice loaded against the accused employees, there had been absolutely nothing to support McCarthy's sensational charges.

This, of course, could not have been apparent at the time, and McCarthy, as was typical of him, went on to a new sensation before the public had a chance to catch its breath. He discovered finally, perhaps for the only time in his career, a man who apparently had been a Communist.

The suspect was Irving Peress, a New York City dentist who had been drafted on October 15, 1952, and had been stationed at Camp Kilmer, New Jersey, outside New Brunswick. In filling out his personnel forms, Peress had claimed the privilege of the Fifth Amendment against possible self-incrimination in answering questions about possible subversive activities and associations. This telltale stain went undetected for months in the flood of paper-work that engulfed the Pentagon, and so on October 23, 1953, Peress was promoted to major. The promotion was not a personal reward; some 7,000 other doctors and dentists also received automatic promotions as provided by newly adopted regulations. But McCarthy, tipped to the possibilities of the Peress case, immediately summoned Peress to testify before him. Peress took the Fifth Amendment to 32 questions dealing with possible Communist affiliations, and McCarthy uttered a scream that made headlines across the nation: "Who promoted Peress?"

In an effort to answer the question, he summoned before him the commanding general of Camp Kilmer, Brig. Gen. Ralph W. Zwicker. Zwicker was a much-decorated hero of World War II. He had led a scouting force ashore in the early hours of the D-Day landing in Normandy. He had commanded a regiment of the Second Infantry Division in the Battle of the Bulge. There could be no question about his patriotism, but McCarthy treated him with contempt.

General Zwicker tried to explain that he had had nothing to say about the promotion of Peress. He had nothing to say about any case involving possible subversion. All such cases were referred to higher echelons in the Pentagon, where army intelligence specialists sifted the evidence and decisions were made as to what action should be taken. These decisions were relayed to General Zwicker through First Army Headquarters in New York. He was only the last man on the conveyor belt. None of this made any impression on McCarthy. He browbeat Zwicker unmercifully and finally denounced him as "unfit to wear that uniform."

This brazen slandering of a heroic general was too much. The Eisenhower administration, which had sat still while the State Department was trampled underfoot, now was faced with an issue it could not dodge; if McCarthy was to be allowed to rage on unchecked in this fashion, the morale of the army also would be destroyed.

The first Republican to see and seize the issue was a much-respected senator from Vermont, Ralph W. Flanders. On March 9, Flanders took the floor of the Senate and flayed McCarthy unmercifully. He accused McCarthy of trying to set up "a one-man party, McCarthyism," and then he launched into this description of McCarthy in action:

> He dons his warpaint. He goes into his war dance. He emits his warwhoops. He goes forth to battle and proudly returns with the scalp of a pink army dentist. We may assume that this represents the depth and seriousness of the Communist penetration at this time.

Secretary of the Army Robert T. Stevens, a mild-mannered former textile manufacturer, had also become enraged. Stevens may have been no army expert, but he knew one thing: He could not permit his officers to be kicked around and insulted by McCarthy and still retain their respect or, more important, have any morale left in the army. And so he denounced McCarthy's methods and announced he would not permit army personnel to appear before McCarthy again and be subjected to such abuse.

The feud grew hotter with every uttered word. The army now leaked to the press the details of the way in which, it said, Cohn had badgered it to get a commission for Schine. It implied that McCarthy's investigations of the army were motivated by spite aroused by the Schine affair. McCarthy roared that Stevens was "a liar," and he accused the army of trying to "blackmail" him to call off his investigations. The conflict now was out in the open. It was so bitter there could be no compromise, and an investigation would have to be held to determine who was telling the truth.

A reluctant U.S. Senate ordered hearings, and these began in the full glare of television lights on April 22, 1954. It was a show that captured the attention of the entire nation. For the next several weeks, millions of Americans would eat their evening meals from television trays in their livings rooms, their eyes glued to the evening newscasts, anxious not to miss a single act of the proceedings.

The setting, the personalities, the showdown nature of the issues—all were made to order for the kind of drama one usually sees only on the stage. The hearings were held in the plush Senate Caucus Room, its high ceiling supported by majestic columns, the scene of many stormy McCarthy hearings in the past. Senator Karl Mundt, a Republican from South Dakota, a longtime supporter of McCarthy, presided. The committee members sat in comfortable chairs on a raised dais behind a long, continuous judge's bench, the American flag draped in the background.

Before this row of judges, behind a long low counsel table, sat the contending parties. At one end was Joe McCarthy, dark-browed, sharp-nosed, a scowl on his swarthy features as he leaned his head sidewise to listen to the whispered words of Roy Cohn, who was serving as his personal counsel. Farther down the table was Ray H. Jenkins, 57, a rugged, square-jawed six-footer from Knoxville, Tennessee, the committee counsel.

Toward the other end of the table sat Secretary Stevens, stocky, solid-faced, unemotional; and beside him sat the man who was to become the star of the show—Joseph Nye Welch, a 63-year-old Boston lawyer who specialized in trial work. Welch was a chunky man with a deceptively pixie-like look about him. He had wide lips, a long face, a large broad nose, and high-arched quizzical eyebrows. He dressed like the proper Bostonian in conservative suits, little bow ties, and vest. He seemed at times almost asleep, and he spoke in the softest tones. But his wit was rapier-sharp, and many a startled witness was to find that this mild-seeming man could skewer him with the harshest of harsh questions.

The hearing had hardly begun before Joe McCarthy propelled himself before the eyes of the watching television cameras.

"A point of order, Mr. Chairman, may I raise a point of order?" he cried in his shrill voice.

His objection was a highly technical one. Welch, he said, had represented himself as counsel for the army, and McCarthy contended Welch did not represent the army, but Stevens personally. The whole point seemed a bit silly, but McCarthy argued it as if the fate of the nation were at stake. Mundt finally cut him off and ordered Jenkins to call his first witness.

The brief flareup had served, however, to put Joe McCarthy immediately in the spotlight. It had given the public the first glimpse of McCarthy in action, and his cry—"Point of order, Mr. Chairman"—was one that was to be raised so incessantly in the coming days that it became in time a phrase of ridicule.

The hearings lasted for 36 days and amassed two million words of testimony. And, though many impressions were created, one came to dominate them all—the picture of Joe McCarthy snarling, ramping, raging, injecting himself into every scene, trying any dirty trick that he thought might work, and crying over and over again, "Point of order, Mr. Chairman."

• • • • •

The hearings went on and on, it seemed almost endlessly. McCarthy hounded Secretary Stevens for 14 days. Though every question that could possibly be asked had been asked and answered, McCarthy insisted, when his turn for questioning came, on going over the same old ground again and again. The strain upon the secretary was evident. He became gray-faced under the glaring television lights; his right eye sometimes blinked uncontrollably; and his right cheek twitched.

Through it all, there was another major furor when McCarthy, in cross-examining Stevens, flashed what purported to be an FBI report, dated October 26, 1951, warning of possible espionage dangers at Fort Monmouth. How had McCarthy obtained an FBI "top secret" report? Was it genuine?

These questions occupied the committee for days. It finally developed that the McCarthy report was not a copy of the FBI original. It was a digest of a longer FBI document. And there was one striking difference between the two. The FBI report had not attempted to judge; it had merely recited what information had been obtained about various employees. McCarthy's version, however, had the word "derogatory" printed after some of the names.

• • • • •

The dispute over the purloined and abbreviated FBI report led to the final, climactic scene. The hearings would drag on after it, twitching in a kind of final dying agony, but after this one unforgettable moment, nothing else really mattered.

This highlight came on June 9, 1954, while Welch was cross-examining Roy Cohn. Welch established that Cohn and McCarthy had had their version of the FBI report in their possession for months, yet they hadn't informed Secretary Stevens in their own Republican administration about it.

• • • • •

Welch wanted to know if Cohn had any doubts about Stevens's fidelity. "No, sir." Or his honor? "No, sir." Or his patriotism? "No, sir." Welch drove home his point. "And yet, Mr. Cohn, you didn't tell him what you knew?" Cohn could only repeat helplessly that he did not know.

Then Welch, in his most puckish manner, suggested that when one had such information one should move "before sundown" to do something about it. "May I add my small voice, sir," he said in his gently sarcastic way, "and say whenever you know about a subversive or a Communist or a spy, please hurry. Will you remember those words?"

Ridicule is the deadliest weapon, and Joe McCarthy could no longer restrain himself.

"Point of order," he cried, and he charged one last fatal time before the television cameras.

"In view of Mr. Welch's request that information be given," he began, "I think we should tell him that he has in his law firm a young man named [Frederick H.] Fisher whom he recommended, incidentally, to do the work on this committee, who has been for a number of years a member of an organization which was named . . . as the legal bulwark of the Communist party . . ."

Roy Cohn sat slumped in the witness chair, shaking his head in silent protest, but McCarthy charged recklessly on. He explained that Fisher had belonged to the National Lawyers' Guild, an organization that had been labeled subversive by the House Un-American Activities Committee, and he accused Welch of having tried to get Fisher named, despite this, "as the assistant counsel for this committee."

"Now I have hesitated bringing that up," McCarthy said, adopting his pose as the fairest of men, "but I have been bored with your phony request to Mr. Cohn here that he personally get every Communist out of government before sundown. Therefore we will give you the information about the young man in your own organization.

"Now I'm not asking you at this time why you tried to force him on this committee. That you did, the committee knows . . ."

It instantly became apparent that the committee knew nothing of the sort. Senator Mundt, who in the past had supported McCarthy, broke into McCarthy's tirade, saying:

"The Chair wishes to say that he has no recognition or no memory of Mr. Welch recommending Mr. Fisher or anybody else as counsel for this committee."

Welch was staring at McCarthy. He no longer resembled the puckish actor. His face had gone white with anger.

"Senator McCarthy," he began in a voice that shook, "I did not know, Senator—Senator, sometimes you say, 'May I have your attention.' May I have yours, Senator?"

McCarthy turned his back . . . , calling loudly for a newspaper clipping about Fisher.

"I'm listening to someone in one ear and you in the other," he told Welch.

"Now this time, sir, I want you to listen with both," Welch snapped.

"Yes, sir."

McCarthy, boldly indifferent, went right on giving instructions about material he wanted to place in the record.

"Senator, you won't need anything in the record when I finish telling you this," Welch said, his voice still shaking with emotion, tears glistening in his eyes. "Until this moment, Senator, I think I never really gauged your cruelty or your recklessness.

"Fred Fisher is a young man who went to Harvard Law School and came into my firm and is starting what looks to be a brilliant career with us. When I decided to work for this committee I asked Jim St. Clair, who sits on my right, to be my first assistant. I said to him, 'Jim, pick somebody in the firm to work under you that you would like.'

"He chose Fred Fisher and they came down on an afternoon plane. That night when we had taken a little stab at trying to see what the case was about, Fred Fisher and Jim St. Clair and I went to dinner together.

"I then said to these young men: 'Boys, I don't know anything about you except I've always liked you, but if there's anything funny in the life of either one of you that would hurt anybody in this case, you had better speak up quick.'

"And Fred Fisher said: 'Mr. Welch, when I was in law school and for a period of months after, I belonged to the Lawyers' Guild,' as you have suggested, Senator.

"He went on to say, 'I am the secretary of the Young Republicans' League with the son of the Massachusetts governor and I have the respect and admiration of the 25 lawyers or so in Hale and Dorr [Welch's law firm].'

"And I said, 'Fred, I just don't think I'm going to ask you to work on the case. If I do, one of these days that will come out and go over national television and it will hurt like the dickens.'

"So, Senator, I asked him to go back to Boston. Little did I dream you could be so reckless and so cruel as to do an injury to that lad. It is true he is still with Hale and Dorr. It is true he will continue to be with Hale and Dorr.

"It is, I regret to say, equally true that I fear he shall always bear a scar, needlessly inflicted by you. If it were in my power to forgive you for your reckless cruelty, I would do so. I like to think I'm a gentle man, but your forgiveness will have to come from someone other than me."

The Senate Caucus Room was hushed, its audience spellbound. Few there probably realized how thoroughly McCarthy had exposed himself. Far from trying to get the committee to hire Fisher, Welch had sent him back to Boston as he had said; and in trying to anticipate McCarthy's moves and lessen the damage he might do, he had disclosed the action and the reasons for it at the time. The *New York Times* had carried the story and had used Fisher's picture; but, despite all this, McCarthy had not been able to resist the savage lunge and the unprincipled accusation before a nationwide television audience.

Having made the gamble, even McCarthy could now feel the force of Welch's anger and contempt. He fumbled with some papers before him, and then he tried to bluster his way through the gathering storm, rumbling that Welch "has been baiting Mr. Cohn here for hours" and "I just want to give him this man's record . . ."

Welch, the tears gone from his eyes, now had full control of himself. His eyes were cold and hard, his voice icy as he said: "Senator, may we not drop this? We know he belonged to the Lawyers' Guild."

"Let me finish this," cried McCarthy.

"And Mr. Cohn nods his head at me. I did you, I think, no personal injury, Mr. Cohn."

"No, sir."

"I meant to do you no personal injury, and if I did, I beg your pardon. Let us not assassinate this lad further, Senator. You've done enough. Have you no sense of decency, sir? At long last, have you left no sense of decency?"

"I know this hurts you, Mr. Welch," snarled McCarthy.

"I'll say it hurts."

"May I say, Mr. Chairman, as a point of personal privilege, that I'd like to finish this."

"Senator, I think it hurts you, too, sir," said Welch.

McCarthy rumbled on, trying to show that Welch had attempted to force Fisher upon the committee, a charge whose truth Mundt again denied. McCarthy then attempted to ask Welch a question, but Welch froze him with this final rejoinder:

"Mr. McCarthy, I will not discuss this further with you. You have sat within six feet of me and could ask, could have asked me about Fred Fisher. You have seen fit to bring it out, and if there is a God in Heaven it will do neither you nor your cause any good.

"I will not discuss it further. I will not ask Mr. Cohn any more questions. You, Mr. Chairman, may, if you will, call the next witness."

•••••

Joe McCarthy was destroyed in that one, dramatic scene. He had been exposed to millions as a low, unprincipled battler. He would never recover.

The Senate, so long cowed by him, was now prodded by Senator Flanders to censure him. Senators always hate to take action against one of their exclusive club, and it was perhaps a measure of McCarthy's offenses against decency that the Senate was finally impelled to investigate him.

There were more hearings, more wild flailing about by McCarthy. In typical McCarthy fashion, he denounced mild-mannered Senator Arthur V. Watkins, a Utah Republican and chairman of the investigating committee. Watkins, he charged, was "cowardly" and "stupid"; the Watkins committee was serving as the "unwitting handmaiden," the "involuntary agent," and "attorneys in fact" of the Communist party.

It was too much to be borne. The Senate voted 67–22 to "condemn" McCarthy, not to "censure" him. His followers attempted to find some hope in that fact, but the effect was the same. McCarthy had been discredited and repudiated.

His collapse, both politically and physically, was incredibly swift. He wandered the halls of the Senate like some pale ghost of his former self. Where the press had hung on his every word in the glory days of the witch-hunt, his speeches were now almost automatically consigned to the wastebasket. Always a heavy drinker, he drank more and more heavily—and carried it less well. Finally, on April 28, 1957, he was taken to the Bethesda Naval Hospital, where he had been treated several times previously, and there at 6:02 P.M. on May 2, he died. The cause of death was described as "peripheral neuritis," an affliction of the nervous system often associated with the disease of alcoholism.

Even in death, he was not forgotten, not without influence. There were still millions of Americans who believed that he really had been leading a great "crusade" against communism. A Gallup poll taken in August 1954, after his damaging self-exposure at the Army–McCarthy hearings, showed that 51 percent of all Americans opposed McCarthy, but—what was truly surprising—36 percent, an enormous number, still had unshaken faith in him. They still believed—and much evidence indicates that many still do—that there were Communists everywhere and that all our troubles had been caused by conspiracy and betrayal.

Yet the facts were undeniable. Beginning in the Truman administration, every government employee, no matter how low his position, was investigated by departmental security agencies and the FBI. If there was *anything* in his record to cause a doubt or a suspicion, the employee was automatically suspended. He could appeal, but he was always at a disadvantage. He was not permitted to face his accusers; he could not cross-examine them. He was not permitted even to know who they were. In a reversal of all American tradition, the government did not have to prove an employee's guilt; it did not really have to prove anything. He had to prove—and prove beyond a shadow of a doubt—his complete innocence and trustworthiness.

This evidence, taken at appeal hearings, was passed on by loyalty boards composed of conservative Democrats and Republicans. President Truman, in an effort to avoid just the kind of demagogic hue and cry McCarthy had raised, had placed conservative and lifelong Republicans in charge of the State Department's Loyalty Board and the top Loyalty Review Board. Under these circumstances it is hardly enough to say the dice were loaded; they were double-loaded.

Yet out of nearly 5 million federal employees screened during the Truman administration, only 560—about one-hundredth of 1 percent—were dismissed "on grounds relating to loyalty." McCarthy and the Republicans, of course, clamored that the Truman system was too lax; they would tighten the net so that not even a gnat could get through. Yet the Eisenhower administration found it practically impossible to justify this pet theory. On February 18, 1954, it reported there had been some 2,200 "security risk" firings, but only 29 involved disloyalty. This figure was so small it was ridiculous, and so repeated and transparent efforts were made to revise it upward. In the next month, the figures were changed again and again until the administration finally proclaimed in March 1954 that out of 2,429 dismissals, 422 involved "subversives." Even if one discounts the constant shifting of the figures, even if one accepts this 422 tally as genuine, it didn't spell out the presence of a menace. There were then some 2.5 million federal employees; and even if 422 had finally rested under the shadow of a "doubt," this still represented less than two-hundredths of 1 percent of all government workers.

Those were the facts, but a demagogue does not deal in facts. He deals in fear, in blind unreasoning emotion, in hate and prejudice. Joe McCarthy knew and practiced the art as has no other demagogue in American history. He turned the nonexistent into a menace. He trampled on justice and fair play. He disgraced his country at home and abroad—and made millions believe they were following him in a holy crusade. Such is the power of the supreme demagogue; such, the lesson of Joe McCarthy.

NSC/68

The events that gave rise to McCarthyism also prompted important changes in U.S. foreign policy. At about the same time that McCarthy was making his Wheeling address, President Truman authorized a comprehensive reassessment of the nation's international commitments. The resulting study, NSC/68, was one of the most important policy statements of the entire Cold War era. In it, administration advisors urged that the United States accept the role of world policeman and develop free-world military capabilities on an international scale. The following excerpts from the report state its underlying assumptions and main recommendations.

• • • • •

The fundamental design of those who control the Soviet Union and the international Communist movement is to retain and solidify their absolute power, first in the Soviet Union and second in the areas now under their control. In the minds of the Soviet leaders, however, achievement of this design requires the dynamic extension of their authority and the ultimate elimination of any effective opposition to their authority.

The design, therefore, calls for the complete subversion or forcible destruction of the machinery of government and structure of society in the countries of the non-Soviet world and their replacement by an apparatus and structure subservient to and controlled from the Kremlin. To that end Soviet efforts are now directed toward the domination of the Eurasian land mass. The United States, as the principal center of power in the non-Soviet world and the bulwark of opposition to Soviet expansion, is the principal enemy whose integrity and vitality must be subverted or destroyed by one means or another if the Kremlin is to achieve its fundamental design.

• • • • •

A more rapid buildup of political, economic, and military strength and thereby of confidence in the free world than is now contemplated is the only course which is consistent with progress toward achieving our fundamental purpose. The frustration of the Kremlin design requires the free world to develop a successfully functioning political and economic system and a vigorous political offensive against the Soviet Union. These, in turn, require an adequate military

Source: Copyright © 1993 from: *American Cold War Strategy* by: May. Reprinted with permission of St. Martin's Press, Inc.

shield under which they can develop. It is necessary to have the military power to deter, if possible, Soviet expansion, and to defeat, if necessary, aggressive Soviet or Soviet-directed actions of a limited or total character. The potential strength of the free world is great; its ability to develop these military capabilities and its will to resist Soviet expansion will be determined by the wisdom and will with which it undertakes to meet its political and economic problems.

• • • • •

A comprehensive and decisive program to win the peace and frustrate the Kremlin design should be so designed that it can be sustained for as long as necessary to achieve our national objectives. It would probably involve:

1. The development of an adequate political and economic framework for the achievement of our long-range objectives.
2. A substantial increase in expenditures for military purposes adequate to meet the requirements . . .
3. A substantial increase in military assistance programs, designed to foster cooperative efforts, which will adequately and efficiently meet the requirements of our allies . . .
4. Some increase in economic assistance programs and recognition of the need to continue these programs until their purposes have been accomplished.
5. A concerted attack on the problem of the United States balance of payments . . .
6. Development of programs designed to build and maintain confidence among other peoples in our strength and resolution, and to wage overt psychological warfare calculated to encourage mass defections from Soviet allegiance and to frustrate the Kremlin design in other ways.
7. Intensification of affirmative and timely measures and operations by covert means in the fields of economic warfare and political and psychological warfare with a view to fomenting and supporting unrest and revolt in selected strategic satellite countries.
8. Development of internal security and civilian defense programs.
9. Improvement and intensification of intelligence activities.
10. Reduction of federal expenditures for purposes other than defense and foreign assistance, if necessary by the deferment of certain desirable programs.
11. Increased taxes.

• • • • •

QUESTIONS

1. Why did McCarthy wait until 1950 before focusing attention on the "Communists in government" issue? What do the tactics that McCarthy used to spotlight the issue tell us about the Wisconsin senator? Do you think he genuinely believed the State Department was riddled with Communists?

2. How was McCarthy able to become so powerful during the early 1950s? Was his rise to power simply a reflection of Cold War fears? To what extent was partisan politics a factor? Why didn't the Democrats respond more forcefully to McCarthy's charges?

3. What effect did the 1952 elections have on McCarthy's stature as a national political figure? How would you characterize McCarthy's relationship with the Eisenhower administration?

4. Why were U.S. allies so appalled by McCarthy's actions? What effect do you think McCarthyism had on the operation of the U.S. government? How did the Army–McCarthy hearings contribute to the Wisconsin senator's downfall?

5. What influence did McCarthy have on the times in which he lived? Was the threat that McCarthy posed to democracy as grave as Cook implies in the essay?

6. What challenges does a biographer who has chosen to write about McCarthy confront? How well do you think Cook met those challenges?

7. Implementation of the proposals contained in NSC/68 marked an important turning point in the evolution of the Cold War. That conflict is now over, but the country has yet to develop a coherent foreign policy for a post–Cold War world. If you were asked to prepare a major reassessment of contemporary U.S. foreign policy, what recommendations would you make?

BIBLIOGRAPHY

Recent biographies of the Wisconsin senator include David M. Oshinsky, *A Conspiracy So Immense: The World of Joe McCarthy* (1983), and Thomas C. Reeves, *The Life and Times of Joe McCarthy: A Biography* (1982). A particularly insightful older work is Richard H. Rovere, *Senator Joe McCarthy* (1959), which contains a shrewd analysis of McCarthy's tactics. Important aspects of McCarthy's career are examined in Edwin R. Bayley, *McCarthy and the Press* (1981), and Robert Griffith, *The Politics of Fear: Joseph R. McCarthy and the Senate* (1970). Those wishing to learn more about the social and political consequences of McCarthyism and the postwar Red Scare should consult David Caute, *The Great Fear: The Anti-Communist Purge under Truman and Eisenhower* (1978); Earl Latham, *The Communist Conspiracy in Washington: From the New Deal to McCarthy* (1966); and Stanley I. Kutler, *The American Inquisition: Justice and Injustice in the Cold War* (1982).

Martin Luther King, Jr.

During the mid-1950s, Montgomery, Alabama, the former capital of the Confederacy, differed little from other southern cities of the time. The majority of its African-American residents worked as laborers or domestics and had a median income that was about half that of local whites. It was also a place where local authorities rigidly enforced regional racial codes. Regardless of their personal accomplishments, all blacks were expected to behave deferentially toward whites. No African American could register at a white hotel, dine at a white restaurant, play on a white playground, or drink from a white water fountain. On the city's buses, blacks paid at the front, then stepped back off and reentered through the rear door. Once on the bus, black riders sat from back to front; and as the bus filled, they abandoned their seats from front to back. Moreover, they had to do so row by row, so that no white would be forced to sit in the same row as a black.

That was the situation on the Montgomery bus lines when, on December 1, 1955, a black seamstress named Rosa Parks refused to give up her seat in a half-filled row. She had been working all day and said her feet were tired. This made no impression on Montgomery authorities, who immediately arrested Parks for violating municipal segregation laws. As word of her arrest spread, the city's black leaders began mobilizing for action. Many had been waiting for just such an opportunity, and by the following afternoon, local activists had distributed 40,000

leaflets calling for a bus boycott. The first major battle of the mass action phase of the Civil Rights movement had begun.

It was here that Martin Luther King, Jr., first captured widespread attention. After the boycott began, he quickly emerged as one of the movement's leaders. He did so in the same way that he would time and again in the future: through his unmatched ability to give expression to the most deeply felt aspirations of southern blacks. "My friends," he told local boycotters in his first political address, "I want it to be known—that we are going to work with grim and bold determination—to gain justice on the buses in this city." "And we are not wrong," he continued, employing the rhythmic cadences that were a hallmark of his oratorical genius:

> *If we are wrong—the Supreme Court of this nation is wrong. If we are wrong—God Almighty is wrong! If we are wrong—Jesus of Nazareth was merely a utopian dreamer and never came down to earth! If we are wrong—justice is a lie. And we are determined here in Montgomery—to work and fight until justice runs down like water, and righteousness like a mighty stream!*

It was an electrifying performance. And this was just the beginning for the 26-year-old minister. He would be dead in another 13 years, the victim of an assassin's bullet, but much would change before then.

Although King played a major role in bringing about those changes, he was in many respects an unlikely candidate to head a movement that would transform American social relations. By the standards of black southern society, he came from an extremely privileged background; and whatever plans his profoundly conservative father had for Martin, Jr., they did not include his leading a mass protest movement. In the essay that follows, Stephen B. Oates examines the forces that impelled King to choose the path that he did and discusses his changing conceptions regarding the movement's objectives.

Martin Luther King

Stephen B. Oates

He was M.L. to his parents, Martin to his wife and friends, Doc to his aides, Reverend to his male parishioners, Little Lord Jesus to adoring churchwomen, De Lawd to his young critics in the Student Nonviolent Coordinating Committee, and Martin Luther King, Jr., to the world. At his pulpit or a public rostrum, he seemed too small for his incomparable oratory and international fame as a civil rights leader and spokesman for world peace. He stood only five feet

Source: This article is reprinted from the April 1988 issue of *American History Illustrated* with the permission of Cowles History Group, Inc. Copyright *American History Illustrated* magazine.

seven, and had round cheeks, a trim mustache, and sad, glistening eyes—eyes that revealed both his inner strength and his vulnerability.

He was born in Atlanta on January 15, 1929, and grew up in the relative comfort of the black middle class. Thus he never suffered the want and privation that plagued the majority of American blacks of his time. His father, a gruff, self-made man, was pastor of Ebenezer Baptist Church and an outspoken member of Atlanta's black leadership. M.L. joined his father's church when he was five and came to regard it as his second home. The church defined his world, gave it order and balance, taught him how to "get along with people." Here M.L. knew who he was—"Reverend King's boy," somebody special.

At home, his parents and maternal grandmother reinforced his self-esteem, praising him for his precocious ways, telling him repeatedly that he was *somebody*. By age five, he spoke like an adult and had such a prodigious memory that he could recite whole Biblical passages and entire hymns without a mistake. He was acutely sensitive, too, so much so that he worried about all the blacks he saw in Atlanta's breadlines during the Depression, fearful that their children did not have enough to eat. When his maternal grandmother died, 12-year-old M.L. thought it was his fault. Without telling anyone, he had slipped away from home to watch a parade, only to find out when he returned that she had died. He was terrified that God had taken her away as punishment for his "sin." Guilt-stricken, he tried to kill himself by leaping out of his second-story window.

He had a great deal of anger in him. Growing up a black in segregated Atlanta, he felt the full range of southern racial discrimination. He discovered that he had to attend separate, inferior schools, which he sailed through with a modicum of effort, skipping grades as he went. He found out that he—a preacher's boy—could not sit at lunch counters in Atlanta's downtown stores. He had to drink from a "colored" water fountain, relieve himself in a rancid "colored" restroom, and ride a rickety "colored" elevator. If he rode a city bus, he had to sit in the back as though he were contaminated. If he wanted to see a movie in a downtown theater, he had to enter through a side door and sit in the "colored" section in the balcony. He discovered that whites referred to blacks as "boys" and "girls" regardless of age. He saw "WHITES ONLY" signs staring back at him in the windows of barber shops and all the good restaurants and hotels, at the YMCA, the city parks, golf courses, swimming pools, and in the waiting rooms of the train and bus stations. He learned that there were even white and black sections of the city and that he resided in "nigger town."

Segregation caused a tension in the boy, a tension between his parents' injunction ("Remember, you are *somebody*") and a system that constantly demeaned and insulted him. He struggled with the pain and rage

prurient   An inordinate interest in matters of sex or appealing to that interest.

Hegelian   Relating to the philosophy or dialectic method of the German philosopher Hegel, in which the thesis, antithesis, and synthesis are used as an analytic tool to approach a higher unity or new thesis.

he felt when a white woman in a downtown store slapped him and called him "a little nigger" . . . when a bus driver called him "a black son-of-a-bitch" and made him surrender his seat to a white . . . when he stood on the very spot in Atlanta where whites had lynched a black man . . . when he witnessed nightriding Klansmen beating blacks in the streets. How, he asked defiantly, could he heed the Christian injunction and love a race of people who hated him? In retaliation, he determined "to hate every white person."

Yes, he was angry. In sandlot games, he competed so fiercely that friends could not tell whether he was playing or fighting. He had his share of playground combat, too, and could outwrestle any of his peers. He even rebelled against his father, vowing never to become a preacher like him. Yet he liked the way Daddy King stood up to whites: He told them never to call him a boy and vowed to fight this system until he died.

Still, there was another side to M.L., a calmer, sensuous side. He played the violin, enjoyed opera, and relished soul food—fried chicken, cornbread, and collard greens with ham hocks and bacon drippings. By his mid-teens, his voice was the most memorable thing about him. It had changed into a rich and resonant baritone that commanded attention whenever he held forth. A natty dresser, nicknamed "Tweed" because of his fondness for tweed suits, he became a connoisseur of lovely young women. His little brother A.D. remembered how Martin "kept flitting from chick to chick" and was "just about the best jitterbug in town."

At 15, he entered Morehouse College in Atlanta, wanting somehow to help his people. He thought about becoming a lawyer and even practiced giving trial speeches before a mirror in his room. But thanks largely to Morehouse President Benjamin Mays, who showed him that the ministry could be a respectable forum for ideas, even for social protest, King decided to become a Baptist preacher after all. By the time he was ordained in 1947, his resentment toward whites had softened some, thanks to positive contact with white students on an intercollegiate council. But he hated his segregated world more than ever.

Once he had his bachelor's degree, he went north to study at Crozer Seminary near Philadelphia. In this mostly white school, with its polished corridors and quiet solemnity, King continued to ponder the plight of blacks in America. How, by what method and means, were blacks to improve their lot in a white-dominated country? His study of history, especially of Nat Turner's slave insurrection, convinced him that it was suicidal for a minority to strike back against a heavily armed majority. For him, voluntary segregation was equally unacceptable, as was accommodation to the status quo. King shuddered at such negative approaches to the race problem. How indeed were blacks to combat discrimination in a country ruled by the white majority?

As some other blacks had done, he found his answer in the teachings of Mohandas Gandhi—for young King, the discovery had the force of a conversion experience. Nonviolent resistance, Gandhi taught, meant noncooperation with evil, an idea he got from Henry David Thoreau's essay "On Civil Disobedience." In India, Gandhi gave Thoreau's theory practical application in the form of strikes, boycotts, and protest marches, all conducted nonviolently and all predicated on love for the oppressor and a belief in divine justice. In gaining Indian independence, Gandhi sought not to defeat the British, but to redeem them through love, so as to avoid a legacy of bitterness. Gandhi's term for this—*Satyagraha*—reconciled love and force in a single, powerful concept.

As King discovered from his studies, Gandhi had embraced nonviolence in part to subdue his own violent nature. This was a profound revelation for King, who had felt much hatred in his life, especially toward whites. Now Gandhi showed him a means of harnessing his anger and channeling it into a positive and creative force for social change.

At this juncture, King found mostly theoretical satisfaction in Gandhian nonviolence; he had no plans to become a radical activist in the segregated South. Indeed, he seemed destined to a life of the mind, not of social protest. In 1951, he graduated from Crozer and went on to earn a Ph.D. in theology from Boston University, where his advisor pronounced him "a scholar's scholar" of great intellectual potential. By 1955, a year after the school desegregation decision, King had married comely Coretta Scott and assumed the pastorship of Dexter Avenue Baptist Church in Montgomery, Alabama. Immensely happy in the world of ideas, he hoped eventually to teach theology at a major university or seminary.

But, as King liked to say, the *Zeitgeist,* or spirit of the age, had other plans for him. In December 1955, Montgomery blacks launched a boycott of the city's segregated buses and chose the articulate 26-year-old minister as their spokesman. As it turned out, he was unusually well prepared to assume the kind of leadership thrust on him. Drawing on Gandhi's teachings and example, plus the tenets of his own Christian faith, King directed a nonviolent boycott designed both to end an injustice and redeem his white adversaries through love. When he exhorted blacks to love their enemies, King did not mean to love them as friends or intimates. No, he said, he meant a disinterested love in all humankind, a love that saw the neighbor in everyone it met, a love that sought to restore the beloved community. Such love not only avoided the internal violence of the spirit, but severed the external chain of hatred that only produced more hatred in an endless spiral. If American blacks could break the chain of hatred, King said, true brotherhood could begin. Then posterity would have to say that there had lived a race of people, of black people, who "injected a new meaning into the veins of history and civilization."

During the boycott King imparted his philosophy at twice-weekly mass meetings in the black churches, where overflow crowds clapped and cried as his mellifluous voice swept over them. In these mass meetings King discovered his extraordinary power as an orator. His rich religious imagery reached deep into the black psyche, for religion had been the black people's main source of strength and survival since slavery days. His delivery was "like a narrative poem," said a woman journalist who heard him. His voice had such depths of sincerity and empathy that it could "charm your heart right out of your body." Because he appealed to the best in his people, articulating their deepest hurts and aspirations, black folk began to idolize him; he was their Gandhi.

Under his leadership, they stood up to white Montgomery in a remarkable display of solidarity. Pitted against an obdurate city government that blamed the boycott on Communist agitation and resorted to psychological and legal warfare to break it, the blacks stayed off the buses month after month, and walked or rode in a black-operated carpool. When an elderly woman refused the offer of a ride, King asked her, "But don't your feet hurt?" "Yes," she replied, "my feet is tired but my soul is rested." For King, her irrepressible spirit was proof that "a new Negro" was emerging in the South, a Negro with "a new sense of dignity and destiny."

That "new Negro" menaced white supremacists, especially the Ku Klux Klan, and they persecuted King with a vengeance. They made obscene phone calls to his home, sent him abusive, sickening letters, and once even dynamited the front of his house. Nobody was hurt, but King, fearing a race war, had to dissuade angry blacks from violent retaliation. Finally, on November 13, 1956, the U.S. Supreme Court nullified the Alabama laws that enforced segregated buses and handed King and his boycotters a resounding moral victory. Their protest had captured the imagination of progressive people all over the world and marked the beginning of a southern black movement that would shake the segregated South to its foundations. At the forefront of that movement was a new organization, the Southern Christian Leadership Conference (SCLC), which King and other black ministers formed in 1957, with King serving as its president and guiding spirit. Operating through the southern black church, SCLC sought to enlist the black masses in the freedom struggle by expanding "the Montgomery way" across the South.

The "Miracle of Montgomery" changed King's life, catapulting him into international prominence as an inspiring new moral voice for civil rights. Across the country, blacks and whites alike wrote him letters of encouragement; *Time* magazine pictured him on its cover; the National Association for the Advancement of Colored People (NAACP) and scores of church and civic organizations vied for his services as a speaker. "I am really disturbed how fast all this has happened to me," King told his wife. "People will expect me to perform miracles for the rest of my life."

But fame had its evil side, too. When King visited New York in 1958, a deranged black woman stabbed him in the chest with a letter opener. The weapon was lodged so close to King's aorta, the main artery from the heart, that he would have died had he sneezed. To extract the blade, an interracial surgical team had to remove a rib and part of his breastbone; in a burst of inspiration, the lead surgeon made the incision over King's heart in the shape of a cross.

That he had not died convinced King that God was preparing him for some larger work in the segregated South. To gain perspective on what was happening there, he made a pilgrimage to India to visit Gandhi's shrine and the sites of his "War for Independence." He returned home with an even deeper commitment to nonviolence and a vow to be more humble and ascetic like Gandhi. Yet he was a man of manifold contradictions, this American Gandhi. While renouncing material things and giving nearly all of his extensive honorariums to SCLC, he liked posh hotels and zesty meals with wine, and he was always immaculately dressed in a gray or black suit, white shirt, and tie. While caring passionately for the poor, the downtrodden, and the disinherited, he had a fascination with men of affluence and enjoyed the company of wealthy SCLC benefactors. While trumpeting the glories of nonviolence and redemptive love, he could feel the most terrible anger when whites murdered a black or bombed a black church; he could contemplate giving up, turning America over to the haters of both races, only to dedicate himself anew to his nonviolent faith and his determination to redeem his country.

In 1960, he moved his family to Atlanta so that he could devote himself full time to SCLC, which was trying to register black voters for the upcoming federal elections. That same year, southern black students launched the sit-in movement against segregated lunch counters, and King not only helped them form the Student Nonviolent Coordinating Committee (SNCC) but raised money on their behalf. In October he even joined a sit-in protest at an Atlanta department store and went to jail with several students on a trespassing charge. Like Thoreau, King considered jail "a badge of honor." To redeem the nation and arouse the conscience of the opponent, King explained, you go to jail and stay there. "You have broken a law which is out of line with the moral law and you are willing to suffer the consequences by serving the time."

He did not reckon, however, on the tyranny of racist officials, who clamped him in a malevolent state penitentiary, in a cell for hardened criminals. But state authorities released him when Democratic presidential nominee John F. Kennedy and his brother Robert interceded on King's behalf. According to many analysts, the episode won critical black votes for Kennedy and gave him the election in November. For King, the election demonstrated what he had long said: that one of the most significant steps a black could take was the short walk to the voting booth.

The trouble was that most blacks in Dixie, especially in the Deep South, could not vote even if they so desired. For decades, state and local authorities had kept the mass of black folk off the voting rolls by a welter of devious obstacles and outright intimidation. Through 1961 and 1962, King exhorted President Kennedy to sponsor tough new civil rights legislation that would enfranchise southern blacks and end segregated public accommodations as well. When Kennedy shied way from a strong civil rights commitment, King and his lieutenants took matters into their own hands, orchestrating a series of southern demonstrations to show the world the brutality of segregation. At the same time, King stumped the country, drawing on all his powers of oratory to enlist the black masses and win white opinion to his cause.

Everywhere he went his message was the same.

The civil rights issue is an eternal moral issue that will determine the destiny of our nation and our world. As we seek our full rights, we hope to redeem the soul of our country. For it is our country, too, and we will win our freedom because the sacred heritage of America and the eternal will of God are embodied in our echoing demands. We do not intend to humiliate the white man, but to win him over through the strength of our love. Ultimately, we are trying to free all of us in America—Negroes from the bonds of segregation and shame, whites from the bonds of bigotry and fear.

We stand today between two worlds—the dying old order and the emerging new. With men of ill-will greeting this change with cries of violence, of interposition and nullification, some of us may get beaten. Some of us may even get killed. But if you are cut down in a movement designed to the save the soul of a nation, no other death could be more redemptive. We must realize that change does not roll in "on the wheels of inevitability," but comes through struggle. So "let us be those creative dissenters who will call our beloved nation to a higher destiny, to a new plateau of compassion, to a more noble expression of humaneness."

That message worked like magic among America's long-suffering blacks. Across the South, across America, they rose in unprecedented numbers to march and demonstrate with Martin Luther King. His singular achievement was that he brought the black masses into the freedom struggle for the first time. He rallied the strength of broken men and women, helping them overcome a lifetime of fear and feelings of inferiority. After segregation had taught them all their lives that they were *nobody*, King taught them that they were *somebody*. Because he made them believe in themselves and in the beauty of chosen suffering, he taught them how to straighten their backs ("a man can't ride you unless your back is bent") and confront those who oppressed them. Through the technique of nonviolent resistance, he furnished them something no previous black leader had been able to provide. He showed them a way of controlling their pent-up anger, as he had controlled his own, and using it to bring about constructive change.

The mass demonstrations King and SCLC choreographed in the South produced the strongest civil rights legislation in American history. This was the goal of King's major southern campaigns from 1963 to 1965. He would single out some notoriously segregated city with white officials prone to violence, mobilize the local blacks with songs, scripture readings, and rousing oratory in black churches, and then lead them on protest marches conspicuous for their grace and moral purpose. Then he and his aides would escalate the marches, increase their demands, even fill up the jails, until they brought about a moment of "creative tension," when whites would either agree to negotiate or resort to violence. If they did the latter, King would thus expose the brutality inherent in segregation and stab the national conscience so that the federal government would be forced to intervene with corrective measures.

The technique succeeded brilliantly in Birmingham, Alabama, in 1963. Here Police Commissioner Eugene "Bull" Connor, in full view of reporters and television cameras, turned firehoses and police dogs on the marching protestors. Revolted by such ghastly scenes, stricken by King's own searching eloquence and the bravery of his unarmed followers, Washington eventually produced the 1964 Civil Rights Act, which desegregated public facilities—the thing King had demanded all along from Birmingham. Across the South, the "WHITES ONLY" signs that had hurt and enraged him since boyhood now came down.

Although SNCC and others complained that King had a Messiah complex and was trying to monopolize the Civil Rights movement, his technique worked with equal success in Selma, Alabama, in 1965. Building on a local movement there, King and his staff launched a drive to gain southern blacks the unobstructed right to vote. The violence he exposed in Selma—the beating of black marchers by state troopers and deputized posse men, the killing of a young black deacon and a white Unitarian minister—horrified the country. When King called for support, thousands of ministers, rabbis, priests, nuns, students, lay leaders, and ordinary people—black and white alike—rushed to Selma from all over the country and stood with King in the name of human liberty. Never in the history of the movement had so many people of all faiths and classes come to the southern battleground. The Selma campaign culminated in a dramatic march over the Jefferson Davis Highway to the state capital of Montgomery. Along the way, impoverished local blacks stared incredulously at the marching, singing, flag-waving spectacle moving by. When the column reached one dusty crossroads, an elderly black woman ran out from a group of old folk, kissed King breathlessly, and ran back crying, "I done kissed him! The Martin Luther King! I done kissed the Martin Luther King!"

In Montgomery, first capital and much-heralded "cradle" of the Confederacy, King led an interracial throng of 25,000—the largest civil rights demonstration the South had ever witnessed—up Dexter Avenue with banners waving overhead. The pageant was as ironic as it was extraordinary, for it was up Dexter Avenue that Jefferson Davis's first inaugural parade had marched, and in the portico of the capitol Davis had taken his oath of office as president of the slave-based Confederacy. Now, in the spring of 1965, Alabama blacks—most of them descendants of slaves—stood massed at the same statehouse, singing a new rendition of "We Shall Overcome," the anthem of the Civil Rights movement. They sang, "Deep in my heart, I do believe, We have overcome—*today*."

Then, within view of the statue of Jefferson Davis, and watched by cordons of state troopers and television cameras, King mounted a trailer. His vast audience listened, transfixed, as his words rolled and thundered over the loudspeaker:

> My people, my people listen. The battle is in our hands . . . We must come to see that the end we seek is a society at peace with itself, a society that can live with its conscience. That day will be a day not of the white man, not of the black man. That will be the day of man as man.

And that day was not long in coming, King said, whereupon he launched into the immortal refrains of "The Battle Hymn of the Republic," crying out, "Our God is marching on! Glory, glory hallelujah!"

Aroused by the events in Alabama, Washington produced the 1965 Voting Rights Act, which outlawed impediments to black voting and empowered the attorney general to supervise federal elections in seven southern states where blacks were kept off the rolls. At the time, political analysts almost unanimously attributed the act to King's Selma campaign. Once federal examiners were supervising voter registration in all troublesome southern areas, blacks were able to get on the rolls and vote by the hundreds of thousands, permanently altering the pattern of southern and national politics.

In the end, the powerful civil rights legislation generated by King and his tramping legions wiped out statutory racism in America and realized at least the social and political promise of emancipation a century before. But King was under no illusion that legislation alone could bring on the brave new America he so ardently championed. Yes, he said, laws and their vigorous enforcement were necessary to regulate destructive habits and actions and to protect blacks and their rights. But laws could not eliminate the "fears, prejudice, pride, and irrationality" that were barriers to a truly integrated society, to peaceful inter-group and interpersonal living. Such a society could be achieved only when people accepted that inner, invisible law that etched on their hearts the conviction "that all men are brothers and that love is mankind's most potent weapon for personal and social transformation. True integration will be achieved by true neighbors who are willingly obedient to unenforceable obligations."

Even so, the Selma campaign was the movement's finest hour, and the Voting Rights Act the high point of a broad civil rights coalition that included the federal government, various white groups, and all the other civil rights organizations in addition to SCLC. King himself had best expressed the spirit and aspirations of that coalition when, on August 28, 1963, standing before the Lincoln Memorial, he electrified an interracial crowd of 250,000 with perhaps his greatest speech, "I Have a Dream," in which he described in rhythmic, hypnotic cadences his vision of an integrated America. Because of his achievements and moral vision, he won the 1964 Nobel Peace Prize, at 34 the youngest recipient in Nobel history.

Still, King paid a high price for his fame and his cause. He suffered from stomachaches and insomnia, and even felt guilty about all the tributes he received, all the popularity he enjoyed. Born in relative material comfort and given a superior education, he did not think he had earned the right to lead the impoverished black masses. He complained, too, that he no longer had a personal self and that sometimes he did not recognize the Martin Luther King people talked about. Lonely, away from home for protracted periods, beset with temptation, he slept with other women, for some of whom he had real feeling. His sexual transgressions only added to his guilt, for he knew he was imperiling his cause and hurting himself and those he loved.

Alas for King, FBI Director J. Edgar Hoover found out about the black leader's infidelities. The director already abhorred King, certain that Communist spies influenced him and masterminded his demonstrations. Hoover did not think blacks capable of organizing such things, so Communists had to be behind them and King as well. As it turned out, a lawyer in King's inner circle and a man in SCLC's New York office did have Communist backgrounds, a fact that only reinforced Hoover's suspicions about King. Under Hoover's orders, FBI agents conducted a ruthless crusade to destroy King's reputation and drive him broken and humiliated from public life. Hoover's men tapped King's phones and bugged his hotel rooms; they compiled a **prurient** monograph about his private life and showed it to various editors, public officials, and religious and civic leaders; they spread the word, Hoover's word, that King was not only a reprobate but a dangerous subversive with Communist associations.

King was scandalized and frightened by the FBI's revelations of his extra-marital affairs. Luckily for him, no editor, not even a racist one in the South, would touch the FBI's salacious materials. Public officials such as Robert Kennedy were shocked, but argued that King's personal life did not affect his probity as a civil rights leader. Many blacks, too, declared that what he did in private was his own business. Even so, King vowed to refrain from further af-fairs—only to succumb again to his own human frailties.

As for the Communist charge, King retorted that he did not need any Rus-sians to tell him when someone was standing on his neck; he could figure that out by himself. To mollify his political friends, however, King did banish from SCLC the two men with Communist backgrounds (later he resumed his ties with the lawyer, a loyal friend, and let Hoover be damned). He also denounced communism in no uncertain terms. It was, he believed, profoundly and funda-mentally evil, an atheistic doctrine no true Christian could ever embrace. He hated the dictatorial Soviet state, too, whose "crippling totalitarianism" subor-dinated everything—religion, art, music, science, and the individual—to its terrible yoke. True, communism started with men like Karl Marx who were "aflame with a passion for social justice." Yet King faulted Marx for rejecting God and the spiritual in human life. "The great weakness in Karl Marx is right here," King once told his staff, and he went on to describe his ideal Christian commonwealth in **Hegelian** terms: "Capitalism fails to realize that life is so-cial. Marxism fails to realize that life is individual. Truth is found neither in the rugged individualism of capitalism nor in the impersonal collectivism of com-munism. The kingdom of God is found in a synthesis that combines the truths of these two opposites. Now there is where I leave brother Marx and move on toward the kingdom."

But how to move on after Selma was a perplexing question King never successfully answered. After the devastating Watts riot in August 1965, he took his movement into the racially troubled urban North, seeking to help the suf-fering black poor in the ghettos. In 1966, over the fierce opposition of some of his own staff, he launched a campaign to end the black slums in Chicago and forestall rioting there. But the campaign foundered because King seemed un-able to devise a coherent antislum strategy, because Mayor Richard Daley and his black acolytes opposed him bitterly, and because white America did not seem to care. King did lead open-housing marches into segregated neighbor-hoods in Chicago, only to encounter furious mobs who waved Nazi banners, threw bottles and bricks, and screamed, "We hate niggers!" "Kill the niggers!" "We want Martin Luther Coon!" King was shocked. "I've been in many demonstrations all across the South," he told reporters, "but I can say that I have never seen—even in Mississippi and Alabama—mobs as hostile and as hate-filled as I've seen in Chicago." Although King prevented a major riot there and wrung important concessions from City Hall, the slums remained, as wretched and seemingly unsolvable as ever.

That same year, angry young militants in SNCC and the Congress of Racial Equality (CORE) renounced King's teachings—they were sick and tired of "De Lawd" telling them to love white people and work for integration. Now they advocated "Black Power," black separatism, even violent resistance to liberate blacks in America. SNCC even banished whites from its ranks and went on to drop "nonviolent" from its name and to lobby against civil rights legislation.

Black Power repelled the older, more conservative black organizations such as the NAACP and the Urban League and fragmented the Civil Rights Movement beyond repair. King, too, argued that black separatism was chimerical, even suicidal, and that nonviolence remained the only workable way for black people. "Darkness cannot drive out darkness," he reasoned: "only light can do that. Hate cannot drive out hate: only love can do that." If every other black in America turned to violence, King warned, then he would still remain the lone voice preaching that it was wrong. Nor was SCLC going to reject whites as SNCC had done. "There have been too many hymns of hope," King said, "too many anthems of expectation, too many deaths, too many dark days of standing over graves of those who fought for integration for us to turn back now. We must still sing 'Black and White Together, We Shall Overcome.'"

In 1967, King himself broke with the older black organizations over the ever-widening war in Vietnam. He had first objected to American escalation in the summer of 1965, arguing that the Nobel Peace Prize and his role as a Christian minister compelled him to speak out for peace. Two years later, with almost a half-million Americans—a disproportionate number of them poor blacks—fighting in Vietnam, King devoted whole speeches to America's "immoral" war against a tiny country on the other side of the globe. His stance provoked a fusillade of criticism from all directions—from the NAACP, the Urban League, white and black political leaders, *Newsweek, Life, Time,* and the *New York Times,* all telling him to stick to civil rights. Such criticism hurt him deeply. When he read the *Times*'s editorial against him, he broke down and cried. But he did not back down. "I've fought too long and too hard now against segregated accommodations to end up segregating my moral concerns," he told his critics. "Injustice *any*where is a threat to justice everywhere."

That summer, with the ghettos ablaze with riots, King warned that American cities would explode if funds used for war purposes were not diverted to emergency antipoverty programs. By then, the Johnson administration, determined to gain a military victory in Vietnam, had written King off as an antiwar agitator, and was now cooperating with the FBI in its efforts to defame him.

The fall of 1967 was a terrible time for King, the lowest ebb in his civil rights career. Everybody seemed to be attacking him—young black militants for his stubborn adherence to nonviolence, moderate and conservative blacks, labor leaders, liberal white politicians, the White House, and the FBI for his stand on Vietnam. Two years had passed since King had produced a nonviolent victory, and contributions to SCLC had fallen off sharply. Black spokesman Adam Clayton Powell, who had once called King the greatest Negro in America, now derided him as Martin Loser King. The incessant attacks began to irritate him, creating such anxiety and depression that his friends worried about his emotional health.

Worse still, the country seemed dangerously polarized. On one side, back-lashing whites argued that the ghetto explosions had "cremated" nonviolence and that white people had better arm themselves against black rioters. On the other side, angry blacks urged their people to "kill the Honkies" and burn the cities down. All around King, the country was coming apart in a cacophony of hate and reaction. Had America lost the will and moral power to save itself? he wondered. There was such rage in the ghetto and such bigotry among whites that he feared a race war was about to break out. He felt he had to do something to pull America back from the brink. He and his staff had to mount a new campaign that would halt the drift to violence in the black world and combat stiffening white resistance, a nonviolent action that would "transmute the deep rage of the ghetto into a constructive and creative force."

Out of his deliberations sprang a bold and daring project called the poor people's campaign. The master plan, worked out by February 1968, called for SCLC to bring an interracial army of poor people to Washington, D.C., to dramatize poverty before the federal government. For King, just turned 39, the time had come to employ civil disobedience against the national government itself. Ultimately, he was projecting a genuine class movement that he hoped would bring about meaningful changes in American society—changes that would redistribute economic and political power and end poverty, racism, "the madness of militarism," and war.

In the midst of his preparations, King went to Memphis, Tennessee, to help black sanitation workers there who were striking for the right to unionize. On the night of April 3, with a storm thundering outside, he told a black audience that he had been to the mountaintop and had seen what lay ahead. "I may not get there with you. But I want you to know tonight that we as a people *will* get to the promised land."

The next afternoon, when King stepped out on the balcony of the Lorraine Motel, an escaped white convict named James Earl Ray, stationed in a nearby building, took aim with a high-powered rifle and blasted King into eternity. Subsequent evidence linked Ray to white men in the St. Louis area who had offered "hit" money for King's life.

For weeks after the shooting, King's stricken country convulsed in grief, contrition, and rage. While there were those who cheered his death, the *New York Times* called it a disaster to the nation, the *London Times,* an enormous loss to the world. In Tanzania, Reverend Trevor Huddleston, expelled from South Africa for standing against apartheid, declared King's death the greatest single tragedy since the assassination of Gandhi in 1948, and said it challenged the complacency of the Christian Church all over the globe.

On April 9, with 120 million Americans watching on television, thousands of mourners—black and white alike—gathered in Atlanta for the funeral of a man who had never given up his dream of creating a symphony of brotherhood on these shores. As a black man born and raised in segregation, he had had every reason to hate America and to grow up preaching cynicism and retaliation. Instead, he had loved the country passionately and had sung of her promise and glory more eloquently than anyone of his generation.

They buried him in Atlanta's South View Cemetery, then blooming with dogwood and fresh green boughs of spring. On his crypt, hewn into the marble, were the words of an old Negro spiritual he had often quoted: "Free at Last, Free at Last, Thank God Almighty I'm Free at Last."

JO ANN ROBINSON AND THE WOMEN'S POLITICAL COUNCIL OF MONTGOMERY

Though best remembered as the event that catapulted Martin Luther King, Jr., onto the national stage, the Montgomery bus boycott was a collective effort that involved the city's entire black community. Long before King assumed his Montgomery pastorate, local activists had been planning for just such an occasion. Without their organizational work, the boycott could not have been sustained for a week, much less 13 months. In the selection below, Jo Ann Robinson describes the actions taken by the Women's Political Council to launch the boycott. Her recollections provide a salutary reminder of the vital role women played in the Civil Rights movement.

The Women's Political Council was an organization begun in 1946 after dozens of black people had been arrested on the buses. We witnessed the arrests and humiliations and the court trials and the fines paid by people who just sat down on empty seats. We knew something had to be done.

We organized the Women's Council and within a month's time we had over a hundred members. We organized a second chapter and a third, and soon we had more than 300 members. We had members in every elementary, junior high, and senior high school. We had them organized from federal and state and local jobs; wherever there were more than 10 blacks employed, we had a member there. We were organized to the point that we knew that in a matter of hours we could corral the whole city.

The evening that Rosa Parks was arrested, Fred Gray called me and told me that her case would be [heard] on Monday. As president of the main body of the Women's Political Council, I got on the phone and called all the officers of the three chapters. I told them that Rosa Parks had been arrested and she would be tried. They said, "You have the plans, put them into operation."

I didn't go to bed that night. I cut those stencils and took them to [the] college . . .

I talked with every member [of the Women's Council] in the elementary, junior high, and senior high schools and told them to have somebody on the campus. I told them that I would be there to deliver them [the handbills]. I taught my classes from 8:00 to 10:00. When my 10:00 class was over, I took two senior students with me. I would drive to the place of dissemination and a kid would be there to grab [the handbills].

Source: Juan Williams, with the Eyes on the Prize Production Team, *Eyes on the Prize: America's Civil Rights Years, 1954–1965* (New York: Viking, 1987), pp. 70–71.

After we had circulated those 35,000 circulars, we went by the church. That was about 3:30 in the afternoon. We took them to the minister . . . The [ministers] agreed to meet that night to decide what should be done about the boycott after the first day. You see, the Women's Council planned it only for Monday, and it was left up to the men to take over after we had forced them really to decide whether or not it had been successful enough to continue, and how long it was to be continued.

They had agreed at the Friday night meeting that they would call this meeting at Holt Street Church and they would let the audience determine whether or not they would continue the bus boycott or end it in one day.

Monday night, the ministers held their meeting. The church itself holds four or five thousand people. But there were thousands of people outside of the church that night. They had to put up loudspeakers so they would know what was happening. When they got through reporting that very few people had ridden the bus, that the boycott was really a success—I don't know if there was one vote that said "No, don't continue that boycott"—they voted unanimously to continue the boycott. And instead of it lasting one day as the Women's Council had planned it, it lasted for 13 months.

The spirit, the desire, the injustices that had been endured by thousands of people through the years . . . I think people were fed up, they had reached the point that they knew there was no return. That they had to do it or die. And that's what kept it going. It was the sheer spirit for freedom, for the feeling of being a man or a woman.

Now when you ask why the courts had to come in, they had to come in. You get 52,000 people in the streets and nobody's showing any fear, something had to give. So the Supreme Court had to rule that segregation was not the way of life . . . We [met] after the news came through. All of these people who had fought got together to communicate and to rejoice and to share that built-up emotion and all the other feelings they had lived with during the past 13 months. And we just rejoiced together.

QUESTIONS

1. In what ways was King's boyhood different from that of most other black children growing up in the South during the 1930s and 1940s? What childhood experiences made the greatest impression on King? *grew to hate whites*
2. How did the writings of Thoreau and Gandhi influence the development of King's social thought? What did Oates mean when he described King as a "man of contradictions"?
3. Why, according to Jo Ann Robinson, did the Montgomery bus boycott prove so successful? What do her recollections tell us about gender relations within the Civil Rights movement?
4. What were King's greatest strengths as a civil rights leader? Why did King conduct his major campaigns in southern cities that were particularly notorious for their harsh treatment of African Americans? How would you characterize King's relationship with the various groups involved in the Civil Rights movement?

5. Why did King come to believe that legislation alone would provide inadequate protection of black rights? In what ways did King's view of the movement's objectives change during the final years of his life?

6. Could the Civil Rights movement of the 1960s have made the advances that it did without King's leadership? Would W. E. B. Du Bois or Henry McNeal Turner have been able to play a similar role had they been given the opportunity during their most active years? What was King's most enduring achievement as a civil rights leader?

BIBLIOGRAPHY

Stephen B. Oates, the author of this chapter's essay, also has written a full-length biography of the civil rights leader: *Let the Trumpet Sound: The Life of Martin Luther King, Jr.* (1983). Other biographies of King include David L. Lewis, *King: A Biography*, 2d ed. (1978), and Lerone Bennett, Jr., *What Manner of Man: A Biography of Martin Luther King, Jr.*, 6th ed. (1986). Two important studies of King's role in the broader movement for black rights are David J. Garrow, *Bearing the Cross: Martin Luther King, Jr., and the Southern Christian Leadership Conference* (1986), and Taylor Branch, *Parting the Waters: America in the King Years, 1954–1963* (1988). A fine retrospective account of the civil rights struggle is Howell Raines, *My Soul Is Rested: Movement Days in the Deep South Remembered* (1977). For a well-crafted survey that moves beyond the King years, see Harvard Sitkoff, *The Struggle for Black Equality, 1954–1992*, rev. ed. (1993). J. Edgar Hoover's harassment of King is examined in David J. Garrow, *The FBI and Martin Luther King, Jr.: From "Solo" to Memphis* (1981), and Kenneth O'Reilly, *Racial Matters: The FBI's Secret File on Black America, 1960–1972* (1989).

Betty Friedan

With the passage of the Nineteenth Amendment in 1920, women appeared ready to assume an increasingly prominent role in American public life. But this was not to be. The movement that gave women the right to vote did not survive the twenties, and by the 1950s many people had forgotten that it ever existed. Meanwhile, as the postwar domestic revival gave the doctrine of separate spheres a new lease on life, women seemed more firmly tied to family and household duties than they had ever been. Yet, beneath the seemingly placid surface of 1950s homelife, a number of important changes were taking place—changes that would result in the formation of the modern women's movement.

One important change was the fact that increasing numbers of women were entering the labor force. By 1960, 40 percent of all women over the age of 16 held jobs outside the home. And with each passing year, a grow-ing proportion of these women were married: Whereas 15 percent of wives worked in 1930, 30 percent did so in 1960. This development contributed to the resurgence of feminism by exposing more women to the inequities that made them second-class citizens in the workplace. Everywhere they looked, women ran up against long-standing assumptions that their natural place was in the home; that they were working only to pick up a little "pin money" or to supplement male incomes; that they were in effect casual workers who lacked real commitment to their jobs;

and that, as a consequence, they did not have the same rights as their male counterparts.

At the same time, as Betty Friedan soon would show, there was growing discontent among suburban housewives. It is not often that a book has the impact that its author would like. One of those rare exceptions was Friedan's The Feminine Mystique *(1963). Unlike most books, this one really struck a nerve. In it, Friedan used a number of case studies to examine the alienation felt by many American housewives—to look at what she called "the problem that has no name." These were women who had been told that marriage, family, and the homemaker's role would provide them all that one could reasonably expect from life: a sense of self-worth, dignity, and personal fulfillment. They tried it, and years later they found that they did not feel any of these things. Friedan attempted to explain the discrepancy by looking at the ways in which women's magazines, advertisers, and educators manipulated the feminine mystique to convince women that they could best attain happiness by accepting a "voluntary servitude" within the home.*

Those women who responded to Friedan's message did not immediately take their case into the streets. But they did begin to reexamine their lives. Many also began searching, often outside the household, for a means of achieving that sense of fulfillment their domestic lives denied them. And regardless of what they did on their own behalf, they vowed that their daughters would never be put in a similar position. In the essay that follows, David Halberstam examines the process by which Friedan came to write her pathbreaking work, while surveying the developments that made her observations in The Feminine Mystique *so compelling to suburban housewives of the early 1960s.*

Betty Friedan

David Halberstam

It was all part of a vast national phenomenon. The number of families moving into the middle class—that is, families with more than $5,000 in annual earnings after taxes—was increasing at the rate of 1.1 million a year, *Fortune* noted. By the end of 1956 there were 16.6 million such families in the country, and by 1959, in the rather cautious projections of *Fortune*'s editors, there would be 20 million such families—virtually half the families in America. *Fortune* hailed "an economy of abundance" never seen before in any country in the world. It reflected a world of "optimistic philoprogenitive [the word means that Americans were having a lot of children], high-spending, debt-happy, bargain-conscious, upgrading, American consumers."

Source: From *The Fifties* by David Halberstam. Copyright © 1995 by The Ameteurs Limited. Reprinted by permission of Villard Books, a division of Random House, Inc.

In all of this no one was paying very close attention to what the new home-oriented, seemingly drudgery-free life was doing to the psyche and outlook of American women. The pictures of them in magazines showed them as relentlessly happy, liberated from endless household tasks by wondrous new machines they had just bought. Since the photos showed them happy, and since there was no doubt that there were more and better household appliances every year, it was presumed that they were in fact happy. That was one of the more interesting questions of the era, for the great migration to the suburbs reflected a number of profound trends taking place in the society, not the least important of which was the changing role of women, particularly middle-class women. Up until then during this century women had made fairly constant progress in the spheres of politics, education, and employment opportunities. Much of their early struggle focused on the right of married women to work (and therefore to take jobs away from men who might be the heads of families). In the thirties a majority of states, 26 of 48, still had laws prohibiting the employment of married women. In addition, a majority of the nation's public schools, 43 percent of its public utilities, and 13 percent of its department stores enforced rules on not hiring of wives. A poll of both men and women in the thirties that asked "Do you approve of a married woman earning money in business or industry if she has a husband capable of supporting her?" showed that 82 percent of the men and women polled disapproved.

During the Depression, large numbers of women went to work because their homes needed every bit of cash they could bring home. In addition women were always welcome in those parts of industry that offered poorer-paying jobs. At the beginning of the New Deal in the garment district of New York, where traditionally workers were the wives of immigrants, women worked 48 hours a week for 15 cents an hour, which meant that after a long, exhausting work week they brought home $7.20.

But in general there was an assumption that as society began to change and more and more women were better educated, there would be more women working in the professions for better wages. World War II dramatically (if only temporarily) changed how the nation regarded the employment of women. Overnight, that which had been perceived as distinctly unfeminine—holding heavy-duty industrial jobs—became a patriotic necessity. Four million additional workers were needed in industry and in the armed forces and a great many of them had to be women. The *Ladies' Home Journal* even put a woman combat pilot on its cover. Suddenly, where women had not gone before they were very welcome indeed; some 8 million women entered the workforce during the war.

That trend came to a stunning halt in the years after the war. Part of it was the traditional tilt of the society toward men—if there were good, well-paying jobs, then the jobs obviously belonged to men as they came

Seven Sister schools   Elite colleges made up of Smith, Mt. Holyoke, Barnard, Vassar, Radcliffe, Wellesley, and Bryn Mawr.

Charles Addams   Famed cartoonist whose drawings appeared frequently in the *New Yorker*.

home from the war to head families. Within two months after the end of the war, some 800,000 women had been fired from jobs in the aircraft industry; the same thing was happening in the auto industry and elsewhere. In the two years after the war, some 2 million women had lost their jobs.

In the postwar years the sheer affluence of the country meant that many families could now live a middle-class existence on only one income. In addition, the migration of the suburbs physically separated women from the workplace. The new culture of consumerism told women they should be homemakers and saw them merely as potential buyers for all the new washers and dryers, freezers, floor waxers, pressure cookers, and blenders.

There was in all this a retreat from the earlier part of the century. Now, there was little encouragement for women seeking professional careers, and in fact there was a good deal of quite deliberate discouraging of it. Not only were women now reared in homes where their mothers had no careers, but male siblings were from the start put on a very different track: The boys in the family were to learn the skills critical to supporting a family, while daughters were to be educated to get married. If they went to college at all they might spend a junior year abroad studying art or literature. Upon graduation, if they still had ideas of a professional career, the real world did not give them much to be optimistic about.

The laws about married women working might have changed, but the cultural attitudes had not. The range of what women were allowed to do professionally in those days was limited, and even in those professions where they were welcome, they were put on a lower, slower track. Gender, not talent, was the most important qualification. Men and women who graduated at the same time from the same colleges and who had received the same grades (in many cases the women received better grades), then arrived at the same publishing or journalistic companies only to be treated very differently.

Men were taken seriously. Women, by contrast, were doomed to serve as support troops. Often they worked harder and longer for less pay with lesser titles, usually with the unspoken assumption that if they were at all attractive, they would soon get married, become pregnant, and leave the company. Only someone a bit off-center emotionally would stay the course. It was a vicious circle: Because young women were well aware of this situation, there was little incentive to commit an entire life to fighting it and becoming what was then perceived of as a hard and brittle career woman. ("Nearly Half the Women in Who's Who Are Single," went one magazine title in that period trying to warn young women of the pitfalls of careerism.) If there were short stories in women's magazines about career women, then it turned out they, by and large, portrayed women who were unhappy and felt themselves emotionally empty. Instead, the magazines and the new television sitcoms glorified dutiful mothers and wives.

Even allegedly serious books of the era (for instance, an influential book of pop sociology by a man named Ferdinand Lundberg and his psychoanalyst collaborator Marynia Farnham, entitled *Modern Woman: The Lost Sex*) attacked the idea of women with careers. "The independent woman is a contradiction in terms," Lundberg and Farnham had written. Feminism itself, in their words, "was a deep illness." "The psychosocial rule that takes form, then, is this: The more educated a woman is, the greater chance there is of sexual disorder, more or less severe. The greater the disordered sexuality in a given group of women, the fewer children they have," they wrote. They also suggested that the federal government give rewards to women for each child they bore after the first.

A postwar definition of femininity evolved. To be feminine, the American woman first and foremost did not work. If she did, that made her competitive with men, which made her hard and aggressive and almost surely doomed to loneliness. Instead, she devotedly raised her family, supported her husband, kept her house spotless and efficient, got dinner ready on time, and remained attractive and optimistic; each hair was in place. According to studies, she was prettier than her mother, she was slimmer, and she even smelled better than her mother.

At this particular moment, it was impossible to underestimate the importance and influence of the women's magazines—the *Ladies' Home Journal*, *Redbook*, *McCall's*, and *Mademoiselle*—on middle-class young women. Isolated in the suburbs they felt uneasy and lonely and largely without guidance. More often than not, they were newly separated from their original families and the people they had grown up with. They were living new lives, different from those of their parents, with new and quite different expectations on the part of their husbands. Everything had to be learned.

In an age before the coming of midday television talk shows largely designed for housewives, women's magazines comprised the core reading material for the new young suburban wives. If the magazines' staffs at the lower rungs were comprised mostly of women, the magazines were almost always edited by men; in addition, editorial content, much more than in most general-circulation magazines, echoed the thrust of the advertising. Research showed, or seemed to show, that husbands made the critical decisions in terms of which political candidate a family might support, but the wives made the decisions on which refrigerator and which clothes washer to buy. If the advertising was designed to let women know what the newest appliances were and how to use them, then the accompanying articles were designed to show they could not live up to their destinies without them.

This was not done deliberately. There were no editorial meetings where male editors sat around and killed ideas that showed the brave new suburban world as populated with a significant percentage of tense, anxious female college graduates who wondered if they were squandering the best years of their lives. But there was an instinctive bias about what women needed to hear and that it should all be upbeat, and that any larger doubts were unworthy.

The magazines explained their new lives to them: how to live, how to dress, what to eat, why they should feel good about themselves and their husbands and their children. Their sacrifices, the women's magazines emphasized, were not really sacrifices, they were about fulfillment. All doubts were to be conquered.

The ideal fifties women were to strive for was articulated by *McCall's* in

1954: togetherness. A family was as one, its ambitions were twined. The husband was designated leader and hero, out there every day braving the treacherous corporate world to win a better life for his family; the wife was his mainstay on the domestic side, duly appreciative of the immense sacrifices being made for her and her children. There was no divergence within. A family was a single perfect universe—instead of a complicated, fragile mechanism of conflicting political and emotional pulls. Families portrayed in women's magazines exhibited no conflicts or contradictions or unfulfilled ambitions. Thanks, probably, to the drive for togetherness, the new homes all seemed to have what was called a family room. Here the family came together, ate, watched television, and possibly even talked. "When Jim comes home," said a wife in a 1954 advertisement for prefabricated homes, "our family room seems to draw us closer together." And who was responsible ultimately for togetherness if not the wife?

"The two big steps that women must take are to help their husbands decide where they are going and use their pretty heads to help them get there," wrote Mrs. Dale Carnegie, wife of one of the nation's leading experts on how to be likable, in the April 1955 *Better Homes and Gardens.* "Let's face it, girls. That wonderful guy in your house—and in mine—is building your house, your happiness, and the opportunities that will come to your children." Split-level houses, Mrs. Carnegie added, were fine for the family, "but there is simply no room for split-level thinking—or doing—when Mr. and Mrs. set their sights on a happy home, a host of friends, and a bright future through success in HIS job."

Those women who were not happy and did not feel fulfilled were encouraged to think that the fault was theirs and that they were the exception to blissful normality. That being the case, women of the period rarely shared their doubts, even with each other. If anything, they tended to feel guilty about any qualms they had: Here they were living better than ever—their husbands were making more money than ever, and there were ever bigger, more beautiful cars in the garage and appliances in the kitchen. Who were they to be unhappy?

One of the first women to challenge the fallacy of universal contentment among young suburban wives was a young woman from the heartland of the country. Born and reared in Peoria, Illinois, she did well enough in school to be admitted to an elite Eastern women's college, one of the **Seven Sister schools.** She entered Smith College in 1939, finding everything that she had longed for as a small-town girl in Peoria: a world where women were rewarded for being smart and different instead of being punished for it. She graduated in 1942, summa cum laude, full of optimism about the future even though the war was still going on. Several scholarships were offered her. Ambitious, admired by her classmates, Betty Goldstein was certain that she would lead a life dramatically different from her mother's. Miriam Goldstein had been a society-page writer for the Peoria, Illinois, paper, before marrying a local storeowner and becoming a housewife. In her daughter's eyes, she took out her own frustrated ambitions by pushing her children to achieve. But at graduation time, Betty Goldstein turned down the fellowships because she was interested in a young man; since he had not been offered a comparable scholarship, she was afraid it would tear their relationship apart if she accepted hers. That decision, she later wrote, turned her instantly into a cliché. Looking back on her life, Betty Goldstein Friedan, one of the first voices of the feminist movement, noted the young man's face was more quickly forgotten than the terms of the scholarship itself.

Instead of getting married, she moved to the exciting intellectual world of Greenwich Village and became part of a group of liberal young people involved in labor issues and civil rights before it was fashionable. The women all seemed to be graduates of Smith, Vassar, and Radcliffe; they were bright and optimistic, eager to take on a static society. Betty Goldstein worked as a reporter for a left-wing labor paper. As a journalist, she had got a reputation of knowing her way around and having lots of contacts. She became the person designated to arrange illegal abortions for involuntarily pregnant friends. This, she found, she was able to do with a few discreet phone calls. The going price was $1,000. Once it was also her job to find a minister for two Protestant friends who wanted to marry. Because the groom was a divorced man, she noted with some irony, it was harder to find a willing minister than an abortionist.

When the war was over, the men returned from Europe and the South Pacific, and the women were gradually squeezed out of their jobs. Betty Goldstein, unsure of her role and her future, not liking the idea of a life alone (she had, she noted, "a pathological fear of being alone"), met a young veteran named Carl Friedan, who seemed funny and charming, and in 1947, two years after the war had ended, they were married. In 1949 they had their first child. When she was pregnant with her second child she was fired from the labor paper, whose radicalism, it appeared, did not yet extend to women's rights. When she took her grievance to the newspaper guild, she was told that the second pregnancy, which had cost her job, was her fault. There was, she later realized, no union term for sex discrimination.

Ms. Friedan soon found herself part of the great suburban migration as she moved further and further away from the Village, which had been the center of her professional and intellectual world. There, ideas had always seemed important. As she and her husband moved to larger and larger living quarters, first to Queens, where the Friedans lived in a pleasant apartment, and then to houses in the suburbs, her time was gradually more and more taken by children and family. As that happened, she was cut off, first physically, from what she had been, and then increasingly intellectually and socially as well. Betty Friedan now poured her energy into being a housewife and mother, into furnishing the apartment and houses and shopping, cooking, and cleaning for her family.

The Friedan family, she later realized, had been almost unconsciously caught up in the postwar migration to the suburbs. It was an ascent to an ever better style of living; but she also began to see it as a retreat as well from her earlier ambitions and standards. She liked doing the domestic things that Americans now did in their new, ever more informal social lives—grilling hamburgers on the outdoor barbecue, attending spur-of-the-moment cocktail parties, sharing summer rentals on Fire Island with friends. Finally, the Friedans bought an old house, worthy of **Charles Addams,** in Rockland

County for $25,000 (with $2,500 down), where Betty Friedan, Smith summa cum laude and future feminist leader, spent her time, scraping eight layers of paint off a fireplace ("I quite liked it"), chauffeuring children to and from school, helping to run the PTA, and coming as close as someone as fiercely independent as she was could to being a good housewife, as portrayed in the women's magazines of that day. In some ways her life was full, she would later decide, and in some ways it was quite empty. She liked being a mother, and she liked her friends, but she missed the world of social and political involvement back in New York. She also worried that she had not lived up to her potential. By the time they were living in Rockland County, she had begun to write freelance for various women's magazines. It was a clear sign, she realized later, that while the domestic side of her life was rich, it was not rich enough.

The deal she made with herself then was a revealing one. It was her job as a writer to make more money than she and Carl spent on a maid—otherwise her writing would be considered counterproductive and would be viewed as subtracting from rather than adding to the greater good of the family. Her early articles, "Millionaire's Wife" (*Cosmopolitan*, September 1956); "Now They're Proud of Peoria" (*Reader's Digest*, August 1955); "Two Are an Island" (*Mademoiselle*, July 1955); and "Day Camp in the Driveways" (*Parents' Magazine*, May 1957) were not exactly the achievements she had had in mind when she left Smith.

She was also very quickly finding out the limits of what could be done in writing for women's magazines at that time. In 1956, when she was pregnant with her third child, she read in a newspaper about Julie Harris, the actress, then starring in a play called *The Lark*. Ms. Harris had had natural childbirth, something that Betty Friedan, who had undergone two cesareans, admired and even envied. She decided, with the ready agreement of the magazines, to do a piece on Ms. Harris and her childbirth. She had a glorious time interviewing the actress and was completely captivated by her. She wrote what she thought was one of her best articles on the joys of natural childbirth. To her surprise, the article was turned down at first because it was too graphic.

That was hardly her only defeat with the magazines. When she suggested an article about Beverly Pepper, just beginning to experience considerable success as a painter and sculptor, and who was also raising a family, the editors of one magazine were scornful. American women, they told her, were not interested in someone like this and would not identify with her. Their market research, of which they were extremely confident, showed that women would only read articles that explained their own roles as wives and mothers. Not many American women out there had families and were successful as artists—therefore it would have no appeal. Perhaps, one editor said, they might do the article with a photograph of Mrs. Pepper painting the family crib.

At the time one of her children was in a play group with the child of a neighboring woman scientist. Ms. Friedan and the woman talked on occasion and her friend said she believed that a new ice age was approaching. The subject had interested Friedan, not normally a science writer, and she had suggested an article for *Harper's*. The resulting article, "The Coming Ice Age" was a considerable success and won a number of prizes. In New York George Brockway, a book editor at Norton, saw the piece and liked it. He called to ask if she was interested in writing a book. She was excited by his interest but had no desire to expand the piece into a book; the scientific work was not really hers, in the sense that it did not reflect her true interests and feelings. It was, she later said, as if she had served as a ghostwriter for another person on it.

Then something happened that changed her life. She and two friends were asked to do a report on what had happened to the members of the Smith class of '42 as they returned for their 15th reunion in 1957. She made up a questionnaire and got an assignment from *McCall's* to pay for her time. The piece was supposed to be called "The Togetherness Woman." The questions were: "What difficulties have you found in working out your role as a woman?" "What are the chief satisfactions and frustrations of your life today?" "How do you feel about getting older?" "How have you changed inside?" "What do you wish you had done differently?" The answers stunned her: She had tapped into a great reservoir of doubt, frustration, anxiety, and resentment. The women felt unfulfilled and isolated with their children; they often viewed their husbands as visitors from a far more exciting world.

The project also emphasized Friedan's own frustrations. All those years trying to be a good wife and mother suddenly seemed wasted; it had been wrong to suppress her feelings rather than to deal with them. The surprise was that there were thousands of women like her out there. As she wrote later in *The Feminine Mystique:*

> It was a strange stirring, a sense of dissatisfaction, a yearning that women suffered in the middle of the twentieth century in the United States. Each suburban wife struggled with it alone. As she made the beds, shopped for groceries, matched slip cover materials, ate peanut butter sandwiches with her children, chauffeured Cub Scouts and Brownies, lay beside her husband at night, she was afraid to ask of herself the silent question—"Is this all?"

As she had walked around the Smith campus during her reunion, she was struck by the passivity of the young women of the class of 1957. Upon graduation, her generation had been filled with excitement about the issues of the day: When Ms. Friedan asked these young women about their futures, they regarded her with blank looks. They were going to get engaged and married and have children, of course. She thought: This is happening at Smith, a place where I found nothing but intellectual excitement when I was their age. Something had gotten deep into the bloodstream of this generation, she decided.

She left and started to write the piece for *McCall's*, but it turned out very different from the one that she had intended to write. It reflected the despair and depression she had found among her contemporaries, and it was critical of women who lived through their husbands and children. *McCall's*, the inventor of "togetherness"—not surprisingly—turned it down. She heard that all the women editors there wanted to run it but that they had been overruled by their male superiors. That did not entirely surprise her, but she was sure someone else would want it. So she sent it to the *Ladies' Home Journal*, where it was accepted. There, to her amazement, it was rewritten so completely that it seemed to make the opposite points, so she pulled it. That left *Redbook,* where Bob Stein, an old friend, worked. He suggested that she do more interviews, particularly with younger women. She did, and sent the piece back to him. He was stunned by it. How could Betty Friedan write a piece so out of sync with what his magazine wanted? Why was she so angry? What in God's name had come over her? he wondered. He turned it down and called her agent. "Look," he said over the phone. "Only the most neurotic housewife would identify with this."

She was, she realized later, challenging the magazines themselves. She was saying that it was wrong to mislead women to think they should feel one way when in fact they often felt quite differently. She had discovered a crisis of considerable proportions, and these magazines would only deny it.

She was angry. It was censorship, she believed. Women's magazines had a single purpose, she decided—to sell a vast array of new products to American housewives—and anything that worked against that, that cast doubt about the happiness of the housewives using such products, was not going to be printed. No one from the advertising department sat in on editorial meetings saying which articles could run and which could not, she knew, but the very purpose of the magazine was to see women first and foremost as consumers, not as people.

At about that time she went to New York to attend a speech by Vance Packard, the writer. He had just finished his book, *The Hidden Persuaders,* about subliminal tactics in advertising. His efforts to write about this phenomenon in magazines had been completely unsuccessful, he said, so he turned it into a book, which had become a major best-seller. The parallels between his problems and hers were obvious. Suddenly, she envisioned "The Togetherness Woman" as a book. She called George Brockway at Norton, and he seemed delighted with the idea.

The economics of publishing were significantly different from those of magazines. Books were not dependent upon ads, they were dependent upon ideas, and the more provocative the idea, the more attention and, often, the better the sales. Brockway knew there had already been a number of attacks on conformity in American society, particularly as it affected men. Here was an attack that would talk about its effect on women, who were, of course, the principal buyers of books. He was impressed by Ms. Friedan. She was focused and, to his mind, wildly ambitious.

She told Brockway she would finish it in a year; instead, it took five years. Later she wrote that no one, not her husband, her editor, or anyone who knew her, thought she would ever finish it. She did so while taking care of three children. She later described herself as being like all the other mothers in suburbia, where she "hid, like secret drinking in the morning, the book I was writing when my suburban neighbors came for coffee . . ."

Her research was prodigious. Three days a week she went to the New York City Public Library for research. The chief villains, she decided, were the women's magazines. What stunned her was the fact that this had not always been true. In the same magazines in the late thirties and forties, there had been a sense of women moving steadily into the male professional world; then women's magazines had created a very different kind of role model, of a career woman who knew how to take care of herself and who could make it on her own.

But starting around 1949, these magazines changed dramatically. It was as if someone had thrown a giant switch. The new woman did not exist on her own. She was seen only in the light of supporting her husband and his career and taking care of the children.

The more Ms. Friedan investigated, the more she found that the world created in the magazines and the television sitcoms was, for many women at least, a fantasy world. Despite all the confidence and happiness among women portrayed in the magazines, there was underneath it all a crisis in the suburbs. It was the crisis of a generation of women who had left college with high idealism and who had come to feel increasingly frustrated and who had less and less a sense of self-esteem.

Nor, she found, did all the marvelous new appliances truly lighten the load of the housewife. If anything they seemed to extend it—there was some kind of Gresham's law at work here: The more time-saving machines there were, the more things there were to do with them. She had stumbled across something that a number of others, primarily psychiatrists, had noticed: a certain emotional malaise, bordering on depression, among many women of the era. One psychiatrist called it "the housewife's syndrome," another referred to it as "the housewife's blight." No one wrote about it in popular magazines, certainly not in the monthly women's magazines.

So, gathering material over several years, she began to write a book that would come out in 1963, not as *The Togetherness Woman*, but as *The Feminine Mystique*. She was approaching 40 as she began, but she was regenerated by the importance of the project; it seemed to give her her own life back. The result was a seminal book on what had happened to women in America. It started selling slowly but word of it grew and grew, and eventually, with 3 million copies in print, it became a handbook for the new feminist movement that was gradually beginning to come together.

THE FEMININE MYSTIQUE

The best way to understand why Friedan's analysis evoked such a strong response is to read what she had to say. In the selection below from her influential work, she discusses that mysterious ailment, "the problem that has no name."

•••••

Source: From *The Feminine Mystique* by Betty Friedan. Copyright © 1983, 1974, 1973, 1963 by Betty Friedan. Reprinted by permission of W. W. Norton & Company, Inc.

If a woman had a problem in the 1950s and 1960s, she knew that something must be wrong with her marriage or with herself. Other women were satisfied with their lives, she thought. What kind of a woman was she if she did not feel this mysterious fulfillment waxing the kitchen floor? She was so ashamed to admit her dissatisfaction that she never knew how many other woman shared it. If she tried to tell her husband, he didn't understand what she was talking about. She did not really understand it herself. For over 15 years women in America found it harder to talk about this problem than about sex. Even the psychoanalysts had no name for it. When a woman went to a psychiatrist for help, as many women did, she would say, "I'm so ashamed," or "I must be hopelessly neurotic." "I don't know what's wrong with women today," a suburban psychiatrist said uneasily. "I only know something is wrong because most of my patients happen to be women. And their problem isn't sexual." Most women with this problem did not go to see a psychoanalyst, however. "There's nothing wrong really," they kept telling themselves. "There isn't any problem."

But on an April morning in 1959, I heard a mother of four, having coffee with four other mothers in a suburban development 15 miles from New York, say in a tone of quiet desperation, "the problem." And the others knew, without words, that she was not talking about a problem with her husband, or her children, or her home. Suddenly they realized they all shared the same problem, the problem that has no name. They began, hesitantly, to talk about it. Later, after they had picked up their children at nursery school and taken them home to nap, two of the women cried, in sheer relief, just to know they were not alone.

•••••

Even so, most men, and some women, still did not know that this problem was real. But those who had faced it honestly knew that all the superficial remedies, the sympathetic advice, the scolding words and the cheering words were somehow drowning the problem in unreality. A bitter laugh was beginning to be heard from American women. They were admired, envied, pitied, theorized over until they were sick of it, offered drastic solutions or silly choices that no one could take seriously. They got all kinds of advice from the growing armies of marriage and child-guidance counselors, psychotherapists, and armchair psychologists, on how to adjust to their role as housewives. No other road to fulfillment was offered to American women in the middle of the twentieth century. Most adjusted to their role and suffered or ignored the problem that has no name. It can be less painful, for a woman, not to hear the strange, dissatisfied voice stirring within her.

It is no longer possible to ignore that voice, to dismiss the desperation of so many American women. This is not what being a woman means, no matter what the experts say. For human suffering there is a reason; perhaps the reason has not been found because the right questions have not been asked, or pressed far enough. I do not accept the answer that there is no problem because American women have luxuries that women in other times and lands never dreamed of; part of the strange newness of the problem is that it cannot be understood in terms of the age-old material problems of man: poverty, sickness, hunger, cold. The women who suffer this problem have a hunger that food cannot fill. It persists in women whose husbands are struggling interns and law clerks, or prosperous doctors and lawyers; in wives of workers and executives who make $5,000 a year or $50,000. It is not caused by lack of material advantages; it may not even be felt by women preoccupied with desperate problems of hunger, poverty, or illness. And women who think it will be solved by more money, a bigger house, a second car, moving to a better suburb, often discover it gets worse.

•••••

QUESTIONS

1. According to women's magazines, what qualities were required for the ideal woman of the 1950s to achieve happiness and fulfillment? What were Friedan's feelings about life in the suburbs? Were they entirely negative?
2. Why did the media discourage women from pursuing careers outside the home during the 1950s? What obstacles did wage-earning women typically confront during the period?
3. Why was the popular image of women's domestic role so positive during the 1950s? Why did Friedan decide to challenge that image? What influence did her association with Smith College have on her development as a social critic?
4. Why were Friedan's ideas for *The Feminine Mystique* so much more acceptable to a book publisher than to a women's magazine? What did her research reveal about the changing portrayal of women in these magazines?
5. Why do you think Friedan believed "the problem that has no name" was the most apt description of the frustration that many suburban housewives felt during the 1950s? Based on the above excerpts from *The Feminine Mystique,* how would you define "the problem that has no name"? Would Friedan's work have been more or less influential if it had been written 20 years earlier?
6. Do you see any similarities between Friedan, Eleanor Roosevelt, and Margaret Sanger? In what ways did the three women differ? Which of them faced the greatest obstacles? Which of them did more to advance the cause of women's rights?

BIBLIOGRAPHY

Although there is no full-length treatment of Friedan's life, autobiographical observations appear in three of the books she has written: *The Feminine Mystique* (1963); *It Changed My Life: Writings of the Women's Movement* (1976); and *The Second Stage* (1981). Those seeking to learn more about the postwar expansion of suburbia should consult Kenneth Jackson, *Crabgrass Frontier: The Suburbanization of the United States* (1985). For a provocative examination of postwar domesticity, see Elaine Tyler May, *Homeward Bound: American Families in the Cold War Era* (1988). Major studies of the rebirth of feminism during the 1960s include Susan M. Hartmann, *From Margin to Mainstream: American Women and Politics Since 1960* (1989), and Sara Evans, *Personal Politics: The Roots of Women's Liberation in the Civil Rights Movement and the New Left* (1980). Two ably executed surveys that place these developments in a broader historical context are William Chafe, *The Paradox of Change: American Women in the Twentieth Century* (1991), and Rosalind Rosenberg, *Divided Lives: American Women in the Twentieth Century* (1992).

Cesar Chavez

In the immediate postwar decades, unions in mass-production industries such as autos and steel achieved impressive advances at the bargaining table. In addition to providing substantial wage increases, union-negotiated contracts contained provisions for paid vacations, health insurance programs, pension plans, cost-of-living allowances, and other security measures. When the United Auto Workers (UAW) established an employer-funded system of supplemental unemployment benefits in 1955, organized labor appeared to be on the verge of obtaining its long-sought goal of a guaranteed annual wage. And when UAW President Walter Reuther later observed that the union movement was "developing a whole new middle class," countless workers doubtless agreed.

But Reuther did not speak for all wage earners. Far away from the na-

tion's mass-production industries, America's agricultural workers continued to live and labor in a world of grinding poverty that had changed little during the previous century. Federal laws mandating collective bargaining did not apply to these workers; and a series of organizational efforts, extending back to the turn of the century, had all been defeated by the politically powerful growers who employed them and who dominated the areas in which they worked. Without protection and often without hope, farm workers had become the forgotten people of the American labor

force. It was little wonder that when Cesar Chavez decided to organize Cali-
fornia farmworkers during the early 1960s, he spoke of the mission as "an all
but impossible task."

Yet the sixties was a unique time in American life, when anything seemed
possible. Civil rights demonstrators had shown that courage and determina-
tion could undermine the most intractable forms of oppression. And Chavez
possessed just the qualities needed to channel that movement's energy and
hope toward his own ends. An intense man of single-minded purpose, he con-
vinced farmworkers that they too could create a better world for themselves
and their children. At the same time, he took steps to mobilize national sup-
port for his efforts, thus shattering the isolation that had long abetted growers'
exploitation of agricultural laborers. As much a social activist as a labor orga-
nizer, Chavez established a union that exhibited the same dual personality.

It was an extraordinary achievement. In the essay that follows, Cletus E.
Daniel describes the numerous obstacles that Chavez had to overcome. In the
process, Daniel not only provides an insightful examination of the character
traits that enabled Chavez to persevere in his seemingly hopeless task; he also
offers a judicious assessment of Chavez's strengths and shortcomings as a
labor leader.

Cesar Chavez

Cletus E. Daniel

It was, Cesar Chavez later wrote, "the strangest meeting in the history of California agriculture." Speaking by telephone from his cluttered headquarters in
La Paz to Jerry Brown, the new governor of California, Chavez had been asked
to repeat for the benefit of farm employers crowded into Brown's Sacramento
office the farmworker leader's acceptance of a farm labor bill to which they
had already assented. And as the employers heard Chavez's voice repeating
the statement of acceptance he had just made to the governor, they broke into
wide smiles and spontaneous applause.

That representatives of the most powerful special interest group in California history should have thus expressed their delight at the prospect of realizing still another of their legislative goals does not account for Chavez's assertion of the meeting's strange character. These were, after all, men long
accustomed to having their way in matters of farm labor legislation. What was
strange about that meeting on May 5, 1975, was that the state's leading farm
employers should have derived such apparent relief and satisfaction from
hearing the president of the United Farm Workers of America, AFL-CIO, agree
to a legislative proposal designed to afford farmworkers an opportunity to es-

Source: From *Labor Leaders in America.* Copyright 1987 by the Board of Trustees of the University of
Illinois. Used with the permission of the author and the University of Illinois Press.

cape their historic powerlessness through unionism and collective bargaining.

Beyond investing the state's farmworkers with rights that those who labored for wages on the land had always been denied, the passage of California's Agricultural Labor Relations Act (ALRA) was a seismic event, one that shattered the foundation upon which rural class relations had rested for a century and more. For the state's agribusinessmen, whose tradition it had been to rule the bounteous fields and orchards of California with a degree of authority and control more appropriate to potentates than mere employers, supporting the ALRA was less an act of culpable treason against their collective heritage than one of grudging resignation in the face of a suddenly irrelevant past and an apparently inescapable future. For the state's farmworkers, whose involuntary custom it had always been to surrender themselves to a system of industrialized farming that made a captive peasantry of them, the new law made possible what only the boldest among them had dared to image: a role equal to the employer's in determining terms and conditions of employment. Yet if the ALRA's enactment was a victory of unprecedented dimensions for California farmworkers as a class, it was a still greater personal triumph for Cesar Chavez.

More than any other labor leader of his time, and perhaps in the whole history of American labor, Cesar Chavez leads a union that is an extension of his own values, experience, and personality. This singular unity of man and movement has found its most forceful and enduring expression in the unprecedented economic and political power that has accrued to the membership of the United Farm Workers (UFW) under Chavez's intense and unrelenting tutelage. Indeed, since 1965, when Chavez led his then small following into a bitter struggle against grape growers around the lower San Joaquin valley town of Delano, the UFW has, despite the many crises that have punctuated its brief but turbulent career, compiled a record of achievement that rivals the accomplishments of the most formidable industrial unions of the 1930s.

While this personal domination may well be the essential source of the UFW's extraordinary success, it has also posed risks for the union. For just as Chavez's strengths manifest themselves in the character of his leadership, so, too, must his weaknesses. Certainly the UFW's somewhat confused sense of its transcending mission—whether to be a trade union or a social movement; whether to focus on narrow economic gains or to pursue broader political goals—reflects in some degree Chavez's personal ambivalence toward both the ultimate purpose of worker organization and the fundamental objective of his own prolonged activism.

Had his adult life followed the pattern of his early youth, Cesar Chavez need not have concerned

---

"Okie"   Poor people of Oklahoma who left the "dust bowl" and sought a better life in California.

bracero   A Mexican laborer admitted to the U.S. especially for seasonal contract labor in agriculture.

St. Francis of Assisi   Founder of the Franciscans and one of the greatest Christian saints.

Gandhi   Leader of the Indian Nationalist movement against British rule who advocated nonviolent protest.

himself with the task of liberating California farmworkers from an exploitive labor system that had entombed a succession of Chinese, Japanese, Filipino, Mexican, and other non-Anglo immigrants for more than a hundred years. Born on March 31, 1927, the second child of Librado and Juana Chavez, Cesar Estrada Chavez started his life sharing little beyond language and a diffuse ethnic heritage with the Chicano—Mexican and Mexican-American—workers who constitute nearly the entire membership of the United Farm Workers of America. Named after his paternal grandfather Cesario, who had home-steaded the family's small farm in the north Gila River valley near Yuma three years before Arizona claimed statehood, Chavez enjoyed during his youth the kind of close and stable family life that farmworkers caught in the relentless currents of the western migrant stream longed for but rarely attained. And al-though farming on a small scale afforded few material rewards even as it de-manded hard and unending physical labor, it fostered in Chavez an apprecia-tion of independence and personal sovereignty that helps to account for the special force and steadfastness of his later rebellion against the oppressive de-pendence into which workers descended when they joined the ranks of Cali-fornia's agricultural labor force.

It is more than a little ironic that until 1939, when unpaid taxes put the family's farm on the auction block, Chavez could have more reasonably as-pired to a future as a landowner than as a farmworker. "If we had stayed there," he later said of the family's farm, "possibly I would have been a grower. God writes in exceedingly crooked lines."

The full significance of the family's eviction from the rambling adobe ranch house that had provided not only shelter but also a sense of place and social perspective was not at once apparent to an 11 year old. The deeper meaning of the family's loss was something that accumulated in Chavez's mind only as his subsequent personal experience in the migrant stream dis-closed the full spectrum of emotional and material hardship attending a life set adrift from the roots that had nurtured it. At age 11 the sight of a bulldozer ef-fortlessly destroying in a few minutes what the family had struggled over nearly three generations to build was meaning enough. The land's new owner, an Anglo grower impatient to claim his prize, dispatched the bulldozer that became for Chavez a graphic and enduring symbol of the power that the "haves" employ against the "have-nots" in industrialized agriculture. . .

• • • • •

"When we were pushed off our land," Chavez said, "all we could take with us was what we could jam into the old Studebaker or pile on its roof and fenders, mostly clothes and bedding . . . I realized something was happening because my mother was crying, but I didn't realize the import of it at the time. When we left the farm, our whole life was upset, turned upside down. We have been part of a very stable community, and we were about to become mi-gratory workers."

Yet if Chavez's experience was in some ways similar to that of the dispos-sessed dust-bowl migrant whose pilgrimage to California was also less an act of hope than of despair, it was fundamentally unlike that of even the most destitute Anglo—John Steinbeck's generic **"Okie"**—because of virulent racial attitudes among the state's white majority that tended to define all persons "of color" as unequal. For the Chavez family, whose standing as landowners in a region populated by people mainly like themselves had insulated them from many of the meanest forms of racism, following the crops in California as undifferentiated members of a brown-skinned peasantry afforded an unwelcome education. To the familiar varieties of racial humiliation and mistreatment—being physically punished by an Anglo teacher for lapsing into your native tongue; being in the presence of Anglos who talked about you as if you were an inanimate object—were added some new and more abrasive forms: being rousted by border patrolmen who automatically regarded you as a "wetback" until you proved otherwise; being denied service at a restaurant or made to sit in the "Mexican only" seats at the local movie house; being stopped and searched by the police for no reason other than your skin color announced your powerlessness to resist; being cheated by an employer who smugly assumed that you probably wouldn't object because Mexicans were naturally docile.

But, if because of such treatment Chavez came to fear and dislike Anglos—*gringos* or *gabachos* in the pejorative lexicon of the barrio—he also came to understand that while considerations of race and ethnicity compounded the plight of farmworkers, their mistreatment was rooted ultimately in the economics of industrialized agriculture. As the family traveled the state from one crop to the next, one hovel to the next, trying desperately to survive on the meager earnings of parents and children alike, Chavez quickly learned that Chicano labor contractors and Japanese growers exploited migrants as readily as did Anglo employers. And, although the complex dynamics of California's rural political economy might still have eluded him, Chavez instinctively understood that farmworkers would cease to be victims only when they discovered the means to take control of their own lives.

The realization that unionism must be that means came later. Unlike the typical Chicano family in the migrant stream, however, the Chavez family included among its otherwise meager possessions a powerful legacy of the independent life it had earlier known, one that revealed itself in a stubborn disinclination to tolerate conspicuous injustices. "I don't want to suggest we were that radical," Chavez later said, "but I know we were probably one of the strikingest families in California, the first ones to leave the fields if anyone shouted Huelga!—which is Spanish for Strike! . . . If any family felt something was wrong and stopped working, we immediately joined them even if we didn't know them. And if the grower didn't correct what was wrong, then they would leave, and we'd leave."

· · · · ·

Although the United Cannery, Agricultural, Packing and Allied Workers of America, a CIO-affiliated union, was conducting sporadic organizing drives among California farmworkers when Chavez and his family joined the state's farm labor force at the end of the 1930s, he was too young and untutored to appreciate "anything of the real guts of unions." Yet because his father harbored a strong, if unstudied, conviction that unionism was a manly act of resistance to the employers' authority, Chavez's attitude toward unions quickly progressed from vague approval to ardent endorsement. His earliest participation in a union-led struggle did not occur until the late 1940s, when the AFL's National Farm Labor Union conducted a series of ultimately futile strikes in the San Joaquin valley. This experience, which left Chavez with an acute sense of frustration and disappointment as the strike inevitably withered in the face of overwhelming employer power, also produced a brief but equally keen feeling of exhilaration because it afforded an opportunity to vent the rebelliousness that an expanding consciousness of his own social and occupational captivity awakened within him. Yet to the extent that unionism demands the subordination of individual aspirations to a depersonalized common denomination of the group's desires, Chavez was not in his youth the stuff of which confirmed trade unionists are made. More than most young migrant workers, whose ineluctable discontent was not heightened further by the memory of an idealized past, Chavez hoped to escape his socioeconomic predicament rather than simply moderate the harsh forces that governed it.

To be a migrant worker, however, was to learn the hard way that avenues of escape were more readily imagined than traveled. As ardently as the Chavez family sought a way out of the migrant orbit, they spent the early 1940s moving from valley to valley, from harvest to harvest, powerless to fend off the corrosive effects of their involuntary transiency. Beyond denying them the elementary amenities of a humane existence—a decent home, sufficient food, adequate clothing—the demands of migrant life also conspired to deny the Chavez children the educations that their parents valiantly struggled to ensure. For Cesar school became a "nightmare," a dispiriting succession of inhospitable places ruled by Anglo teachers and administrators whose often undisguised contempt for migrant children prompted him to drop out after the eighth grade.

Chavez's inevitable confrontation with the fact of his personal powerlessness fostered a sense of anger and frustration that revealed itself in a tendency to reject many of the most visible symbols of his cultural heritage. This brief episode of open rebellion against the culture of his parents, which dates from the family's decision to settle down in Delano in late 1943 until he reluctantly joined the navy a year later, was generally benign: *Mariachis* were rejected in favor of Duke Ellington; his mother's *dichos* and *consejos*—the bits of Mexican folk wisdom passed from one generation to the next—lost out to less culture-bound values; religious customs rooted in the rigid doctrines of the Catholic church gave way to a fuzzy existentialism . . . In the end, Chavez reacted most decisively against the debilitating circumstances of his life by joining the navy, a reluctant decision whose redeeming value was that it offered a means of escape, a way "to get away from farm labor."

The two years he spent in the navy ("the worst of my life") proved to be no more than a respite from farm labor. If Chavez had hoped to acquire a trade while in the service, he soon discovered that the same considerations of race and ethnicity that placed strict limits on what non-Anglos could reasonably aspire to achieve at home operated with equal efficiency in the navy to keep them in the least desirable jobs. Without the training that might have allowed him to break out of the cycle of poverty and oppression that the labor system of industrialized agriculture fueled, Chavez returned to Delano in 1946 to the only work he knew.

Finding work had always been a problem for farmworkers due to a chronic oversupply of agricultural labor in California. The problem became even more acute for migrant families after the war because agribusiness interests succeeded in their political campaign to extend the so-called *Bracero* program, a treaty arrangement dating from 1942 that permitted farm employers in California and the Southwest to import Mexican nationals under contract to alleviate real and imagined wartime labor shortages.

For Chavez, the struggle to earn a living took on special urgency following his marriage in 1948 to Helen Fabela, a Delano girl whom he had first met when his family made one of its periodic migrations through the area in search of work. Being the daughter of farmworkers, and thus knowing all too well the hardships that attended a family life predicated upon the irregular earnings of agricultural work, did nothing to cushion the hard times that lay ahead for Helen Chavez and her new husband, a 21-year-old disaffected farm laborer without discernable prospects.

Chavez met the challenge of making a living, which multiplied with the arrival of a new baby during each of the first three years of marriage, in the only way he knew: He took any job available, wherever it was available. Not until 1952, when he finally landed a job in a San Jose lumberyard, was Chavez able to have the settled life that he and Helen craved. The Mexican barrio in San Jose, known to its impoverished inhabitants as Sal Si Puedes—literally "get out if you can"—was a few square blocks of ramshackle houses occupied by discouraged parents and angry children who, in their desperation to do just what the neighborhood's morbid nickname advised, too often sought ways out that led to prison rather than to opportunity. Long before it became home to Chavez and his family, Sal Si Puedes had earned a reputation among the sociologists who regularly scouted its mean streets as a virtual laboratory of urban social pathology. In the early 1950s, however, the area also attracted two men determined in their separate ways to alleviate the powerlessness of its residents rather than to document or measure it. More than any others, these two activists, one a young Catholic priest, the other a veteran community organizer, assumed unwitting responsibility for the education of Cesar Chavez.

When Father Donald McDonnell established his small mission church in Sal Si Puedes, he resolved to attend to both the spiritual need of his destitute parishioners and their education in those doctrines of the Catholic church relating to the inherence rights of labor. To Cesar Chavez, the teachings of the church, the rituals and catechism that he absorbed as an obligation of culture rather than a voluntary and knowing act of religious faith, had never seemed to have more than tangential relevance to the hard-edged world that poor people confronted in their daily lives. But in the militant example and activist ped-

agogy of Father McDonnell, Chavez discovered a new dimension of Catholi-
cism that excited him precisely because it was relevant to his immediate circumstances . . .

More than anyone else, Father McDonnell awoke Chavez to a world of
pertinent ideas that would become the essential source of his personal philosophy; introduced him to a pantheon of crusaders for social justice (Gandhi
among them) whose heroic exertions would supply the inspiration for his own
crusade to empower farmworkers. Yet the crucial task of instructing Chavez in
the practical means by which his nascent idealism might achieve concrete expression was brilliantly discharged by Fred Ross, an indefatigable organizer
who had spent the better part of his adult life roaming California trying to
show the victims of economic, racial, and ethnic discrimination how they
might resist further abuse and degradation through organization.

Drawn to Sal Si Puedes by the palpable misery of its Chicano inhabitants,
Ross began to conduct the series of informal house meetings through which he
hoped to establish a local chapter of the Community Service Organization
(CSO), a self-help group that operated under the sponsorship of radical activist
Saul Alinsky's Chicago-based Industrial Areas Foundation. Always on the look-
out for the natural leaders in the communities he sought to organize, Ross at
once saw in Chavez, despite his outwardly shy and self-conscious demeanor,
the telltale signs of a born organizer. "At the very first meeting," Ross recalled:
"I was very much impressed with Cesar. I could tell he was intensely interested,
a kind of burning interest rather than one of those inflammatory things that
lasts one night and is then forgotten. He asked many questions, part of it to see
if I really knew, putting me to the test. But it was much more than that." Ross
also discovered that Chavez was an exceedingly quick study . . .

The confidence that Ross expressed in Chavez's leadership potential was
immediately confirmed. Assigned to the CSO voter registration project in San
Jose, Chavez displayed a natural aptitude for the work; so much in fact that
Ross turned over control of the entire drive to him. And if his style of leadership proved somewhat unconventional, his tactical sense was unerring. While
Ross had relied upon local college students to serve as registrars for the campaign, Chavez felt more could be gained by using people from the barrio. "Instead of recruiting college guys," he said, "I got all my friends, my beer-drink-
ing friends. With them it wasn't a question of civic duty, they helped me
because of friendship, and because it was fun." With nearly 6,000 new voters
registered by the time the campaign ended, Chavez's reputation as an organizer was established.

• • • • •

After watching his protégé in action for only a few months, Fred Ross persuaded Saul Alinsky that the CSO should employ the talents of so able an organizer on a full-time basis. Becoming a professional organizer, however, was
a prospect that frightened Chavez nearly as much as it excited him. Helping
Fred Ross was one thing, organizing on his own among strangers was quite

another. Yet in the end, his desire to oppose what seemed unjust outweighed his fears.

From the end of 1952 until he quit the organization 10 years later to build a union among farmworkers, the CSO was Chavez's life. He approached the work of helping the poor to help themselves in the only way his nature allowed, with a single-mindedness that made everything else in his life—home, family, personal gain—secondary. For Chavez, nothing short of total immersion in the work of forcing change was enough. If his wife inherited virtually the entire responsibility for raising their children (who were to number eight in all), if his children became resentful at being left to grow up without a father who was readily accessible to them, if he was himself forced to abandon any semblance of personal life, Chavez remained unshaken in his belief that the promotion of the greater good made every such sacrifice necessary and worthwhile.

• • • • •

In the beginning, helping people to deal with problems they felt otherwise powerless to resolve was an end in itself. In time, however, Chavez saw that if his service work was going to produce a legacy of activist sentiment in Chicano neighborhoods, it was necessary to recast what had typically been an act of unconditional assistance into a mutually beneficial transaction. And, when he discovered that those whom he was serving were not just willing, but eager, to return the favor, Chavez made that volition the basis upon which he helped to build the CSO into the most formidable Mexican–American political organization in the state. "Once I realized helping people was an organizing technique," he said, "I increased that work. I was willing to work day and night and to go to hell and back for people—provided they also did something for the CSO in return. I never felt bad asking for that . . . because I wasn't asking for something for myself. For a long time we didn't know how to put that work together into an organization. But we learned after a while—we learned how to help people by making them responsible."

Because agricultural labor constituted a main source of economic opportunity in most Chicano communities, many of those whom Chavez recruited into the CSO were farmworkers. Not until 1958, however, did Chavez take his first halting steps toward making work and its discontents the essential focus of his organizing activities. This gradual shift from community to labor organization occurred over a period of several months as Chavez struggled to establish a CSO chapter in Oxnard, a leading citrus-growing region north of Los Angeles. Asked by Saul Alinsky to organize the local Chicano community in order that it might support the flagging efforts of the United Packinghouse Workers to win labor contracts covering the region's citrus-packing sheds, Chavez embarked upon his task intending to exploit the same assortment of grievances that festered in barrios throughout the state.

His new clients, however, had other ideas. From the beginning, whenever he sought to impress his agenda upon local citizens, they interrupted with their own: a concern that they were being denied jobs because growers in the region relied almost entirely on **braceros** to meet their needs for farm labor. It proved to be an issue that simply would not go away. "At every house meeting," Chavez recalled, "they hit me with the bracero problem, but I would dodge it. I just didn't fathom how big that problem was. I would say, 'Well, you know, we really can't do anything about that, but it's a bad problem. Something should be done.'" An apparently artless dodger, he was, in the end, forced to make the bracero problem the focus of his campaign. "Finally," he admitted, "I decided this was the issue I had to tackle. The fact that braceros were also farmworkers didn't bother me . . . The jobs belonged to local workers. The braceros were brought only for exploitation. They were just instruments for the growers. Braceros didn't make any money, and they were exploited viciously, forced to work under conditions the local people wouldn't tolerate. If the braceros spoke up, if they made the minimal complaints, they'd be shipped back to Mexico."

In attacking Oxnard's bracero problem, Chavez and his followers confronted the integrated power of the agribusiness establishment in its most forceful and resilient aspect. While farm employers around Oxnard and throughout the state were permitted under federal regulations to employ braceros only when they had exhausted the available pool of local farmworkers, they had long operated on the basis of a collusive arrangement with the California Farm Placement Service that allowed them to import Mexican nationals without regard to labor market conditions in the region.

Although Chavez and the large CSO membership he rallied behind him sought nothing more than compliance with existing rules regarding the employment of braceros, the 13-month struggle that followed brought them into bitter conflicts with politically influential employers, state farm placement bureaucrats, and federal labor department officials. Yet through the use of picket lines, marches, rallies, and a variety of innovative agitational techniques that reduced the Farm Placement Service to almost total paralysis, Chavez and his militant following had by the end of 1959 won a victory so complete that farm employers in the region were recruiting their labor through a local CSO headquarters that operated as a hiring hall.

Chavez emerged from the Oxnard campaign convinced that work-related issues had greater potential as a basis for organizing Chicanos than any that he had earlier stressed. The response to his organizing drive in Oxnard was overwhelming, and he saw at once "the difference between that CSO chapter and any other CSO up to that point was that jobs were the main issue." And at the same juncture, he said: "I began to see the potential of organizing the Union."

• • • • •

In Chavez's view, nothing less than fanaticism would suffice if farmworkers were to be emancipated from a system of wage slavery that had endured for a century. When a reporter observed during one of the UFW's later struggles that he "sounded like a fanatic," Chavez readily admitted the charge. "I am," he confessed. "There's nothing wrong with being a fanatic. Those are the only ones that get things done."

In many ways, Chavez's supreme accomplishment as an organizer came long before he signed up his first farmworker. Attracting disciples willing to embrace the idea of a farmworkers' movement with a passion, single-mindedness, and spirit of sacrifice equal to his own was at once Chavez's greatest challenge and his finest achievement. By the fall of 1962, when he formally established the National Farm Workers Association (NFWA) in a derelict Fresno theater, Chavez had rallied to "La Causa"—the iconographic designation soon adopted by the faithful—an impressive roster of "co-fanatics": Dolores Huerta, a small, youthful-looking mother of six (she would have 10 in all) whose willingness to do battle with Chavez over union tactics was exceeded only by her fierce loyalty to him; Gilbert Padilla, like Huerta another CSO veteran, whose activism was rooted in a hatred for the migrant system that derived from personal experience; Wayne Hartimire and Jim Drake, two young Anglo ministers who were to make the California Migrant Ministry a virtual subsidiary of the union; Manuel Chavez, an especially resourceful organizer who reluctantly gave up a well-paying job to join the union when the guilt his cousin Cesar heaped upon him for not joining became unbearable. Most important, there was Helen Chavez, whose willingness to sacrifice so much of what mattered most to her, including first claim on her husband's devotion, revealed the depth of her own commitment to farmworker organization.

Working out of Delano, which became the union's first headquarters, Chavez began the slow and often discouraging process of organizing farm laborers whose strong belief in the rightness of his union-building mission was tempered by an even deeper conviction that "it couldn't be done, that the growers were too powerful." With financial resources consisting of a small savings account, gifts and loans from relatives, and the modest wages Helen earned by returning to the fields, the cost of Chavez's stubborn idealism to himself and his family was measured in material deprivation and emotional tumult. Had he been willing to accept financial assistance from such sources as the United Packinghouse Workers or the Agricultural Workers Organizing Committee (AWOC), a would-be farmworkers' union established in 1959 by the AFL-CIO, the worst hardships that awaited Chavez and his loyalists might have been eased or eliminated. Yet, following a line of reasoning that was in some ways reminiscent of the voluntarist logic of earlier trade unionists, Chavez insisted that a farmworkers' union capable of forging the will and stamina required to breach the awesome power of agribusiness could only be built on the sacrifice and suffering of its own membership.

During the NFWA's formative years there was more than enough sacrifice and suffering to go around. But due to the services it provided to farmworkers and the promise of a better life it embodied, the union slowly won the allegiance of a small but dedicated membership scattered through the San Joaquin valley. By the spring of 1965, when the union called its first strike, a brief walkout by rose grafters in Kern County that won higher wages but no contract, Chavez's obsession was on its way to becoming a functioning reality.

Despite the studied deliberateness of its leaders, however, the struggle that catapulted the union to national attention, and invested its mission with the same moral authority that liberal and left-wing activists of the 1960s attributed to the decade's stormy civil rights, antipoverty, and antiwar movements, began in the fall of 1965 as a reluctant gesture of solidarity with an AWOC local whose mainly Filipino membership was on strike against grape growers around Delano. Given the demonstrated ineptitude of the old-time trade unionists who directed the AFL-CIO's organizing efforts among California farmworkers, Chavez had reason to hesitate before committing his still small and untested membership to the support of an AWOC strike. But the strike was being led by Larry Itliong, a Filipino veteran of earlier agricultural strikes and the ablest of the AWOC organizers, and Chavez did not have it in him to ignore a just cause . . .

The Delano strike, which soon widened beyond the table grape growers who were its initial targets to include the state's major wineries, was a painful five-year struggle destined to test not only the durability of agricultural unionism in California but also the wisdom and resourcefulness of Chavez's leadership. Because growers had little difficulty in recruiting scabs to take the place of strikers, Chavez recognized immediately that a strike could not deny employers the labor they required to cultivate and harvest their crops. Even so, picket lines went up on the first day of the strike and were maintained with unfailing devotion week after week, month after month. Chavez emphasized the need for picketing because he believed that no experience promoted a keener sense of solidarity or afforded strikers a more graphic and compelling illustration of the struggle's essential character. "Unless you have been on a picket line," he said, "you just can't understand the feeling you get there, seeing the conflict at its two most acid ends. It's a confrontation that's vivid. It's a real education." It was an education, however, for which pickets often paid a high price: threats, physical intimidation, and outright violence at the hands of growers and their agents and arbitrary arrests and harassment by local lawmen who made no effort to mask their pro-employer sympathies. Yet, no matter how great the provocation, no matter how extreme the violence directed against them, strikers were sworn by Chavez not to use violence. Chavez's unwavering commitment to nonviolence was compounded from equal measures of his mother's teachings, the affecting example of **St. Francis of Assisi,** and the moral philosophy of **Gandhi.** In the end, though, it was the power of nonviolence as a tactical method that appealed to him. Convinced that the farmworkers' greatest asset was the inherent justice of their cause, Chavez believed that the task of communicating the essential virtue of the union's struggle to potential supporters, and to the general public, would be subverted if strikers resorted to violence . . .

Winning and sustaining public sympathy, as well as the active support of labor, church, student, civic, and political organizations, was indispensable to the success of the Delano struggles because the inefficacy of conventional strike tactics led Chavez to adopt the economic boycott as the union's primary weapon in fighting employers. Newly sensitized to issues of social justice by the civil rights struggles that reverberated across the country, liberals and left-ists enthusiastically embraced the union's cause, endorsing its successive boy-cotts and not infrequently showing up in Delano to bear personal witness to the unfolding drama of the grape strike. Many unions—from dockworkers who refused to handle scab grapes to autoworkers, whose president, Walter Reuther, not only pledged generous financial assistance to the strikers but also traveled to Delano to join their picket lines—also supported the NFWA. Even the AFL-CIO, which had been sponsoring the rival Agricultural Workers Orga-nizing Committee, ended up embracing the NFWA when Bill Kircher, the fed-eration's national organizing director, concluded that the future of farmworker unionism lay with Chavez and his ragtag following rather than with the more fastidious, but less effective, AWOC. Kircher's assessment of the situation also led him to urge a merger of the NFWA and AWOC. And although their long-standing suspicion of "Big Labor" impelled many of the Anglo volunteers who had joined his movement to oppose the idea, Chavez and the union's farm-worker membership recognized that the respectability and financial strength to be gained from such a merger outweighed any loss of independence that AFL-CIO affiliation might entail. With Chavez at its helm and Larry Itliong as its second-in-command, the United Farm Workers Organizing Committee (UFWOC) was formally chartered by the AFL-CIO in August 1966.

•••••

"Alone, the farm workers have no economic power," Chavez once observed, "but with the help of the public they can develop the economic power to counter that of the growers." The truth of that maxim was first revealed in April 1966, when a national boycott campaign against its product line of wines and spirits caused Schenley Industries, which had 5,000 acres of vineyards in the San Joaquin valley, to recognize the farmworkers' union and enter into contract negotiations. For Chavez, who received the news as he and a small band of union loyalists were nearing the end of an arduous, but exceedingly well-publicized, 300-mile march from Delano to Sacramento, Schenley's capit-ulation was "the first major proof of the power of the boycott."

•••••

The victories won during the first two years of the Delano struggle, while they propelled the cause of farmworker organization far beyond the boundaries of any previous advance, left Chavez and his followers still needing to overcome table grape growers in the San Joaquin and Coachella valleys before the union could claim real institutional durability. The state's table grape industry, com-prised for the most part of family farms whose hardworking owners typically viewed unionism as an assault on their personal independence as well as a threat to their prerogatives as employers, remained unalterably opposed to UFWOC's demands long after California's largest wineries had acceded to them. Thus when Chavez made them the main targets of the union's campaign toward the end of 1967, table grape growers fought back with a ferocity and tactical ingenuity that announced their determination to resist unionism at whatever cost.

While the boycott continued to serve as the union's most effective weapon, especially after employers persuaded compliant local judges to issue injunctions severely restricting picketing and other direct action in the strike region, the slowness with which it operated to prod recalcitrant growers toward the bargaining table produced in farmworkers and volunteers alike an impatience that reduced both morale and discipline. It also undermined La Causa's commitment to nonviolence. "There came a point in 1968," Chavez recalled, "when we were in danger of losing . . . Because of a sudden increase in violence against us, and an apparent lack of progress after more than two years of striking, there were those who felt that the time had come to overcome violence by violence . . . There was demoralization in the ranks, people becoming desperate, more and more talk about violence. People meant it, even when they talked to me. They would say, 'Hey, we've got to burn these sons of bitches down. We've got to kill a few of them.'"

In responding to the crisis, Chavez chose a method of restoring discipline and morale that was as risky and unusual as it was revealing of the singular character of his leadership. He decided to fast. The fast, which continued for 25 painful days before it was finally broken at a moving outdoor mass in Delano that included Robert Kennedy among its celebrants, was more than an act of personal penance. "I thought I had to bring the Movement to a halt," Chavez explained, "do something that would force them and me to deal with the whole question of violence and ourselves. We had to stop long enough to take account of what we were doing." Although the fast's religious overtones offended the secular sensibilities of many of his followers, it was more a political than a devotional act; an intrepid and dramatic, if manipulative, device by which Chavez established a compelling standard of personal sacrifice against which his supporters might measure their own commitment and dedication to La Causa, and thus their allegiance to its leader . . .

Those in the union who were closest to Chavez, whatever their initial reservations, found the fast's effect undeniably therapeutic. Jerry Cohen, the union's able young attorney, while convinced that it had been "a fantastic gamble," was deeply impressed by "what a great organizing tool the fast was." "Before the fast," Cohen noted, "there were nine ranch committees [the rough equivalent of locals within the UFW's structure], one for each winery. The fast, for the first time, made a union out of those ranch committees . . . Everybody worked together." Dolores Huerta also recognized the curative power of Chavez's ordeal. "Prior to that fast," she insisted, "there had been a lot of bickering and backbiting and fighting and little attempts at violence. But Cesar brought everybody together and really established himself as a leader of the farmworkers."

While a chronic back ailment, apparently exacerbated by his fast and a schedule that often required him to work 20 hours a day, slowed Chavez's pace during much of 1968 and 1969, the steadily more punishing economic effects of the grape boycott finally began to erode the confidence and weaken the resistance of growers. With the assistance of a committee of strongly pro-union Catholic bishops who had volunteered to mediate the conflict, negotiations between the union and the first defectors from the growers' ranks finally began in the spring of 1970. And by the end of July, when the most obdurate growers in the Delano area collapsed under the combined weight of a continuing boycott and their own mounting weariness, Chavez and his tenacious followers had finally accomplished what five years before seemed impossible to all but the mot sanguine forecasters.

The union's victory, which extended to 85 percent of the state's table grape industry, resulted in contracts that provided for substantial wage increases and employer contributions to UFWOC's health and welfare and economic development funds. Even more important, however, were the noneconomic provisions: union-run hiring halls that gave UFWOC control over the distribution of available work; grievance machinery that rescued the individual farmworker from the arbitrary authority of the boss; restrictions on the use of pesticides that endangered the health of workers; in short, provisions for the emancipation of workers from the century-old dictatorship of California agribusiness.

After five years of struggle and sacrifice, of anguish and uncertainty, Chavez and his followers wanted nothing so much as an opportunity to recuperate from their ordeal and to savor their victory. It was not to be. On the day before the union concluded its negotiations with Delano grape growers, Chavez received the distressing news that lettuce growers in the Salinas and Santa Maria valleys, knowing that they would be the next targets of UFWOC's organizing campaign, had signed contracts providing for the Teamsters' union to represent their field workers. In keeping with the pattern of the Teamsters' involvement with agricultural field labor, no one bothered to consult the Chicano workers whose incessant stooping and bending, whose painful contortions in the service of the hated short-handle hoe, made possible the growers' proud boast that the Salinas valley was the "salad bowl of the nation."

• • • • •

The challenge presented by the Teamsters-grower alliance in the lettuce industry forced UFWOC to divert precious resources into the reconstruction of its far-flung boycott network. It also distracted Chavez and his most competent aides at a time when the union was in the process of transforming itself from an organization expert in agitation into one equipped to administer contracts covering thousands of workers in the grape industry. Meeting the demands of the hiring hall and the grievance process, which were the union's greatest potential sources of institutional strength, also became its most worrisome and debilitating problem as ranch committees composed of rank-and-file members struggled against their own inexperience, and sometimes powerful tendencies toward vindictiveness, favoritism, and a residual servility, to satisfy the labor requirements of employers and to protect the contractual rights of their fellow workers.

Although Chavez instituted an administrative training program designed by his old mentor Fred Ross, he rejected an AFL-CIO offer of assistance because of his stubborn conviction that a genuinely democratic union must entrust its operation to its own members even at the risk of organizational inefficiency and incompetence. And when he shifted the union's headquarters 50 miles southeast of Delano to an abandoned tuberculosis sanitorium in the Tehachapi mountains that he called La Paz—short for Nuestra Senora de la Paz (Our Lady of Peace)—Chavez claimed the move was prompted by a concern that his easy accessibility to members of the union's ranch committees discouraged self-reliance. "It was my idea to leave for La Paz," he explained, "because I wanted to remove my presence from Delano, so they could develop their own leadership, because if I am there, they wouldn't make the decisions themselves. They'd come to me." But the move intensified suspicions of internal critics like Larry Itliong, who left the union partly because Chavez's physical isolation from the membership seemed to enhance the influence of the Anglo "intellectuals" while diminishing that of the rank and file. The greatest barrier to broadening the union's leadership and administrative operation, however, was posed neither by geography nor the influence of Anglo volunteers, but by Chavez himself, whose devotion to the ideal of decentralization was seldom matched by an equal disposition to delegate authority to others. Journalist Ron Taylor, who observed Chavez's style of leadership at close range, wrote: "He conceptually saw a union run in the most democratic terms, but in practice he had a difficult time trying to maintain his own distance; his tendencies were to step in and make decisions . . . Even though he had removed himself from Delano, he maintained a close supervision over it, and all of the other field offices. Through frequent staff meetings and meetings of the executive board, he developed his own personal involvement with the tiniest of union details."

If Chavez's deficiencies as an administrator troubled sympathetic AFL-CIO officials like Bill Kircher, they tended to reinforce the suspicion privately harbored by such trade-union traditionalists as federation president George Meany that viable organization was probably beyond the compass of farmworkers, no matter how driven and charismatic their leader. Indeed, what appeared to be at the root of Meany's personal skepticism was Chavez's eccentric style of leadership and somewhat alien trade-union philosophy: his well-advertised idealism, which uncharitably rendered was a species of mere self-righteousness; his overweening presence, which seemingly engendered an unhealthy cult of personality; his extravagant sense of mission, which left outsiders wondering whether his was a labor or a social movement; his apparently congenital aversion to compromise, which, in Meany's view, negated the AFL-CIO's repeated efforts to negotiate a settlement of UFWOC's jurisdictional dispute with the Teamsters. None of these reservations were enough to keep the AFL-CIO in early 1972 from changing the union's status from that of organizing committee to full-fledged affiliate—the United Farm Workers of America—but in combination they were apparently enough to persuade Meany that Chavez was no longer deserving of the same levels of financial and organizational support previously contributed by the federation.

Yet if trade union administration of an appropriately conventional style was not his forte, Chavez demonstrated during the course of several legislative battles in 1971 and 1972 that his talents as a political organizer and tactician were exceptional. When the Oregon legislature passed an anti-union bill sponsored by the American Farm Bureau Federation, Chavez and his followers, in only a week's time, persuaded the governor to veto it. Shortly thereafter, Chavez initiated a far more ambitious campaign to recall the governor of Arizona for signing a similar grower-backed bill into law. And while the recall drive ultimately bogged down in a tangle of legal disputes, Chavez's success in registering nearly 100,000 mostly poor, mostly Chicano voters fostered fundamental changes in the political balance of power in Arizona.

It was in California, however, that the UFW afforded its opponents the most impressive demonstration of La Causa's political sophistication and clout, and Chavez revealed to friends and foes alike that his ability to influence public debate extended well beyond the normal boundaries of trade-union leadership. With the backing of the state's agribusiness establishment, the California Farm Bureau launched during 1972 a well-financed initiative drive— popularly known as Proposition 22—designed to eliminate the threat of unionism by banning nearly every effective weapon available to the UFW, including the boycott. Having failed the year before to win legislative approval for an equally tough anti-union measure, farm employers were confident that they could persuade the citizens of California, as they had so often before, that protecting the state's highly profitable agricultural industry was in the public interest. Aware that the UFW could not survive under the restrictive conditions that Proposition 22 contemplated, but without the financial resources needed to counter the growers' expensive media campaign, Chavez and his aides masterfully deployed what they did have: an aroused and resourceful membership. In the end, the growers' financial power proved to be no match for the UFW's people power. In defeating Proposition 22 by a decisive margin—58 percent to 42 percent—the UFW not only eliminated the immediate threat facing the union, but also announced to growers in terms too emphatic to ignore that the time was past when farm employers could rely upon their political power to keep farmworkers in their place.

The political battles that occupied Chavez and the UFW during much of 1972 involved issues so central to the union's existence that they could not be avoided. But even in the course of winning its political fights with agribusiness, the union lost ground on other equally crucial fronts. Organizing activities all but ceased as the UFW turned its attention to political action, and further efforts aimed at alleviating the administrative problems that plagued the union's operation in the grape industry and increasing the pressures on Salinas valley lettuce growers were neglected. At the beginning of 1973 the UFW was in the paradoxical situation of being at the height of its political strength while its vulnerability as a union was increasing.

Just how vulnerable the union was became apparent as the contracts it had negotiated in 1970 with Coachella valley grape growers came up for renewal. Chavez had heard rumors that the Teamsters were planning to challenge the

UFW in the region, but not until growers made plain their intention to reclaim complete control over the hiring, dispatching, and disciplining of workers did he suspect that a deal was already in the making. The UFW retained the allegiance of a vast majority of the industry's workers, but neither the growers nor the Teamsters seemed to care. As soon as the UFW contracts expired, all but two growers announced that they had signed new four-year agreements with the Teamsters. Hiring halls, grievance procedures, and protections against dangerous pesticides disappeared along with the workers' right to a union of their own choice.

•••••

In the face of the Teamsters onslaught, the UFW, reinforced by a familiar coalition of religious, student, liberal, and labor volunteers, resorted to its customary arsenal: picket lines, rallies, marches, boycotts, and appeals to the public's sense of justice. Yet with hundreds of beefy Teamster goons conducting a reign of terror through the region, and UFW activists being jailed by the hundreds for violating court orders prohibiting virtually every form of resistance and protest the union employed, the Chavez forces never had a chance of winning back what they had lost in the Coachella valley, or of stopping the Teamsters when they later moved in on the UFW's remaining contracts with Delano-area table grape growers and the state's major wineries. George Meany, who described the Teamsters' raids as "the most vicious strikebreaking, union-busting effort I've seen in my lifetime," persuaded the AFL-CIO executive council to contribute $1.6 million to the UFW's support. But the money could only ease the union's predicament, not solve it. After five months of bitter struggle, more than 3,500 arrests, innumerable assaults, and the violent deaths of two members—one at the hands of a deputy sheriff who claimed that his victim was "resisting arrest," the other at the hands of a gun-toting young strikebreaker who said he felt menaced by pickets—Chavez, his union in ruins, called off any further direct action in favor of the UFW's most effective weapon: the boycott. The UFW, which only a year before had more than 150 contracts and nearly 40,000 members, was reduced by September 1973 to a mere handful of contracts and perhaps one-quarter of its earlier membership.

In the wake of the UFW's stunning defeat in the grape industry, writing the union's obituary became a favorite pastime not only of its long-time adversaries but of some of its traditional sympathizers as well. Most acknowledged the irresistible pressures that a Teamsters–grower alliance unleashed against the union, but many also found fault with the leadership of Cesar Chavez, especially his real or imagined failure to progress from unruly visionary to orderly trade unionist. Chavez's "charisma," said one sympathizer, was no longer "as marketable a commodity as it once was" . . .

Yet if Chavez left something to be desired as a union administrator, his alleged deficiencies scarcely explained the UFW's precipitous descent. The union's battered condition was not a product of its failure to behave conventionally, or of Chavez's disinclination to abandon his assertedly quixotic proclivities in favor of the pure and simple ethic that informed the thinking and demeanor of the more typical trade-union leader. Rather, the UFW's sudden decline was, for the most part, not of its own making: Grape growers had never resigned themselves to sharing power with their workers, and when the Teamsters proffered an alternative brand of unionism that did not impinge upon their essential prerogatives they happily embraced it.

It was precisely because Chavez was "a bit of a dreamer" that the idea of farmworker organization gathered the initial force necessary to overcome the previously insurmountable opposition of employers, and it was because he remained stubbornly devoted to his dream even in the face of the UFW's disheartening setbacks that those who had rushed to speak eulogies over the momentarily prostrated union were ultimately proven wrong. The resources available to him after the debacle of 1973 were only a fraction of what they had been, but Chavez retained both the loyalty of his most able assistants and his own exceptional talents as an organizer and agitator. As the nationwide boycotts he revived against grape and lettuce growers and the country's largest wine producers, the E. and J. Gallo Wineries, slowly gained momentum during 1974, Chavez reminded his Teamsters-employer adversaries in the only language they seemed to understand that the UFW was not going away no matter how diligently they conspired to that end.

•••••

Since 1975 the union's record testifies to a mixed performance on Chavez's part. After reaching a membership of approximately 50,000 by the late 1970s, the union has slowly dwindled in size, comprising roughly 40,000 members by the early 1980s, nearly all of whom, except for isolated outposts in Florida, Arizona, and a couple of other states, are confined to California . . .

It is also the case, however, that the UFW's drift from vitality toward apparent stagnation is partially rooted in a web of complex factors related to the sometimes contradictory leadership of Cesar Chavez: a sincere devotion to democratic unionism that is undermined by a tendency to regard all internal dissidents as traitors at best and anti-union conspirators at worst; a professed desire to make the UFW a rank-and-file union governed from the bottom up that is contradicted by a strong inclination to concentrate authority in his own hands and those of close family members; a commitment to professionalize the administration of the UFW that is impeded by a reliance on volunteerism so unyielding as to have caused many of the union's most loyal and efficient staff members to quit.

In fairness, however, Chavez's performance must be assessed on a basis that encompasses far more than the normal categories of trade-union leadership. For unlike most American labor leaders, who had stood apart from the traditions of their European counterparts by insisting that unionism is an end in itself, Chavez has, in his own somewhat idiosyncratic way, remained determined to use the UFW and the heightened political consciousness of his Chicano loyalists as a means for promoting changes more fundamental than those attainable through collective bargaining and other conventional avenues of trade-union activism. In defining the UFW's singular mission, Chavez once declared: "As a continuation of our struggle, I think that we can develop economic power and put it in the hands of the people so they can have more control of their own lives, and then begin to change the system. We want radical change. Nothing short of radical change is going to have any impact on our lives or our problems. We want sufficient power to control our own destinies. This is our struggle. It's a lifetime job. The work for social change and against social injustice is never ended."

When measured against the magnitude of his proposed enterprise, and against his extraordinary achievements on behalf of workers who were among the most powerless and degraded in America prior to his emergence, Chavez's real and alleged deficiencies in guiding the UFW across the hostile terrain of California's industrialized agriculture in no way detract from his standing as the most accomplished and far-sighted labor leader of his generation.

• • • • •

DOLORES HUERTA

Though their contributions are often overlooked, women have long played a major part in the American labor movement. They continue to do so. With the dramatic rise in dual-income and single-parent families in recent decades, unprecedented numbers of women have entered the labor force; and with the displacement of male-dominated manufacturing work by service employment, unions today must pay particular attention to the needs of their women members if they are to regain their position as major actors in American social and economic life. In the excerpt that follows, Dolores Huerta of the United Farm Workers speaks about some of the problems she has encountered in attempting to combine her roles as single parent and labor organizer.

• • • • •

When I first started working with Cesar I had this problem worrying about whether my kids were going to eat or not, because at the time I started working for the union I was making pretty good money, and I knew I was going to start working without *any* money, and I wondered how I could do it. But the kids have never gone hungry. We've had some rough times, particularly in Delano during the strike, because my kids went without fresh milk for two years. They just had powdered milk we got through donations. It's made them understand what hardship is, and this is good because you can't really relate to suffering unless you've had a little bit of it yourself. But the main thing is that they have their dignity and identity.

My family used to criticize me a lot. They thought that I was a traitor to

Source: Dolores Huerta, "Dolores Huerta Talks about Republicans, Cesar, and Her Home Town," in *Awakened Minority: The Mexican-Americans,* ed. Manuel P. Seruin (Beverly Hills, CA: Glencoe Press, 1974), pp. 287–88.

my Raza, to my family, and to everybody else. But I think they finally realized that what I'm doing is important and they're starting to appreciate it now. They thought that I was just neglecting my children and that what I was doing was just for selfish reasons.

The criticism came mostly from my dad and other relatives, but my brothers are very understanding. My mother was a very active woman, and I just followed her. She's dead now, but she always got the prizes for registering the most voters, and she raised us without any hang-ups about things like that.

You could expect that I would get a lot of criticisms from the farmworkers themselves, but it mostly comes from middle-class people. They're more hung-up about these things than the poor people are, because the poor people have to haul their kids around from school to school, and the women have to go out and work and they've got to either leave their kids or take them out to the fields with them. So they sympathize a lot more with my problem in terms of my children. Sometimes I think it's bad for people to shelter their kids too much. Giving kids clothes and food is one thing, you know, but it's much more important to teach them that other people besides themselves are important, and that the best thing they can do with their lives is to use it in the service of other people. So my kids know that the way that we live is poor, materially speaking, but it's rich in a lot of other ways. They get to meet a lot of people and their experiences are varied.

I know people who work like fools just to give their kids more material goods. They're depriving their family of themselves, for what? At least my kids know why I'm not home. They know that I'm doing this for something in which we're all working—it makes a whole different thing. My children don't have a lot of material things but they work hard for what they do get, just like everybody else, and that makes them really self-sufficient. They make their own arrangements when they go places. They all have a lot of friends and they don't get all hung-up about having a lot of goodies. I think my kids are very healthy both mentally and physically. All the women in the union have similar problems. They don't have to leave their families for as long as I do. But everybody shares everything, we share the work.

QUESTIONS

1. What influence did Father Donald McDonnell and Fred Ross have on the development of Chavez's social thought? Why did Chavez shift from community to labor organization during the early 1960s?
2. What role did women play in the development of the United Farm Workers? What do Dolores Huerta's general beliefs and reflections on her personal life suggest about her effectiveness as a labor organizer?
3. Why did Chavez urge union members to avoid the use of violence? Why did he adopt the economic boycott as the union's main weapon against growers? Why did he place such great stress on political action?
4. How would you characterize Chavez's relationship with mainstream labor leaders such as George Meany? Why did the latter sometimes view Chavez with suspicion?

5. What were Chavez's greatest strengths as a labor leader? What were his most notable shortcomings? In what ways was Chavez similar to Martin Luther King, Jr.? In what ways were the two men different?
6. Given the current emphasis on organizing low-wage workers from diverse cultural backgrounds, what can contemporary labor leaders learn from Chavez's career?
7. Which of the historical figures profiled in this unit would you most like to write about? What questions would you ask in a study of that person? What types of sources would you consult to answer those questions?

BIBLIOGRAPHY

Those seeking additional information on Chavez might consult Jacque Levy, *Cesar Chavez: Autobiography of La Causa* (1975); Sam Kushner, *Long Road to Delano* (1975); Joan London and Henry Anderson, *So Shall Ye Reap: The Story of Cesar Chavez and the Farm Labor Movement* (1970); Dick Meister and Ann Loftis, *A Long Time Coming: The Struggle to Unionize America's Farm Workers* (1977); and Ronald B. Taylor, *Chavez and the Farm Workers* (1975). Historical background on efforts to organize California farmworkers can be found in Cletus E. Daniel, *Bitter Harvest: A History of California Farmworkers, 1870–1941* (1981), and Ernesto Galarza, *Merchants of Labor: The Mexican Bracero Story* (1964). A good general survey of the Mexican–American experience is Matt S. Meier and Feliciano Ribera, *Mexican Americans/American Mexicans: From Conquistadors to Chicanos*, rev. ed. (1994).

Downward Mobility: American Wage Earners in a Changing Economy

By the mid-1970s, the great postwar economic boom had ended. As a host of statistical indexes reveal, the U.S. economy since that time has not performed nearly as well as it did during the preceding three decades. With reduced gross national product (GNP) growth and a falling rate of productive investment in plant, equipment, and the like, unemployment has run consistently higher and real wages have declined. Perhaps the best indicator of how much things have changed is the housing market, one of the major engines of postwar economic expansion. Between 1966 and 1989, the amount of working time needed to purchase a new home nearly doubled: from 4.82 to 8.07 years.

On one level, these developments are a consequence of important changes in the world economy. Most significant was the revival of Japanese and European productive capacity, which created a much more competitive international marketplace. That some U.S. industries responded slowly to the new challenge made a difficult situation even worse. To cite but one example, American steel producers lagged behind foreign competitors in adopting such cost-saving technological innovations as basic oxygen furnaces and continuous casting. The increased bargaining power of Middle Eastern oil producers and other raw materials suppliers further complicated matters, as did the nation's Cold War commitments. Compared with its main allies and foremost economic competitors, the United States throughout

the postwar period devoted a much greater proportion of funds to military spending—funds that might otherwise have been used for productive capital formation.

During the 1980s, most U.S. corporations gradually adapted to the changed economic environment in which they found themselves operating. But they often did so in ways that added to the insecurity of American wage earners. One tactic was to locate new production facilities in developing countries where they could take advantage of low-wage labor. This not only eliminated jobs at home; it also exerted downward pressure on the wages of domestic workers still employed in those industries. Later, as "downsizing" became the watchword of cost-conscious corporate managers, major employers intensified their efforts to reduce the payroll at U.S. plants and offices.

To provide some sense of what these developments have meant for working Americans, we have adopted a somewhat different tack in this chapter. Rather than presenting a biographical essay that profiles a specific individual, we have instead selected an article that provides a collective portrait of various people affected by these economic changes. During the course of writing two books on how contemporary Americans have responded to downward mobility, Katherine Newman has conducted hundreds of in-depth interviews with displaced managers, unemployed blue-collar workers, and other people who have found themselves unable to match the economic achievements of their parents. Major findings of her research are summarized in the essay that follows.

Downward Mobility: American Wage Earners in a Changing Economy

Katherine Newman

· · · · ·

The End of Prosperity

In the expansive years between the end of the Great Depression and the middle of the 1970s, the experience of downward mobility was virtually invisible. Of course, . . . unemployment has always afflicted some Americans, and many fail to recover their previous standard of living. But beginning in the mid-1970s, downward mobility began to afflict groups of Americans who never thought they would have anything in common with the poor. Managerial and executive employees began to feel the brunt of recessions in ways they had not

Source: Excerpt by Katherine S. Newman in Michael A. Bernstein and David E. Adler, *Understanding American Economic Decline.* Reprinted with the permission of Cambridge University Press.

previously experienced. Solid blue-collar citizens began to see their jobs disappear in record numbers. For millions of middle-class and working-class families, this meant the loss of everything they had worked for—jobs, homes, stability, and a secure grip on the future. By the early 1980s, displaced workers found they were unable to find new jobs in a climate where neither educational credentials nor work experience seemed to offer much protection. Pink slips have rained down in the financial services industries as one major bank after another consolidates and sheds its staff.

In the 1990s, high-technology firms, from Apple to IBM to Raytheon, have let thousands go as they downsize in the hope that lower labor costs will put them back in competitive shape. Left behind, stranded in a no-man's-land of persistent joblessness, are the thousands of high-skilled, white-collar workers, now joined on the unemployment lines by millions of working-class colleagues who have had longer and more bitter experience with economic insecurity.

Refugees from the managerial world are undone by the descent into downward mobility. For unlike their blue-collar brethren, who have had to contend with layoffs and callbacks for most of their working life, white-collar managers were accustomed to thinking of themselves as above the fray, valued for their long years of experience, based in turn on their professional credentials. When the axe falls, shock and dismay are quickly followed by an enforced isolation that is almost as hard to endure as the financial duress that unemployment brings. Families that have been independent, cloistered behind suburban hedges, find themselves in need of help and understanding, only to discover that their very independence has become a major handicap. They have no links to trade upon, no meaningful networks that can stand the test of their newfound needy status. Instead, even in the midst of high unemployment across the nation, they discover how quickly they can become the subject of stigma, singled out as blameworthy.

David Patterson was a case in point. He was one of the 40 former managers I interviewed in the course of my study of managerial downward mobility in 1981. A middle manager in a high-tech firm on Long Island, Patterson had moved his whole family from their long-time home in California to the East in the name of an internal promotion. He had been in the new job, a comfortable vice presidency, for less than two years when the company went through a major contraction, shedding over 50 managers in one month. David worked his contacts, scoured *The Wall Street Journal* want ads, and called everyone he knew in the industry to inquire about a new position, initially confident that he would find a job without any trouble. He had been unemployed for nearly a year by the time we met in the smoky corridors of the "Forty Plus Club," a volunteer group for businessmen and -women who are out of work. David's family had "lost" the family home, moved

> **cultural capital**   Cultural wealth, in the form of knowledge, experience, or ideas, which helps to sustain one's position of status and power.
>
> **GI Bill**   A bill passed by Congress that provided educational and other benefits for World War II veterans.

into a small apartment in a suburb outside of the Big Apple, and his wife had struggled to find a job as a receptionist. Their savings depleted and their teenage children in a total uproar, David and his wife were completely bewildered and beginning to tear into each other.

Most damaging for the Pattersons was the sense that no one around them believed their story. No one accepted the notion that there were no jobs to be had. Neighbors and "fair weather" friends had begun asking embarrassing questions that left David's wife, Julia, both traumatized and suspicious:

> Since becoming unemployed there's really nothing, especially for my wife—no place where a woman can talk about things. There are no real relationships. She's hurt. People say to her, "With all the companies on Long Island, your husband can't find a job? Is he really trying? Maybe he likes not working." This really hurts her and it hurts me. People don't understand that you can send out 150 letters to headhunters and get 10 replies. Maybe one or two will turn into something, but there are a hundred qualified people going after each job. The computer industry is contracting all over the place and as it [shrinks], my wife contracts emotionally.

For David, and the others who spend their days at the Forty Plus Club, the dynamics of the American economy, the vagaries of their own particular industries, and the abstract fluctuation of the unemployment figures hold little meaning. These structural facts, these trends which "explain" so much of what has happened to the middle class, pale beside the introspective, self-blaming quality of their downward mobility. When friends become scarce and the phone never rings, the independence of the managerial man becomes his own prison, and his own character takes the center stage. David was forever asking himself what was wrong with *him*, why was *he* unable to find a new job? Even though millions of Americans have found themselves in the same dismal situation, all David can see are his own flaws, magnified a thousand times to expose what he takes to be the "real reasons" he has failed himself and his family. For the trends and statistics do not tell David why others have been more fortunate, even if only a few of them have been able to hang on. There must be something that separates the downwardly mobile from the persistently successful. For David that something can only be found within. He is a product of an individualistic culture that made him feel like a prince, when his life was a Depression-era boy's dream come true, and something of a criminal when it all fell apart. In either case, David—not the international economy—is the protagonist in this story, the one who, as master of his destiny, is responsible for his sorry fate.

Blue-collar workers are less likely to experience downward mobility this way. Those who live in the shadow of shuttered manufacturing plants often live in residential communities for whom the local plant has been the economic mainstay. When General Motors shuts down 11 plants across the country, idling thousands of assembly-line workers with one stroke of the pen, the neighborhoods nearby each reel from the loss of their lifeline. Tertiary businesses—the suppliers of parts, the taverns and restaurants patronized by the workers—and the local governments that rely on the tax dollars of the now unemployed laborers are all cast into the abyss together. If there is a virtue in their loss, it is only that they may have friends to turn to who have been through the same catastrophe and an enemy or series of enemies to blame for their misfortune.

Men and women from the factory world do not see themselves as masters of their own fate in the same way that their white-collar brethren do, recognizing as they do that forces beyond their control have a powerful impact on their well-being. Their personal fates are in the hands of the same large institutions that may have put them in jeopardy in the first place: unions, companies, politicians looking to do some favors. Scanning the newspaper for breakthroughs that will jump-start the plant, they often look in vain. With so many jobs permanently lost, deliverance is not forthcoming. When this reality sinks in and the unemployment compensation has run out, low-paid jobs in the service sector are all that seems to remain.

If they are protected from debilitating self-blame, however, they are also more inclined to feel helpless in their numbers. This much was evident in the course of a year-long study I did in 1983 on the impact of the closure of the Singer Sewing Machine factory in Elizabeth, New Jersey. The Singer Company was a major multinational firm in the mid-nineteenth century, one of the most important manufacturing companies in the U.S. Its empire stretched around the globe, with plants in Russia (confiscated during the Revolution of 1917), Scotland, and many other parts of the world. But the Elizabeth plant was the flagship, the proud home of thousands of craftsmen and assembly-line workers. The town was synonymous with the firm, for Singer provided the bedrock of jobs and security for over 100 years . . .

However, after World War II, the market for sewing machines began to contract. Ready-made clothing became widely available and less expensive, cutting into domestic demand. In the 1960s, the trend toward increased female labor force participation forced the sewing machine market into a deep downturn. Women no longer had time for sewing and they turned away from this mainstay appliance of the past. Singer, in turn, began to diversify away from its original product lines and to withdraw investment from the manufacturing plants. A long, slow bleed turned the Elizabeth factory from a model of industrial innovation into a dinosaur. A moratorium on hiring was followed by layoffs, with the death knell of the factory sounding at last in the early 1980s.

Elena Morales, a Cuban immigrant who settled in Elizabeth, New Jersey, in the early sixties, put nearly 20 years into the Singer Sewing Machine factory. Her job, together with her husband's wages, meant that she could send her kids to parochial school and look forward to a better future for them. She was, in many respects, typical of the plant's work force in its last years of operation. Unfortunately, her experience of post-shutdown downward mobility was typical as well. Having worked her way up from an assembly-line worker to a quality-control inspector, Elena discovered that her track record was of little value in finding a new job that was even close to the quality of the old one:

> I collected unemployment for a year . . . [I worked] part time [in a dry cleaning business]. Then I worked in a restaurant . . . until 1983. Finally I found [my

present] part-time job in the airport cleaning the airplanes. I started as a cleaning lady.

Losing my [Singer] job had a tremendous impact on me. I didn't have
nothing. We still have bills and things . . . Factories are the worst in my mind
now . . . Nothing is secure anymore . . . I think all the companies are going to
close.

Elena's experience has been replicated by millions of others who found
themselves thrown from the unionized, benefit-safe world of stable blue-
collar employment into the universe of unprotected, part-time, low-wage
jobs that do not pay enough to keep a family. Having lost her seniority,
Elena now works the night shift and hopes not only that she can hang on to
this job but that her husband, also a blue-collar worker, will not be jetti-
soned as she was. There is no security left, certainly nothing to look forward to in the future that is half as reliable as the old Singer company once
was.

For Elena, however, more than just the Singer firm is gone. A whole
way of life, an entire social contract, has been destroyed. The loyalty that
bound her family, and hundreds of immigrant families before her, to the
firm has been replaced by a fragile, wary, and instrumental work relationship. She does not put her faith in the airline that employs her now; she
does not believe any firm is likely to return the faith at all. Traditions that
glued workers to management, even in the face of labor conflict, have disappeared across the manufacturing landscape. Craftsmanship, pride in the
product—all of this appears to have gone by the boards as blue-collar
workers discover that they are eminently replaceable: by computers, by
nonunion labor, by hungry people in far away lands willing to work for
nickels.

Yet unlike David Patterson, Elena does not blame herself for the loss of the
Singer job. Her anger is directed at a firm which she believes lost its soul and
its character, and at the government which did nothing to protect blue-collar
workers in the face of imports that beat domestic prices down. She holds herself responsible, as does David, for finding new work, but she does not subject
herself to the withering internal critique that has debilitated him even as he
continued to look for work.

These are two faces of downward mobility, the profiles of people who
never expected to think of themselves as needy. They were the self-reliant
ones who believed until recently that they could manage their own affairs,
requiring help from no one. David Patterson discovered that he needed
others badly, but that there was no one who was interested in his plight.
Elena managed, but at the cost of her standard of living and her prospects
for the future. She cannot look toward retirement, a pension, or health care,
for none of this is provided by her new part-time job. Their experience is
characteristic of the fate of millions of Americans who worked hard and
thought they had it made, only to discover that they have lost virtually
everything.

Generation Gaps

Downward mobility has other faces as well. Americans who came of age after the mid-1970s, including the lion's share of the baby boom generation, have discovered that even if they can keep unemployment at bay, they are not likely to see the standard of living with which they were raised. . . . The generations that entered the labor market after the mid-1970s found themselves at a marked disadvantage in virtually every respect. Jobs, particularly good jobs, were more competitive, with hundreds more people chasing them than there were positions to fill. Housing markets boomed—fine for those already over the hump of home ownership—leaving those not yet in the market stranded by astronomical price increases and escalating interest rates.

According to the National Housing Task Force, a congressional panel formed in 1987 by Senator Alfonso D'Amato and Senator Alan Cranston, nearly two million *fewer* families own their own home today than there would have been if the rates of home ownership common just a decade ago had been sustained throughout the 1980s. Yet even as these numbers went down, some people were doing fairly well in the housing market: Americans over the age of 60 and whites in general increased their share of the home ownership market. For one or two demographic groups to improve their lot while national averages decline can only mean one thing: Somebody has to have done much worse in the housing sweepstakes. The somebodies were members of the baby boom generation who have been locked out of the American dream in increasing numbers.

• • • • •

These trends have had an impact that goes well beyond the roofs over the heads of the nation's boomers. They have taken an equal toll on their confidence, on their sense of belonging, and most especially on their capacity to care for the next generation—the children of the 1990s. This became clear in the course of a two-year study of a suburban enclave in northern New Jersey which I call "Pleasanton." This bedroom community, a mere 20 minutes from New York City, was a modest, middle-income, economically diverse community whose growth—such as it was—dates to the 1950s and 60s. The completion of the highway system that now links suburban New Jersey to the New York orbit made it possible for families to live in places like Pleasanton and ride the freeways to work. Low-cost housing and cheap mortgages put Pleasanton in reach of GIs and their brides, and they moved in droves to this quiet community, a stone's throw from the George Washington Bridge. Thirty years later—and with no visible change in the housing stock—the dream began to fade for the boomers. Throughout the 1970s and 80s, housing prices in Pleasanton skyrocketed. At the same time, job opportunities flattened out, and even with two earners in a household, the bucolic suburbs of their childhood years became untouchable for the boomers. Pleasanton has become an affluent town populated by professionals and well-paid managers. . . .

Wendy Norman . . . spends a lot of time thinking about the advantages her parents conferred upon her: comfort without extravagance, a life of cultural enrichment developed through ballet lessons, the occasional theater trip, and lazy summer days down at the pool. While Wendy was lucky to have all these things, her parents were fortunate, too. The economic history of the 1950s made it possible for them to do far more for Wendy than their own parents had been able to do for them in the dreary days of the Great Depression. The Normans took pride and pleasure in watching Wendy absorb the cultural advantages they could provide. But Wendy is fairly certain she will not feel a similar glow of satisfaction that comes from knowing that she has "done right" by her own kids:

> I guess our grandparents and our parents, what kept them moving and motivated was that they were trying to do for their children. Improve their children's lot. I think they achieved that and for the most part were probably happy in it. That gave them the happiness, the self-fulfillment. I don't think we have that in our generation.

Wendy, and her baby boom counterparts across the nation, are worried that those critical advantages, those aspects of personal biography which sociologists call **"cultural capital,"** may be lost to the children of the 1980s and 1990s. They may have to settle for much less: for mediocre schools, libraries that are closing down for lack of revenue, residence in less affluent communities with fewer amenities.

Today's middle-class parents are only too aware of how problematic such a scenario could be for their children. Kids who do not go to good high schools have a hard time finding their way into competitive colleges. They are disadvantaged in their efforts to get into professional schools or to land high-paying jobs. In short, the connection between cultural advantage and social prestige has never been more definitive, particularly in the eyes of those baby boom parents who were, themselves, the beneficiaries of middle-class advantage. Nancy knows all too well that she would be doing even *worse* in the 1990s were it not for the educational credentials her parents bestowed upon her. She is bombarded daily with news headlines that proclaim education the key to the nation's prosperity, along with daily public hand wringing over the quality of America's schools. The message is abundantly clear: Her child's future depends upon the educational and cultural resources she provides. If these are less than what it takes, Nancy's kid will reap the consequences.

If the baby boom generation is bewildered and disturbed by this sudden turn of events, their parents—the generation that entered adulthood in the affluent years following World War II—are even more confused. They see themselves as living proof of the vitality of the American dream. Children of the Great Depression who were raised in cramped working-class enclaves of the nation's cities, they came of age in a time of war, emerging into peace time along with the benefits of the **GI Bill,** the VA mortgage, cheap land, a booming housing market, and a seemingly endless expansion in every conceivable industry. Young men whose fathers crossed the Atlantic in steerage (and were satisfied if they could land a steady job in a sweat shop), ended up in America's finest universities and fueled an unprecedented expansion of the country's middle class. They became engineers, doctors, lawyers, businessmen— the first professionals in their family lines. The sky was the limit. As these postwar parents tell the story, anyone who was willing to work hard could literally make their dreams come true.

Both generations—those who rode the wave of postwar affluence and those who have fallen into the trough of postindustrial decline—pose questions about their divergent paths, largely in the privacy of their homes and in casual conversation with friends. The declining fortunes of the baby boom cohort, while the subject of an occasional magazine piece or newspaper article, have yet to become the platform for a social movement, or the rallying cry of a new age politician. Indeed, for many Americans the personal strain of coping with disappointed expectations and dashed ambitions is so great that little energy is left over for analyzing their own experience as symptomatic of far-reaching, structural disorders in the U.S. economy.

In the long run these very issues will dominate the policy landscape in America as we move into the twenty-first century. For ultimately the question of who is entitled to the good life in America, and who must pay to help those excluded from the golden circle, must be resolved if we are to avoid the shredding of the social fabric. There is plenty of evidence to show, albeit in isolated ways thus far, that such a shredding process is already underway. If we are to avoid a future characterized by an "every man for himself" philosophy, a credo that cannot sustain any society for long, we must look long and hard at the impact of intergenerational downward mobility and ask what it means in cultural as well as practical terms.

What Happened to the American Dream

Although Pleasanton residents are not economists and do not lay claim to professional expertise in these matters, they have a fairly good grasp of the immediate culprits that have exiled the town's baby boomers from their native community. Four related phenomena come to their minds when they explain how their slice of the American dream has eroded away: escalating housing prices, occupational insecurity, blocked mobility on the job, and the cost-of-living squeeze that has penalized the boomer generation, even when they have more education and better jobs than their parents have.

That housing prices have escalated beyond all comprehension comes as no news to postwar parents. By sitting still and doing almost nothing, they have seen the value of their most important asset rise to levels that are, by their own standards, stratospheric. In the course of the 1980s, real estate became a language and a way of life. Dinner party gossip revolved around how much houses on the block were going for and who was making a killing on what piece of property. It seemed, and still seems to many in Pleasanton, as though there was nothing else to talk about, nothing as captivating as money being made in the form of four bedroom colonials.

The odd thing about this sudden wealth was that it made the process of accumulating capital effortless, almost magical. Compared to the effort involved in working for a living, real estate profits were incredibly easy to pile up. Dumb luck—being in the right place at the right time—and some modest resources were all that was needed to get into the game.

Simon Rittenberg was a salesman for nearly 40 years for a factory that manufactures security devices for use in businesses and homes. He has the hearty, confident character of the ideal salesman even though he has been retired for some time. Like everyone else who grew up in a little apartment during the Depression, it had always been his dream to have a house of his own. Simon was always worried about how he would pay it off. It never occurred to him that he could pile up a little fortune just by hanging on to the house. But when he became a widower and the house was just too big for a lone man, he sold out and discovered how much "doing nothing" had done for his bank account:

> I don't think I had the intelligence to know that by moving, coming to this country, that I would do so well. All I knew was that my father had always rented. He never owned anything. He rented his store, and he rented his apartment. And now I was going to take this big leap into owning a home, which would be mine, my castle. I don't know if that was right or wrong, but I know I was lucky. Because after 35 years, my $17,000 became $285,000 when I sold [the house]. So was that brilliance on my part?
>
> Now I'm a big shot: I made some kind of great deal! The economics of it didn't have anything to do with me. It had to do with the world, what happened.

While Simon is happy enough to have this fat bank account, he takes greater pride in the achievements of his work life than he does the lucrative side effects of the housing mania of the 1980s. He does not feel responsible for his good fortune, though he is not unhappy to have it. It has become emblematic of a kind of real estate madness that seems to have descended on the world, or at least his small corner of it.

Were this madness only positive in its impact, Simon would not be troubled long by its benefits. Yet his son, Ron, has been driven out by the very same forces that provided him with such fantastic rewards. Ron Rittenberg is nearly 40 now and lives in Washington, D.C., where he works for a federal agency that provides information to criminal justice agencies around the country. He has a 3-year-old son and a wife who works full time. They live in suburban Maryland in a community that is nowhere near the level of affluence that Pleasanton represents. Ron just laughs when asked to compare the community he lives in now with the Pleasanton of his youth. The flip side of the father's good fortune is the son's flight to a less expensive community, far away from his kin.

Of course, the escalating cost of housing is not the only divide separating the postwar parents from their baby boom children. Jobs are harder to find and far more insecure in all respects. Pleasanton's progeny were well-educated by any standard and they parlayed that advantage into job qualifications that often exceeded anything their parents had had to offer employers in years gone by. The sons of skilled blue-collar workers got college degrees and became accountants. The daughters of nonworking, high school educated mothers nearly all went on to higher education, often finding jobs as teachers or managers. Yet even with these credentials in hand, success did not come easily to the boomers. Where their parents found an expanding job market with an inexhaustible thirst for their talents, the baby boom generation has found a crowded, competitive market where they are often deemed expendable.

Security is not easy to come by these days; it is a concern that looms very large in the lives of those who were raised in the prosperous, stable 1950s and the roaring, expansive 1960s. Contractions, leveraged buyouts, bankruptcies, layoffs, and general despair over the state of American competitiveness—these are the watchwords of today's business pages. Nothing in the boomers' upbringing, schooling, or early experience in the labor market prepared them for what we must all confront now: the fact that the U.S. economy cannot provide the kind of job opportunities or personal security that the country took for granted in earlier generations.

Martin O'Rourke, now in his early 40s, got a firsthand taste of this nasty medicine when he worked for an auto company in the early 1980s. Martin's father was a blue-collar man through and through, but Martin was a talented artist. Overruling family objections, he decided to go into commercial drawing. Ultimately he ended up starting his own small business where he continues to make a reasonable living today. But his early inclinations were not in an entrepreneurial direction. He thought he'd be a company man, until he witnessed what happens to loyal company men:

> The real reason I quit the company was that my office was next door to a man who had worked for the company since 1955. He was the oldest employee in the company, and he was 62 years old when I met him. On a Friday afternoon at 4:30 they fired him. He had been a very important man in the company and he lived and breathed his work. He was in charge of all the warehouses across the country—all the parts warehouses. They decided to consolidate the warehouses and figured he would be unnecessary. So they just fired him. I'll never forget that day. He was in his office and he was crying and I asked what happened. I thought maybe his wife died or something horrible happened and he just handed me this piece of paper that said he was no longer needed by the company.
>
> I went home and said to my wife, I've got to leave, quit. I can't go on with this job because I'm just as devoted to my work. I lived and breathed my job too and I was 100 percent a company guy and worked insane hours for them. For what? So I could wind up like him? Be just let off? At age 62, where's this man going to go? And my feeling was that I just had to be in control . . .

In the 1980s a new habit began to spread through corporate America, a tradition of declining loyalty of firm to worker and a consequent wariness among younger employees of depending upon any job for permanent security. We are used to the fact that our manufacturing industries are on the skids and few of Pleasanton's progeny were headed in that direction. They were, and are now, white-collar bound. But this has hardly protected them, their parents, or their friends from the shakeouts and shutdowns that have plagued the service industries. New York City, where many Pleasanton boomers work, has lost over 100,000 jobs since 1987, many of them white-collar positions. Martin O'Rourke watched the axe fall on an older, long-time employee, and it scared him enough to abandon the corporate world altogether. His fear was well-justified since few age groups have been spared the pressure of mounting layoffs and white-collar dislocation. . . .

Among those who *have* managed to escape the abyss of unemployment in the 1980s and early 1990s, other problems have contributed to an intergenerational decline. Upward mobility within the ranks of American firms is leveling out at an earlier age for baby boomers than was true for their fathers in the expansive postwar period. When business was booming in the U.S., management pyramids just kept on growing. A large cadre of newly minted BAs (courtesy of the GI Bill) flooded into the marketplace and advanced quickly up the ranks. Business growth remained strong as they reached their 40s and this was reflected in continuous career growth. For these postwar men, careers tended to level off in their 50s and began the slow descent to retirement as they entered their 60s. While some were caught and crushed by the years of high unemployment in the early 1980s, most managed to escape the crunch of the Reagan recession and are coasting still on reasonable pensions and high home equity.

Sons and daughters who began their careers in the 1970s and 1980s have encountered tremendous competition for the "good jobs" and flatter job pyramids that level off at distressingly early ages. Charles Aberstein, whose son Larry graduated from Pleasanton's main high school 10 years ago, has noticed how much harder it is to make one's way in the job market now than it was when he started out:

> We're in a different kind of life environment today than we were 30 years ago. There's lots more competition. There's many more college graduates and fewer and fewer positions. Many of the good jobs have been exported to the Pacific. Major industries have fled the U.S. There are that many fewer executive level positions here and yet many candidates for them. It's a more competitive world than the one that I grew up in. [Larry's] aware of it. He'll find his way, but it won't be easy as it was for me.

Charles climbed the job ladder toward a vice presidency in an insurance firm, but he knows that Larry will find the same kind of ascent less assured. Many baby boomers are discovering that the sheer size of their generation ensures that there are too many of them chasing too few options. Moving up from entry-level positions to middle management seemed easy enough; the next step has become increasingly difficult.

Under the best of circumstances only a few of the millions of baby boomers will see advancement into executive ranks. Many will see the zenith of their careers arrive in their 40s, leaving 20 or 30 more years of their work lives with unchanged horizons (if they are lucky enough to escape the pressures of downsizing or business collapse). Beyond the boredom leveling off entails, its financial consequences are significant as well: Boomers will not see the continued increases in salaries that might eventually pull them up to an even point with their parents . . .

•••••

The End of Entitlement

Financial pressures facing the baby boom generation have profoundly affected every aspect of their private and public lives. From the most intimate decisions about whether or when to have children, to the most pragmatic questions of career choices, virtually every serious decision they have had to make about their lives has been dictated by conflicting desires based on economic limitations. On the one hand, the boomers are loath to give up the critical hallmarks of middle-class life and cling tenaciously to the idea that by working harder (more hours, more workers in a household) they can lay claim to their share of the American dream.

At the same time, they face pressures to conform to ideals of family organization and child rearing that were feasible in the 1950s and 1960s, but are no longer easily achieved. Despite the revolution of the women's movement, which has brought thousands of women (including mothers of young children) into the workplace, the image of nurturing, omnipresent mother has yet to fade away. Indeed, for the boomers themselves, she is a vivid memory, not just an abstraction. The postwar generation was largely raised by women who either retired from the factories and offices they had worked in during World War II or never worked in the paid labor market at all. The domestic front, they were told, was a woman's natural destiny.

While the women's movement did succeed in dismantling the notion that women belong in the kitchen and the kitchen only, it did not succeed in shifting the burden of child rearing to a 50–50 proposition. As Arlie Hochschild has pointed out in her remarkable book, *The Second Shift*, women are still fighting that battle and mainly losing. American society still looks upon women as the crucible of moral development in young children, and charges them with the responsibility for making sure the kids "turn out right." Child-rearing women are told in so many ways that they cannot afford to "mess up." Where social movements encouraged women to broaden their horizons and take up their fair share of the burden of earning a living, personal history and cultural norms tell the same women that they had better be sure they have done a good job raising their children. Can this be done from the vantage point of the workplace? No one is sure it's possible; many are vocally skeptical.

The problem is, of course, that by the early 1980s it became clear that holding on to a middle-class lifestyle would be hard to do absent two income earners in a household. How could husbands support their families alone? How could wives live up to their obligations as moral mothers when their incomes were needed to keep the mortgage payments going? This core contradiction has found no easy resolution; for these cultural and political dilemmas, while usually understood as moral debates, are inseparably tied to the declining fortunes of the baby boom generation.

There are those—even in Pleasanton—who might say, "Why don't the postwar parents help out? If they benefited so much from the boom years, don't they have the resources to rescue their kids?" Even if Pleasanton parents were inclined toward rescue missions, inclined to ignore the cultural prescription that calls for every generation to stand on its own two feet, they lack the wherewithal to prop up their adult children's standard of living. Having had their children at comparatively young ages, the postwar generation of parents find themselves relatively young, with many years of self-financed retirement left. Baby boomers in their 40s often find themselves with parents who are in their 60s, parents who can expect to live for 20 years or more on the resources they garnered during the boom years. In particular, the equity value of their homes—generally the largest single item of value in their personal portfolios—will serve as the main bank account they will draw upon in their retirement years. Where growing old once meant growing poor, social security, public and private pensions, and home equity now mean that the golden generation that hit the postwar boom will also enjoy the most comfortable retirement ever made available to an American generation. They will, that is, if they can hold on to their resources and fund their sunset years themselves.

Medical care costs have skyrocketed in the past decade, as has the cost of maintaining a loved one in a nursing home. Pleasanton parents are all too aware of the expenses involved in the long haul. Moreover, they have little faith that they will be able to depend on anyone else, whether government or members of their own family, to provide for them as they age. Whatever pressure they may feel to help the next generation over the hump, especially over the hump of home ownership, collides with the knowledge that they must husband what they have for the long years ahead.

Were the long-term future the only concern, many Pleasanton parents would undoubtedly try to do something for their struggling boomers. But the present is causing enough problems all by itself, for the fiscal crisis that has beset many a suburban community has generated demands for property tax revenues that are proving ever more difficult for the postwar generation to meet. In Pleasanton itself, property taxes have increased nearly *sixfold* in the past 20 years. For many old timers, who moved to Pleasanton when it was a modest town (on the strength of modest incomes), taxes have proven to be the final straw.

Mary and Sam Kinder moved to Pleasanton in the 1950s, even though they could barely afford a down payment. Sam owned a local hardware store that was bought out by a chain. He now does construction work in the city, driving a tractor trailer on hauling jobs. Mary works for a perfume franchise that has concessions in big department stores and has done so since her youngest child was 10 years old. Married fresh out of high school, the Kinders raised four kids in Pleasanton and lived in one house for almost 38 years. It has not been easy for them financially, but they scraped by and thought things would ease up now that the kids are largely on their own.

Tax increases have put an end to the dream of coasting into retirement. When Sam retires, they are selling out and moving south to join their oldest son who long ago concluded that he too could not afford to live in Pleasanton. Their neighbor Mrs. Floury found the tax problem an even bigger burden since she was a widow and truly unable to meet her legal obligations . . .

•••••

Although many of the postwar migrants to Pleasanton have found themselves sitting on residential gold mines, the tax consequences of this increase have made it increasingly difficult for them to remain in the community they consider to be their own. Pressures to move out grow as they age and face the prospect of declining income.

A growing uneasiness with the social character of Pleasanton is also responsible for making the old timers feel that they are no longer entirely welcome. Pleasanton was, by all accounts, a very ordinary community in the 1950s and 1960s. It was (and still is) pretty and peaceful, but it was not socially exclusive . . . Pleasanton families thought of themselves as ordinary middle-class people (even though by national standards they were quite well off). People who wanted to "put on airs" did not move to Pleasanton; they settled in other, nearby communities that already had established reputations as havens of the wealthy, replete as they were with country clubs, chauffeurs, and genuine mansions.

Yet as the cost of housing grew, the new families who moved to Pleasanton in the 1980s were far more affluent as a group than many of the old timers. A social gap has opened up between the skilled blue-collar workers and middle-level management types who founded the postwar community, and the highly paid professionals who are the only people that can afford to buy into this desirable suburb these days. There are no manual workers, jewelry store clerks, or hardware store owners among today's migrants to Pleasanton. Newcomers are partners in big city law firms, executives in large corporations, and specialist physicians. Their tastes, their desires, and their more privatized lifestyle have subtly eroded the communal flavor of life in Pleasanton, setting the tone for a more genteel, upper-crust local culture. Long-time residents like the James family do not feel entirely comfortable with this shift. Keith James . . . looks back upon the change with the sense that something valuable has been lost in the shuffle:

> By the time I graduated from high school in 1980, the town was just barely affordable. But there were still all the same kind of families. I feel now that Pleasanton has totally turned around. It's become basically a very affluent neighborhood, you know, because it's near Manhattan. You see a lot of new . . . groups coming into town. And we're getting a lot of doctors. It's pushing people out. I can remember when someone's parents lived in town, maybe someone's grandparents lived in Pleasanton, and there was some sort of return to the town. But that's totally changing.

It is not unusual to hear those who know they cannot afford to live in the community now argue that it has changed so much they would not really want to locate there anymore. As one of Keith's classmates put the matter, "I wouldn't really want to live in Pleasanton now. They have a lot of rich people that have moved in that are kind of snobby." As the burden caused by the high cost of living mounts, the change in the social climate in town leaves old timers feeling that the community they may need to vacate is no longer quite the same place anyway. It belongs to a different class of richer Americans.

Mindful of the possibility that their worries will be discounted as so much bleating by spoiled, demanding, perfectly comfortable baby boomers to whom the nation owes nothing, they are quick to point out that in an absolute sense they have much to be grateful for. Neither the boomers nor their parents confuse their experience with that of the poor or believe that they deserve an outpouring of sympathy to soothe their disappointments. They understand that relative to the "truly disadvantaged," they live a charmed existence.

Nonetheless, they live simultaneously with a diffuse sense of dissatisfaction and an underlying desire to fix the blame on someone or some group of individuals who has derailed the journey they thought they had tickets for. They are especially perplexed by the arbitrary character of the trends that have had such a profound influence over their standard of living. It has escaped no one's attention that two generations living side by side have encountered drastically divergent life chances. As Martin O'Rourke puts it, "Times have changed. I don't expect to walk in my parents' footsteps. I won't have the same opportunities they had."

Americans believe themselves to be resourceful people. If there are obstacles in the way of prosperity, we will clear them away. If the rules of the game have changed, we will learn to play by the new ones. Unfortunately, it would appear that we cannot figure out what today's rules really are. We are drowning in a kind of national confusion, floundering in our attempts to find a way out, all the while wondering why the old formula no longer pays off.

With every day that goes by, the unseen hands of the international economy seem to interfere more and more in our most intimate decisions: when to marry, when to have children, where we can live, how easily we can remain in our chosen communities, whether we will be able to enjoy our sunset years or will have to worry about every dime. And on all of these counts, the largest living generation of Americans are doing worse, enjoying less of the good life than those who came before them, most notably their own parents.

The baby boom generation experiences this decline as a boa constrictor wrapped around their eroding sense of freedom. Decisions that were once left to the vagaries of emotion are now calculated down to the last nickel; risks that could once be taken with educational pathways or careers are now out of the question, too dangerous by half. If being careful would cure the disease of downward mobility, baby boomers would at least have a strategy for overcoming the obstacles the economy has placed in their way. But in truth, being careful, making all the right choices, is no guarantee that the future will work the way it is supposed to. Indeed, for many of the nation's youngest boomers—the Reagan generation—who put aside risks and dreams in favor of the pragmatic course, economic history has been unkind in the extreme. No amount of deferred gratification will buy them the gratification they want: skyrocketing prices, stagnating wages, dissipating promotion prospects, and the relentless pressure of an economy that just does not seem to work any more—these are the forces and trends that are closing in like the vise grip of the boa.

But the boomers are hardly the only Americans in trouble. Indeed, there are few generations or regions that have managed to stay out of harm's way. Those who have experienced downward mobility in their own adult lives, who like David Patterson have had to watch their dreams flow down the drain, are often lost in the wilderness of downward mobility. Their numbers have grown as the economy has worsened . . . and as temporary jobs, or poorly paid jobs, come to replace what was once a well-endowed labor market. Politicians and educators alike speak about the importance of training, of skill, of education, issues that are like motherhood and apple pie. What can they say to people like David Patterson—well educated, hard working, and eager to get back into the game—who followed all the rules and now find themselves stranded, diplomas in hand?

• • • • •

THE TREND TOWARD WEALTH BY INHERITANCE

Not all Americans have experienced the downward mobility discussed by Katherine Newman in this chapter. Where recent economic changes have enabled some people to acquire vast wealth, others have benefited from their parents' good fortune during the postwar boom. In the selection that follows, political analyst Kevin Phillips explores the social implications of the increasing significance of inheritance during a period of declining general prosperity.

• • • • •

For young Americans, those under 30 or 35, two decades of polarization had brought a special, though widely unappreciated, irony: Not only were they (and those younger) in danger of being the first generation of Americans to suffer a lower standard of living than their parents, but they would be the first generation to receive—or not receive—much of their economic opportunity from family inheritance, not personal achievement.

By the early 1990s it had become a cottage industry for journalists to show how young Americans were losing ground. Hardly any could buy a home. Many could not even afford to marry. Young men with only a high school education, who could have gone into steel plants or auto factories—and earned blue-collar, middle-class wages—back when postwar America enjoyed the eco-

Source: From *Boiling Point* by Kevin Phillips. Copyright © 1993 by Kevin Phillips. Reprinted by permission of Random House, Inc.

nomic hegemony won at Bastogne and Iwo Jima, now faced what Brookings Institution economist Gary Burtless called "a future of lousy jobs." Only the skilled 25 percent, the college-educated, had middle-class opportunities. Huge numbers of others found themselves caught up in what some called the K-Mart Economy—low-paid employment in retail stores, discount centers, back offices, and fast-food emporia.

• • • • •

Meanwhile, persons between the ages of 45 and 75 controlled the overwhelming bulk of America's household net worth, the proceeds of both the postwar era and the 1980s heyday. Future opportunities were expected to be thinner. Frank Levy and Richard C. Michel, in their book *The Economic Future of American Families*, projected that the baby boom generation at middle age would have only half of the real net worth their parents had at that same stage. With the American economy losing its power, their younger brothers and sisters would fall even further behind.

But not uniformly. For those who were 20, 30, and 35 years old in the 1990s, achievement and inheritance were beginning to reverse their traditional economic roles. Some $8 trillion to $10 trillion in net worth was in the hands of Americans over 50, and as it began to pass to the next generation—largely baby boomers—in the 1990s, the pattern of opportunity and success in the United States would be transformed. Economist Robert Avery of Cornell University, a leading student of the phenomenon, predicted that "we will soon be seeing the largest transfer of income in the history of the world. The passing of the extraordinary wealth created in America in the past five decades will speed up in the 1990s, as those alive and working during those years reach their 70s and 80s."

Inheritance, then, was about to become a critical component of the younger generation's future, something America had never before experienced. Edward Wolff, a New York economist studying the pattern, contended that "if it weren't for gifts and inheritances, most baby boomers would never be able to accumulate any real wealth." Indeed, the process had already begun. In 1973, 56 percent of the total wealth held by persons aged 35 to 39 was given them by their parents. By 1986 the figure for 35- to 39-year-old baby boomers had risen to 86 percent. Higher ratios were still to come, and according to economists, inheritances would peak between 1997 and 2011, with each year's volume equaling roughly 6 percent of GNP.

If these predictions came true, baby boomers would be the most polarized and stratified generation in U.S. history. Economist Wolff projected that if inheritance followed the approximate lines of U.S. wealth concentration in the 1990s, then the wealth going to the top 1 percent would average $3 million, that going to the richest 5 percent (the 95th to 99th percentiles) would average $900,000. Thereafter, the 90th to 94th percentiles would average about $400,000, the 85th to 89th percentiles $200,000, and the 80th to 84th percentiles $100,000. Those in the middle fifth (40th to 59th percentiles) would receive $49,000. For those further down, inheritances would be negligible. Among the upper few percentages, inheritance taxes would take a significant chunk, but the overall pattern would be unmistakable: Inherited wealth would create a hereditary caste; class lines would harden.

•••••

QUESTIONS

1. In what ways did the experience of downward mobility begin to change during the 1970s? What were the primary causes of these changes?
2. Why are displaced managers likely to have a harder time adjusting to downward mobility than unemployed blue-collar workers? Why are displaced managers more likely to blame themselves for downward mobility than unemployed blue-collar workers?
3. Why has it been so much more difficult for members of the baby boom generation to match their parents' economic achievements? Why have so few members of the baby boom generation from Pleasanton been able to establish households in that community?
4. What does Kevin Phillips mean when he says that "achievement and inheritance were beginning to reverse their traditional economic roles" in American social life? In what ways does the evidence presented in Newman's essay support Phillips's contentions? Do you find these arguments persuasive? What kinds of evidence would someone who disagreed with Phillips and Newman use to contest their claims?
5. In the final sentence of this chapter's essay, Katherine Newman asks what politicians can "say to people like David Patterson—well educated, hard working, and eager to get back into the game—who followed all the rules and now find themselves stranded, diplomas in hand?" How would you respond to that question? What are the political implications of the developments Newman discusses in the essay?

BIBLIOGRAPHY

For those seeking more information on the themes discussed in this chapter, two books by Katherine Newman provide the best place to begin: *Falling from Grace: The Experience of Downward Mobility in the American Middle Class* (1988) and *Declining Fortunes: The Withering of the American Dream* (1993). Also see Lillian Rubin, *Families on the Fault Line: America's Working Class Speaks about the Economy, Race, and Ethnicity* (1993). There is a large and growing literature devoted to the economic changes of the past several decades and how the United States might best respond to them. Some of the more notable works include Robert B. Reich, *The Work of Nations: Preparing Ourselves for 21st-Century Capitalism* (1991); Robert Kuttner, *The End of Laissez-Faire: National Purpose and the Global Economy after the Cold War* (1991); Bennett Harrison and Barry Bluestone, *The Great U-Turn: Corporate Restructuring and the Polarizing of America* (1988); Bennett Harrison, *Lean and Mean: The Changing Landscape of Corporate Power in the Age of Flexibility* (1994); and Richard J. Barnett and John Cavanaugh, *Global Dreams: Imperial Corporations and the New World Order* (1994).

Photo Credits

American Portraits, **Volume Two**

1: Stock Montage, Inc.; 2: Courtesy of the Archives and Special Collections on Women in Medicine, Allegheny University of the Health Sciences; 3: Minnesota Historical Society; 4: Stock Montage, Inc.; 5, 6: Corbis-Bettmann; 7: North Wind Picture Archives; 8: Stock Montage, Inc.; 9: Corbis-Bettmann; 10: AP/Wide World; 11: Stock Montage, Inc.; 12, 13: AP/Wide World; 14, 15: Stock Montage, Inc.; 16, 17: AP/Wide World; 18: Courtesy Columbia University, photo by Joe Pineiro